Development in Prosodic Systems

Studies in Generative Grammar 58

Editors

Harry van der Hulst
Jan Koster
Henk van Riemsdijk

Mouton de Gruyter
Berlin · New York

Development in Prosodic Systems

edited by
Paula Fikkert
Haike Jacobs

Mouton de Gruyter
Berlin · New York   2003

Mouton de Gruyter (formerly Mouton, The Hague)
is a Division of Walter de Gruyter GmbH & Co. KG, Berlin.

The series Studies in Generative Grammar was formerly published by
Foris Publications Holland.

⊗ Printed on acid-free paper which falls within the guidelines
of the ANSI to ensure permanence and durability.

Library of Congress Cataloging-in-Publication Data

> Development in prosodic systems / edited by Paula Fikkert, Haike
> Jacobs.
>   p.   cm. − (Studies in generative grammar ; 58)
>   Includes bibliographical references and index.
>   ISBN 3 11 016684 4
>   1. Prosodic analysis (Linguistics)   2. Historical linguistics.
>   I. Fikkert, Johanna Paula Monique, 1965−   II. Jacobs, Haike,
>   1961−   III. Series.
>   P224 .D48   2002
>   414'6−dc21
>   2002151843

ISBN 3-11-016684-4

Bibliographic information published by Die Deutsche Bibliothek

Die Deutsche Bibliothek lists this publication in the Deutsche
Nationalbibliografie; detailed bibliographic data is available in the
Internet at <http://dnb.ddb.de>.

© Copyright 2003 by Walter de Gruyter GmbH & Co. KG, D-10785 Berlin.
All rights reserved, including those of translation into foreign languages. No part of this
book may be reproduced in any form or by any means, electronic or mechanical, including
photocopy, recording, or any information storage and retrieval system, without permission
in writing from the publisher.
Printing & binding: Hubert & Co., Göttingen.
Cover design: Christopher Schneider, Berlin.
Printed in Germany.

Ad memoriam perpetuandam
Mirco Ghini

This volume arose from a workshop on Change in Prosodic Systems, which was part of the 21. Jahrestagung der Deutschen Gesellschaft für Sprachwissenschaft (DGfS) held at Konstanz University in 1999. We would like to thank Twan Geerts for his invaluable assistance in the editing of this book and we dedicate this book to one of the contributors who sadly passed away in January 2001.

Contents

Introduction. 1
Haike Jacobs and Paula Fikkert

The relationship between tone and vowel length in two
neighboring Dutch Limburgian dialects 7
Linda Heijmans

Prosodic change in progress: from quantity language to
accent language 47
Ilse Lehiste

Prosodic change from tone to vowel length in Korean 67
Kyung-Keun Kwon

Diachrony of the Scandinavian accent typology 91
Tomas Riad

Kaluza's Law and the progress of Old English metrics 145
Thomas Cable

Middle English stress doubles: New evidence from Chaucer's
meter 159
Michael Redford

Constraining S and satisfying fit 197
Wim Zonneveld

From phrase-final to post-initial accent in western Basque 249
José Ignacio Hualde

Swiss German vowel length through time 283
Astrid Kraehenmann

The prosodic structure of prefixed words in the history of
West Germanic 315
Paula Fikkert

Left-hand word-stress in the history of English 349
Chris McCully

Why preantepenultimate stress in Latin requires an
OT-account 395
Haike Jacobs

From prosody to place: The development of prosodic contrasts
into place of articulation contrast in the history of Miogliola ... 419
Mirco Ghini

Language index 457

Subject index 459

Introduction

Haike Jacobs and Paula Fikkert

The prosodic system of a language can be defined as the set of organizing principles that govern suprasegmental structure, that is, the structure above the individual sounds of the language. The theory that studies prosodic systems of languages is often referred to as metrical phonology, whereas prosodic phonology is often used as a cover term for phonological adjustments involving more than one word. The studies collected in this book are all written in the framework of metrical phonology or metrical theory, deal with various aspects of change in prosodic systems, and, aim to enlarge our understanding of the range of variation and the types of change that are attested in languages.

Metrical phonology, though, does not consist of one single theory in a definite form, but rather consists of a number of alternative descriptive frameworks (such as, most prominently, the bracketed-grid theory proposed by Halle and Idsardi (1995), the trochee-iamb theory proposed by Hayes (1995)). Furthermore, phonologists have different opinions on how phonological adjustments have to be accounted for. Derivational theories (relying on the use of phonological rules transforming underlying forms into surface representation) compete with constraint-based models (most prominently, Optimality Theory) where the relation between underlying form and surface manifestation is taken care of by relying on a set of universal innate constraints that can be ranked differently in different languages.

We will not attempt to provide an overview of all the different theories currently available (a good and comprehensive overview can be found in Van der Hulst 1999), but rather point where the papers collected here deal with fundamental issues in metrical theory. Broadly, the following four different categories can be distinguished:

(1) Tone, stress and quantity, (2) Evidence from Metrics, (3) Sources of Change: Analogy and Loans, and (4) Sound change as a window on competence.

1. Tone, stress and quantity

The prosodic structure of a language can be studied and inferred from different perspectives. For one thing, typically in languages, a number of phonological phenomena occur, such as, syncope, epenthesis, diphthongization and tonal rules which are sensitive to and therefore directly related to prosodic structure. As such prosodically conditioned segmental processes thus shed light on the prosodic structure of a language.

Also, there is a close relationship between tone, stress and quantity, which becomes particularly evident in change. When tonal distinctions are lost, they are often compensated by vowel quantity distinctions. Another frequently found process involving change in tonal systems is that the loss of inflectional endings can result in new stress contours, which may in turn influence vowel length.

Of particular interest are the changes in languages that have both stress and tone, as is the case in several (southern) Dutch and Scandinavian languages/dialects. If these languages change, do they change in the direction of the standard language or is change determined by other factors such as markedness, frequency, etc? Issues such as these are addressed in the papers by Heijmans, Kwon, Lehiste and Riad.

Heijmans shows that two rather similar neighboring dialects express similar distinctions in different ways: Accent I and Accent II words of the tonal Roermond dialect are rendered by quantity distinctions in Weert.

In a similar vein, Kwon discusses the development from tonal Middle Korean to non-tonal Modern Korean and discusses how and under what conditions tonal distinctions were replaced by vowel quantity distinctions, identifying four factors involved in the prosodic change from tone to length in Korean: tone, word-initial strengthening, abrupt syllable cut and compensatory lengthening.

Lehiste's paper is devoted to a change that Estonian is currently undergoing. Historically, Estonian is assumed to be essentially identical to Finnish with respect to prosodic structure. Due to vowel deletion processes (syncope and apocope) a three-way system of oppositions occurred. Lehiste argues that Estonian is undergoing a change from a quantity language to an accent language, that is, the durational contrasts are still present, but their occurrence is dependent on stress, and their manifestation employs contrastive pitch patterns in addition to contrastive duration.

Riad delves into the diachrony of Scandinavian tone accent. Starting from the hypothesis that Accent II originated from stress clash, Riad adduces arguments supporting the archaic character of the central Swedish (CSw) dialects, both as regards tonal values and the presence of connectivity and sets up a tonal typology for the Scandinavian tones, based on a single set of functions: lexical, prominence and boundary tone.

2. Evidence from Metrics

Another way to study the prosodic structure of older stages of the language is by looking at metrical systems, particularly in poetry with an iambic meter or alliteration. Previous studies have shown that particularly complex words show a considerable amount of prosodic variation in poetry, and this may reflect the changing prosodic structure. The contributions by Cable, Redford and Zonneveld can all be placed in this perspective.

The process of resolution, known as Kaluza's Law, forms the central topic of Cable's paper. Cable discusses the intricacies of resolution in *Beowulf* and shows that vowel quantity and syllable weight follow precise patterns. The *Beowulf* meter is best described as a 'four-position' meter in which stress, quantity and syllable count interact.

Redford addresses the question whether "stress doubles", that is, words that have sometimes initial stress and sometimes final stress, in Chaucer's *Canterbury Tales* provide evidence for Middle English stress or evidence for Chaucer's metrical style. Redford shows that the distribution of stress doubles is very regular: SW line internally and

WS at line-internal phrase boundaries and at the end of a line. He then argues that this specific distribution is caused by to prominence mismatches created at the right-edge of phrasal domains due to the influence of the Romance Stress Rule at the *phrasal* level.

Zonneveld presents a very interesting case of Middle Dutch poetry (*Leven van Sinte Lutgart*). He demonstrates the existence of a constraint on the contents of S (the strong position in the iambic meter), formulated as "No Schwa in S". Normally, constraints on the contents of S co-occur with a liberal setting of the parameter for metrical position (resolution) (Hanson & Kiparsky 1996). Zonneveld shows that the constraint on S in *Lutgart* does not coincide with resolution, but, rather, that more straightforward means are used to make linguistics material match the requirements of the iambic pattern, most notably, synalepha and syncope. He shows that the distribution of determiners, and other schwa containing function words (*te*, *ge*-) is very regular, and that schwa does not occur in a strong position, unless, but very limited, in inversion situations. However, this is only true for schwa in open syllables. He further argues that prosody is independent of metrics (but not vice versa), but metrical patterns do provide insight into the prosodic system of the language, because of FIT: a poet will exploit the vocabulary of the language maximally, under prosodic constraints.

3. Sources of Change: Analogy and Loans

Insight into the prosodic structure of the older stages of the language can also be gained by studying processes that are dependent on prosodic structure, such as, for instance, high vowel deletion and open syllable lengthening in Germanic. Important questions that are addressed in this section are the following. What leads to variation and or change? What is the role of analogy? Which paradigms resist analogical change more than others? What is the role of morphology? What is the role of loans? What triggers change in a prosodic system? Can language contact directly influence prosodic systems?

Hualde, for instance, in his contribution studies the relationship and the historical evolutions of western Basque prosodic systems. Accentual systems different from the basic Gernika-Getxo type, such as the Bilbao and Antzuola, are arguably due to influence from the Spanish accentual/intonational system, and, are demonstrated to be two different manifestations of one and the same phenomenon: convergence of the prosodic system towards the Spanish model.

In her contribution, Kraehenmann traces the historical development of two Swiss German dialects showing that they reacted differently to Open Syllable Lengthening (OSL), which she argues is not due to compensatory lengthening. The differences between the two dialects are explained by the different interaction of OSL with syllable-closing process and the different role of paradigm leveling due to different application domains of OSL.

Fikkert investigates the prosodic structure of prefixed words in the different West-Germanic languages both in native words and in French loans. She argues that the native system determines how words are borrowed into the language. The fact that verbs like *persíst* and *infér* seemed to enter the English language as 'prefixed', was not due to the status of these prefixes per se, but because the language did not usually have initially stressed disyllabic verbal stems. This pattern was extended to the borrowed verbs. For (prefixed) nouns the pattern was quite different, as nouns never ended in superheavy stressed syllables if that could be avoided, and this strategy was extended to loans. The situation in Dutch and German was different: not only did those languages have superheavy stressed syllables, they also had a more varied prefix system.

4. Sound change as a window on competence

There is yet another way in which changing prosodic systems can be studied. As early as 1968, Kiparsky worded the relevance of linguistic change for linguistic theory as follows:

> What we really need is a window on the form of linguistics competence that is not obscured by factors like performance, about which next to nothing is known. In linguistic change we have precisely this window.

Rather than focussing on the motivating forces or sources of change, the contributions by McCully and Jacobs consider prosodic change in this window. McCully studies the prosodic development of English by studying the grammars before and after the changes discussed and tries to provide arguments for evaluating the empirical validity of competing descriptive models.

Jacobs claims that the stress rules of one particular period of the Latin language cannot be adequately described in a rule-based or derivational approach, but instead, require a constraint-based OT-model.

Ghini examines the historical development of the metrical system in the Ligurian (Gallo-Italian) Romance dialect spoken in Miogliola, Northwest Italy. The loss of Latin phonemic length for both vowels and consonants resulted in a new system, where new segmental contrasts developed to compensate the loss of prosodic contrasts. He observes interesting asymmetries between obstruents and sonorants: old prosodic contrasts were maintained as segmental ones among the obstruents through lenition processes. Sonorants, however, did not undergo lenition; nonetheless, they too managed to rescue old prosodic contrasts as new segmental ones, but only for the coronal ones, for an account based on underspecification is provided.

Although quite different in nature that papers in this volume bring together different methodologies and perspectives investigating the same issue – development in prosodic systems – which is still an underresearched are in historical phonology, which so far has mostly focused on sound change.

References

Halle, Morris & William Idsardi
    1995   "General properties of stress and structure". In John A. Goldsmith (ed.), *The handbook of phonological theory.* Cambridge: Blackwell.
Hanson, K. & P. Kiparsky
    1996   "A parametric theory of poetic meter." *Language* 72: 287-335.
Hayes, B.
    1995   *Metrical stress theory: Principles and case studies.* Chicago: University of Chicago Press.
Hulst, H. van der (ed.)
    1999   *Word prosodic systems in the languages of Europe.* Berlin: Mouton.

The relationship between tone and vowel length in two neighboring Dutch Limburgian dialects

Linda Heijmans

1. Introduction

The town of Weert, in the Dutch province of Limburg, close to the provincial boundary with Noord-Brabant and some eight kilometers from the Belgian border, has traditionally been situated on the northwestern periphery of the geographical area with lexical tone (*e.g.* Peters 1936, Goossens 1968, Peeters and Schouten 1989). The dialects spoken in this region are characterized by their singsong intonation, resulting from the interaction of the intonational tones of the sentence with word tones. Two word tones occur, which are referred to in the literature as Accent I (also called 'Schärfung' or 'Stoßton') and Accent II ('Trägheitsakzent' or 'Schleifton'). Although minimal pairs are not frequent, speakers of these dialects can distinguish between two segmentally identical words by using different tones.

The Weert dialect has been described as having such a tonal opposition by Verhoeven (1992) and Verhoeven and Connell (1992). More recently, however, other studies have questioned the existence of a lexical tone contrast in Weert (Van Moorsel 1996, Peeters and Schouten 1989, Schouten and Peeters 1996). The aim of the investigation reported here is to provide experimental evidence that the dialect of Weert is indeed non-tonal, and to show that it uses contrastive vowel length to maintain a contrast in words whose cognates are distinguished by tone in the neighboring tonal dialects. For this purpose, the dialect of Weert will be compared to the nearest dialect with a lexical tone opposition, that of Baexem. The town of Baexem is situated some eight kilometers to the east of Weert, in between Weert and Roermond. The existence of a lexical tone contrast in the latter dialect is undoubted (Gussenhoven, 2000a).

The paper is organized as follows. After a brief discussion of Verhoeven (1992) and Verhoeven and Connell's (1992) account of a tonal contrast in Weert, we will consider data from the dialects of Weert and Baexem that confirm the non-tonal status of the former. Further, a close connection will be shown to exist between vowel length in the non-tonal dialect of Weert and the word tone used in Baexem. A diachronic inspection of the data then serves the purpose of accounting for the relatively few words that fail to comply with this general rule of correspondence. In order to show that the Weert dialect can easily accommodate vowel length oppositions, this section also includes a description of its vowel system. To conclude, we give a brief sketch of how this vowel length contrast, mirroring the tonal contrast of the nearby Baexem dialect, may have arisen in Weert.

2. A lexical tone contrast in Weert?

The only phonetic account of a tonal contrast in the dialect of Weert has been given by Verhoeven and Connell (1992) and Verhoeven (1992). Their acoustic measurements revealed essentially identical pitch contours for Accent I and Accent II, only differing in their alignment with respect to the accented syllable: "tone 1 can be characterized as a rise-fall configuration which occurs proportionally late in the syllable. Tone 2 has a similar configuration, but it occurs relatively early in the accented syllable" (Verhoeven and Connell 1992: 60). This is shown in Figure 1. The average F_0 peaks of Accent I and Accent II are located at 57 and 43 per cent of the total vowel duration after the beginning of the vowel (Verhoeven and Connell 1992: 69).

Besides these differences in peak alignment, Verhoeven and Connell also found significant differences in vowel duration between the two tonal accents. Vowels with Accent II were nearly twice as long as vowels with Accent I: "Mean duration of the vowels with tone 1 is 109 ms, while vowels with tone 2 have an average duration of 209 ms" (Verhoeven and Connell 1992: 65). The authors therefore consider vowel duration and the timing of the rise-fall (relative to the accented vowel) as the main phonetic correlates of the Weert tonal opposition.

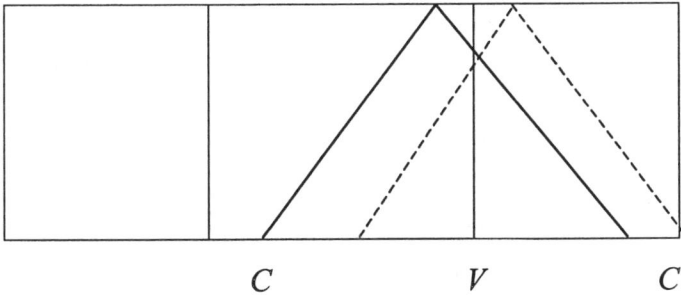

Figure 1. Alignment of the rise-fall pitch configuration in Accent I (dashed line) and Accent II (solid line). The illustration abstracts away from any slope differences. (After: Verhoeven and Connell 1992: 70)

Verhoeven and Connell calculated F_0 peak locations *proportionally* to vowel duration and concluded on that basis that the pitch peak in Accent I occurs later than in Accent II, namely when 57 per cent of the total vowel duration has elapsed (the corresponding value for Accent II is 43 per cent). By doing so, they wanted to eliminate the differences in vowel duration that exist between the two tones, so as not to confound "the location of the F0 peak (...) with the parameter of vowel of duration" (Verhoeven and Connell 1992: 69). This in turn means they assume that the location of the F0 peak is not in any way dependent on vowel duration. However, Rietveld and Gussenhoven (1995), investigating the effects of syllable structure on the alignment of pitch targets in Dutch, found that the alignment point moves rightwards as the coda contains more voiced segments. Also, for (one speaker of) English, Van Santen and Hirschberg (1994: 719) report on a "non-linear rightward stretching of the contour as the durations of onset, vowel nucleus, and coda increase". Rietveld and Gussenhoven (1995: 383) suggest that when more sonorant material is available, the phonetic implementation rules place a target more to the right so that it can be comfortably realized. The alignment of the pitch target can therefore not be discussed without taking into account the segmental structure of the syllable, since the former depends on the latter.

Applied to the Weert dialect, the findings of Rietveld and Gussenhoven (1995) and of Van Santen and Hirschberg (1994) predict that the rise-fall pitch configuration is located further to the right when vowels are longer, that is, in words with Accent II. Indeed, if the location of the pitch peak is expressed in *absolute* terms (relative to the beginning of the vowel), it occurs later in Accent II than in Accent I. This can be seen in Figure 2, which is based on figures (in italics) of Verhoeven and Connell (1992).

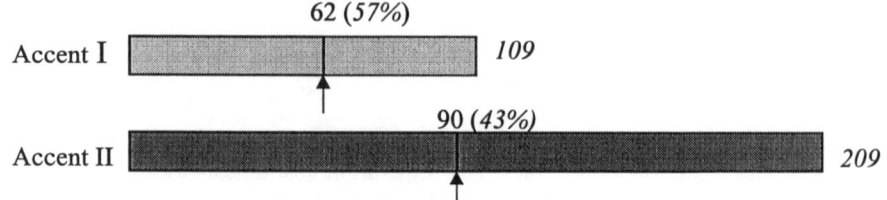

Figure 2. Absolute pitch peak locations (indicated by the arrows) in ms after vowel onset for Accent I (light grey bar) and Accent II (dark grey bar). Total vowel durations are indicated by the numbers behind the bars.

The somewhat later alignment of the rise-fall peak in Accent II is merely a consequence of the longer vowel duration. There is nothing tonal about it. The only acoustic correlate of the Weert lexical tone contrast in the Verhoeven and Connell data that remains intact would thus appear to be vowel duration.

However, if vowel duration is the only distinctive characteristic between Accent I and Accent II in the Weert dialect, it is hardly possible to speak of a *tonal* contrast. As a matter of fact, given the large number of vowel quantity contrasts that the dialect permits (see 4.1.), the huge durational differences that Verhoeven and Connell found might actually represent a phonological vowel length contrast. In other words, a vowel quantity opposition might have been mistaken for a lexical tone contrast, presumably because vowels in words with Accent II are well-known for being phonetically longer. Indeed, all the words with 'tone 2' that feature in Verhoeven and Connell's list of tonal pairs are transcribed as having long vowels, but short vowels are consistently used to transcribe their 'tone 1'. An example of a 'tonal' pair that they give is [kniːn]^{II} 'rabbit', [knin]^{I} 'rabbits', where leaving out the tonal specification might in fact yield more accurate transcriptions. This was also suggested in Laver (1994: 440): "An unusual use of vowel-length relationships is found in many southern dialects of Dutch, where the plural of nouns is signalled by the choice of a short vowel, and the singular by the lengthening of the vowel". Whether or not this is true for all southern Dutch dialects, the point is that the illustrations came from the Weert dialect, were provided by Verhoeven, and included the following pair: [kənin] 'rabbits', [kəni:n] 'rabbit'.

The existence of a lexical tone contrast in the dialect of Weert was questioned by Van Moorsel: "One nowadays doubts the existence of the opposition Accent II-Accent I, in a sense that there is an opposition, but not – at least no more – an intonational one" (1996: 95 transl. LH). Peeters and Schouten (1989) and Schouten and Peeters (1996) were also unable to detect a tonal contrast in the nearby village of Stramproy, some five kilometers to the south of Weert: "There seems to be nothing tonal about the distinction between abrupt [Accent I] and gradual tones [Accent II] – there seem to be only short and long vowels" (Schouten and Peeters 1996: 43). Their data furthermore show that Accent II is on average 50 percent longer than Accent I. We will now turn to the data that support Van Moorsel's claim that a tonal contrast does not in fact exist in the dialect of Weert.

3. Experimental data

3.1. Data collection

The absence of a lexical tone contrast in Weert will be demonstrated by comparing Weert to the nearest dialect with a tonal opposition, that of Baexem, some eight kilometers to the east of Weert (see Appendix 1). This dialect was selected on the basis of the results of a small-scale listening experiment that was conducted in eleven villages lying in between Weert and Roermond, covering a distance of about 15 kilometers.[1] For the dialect of Roermond, a tonal contrast had already been established by Kats (1939) which was analyzed in Gussenhoven (2000a). Per dialect, one speaker was recorded. The same speakers served as listeners some three months later, when they were presented with their own utterances. Subjects were asked to attribute the correct (singular or plural) meaning to the members of six supposedly tonal pairs, /kni:n/ 'rabbit(s)', /bɛin/ 'leg(s)', /æRm/ 'arm(s)', /ʃo:n/ 'shoe(s)', /da:x/ 'day(s)', and /bæRx/ 'mountain(s)'. These were known to be minimal pairs in the Roermond dialect, Accent II being associated with the singular, Accent I with the plural form. In a second set of stimuli, durational differences between the two members of a minimal pair were eliminated, by averaging the durations of the sonorant syllable rhyme. Since Accent II vowels are usually somewhat longer than Accent I vowels, this was done to prevent listeners from basing their jugdments solely on vowel duration, and not on pitch. It was assumed that if a listener could tell the two segmentally identical forms of a minimal pair apart, a lexical tone contrast must be present in his or her dialect. The performance of the Baexem subject showed a sharp increase in the number of correct judgements in comparison to the more westerly villages, *i.e.* those lying closer to Weert. She attributed the right meaning to 78 out of 96 stimuli, or 81 per cent, compared to an average score of 56 per cent in the four villages in between Baexem and Weert. The details of this listening experiment will not be further elaborated upon here; suffice it to say that a tonal contrast could easily be established for the Baexem speaker, and that the speaker of this dialect was therefore chosen as a point of reference for the putatively non-tonal Weert dialect.

A corpus of 145 words was collected in the dialects of Weert and Baexem (see Appendix 2). The lists were compiled on the basis of a large number of segmentally defined classes, each of which allows some generalization to be made concerning the occurrence of either Accent I or Accent II. Goossens' work (1959) on the distribution of the tonal accents in the dialect of Genk (in the Belgian province of Limburg, some 50 km to the south of Weert) served as a starting-point for establishing these segmentally defined classes. Depending on factors such as word-final schwa apocope, vowel height, and consonant voicing, Accent I and Accent II are fairly regularly distributed over the words of the Genk dialect. Presumably, these factors are also involved in the accent distribution of other tonal dialects in the Limburgian-Rhenish region. The segmental compo-sition of the words that were included in our corpus reflected these conditions, so as to provide a representative sample of the dialects. A more detailed account of the structure of the corpus is given in section 4.2 below. The words were realized as part of the declarative and interrogative carrier sentences *Ich zeg noe* (Baexem) / *noow* (Weert) *X*, lit. I say now X, 'I now say X' and *Zeg ich noe / noow X*?, lit. Say I now X?, 'Do I now say X?'. The Weert speaker was a 62-year-old male, the Baexem speaker a 70-year-old female; both were born in their home towns and had lived there all their lives. The lexical tones of the Baexem words were independently transcribed by two trained listeners. The utterances were furthermore acoustically analyzed using the software package PRAAT, available at http://www.fon.hum.uva.nl/praat/.

3.2. The non-tonal dialect of Weert: a comparison with tonal Baexem

The intonational differences between the dialects of Weert and Baexem become particularly clear when studying the pitch contours of one of the minimal pairs, such as the words for 'rabbit' and 'rabbits'. The top panel of Figure 3 illustrates the declarative and interrogative realizations of these words in the dialect of Baexem, whereas the corresponding Weert forms are represented in the bottom panel.

In the dialect of Baexem, the words for 'rabbit' and 'rabbits' have the same segmental structure, namely [kniːn], but the pitch contour of the singular is clearly different from that of the plural form, both in the declarative and in the interrogative contours. In final focused position, the declarative contour for Accent II follows a falling-rising pattern, while a fall inside the accented syllable is observed for Accent I. The interrogative realization of Accent I in phrase-final position is a rise-fall that occurs fairly late in the focused syllable. The corresponding contour for Accent II shows a rise that is preceded by a flat part in the first half of the syllable. The dialect of Baexem thus exemplifies the mechanism underlying a lexical tone contrast; by making use of these distinctions in pitch, speakers of a tonal dialect can distinguish between [kniːn] meaning 'rabbit' with Accent II and the segmentally identical form for 'rabbits' with Accent I.

14 Linda Heijmans

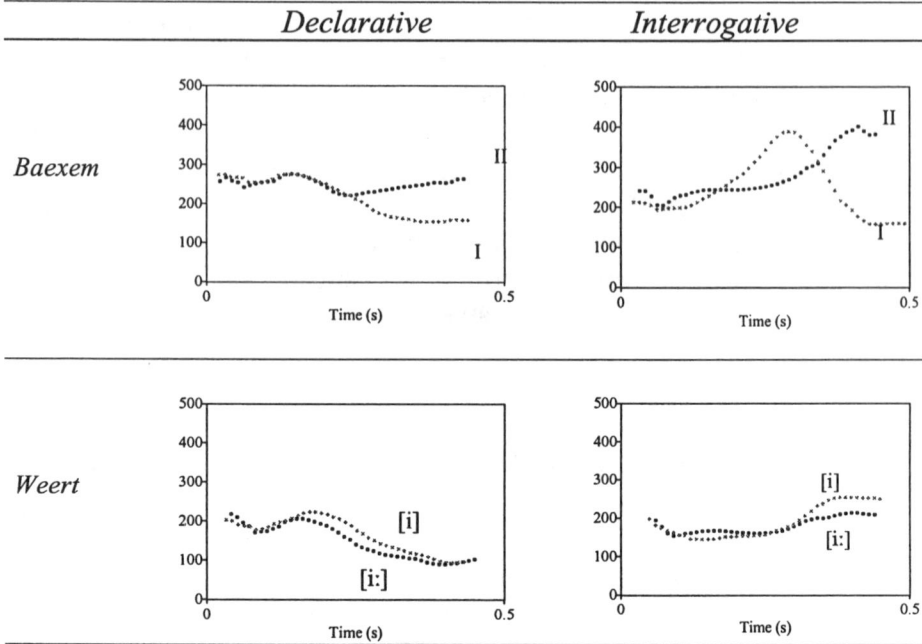

Figure 3. Declarative and interrogative F0 contours of 'rabbit' (black) and 'rabbits' (grey) in Baexem and Weert in final focused position.

The dialect of Weert does not have such a tonal opposition. As can be seen in Figure 3, the Weert F0 contours of 'rabbit' more or less match that of 'rabbits'. Clearly, a lexical tone contrast cannot be established here. However, if the singular form is barely distinguishable from the plural on the basis of F0, there still is a very salient contrast between the two: 'rabbit', [kni:n], has a long vowel in the dialect of Weert, but a short vowel appears in the plural: [knin]. This is indicated in Figure 3 by [i:] and [i], respectively. Vowel durations are given in Table 1, showing that, in Weert, the vowel of the singular form is almost eighty milliseconds longer than that of the plural. Hardly any differences in vowel duration occur in the corresponding Baexem minimal pair. Whereas Baexem has a lexical tone contrast to distinguish the singular from the plural, it is argued that Weert uses vowel length contrastively to achieve the same goal.

Table 1. Average vowel durations in Weert and Baexem (in milliseconds).

Weert		Baexem		gloss
kni:n	220	kni:n^{II}	186	rabbit
knin	143	kni:n^{I}	177	rabbits
stɛin	273	ʃtɛin^{II}	254	stone
stæjn	192	ʃtɛin^{I}	219	stones

Another illustration of the non-tonal status of the dialect of Weert – and of the tonal status of that of Baexem – is provided by the Baexem minimal pair [ʃtɛin]^{II} 'stone' vs. [ʃtɛin]^{I} 'stones' and its Weert cognates [stɛin] 'stone' vs. [stæjn] 'stones'.[2]

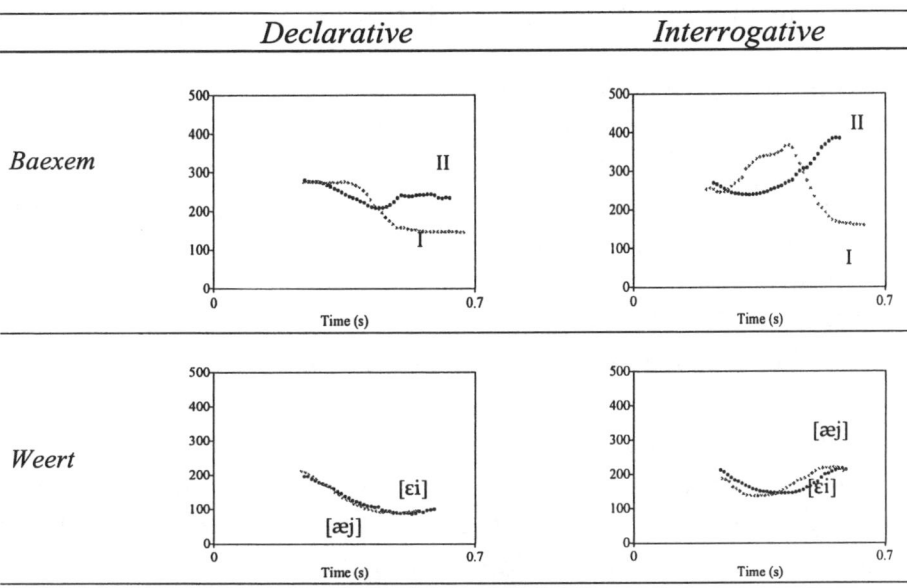

Figure 4. Declarative and interrogative F0 contours of 'stone' (black) and 'stones' (grey) in Baexem and Weert in final focused position.

Figure 4 illustrates the pitch contours of both the Baexem and the Weert words for 'stone' and 'stones', realized as part of a declarative and interrogative sentence. Again, we find Weert using a durational difference to realize these two items (*cf.* Table 1), whereas Baexem employs a tonal difference. It should be stressed that the short vowel plus glide combination [æj] that the Weert dialect uses in the plural form is clearly distinct from the diphthong [ɛi] of the singular. First of all, the first part of the diphthong is somewhat closer than the corresponding element in the short vowel plus glide. Second, the duration of the short vowel plus glide combination [æj] is substantially shorter than that of the diphthong. As a result, [æj] sounds very much as if it were the short counterpart of [ɛi], comparable to the [i] in 'rabbits' that was the short counterpart of the [i:] in 'rabbit'. The contrastive use of diphthongs and vowels that are followed by a glide is extremely rare in the world's languages though. Apart from Weert (and other Limburgian dialects such as Maastricht, Gussenhoven and Aarts, 1999), only Polish seems to contrast diphthongs with short vowel plus glide combinations (Chris Golston, personal communication).

So far, we have only looked at F0 contours of focused monosyllables that appeared in utterance-final position. But also bisyllabic words with a final ə-syllable were inserted at the end of the declarative and interrogative carrier sentences, thus yielding prefinal focused contours. These intonation patterns are illustrated in Figure 5 by means of the declarative and interrogative realizations of ['vɛ:ɣə]^{II} 'to sweep' and ['ne:sə]^{I} 'to sneeze' for Baexem, and of ['vɛ:ɣə] 'to sweep' and ['ne:stə] 'to sneeze' for Weert.

In the Baexem prefinal declarative contours, an early fall during the focused syllable in Accent I ['ne:sə]^{I} 'to sneeze' signals the distinction with a late fall, *i.e.* after the accented syllable, in Accent II ['vɛ:ɣə]^{II} 'to sweep'. The interrogative version of Accent I is realized as a rise throughout the duration of the syllable, while the pitch contour stays level or slightly drops in the Accent II syllable. For Accent I, a sharp fall can be observed at the end of the intonation phrase, but not for Accent II, where the F0 contour is in the process of falling from high. As for the Weert intonation patterns of ['ne:stə] 'to sneeze' and ['vɛ:ɣə] 'to sweep', they perfectly overlap one another. Other word pairs yield similar pitch contours, both in Baexem and in Weert. In other words, a tonal contrast is absent in Weert in the prefinal just as in the final examples, but not in Baexem.

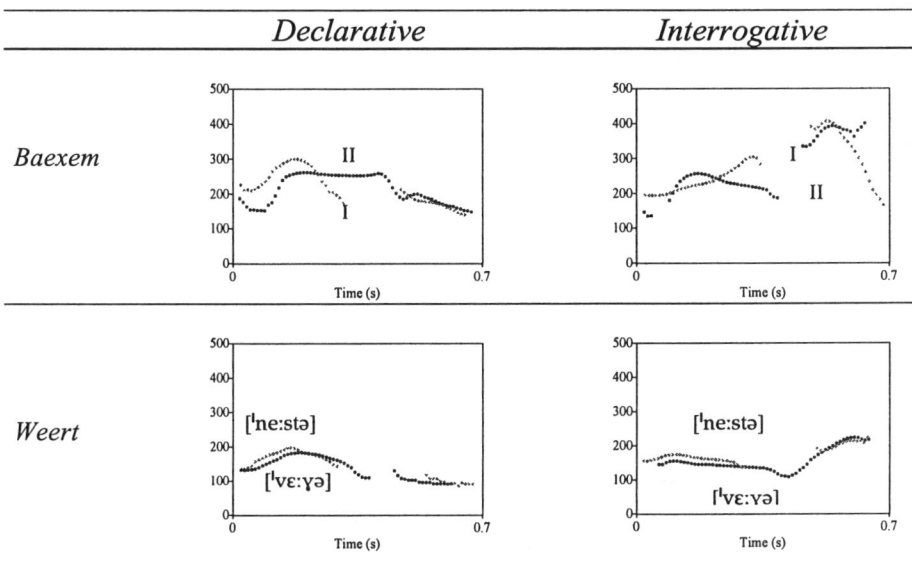

Figure 5. Declarative and interrogative F0 contours of 'to sweep' (black) and 'to sneeze' (grey) in Baexem and Weert in prefinal focused position.

3.3. Theoretical account of the Baexem tonal contrast: a comparison with Roermond

The Baexem realizations of the tonal accents in final and prefinal focused position follow the same F0 contours as in the Roermond dialect, both in declarative and interrogative sentences. The Roermond lexical tone contrast has been analyzed in an autosegmental-metrical framework by Gussenhoven (2000a). The contours of a Roermond tonal pair that is realized with focus in both final and nonfinal position are as in Figure 6.
Gussenhoven (2000a) proposes the following analysis for Roermond, where the lexical tone contrast is restricted to syllables with two sonorant moras. The boundary tones are Li for declaratives and HiLi for interrogatives. To mark focus, Roermond uses a high tone (H*) in declarative utterances, but a low tone (L*) in question intonation.

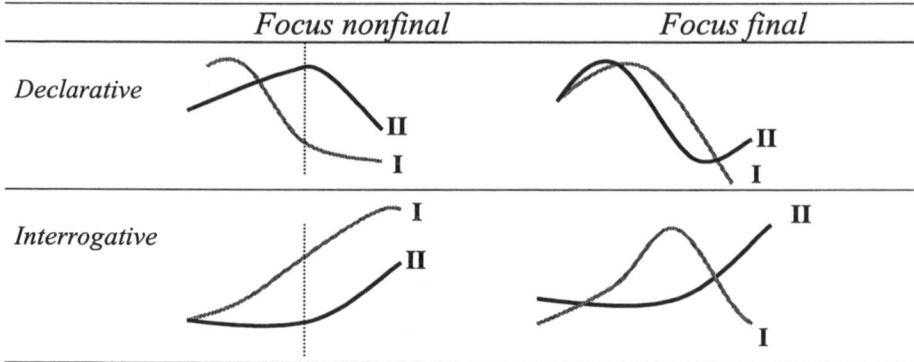

Figure 6. Schematic representations of the contrast between Accent I (grey) and Accent II (black) in Roermond in final and nonfinal focused position with declarative and interrogative intonation (based on Gussenhoven, 2000a, Table I).

The focal tones associate with the first sonorant mora of the main stressed syllable. Accent I is lexically toneless, but Accent II has a lexical H associated to the second sonorant mora.

To account for the steep, early fall in Accent I nonfinal declarative contours, it is assumed that the low boundary tone spreads to the free second sonorant mora of the focal syllable. Since a lexical H is allocated to this position in Accent II words, the nonfinal declarative fall comes somewhat later here. Assimilatory processes take place in the Accent II interrogative contours. First, the Accent II lexical H changes to L under the influence of a preceding L*. Second, if the lexical H occupies the last mora of the intonation phrase, whether in interrogatives or in declaratives, the boundary tone(s) are realized before it. This has far-reaching implications for the final Accent II contours. In declaratives, the boundary low tone is implemented before the lexical H and after the focal H*, thus yielding a falling-rising pattern. In final interrogative realizations, the Accent II lexical H comes after the HiLi boundary tone. Here, it is therefore not the lexical H, but the first element of the boundary tone that assimilates to the preceding L* focal accent. The unusual order of boundary and lexical tones is accounted for in Optimality Theory as resulting from the competition between two conflicting alignment constraints: one that aligns boundary tones at the right edge of the intonation phrase and one that aligns the lexical H at the right edge of the syllable, which is ranked higher (see also Gussenhoven, 2000c).

The analysis that Gussenhoven developed for the dialect of Roermond can also be applied to the intonation patterns that were observed for Baexem. However, a difference between the Baexem and Roermond realizations of the intonational and lexical tones would appear to be that Baexem truncates the interrogative HiLi boundary tone when a focused Accent II syllable appears prefinally (Figure 7; bottom left panel, black contour), while this does not seem to take place in the corresponding Roermond prefinal contour where a full fall occurs at the end of the intonation phrase (Gussenhoven, 2000a and 2000c). Figure 7 brings together the schematic representations of the Baexem contours as illustrated in Figure 3 to 5 as well as Gussenhoven's account of the Roermond tonal contrast as outlined above. Note that although the nonfinal contours of Baexem and Roermond look rather different, these differences can be ascribed to the fact that in Baexem, the focal syllable is actually prefinal, so that the boundary tones are included in the representations of the Baexem lexical tone contrast in Figure 7, but not in Figure 6 for Roermond.

After having elaborated on the representation of the tonal contrast in the dialects of Baexem and Roermond, we have now come to a point where a comparison with the Weert dialect would be appropriate. From the illustrations of two monosyllabic minimal pairs, 'rabbit(s)' and 'stone(s)', and two bisyllabic words carrying different tonal accents in Baexem, it seems reasonable to assume that the dialect currently spoken in Weert is not tonal at all. None of the examined words in the corpus showed intrinsically different intonation contours than those illustrated here. Also, there is no doubt that the dialect of Baexem uses contrasting lexical tones, much in the same way as Roermond. While these tonal dialects can use Accent I and Accent II to express (morphological and lexical) differences between otherwise identical forms, the dialect of Weert was shown to contrast not only short vowels with long vowels (as in [kniːn] 'rabbit', [knin] 'rabbits'), but also short vowel plus glide combinations with diphthongs (as in [stɛin] 'stone', [stæjn] 'stones') to achieve a similar distinction.

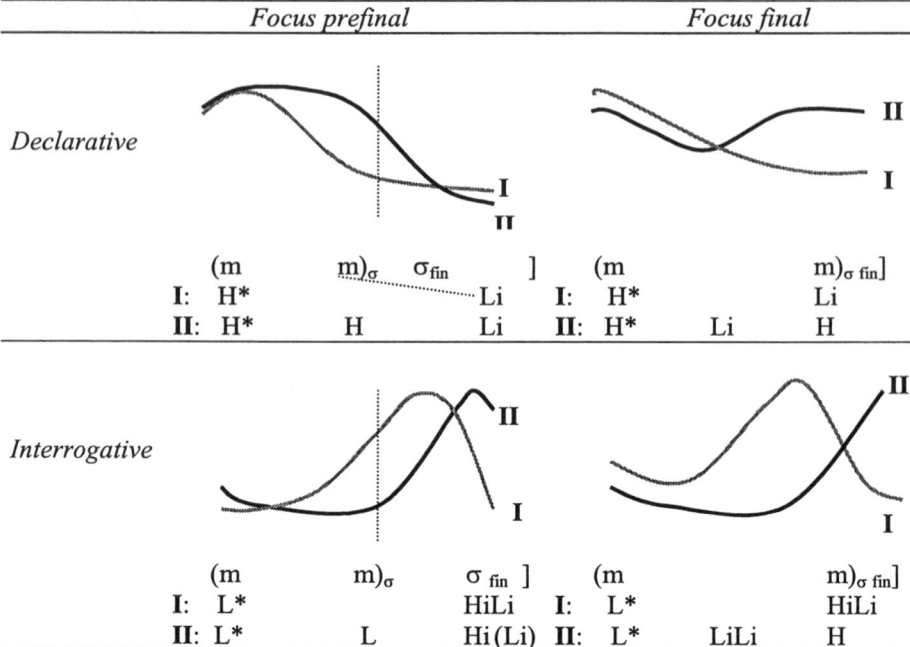

Figure 7. Schematic representations of the contrast between Accent I (grey) and Accent II (black) in Baexem in final and prefinal focused position with declarative and interrogative intonation (σ_{fin} stands for final syllable).

The data presented in this section not only illustrate the non-tonal status of the Weert dialect, they also reveal a fairly systematic correspondence between vowel length in Weert and lexical tone type (Accent I or Accent II) in Baexem. In the 'rabbit(s)' and 'stone(s)' examples, a short vowel (plus a glide) appears whenever the Baexem cognate word has Accent I, *i.e.* in the plural forms, but a long vowel (or diphthong) is used instead of Accent II. In order to see if these correspondences in fact exist on a wider scale, the remaining words of the Baexem corpus will be compared with their non-tonal Weert counterparts. The next section opens with a discussion of the Weert vowel system, so as to bring out the fact that the dialect can readily accommodate a vowel quantity difference.

4. Correspondences between vowel length in Weert and the lexical tones of the Baexem dialect

4.1. The Weert vocalic system[3]

The Weert dialect has 28 stressable oral vocalic nuclei: seven short lax vowels, three short tense vowels, twelve long (tense or lax) monophthongs, and six diphthongs, of which three are centring and three are closing. Among the short vowels, eight have approximately the same quality as their long counterparts. In addition, there is [ə], which occurs in unstressed syllables only. A typologically interesting set is formed by the long monophthongs, which include the series [iː, eː, ɛː, æː, aː, ɑː, ɔː, uː], of which [æː, aː, ɑː] are all unrounded. The vowels [ɑː] and [æː] are restricted to positions before a sonorant consonant in the coda, but in this position contrast with the other vowels, as shown by [keːl] 'smock', [kɛːl] 'throat', [bæːls] 'Belgian', [kaːl] 'bold' and [kɑːl] 'rumours'.[4] Before [ʀ] in the same word, [i, y, u], [iə, yə, uə] and [ɛi, œy, ʌu] do not occur, but all other vowels do. Recordings of the keywords in Table 2 and 3 are available at http://lands.let.kun.nl/projects/weert.html. The speech transcribed is that of a 22-year-old female speaker.

Like many southeastern dialects, Weert allows short lax vowels to be followed by [β̞, j] in the coda, by the side of long vowels. The standard language only has combinations of long vowels and glides. It does, however, not share the possibility of short vowels to be followed by a glide. When preceded by a short vowel, the glide can be followed by a tautosyllabic consonant. The combinations that can occur, figure in Table 3.

The vowel plus glide combinations [æj], [œj], [ɑβ̞] are distinct from the closing diphthongs [ɛi, œy, ʌu], whose qualities are similar to those of the corresponding diphthongs in the standard language. First, the durations of the vowel plus glide combinations are shorter than those of the diphthongs. In the context [β̞æjts] 'luxurious', [zβ̞ɛit] 'sweat' spoken in isolation, the respective durations are 180 ms and 230 ms.

Table 2. Vowels in the Weert dialect.

Short vowels			Long vowels			Diphthongs		
i	ʀit	'Mary'	i:	βi:t	'far'	iə	kiət	'hut'
y	yt	'out'	y:	zy:t	'sees'	yə	ɣʀyəts	'proud of'
ɪ	hɪtst	'heat'	e:	ʀe:t	'reed'	uə	ʀuət	'red'
ʏ	blʏts	'bump'	ø:	zø:t	'sweet'	ɛi	lɛit	'sorrow'
ɛ	ˈzɛgə	'to say'	ɛ:	ˈblɛ:cə	'leaf+DIM'	œy	kœyt	'fun'
œ	nœt	'mean'	œ:	fœ:ts	'slap'	ʌu	stʌut	'naughty'
æ	slæt	'dishcloth'	æ:	tæ:nt	'tent'			
			a:	na:t	'wet'			
ɑ	kʀɑts	'scratch'	ɑ:	lɑ:ŋk	'tall'			
ɔ	kʀɔt	'beet'	ɔ:	kβɔ:t	'angry'			
			o:	blo:t	'blood'			
u	ʀuts	'slide'	u:	ʀu:t	'pane'			
ə	ˈm:xcə	'girl						

Table 3. Vowel plus glide combinations in the Weert dialect

Short vowel plus glide			Long vowel plus glide		
ɪj	blɪj	'happy'	i:β	li:β	'lion'
ʏj	kʏj	'cows'	y:j	py:j	'paws'
			e:j	sne:j	'cut'
			ø:j	zø:j	'she, they'
œj	bœj	'shower'	ɛ:j	bɛ:j	'(I) pray'
æj	dʀæj	'three'	œ:j	sxœ:j	'bolts'
(ɑj)	de:ˈtɑj	'detail'	a:j	sl a:j	'lettuce'
ɑβ	nɑβ	'narrow'			
(ɔj)	hɔj	'hi'	ɔ:j	kɔ:j	'cold'
ɔβ	nɔβ	'new'	o:j	ɣo:j	'good'
			o:β	no:β	'now'
			u:j	ku:j	'cage'

Second, the short vowels are slightly more open than the first elements of the diphthongs, [œ] being considerably opener before [j] than elsewhere. The duration of the long vowel plus glide combination [a:j] is 300 ms. Because the diphthongs [ɛi, œy, ʌu] rarely occur word-finally, there are few minimal pairs with short vowel plus glide combinations in final position. An example of a near-minimal pair is [bœj] 'shower', [nœy] as in [hɛː kʀeːx ɔp sin ˈnœy] 'he was given a good beating'. Preconsonantal (near-)minimal pairs can easily be found: [β̞æjc] '(the wind) blows', [lɛit] 'sorrow', [dœjts] 'German' (adj.), [kœyt] 'fun', [ɑβx] 'eye', [ʌux] 'also'.

In view of our investigation, then, it is important to note that the Weert dialect has no less than eight monophthongal pairs that differ in vowel length. These are [i(ː), ɛ(ː), æ(ː), a(ː), ɑ(ː), ɔ(ː), o(ː), u(ː)]. Interestingly, also the diphthongs [ɛi, œy, ʌu] can be used contrastively with the short vowel plus glide combinations [æj, œj, ɑβ], respectively, and in a way this resembles length contrasts. The remaining part of this chapter examines to what extent words with short vocalic elements[5] in the non-tonal dialect of Weert have cognate words with Accent I in Baexem and, vice versa, to what extent long vocalic elements correspond to Accent II.

4.2. Examining the corpus for correspondences between Weert vowel length and Baexem lexical tone.

4.2.1. Overview of the corpus and general remarks

Out of the 147 word pairs included in our corpus, 74 Baexem words with Accent II contain long vocalic elements in their Weert counterparts. Another 36 have Accent I while having short vocalic elements in Weert. Thus, a total of 110 word pairs agreed in either one of these respects. Within these 110 word pairs, vowels are usually, but not necessarily, of the same phonological length in both dialects. This is illustrated in the four panels of Table 4.

No differences in vowel length occur in the Weert and Baexem words that figure in the lefthand column of Table 4. Here, Baexem Accent I and II associate with syllables that have short and long vocalic elements, respectively, and whose Weert counterparts have the same vowel length. The righthand column presents words that do not

24 Linda Heijmans

Table 4. Vowel length – lexical tone type correspondences

	same vowel length			different vowel length		
	Weert	Baexem	gloss	Weert	Baexem	Gloss
short vocalic elements vs. Accent I	haŋ	hæɲ [I]	'hands'	bœjm	bœym [I]	'trees'
	æʀm	æʀm [I]	'arms'	yl	yːl [I]	'owl'
	stʏm	ʃtʏm [I]	'voice'	mul	muːl [I]	'mouth'
	Weert	Baexem	gloss	Weert	Baexem	Gloss
long vocalic elements vs. Accent II	knœyp	knœyp [II]	'buttons'	sxœːlc	ʃʏlc [II]	'debt, fault'
	iːs	iːs [II]	'ice'	baːŋk	baŋk [II]	'bank'
	beːk	beːk [II]	'brook'	æːʀm	æʀm [II]	'arm'

agree in vowel length across the dialects. These constitute about a quarter of the 110 word pairs. Here, the Baexem Accent I words with long vocalic elements have Weert cognates with short vocalic elements. On the other hand, long vocalic elements are used in Weert if their Baexem counterparts have Accent II and short vocalic elements. In this way, the correspondences between Accent I in Baexem and short vocalic elements in Weert on the one hand (top row), and Accent II and long vocalic elements on the other (bottom row), hold good.

The short vowels in our Baexem examples with Accent II are always followed by a sonorant consonant in the same syllable. In the tonal systems of Maasbracht (Hermans 1985, 1994), Roermond (Gussenhoven 2000a), and Venlo (Gussenhoven and Van der Vliet 1998), the syllable rhyme has to consist of a long vowel, a diphthong, or a short lax vowel and a tautosyllabic sonorant in order for the contrast to exist. Since in the latter two dialects, the tonal contrast is defined as the presence (in case of Accent II) versus absence (in case of Accent I) of a lexical tonal marking, words whose main-stressed syllable contains only a single sonorant could also be said to have Accent I, all the more since Gussenhoven found that these syllables have similar pitch contours to bimoraic syllables with Accent I, both in the dialect of Roermond (2000a) and Venlo (Gussenhoven and Van der Vliet 1999). However, since monomoraic syllables cannot have Accent II, it does not make sense to speak of Accent I – or of a lexical tone opposition – in words of this type, which will therefore be left unspecified for tone in the present study.

The Baexem dialect does not tolerate a lexical tone contrast on monomoraic syllables either. The items 1 through 9 in Appendix 2, whose main stressed syllables contain only one sonorant mora, always pattern in the same way, i.e. like bimoraic syllables with Accent I. This is shown in Figure 8.

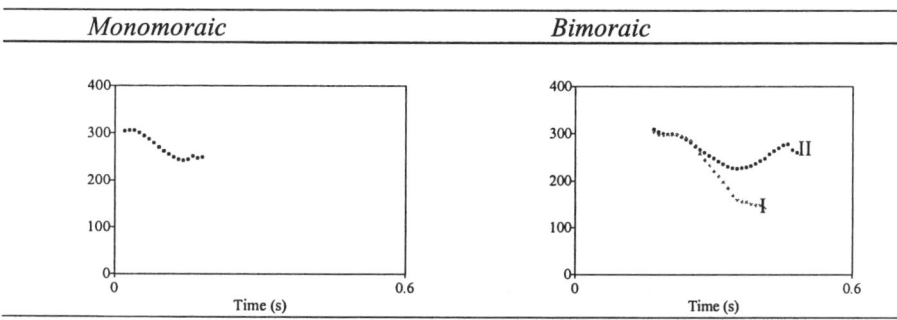

Figure 8. Declarative F0 contours of [pœt] 'pots' (lefthand panel) and [ʃtʏm]^I 'voice' (righthand panel, in grey) and [ʃʏlc]^{II} 'fault, debt' (righthand panel, in black) in Baexem.

It would be inappropriate, however, to lump together words like [pœt] 'pots' and ['kʀɔ.lə] 'curls' with those of the type [ʃtʏm]^I 'voice' and ['hʏɲ.cə]^I 'little dog', because the tonal contrast in the Baexem dialect too, is apparently excluded on syllables with one sonorant mora. Hence, both [ʃtʏm]^I 'voice' with Accent I and [ʃʏlc]^{II} 'fault, debt' with Accent II are actual words in Baexem, distinguishable not only from their segmental structure but also from their pitch contours, but a word like [pœt] 'pots', which has no second sonorant mora, has no such tonally different counterpart. Following Hermans (1994), Gussenhoven (2000a), and Gussenhoven and Van der Vliet (1999), the term Accent I will not be used for words of the type [pœt] or ['kʀɔ.lə], even if these have contour shapes resembling those of Accent I, since it counterfactually implies that Accent II is also possible.

The remaining words in Appendix 2 have at least two sonorant moras, so that Baexem permits a lexical tone contrast here. Below is a more detailed account of the structure of the corpuses that were collected in the dialects of Weert and Baexem, and of the overall tendency that could be observed: when a word has Accent II in Baexem, the chances are that it will have a long vocalic element in its Weert cognate and, conversely, when it has Accent I, a short vocalic element is to be expected in Weert. Attention will also be paid to the relatively small number of words that do not obey this general principle, and at the same time an explanation will be offered for their deviant behavior.

4.2.2. West Germanic[6] short vowels in closed syllables with a sonorant coda

As for the Baexem words with short vowels that are followed by a tautosyllabic sonorant, they either have Accent I or Accent II (see Appendix 2, #10-49). The distribution of the tonal accents in this class of words can be adequately described by making use of two parameters: consonant voicing and schwa apocope. Accent I is commonly found in words where a schwa was apocopated in a weak syllable with a voiced onset. An example illustrating this is the following. From a purely synchronic perspective, it is not clear why [bæRx]^{II} 'mountain' (Appendix 2, #16) and [bæRx]^{I} 'mountains' (Appendix 2, #42) have different tonal accents. But diachronically, the form /bæR.ɣə/ is at the basis of Accent I [bæRx]^{I} 'mountains'. Once the final schwa had been apocopated, the voiced onset of /bæR.ɣə/ became the final coda consonant of /bæRɣ/, which subsequently devoiced. However, in forms where apocope did not apply, like the singular [bæRx]^{II} 'mountain', Accent II is most common.

On the other hand, if schwa apocope took place in a syllable with a voiceless instead of a voiced onset, we do not find Accent I. For instance, [bæŋk]^{II} 'banks', which derives from /bæŋ.kə/, has Accent II, as well as the monosyllabic singular [bɑŋk]^{II} 'bank' (Appendix 2, #11 and 10, respectively), where the final coda consonant is also voiceless underlyingly. Table 5 generalizes the observations that were made regarding the distribution of the tonal accents in the class of words with short vowels that are followed by a sonorant in the same syllable.

Table 5. Distribution of Accent I and Accent II in words with West Germanic short vowels plus tautosyllabic sonorants

	no apocope	*apocope*
underlying voiceless obstruent	Accent II: [baŋk] `II 'bank'	Accent II: [bæŋk] II 'banks'
underlying voiced obstruent	Accent II: [bæRx] II 'mountain'	Accent I: [bæRx] I 'mountains'

To get back to the main point of this chapter, with the exception of a few items[7], the Weert cognates of the Baexem words with Accent I contain short vowels. But on the other hand, so do the Baexem words. For this reason, the Accent II words that have a short vowel in Baexem[8], but are realized with a long vowel in the dialect of Weert are more interesting. For instance, the Weert counterparts of the Accent II examples from Baexem in Table 6 are [bɑːŋk] 'bank', [bæːŋk] 'banks', and [bæːRx] 'mountain', but [bæRx] 'mountains'. Thus, while [bæRx]^{II} 'mountain' and [bæRx]^{I} 'mountains' are tonally distinct in the dialect of Baexem, in Weert, they are distinguished on the basis of vowel length alone.

4.2.3. West Germanic short vowels in open syllables

A similar classification of the tonal accents as that of the West Germanic short vowels in syllables with a sonorant coda obtains to the next couple of items on our list (Appendix 2, #50-74).[9] Although the contemporary forms all have long vowels, both in Baexem and in Weert, these were short in their West Germanic precursors, where they appeared in open syllables.[10] Here, as well as with the abovementioned short vowels that had a (sonorant) coda, it can be observed that the words that have Accent I are the ones where schwa apocope occurred in a syllable with a voiced onset. If apocope did not apply or if the consonant was voiceless all along, or both, Accent II is most likely to occur. An overview of this and some examples are given in Table 6.

Table 6. Distribution of Accent I and Accent II in words with West Germanic short vowels in open syllables

	no apocope	apocope
underlying voiceless obstruent	Accent II: [ˈɛːtə]^{II} 'to eat'	Accent II: [zaːt]^{II} 'drunk'
underlying voiced obstruent	Accent II: [ˈʀɛːɣən]^{II} 'rain'	Accent I: [daːx]^{I} 'days'

Whether the West Germanic short vowels appeared in open syllables or were followed by a tautosyllabic sonorant consonant (see 4.2.2.), the same principles of apocope and consonant voicing underlie the patterning of the lexical tones. By contrast, short vowel lengthening took place in open syllables only.

This brings us to the following. It is fairly uncontroversial that short stressed vowels in open syllables were pervasively changed into long vowels during the thirteenth and fourteenth centuries in all West Germanic languages, a process called Open Syllable Lengthening (OSL) (Lahiri and Dresher 1999). Not surprisingly, the Dutch Limburgian dialects of Baexem and Weert also underwent it. OSL took place independently of the tonal word accents: both dialects have long vowels in the class of words that once had short vowels in open syllables, as illustrated in items 50 through 74 of Appendix 2. As a result, the earlier observed correspondence between Baexem Accent I and Weert short vowels does not apply to the words that underwent OSL. OSL accounts for about a fifth of the non-corresponding cases, which have Accent I in Baexem, but a long vowel in Weert (Appendix 2, #67-74).

4.2.4. West Germanic high long vowels

Moving on now to the West Germanic long vowels on our list, the bulk of them have stayed long in their modern Baexem reflexes, but much less so in Weert. Within the class of long vowels, another factor, vowel height, comes into play. The lexical tones realized on old high long vowels pattern in the same way as the short vowels, that is, Accent II occurs unless the vowel was followed by a voiced consonant in the onset of the next, unstressed syllable of which the word-final schwa was lost. This is further illustrated in Table 7.

Table 7. Distribution of Accent I and Accent II in words with West Germanic high long vowels

	no apocope	apocope
underlying voiceless obstruent	Accent II: [ʃtRuːk]^{II} 'shrub'	Accent II: [ʃtRyːk]^{II} 'shrubs'
underlying voiced obstruent	Accent II: [kniːn]^{II} 'rabbit'	Accent I: [kniːn]^{I} 'rabbits'

The items 75 to 114 in Appendix 2 show a perfect relationship between vowel length in Weert and tonal accent in Baexem. Although they all have vowels that were once long, Weert now has short vowels in words, which have Accent I in their Baexem cognates, but kept the old long vowels otherwise. Compare for instance the Baexem word for 'rabbits' in Table 7, to its Weert counterpart, [knin], number 103 in Appendix 2. Also short vowel plus glide sequences are used in Weert as short counterparts of Baexem Accent I diphthongs, such as [Ræjs] 'journey' and [bœjm] 'trees', corresponding to [Rɛis]^{I} and [bœym]^{I}.

4.2.5. West Germanic non-high long vowels

The final portion of Appendix 2 (#115-147) is full of Accent I words. This tonal accent seems to occur in these words regardless of the (voiced or voiceless) nature of the following consonant, and schwa apocope does not seem to play a role either. If not the segmental structure, the nature of the vowel may be involved: all these Accent I forms have vowels that derive from West Germanic non-high long vowels. Apparently, Accent I is inherently linked up with these vowels.[11] Examples are given in Table 8 below.

Table 8. Accent I in words with West Germanic non-high long vowels

	no apocope	*Apocope*
underlying voiceless obstruent	Accent I: [boːk]¹ 'book'	Accent I: [ʃœːp]¹ 'sheep'
underlying voiced obstruent	Accent I: [ʃtoːl]¹ 'chair'	Accent I: [ʃtøːl]¹ 'chairs'

As a general rule, the vowel quantity of the West Germanic non-high long vowels was not affected either in Baexem or in Weert (see Appendix 2, #115-147). Take, for instance, the Weert words that correspond to the Baexem examples given in Table 8. These are [boːk] 'book', [sxœːp] 'sheep', [stoːl] 'chair' and [støːl] 'chairs'. Both dialects have kept the old long vowels, except sometimes when they appear in front of a glide (often word-finally), as in Baexem [blɔβ]¹ 'blue' and [kyj]¹ 'cows', and their Weert cognates [blɑβ] and [kʏj]. At the same time, this class of words shows up with Accent I in Baexem. This means that Accent I correlates with long vocalic elements in the corresponding Weert words, despite its usual cooccurrence with short vocalic elements. The Weert descendants of the West Germanic non-high long vowels failed to be shortened under the influence of Baexem Accent I.

This leaves us with the following question: why is it that the West Germanic high long vowels, unlike the non-high ones, show short outcomes in Weert when the corresponding Baexem word has Accent I? In other words, why does the Weert dialect tolerate [knin] 'rabbits', [yl] 'owl', and [mul] 'mouth', but not the short vowel variants of [zeːk] 'ill', [vøːt] 'feet', [pɔːl] 'pole'? A partial explanation could be that [e] and [ø] are not part of the Weert phoneme inventory. However, [ɔ] is. Except for [e, ø, o, a], the dialect has short counterparts for all long vowels, including the non-high ones (see section 4.1). The different behavior of the high and non-high vowels can therefore better be explained by looking at their intrinsic properties. It is a well-known fact that high vowels tend to be shorter than low vowels. The latter require more time to be pronounced, since the degree of tongue and jaw lowering is greater than in producing high vowels (Catford 1977: 196-97). This natural tendency of high vowels to be short may have contributed towards the shortening of the West Germanic high long vowels, but not of the non-high vowels, that took place in the dialect of Weert when they had Accent I cognates in Baexem.

4.2.6. OSL and West Germanic non-high vowels: one and the same exceptional category?

Summarizing the diachronic developments, short vocalic elements in the Weert dialect as it is currently spoken can derive from two sources: either they were short already in West Germanic where they appeared in closed syllables (with a sonorant coda)[12] or their West Germanic precursors were long high vowels. In either case, the corresponding forms in the Baexem dialect have Accent I. Conversely, the West Germanic short vowels followed by a tautosyllabic sonorant could also be long in the dialect of Weert, as well as the West Germanic high long vowels. The corresponding words in Baexem, then, have Accent II, but not necessarily a long vowel. However, regardless of the word tone used in Baexem, long vocalic elements turn up in Weert when they are the products of OSL or when they belong to the class of non-high long vowels.

A closer look at the word lists reveals that in the current forms where OSL applied (Appendix 2, #50-74), high vowels never occur, neither in Baexem nor in Weert (except for the Weert form [zuən] 'son'). Indeed, the West Germanic high short vowels ĭ and ŭ that appeared in open syllables were lengthened to ē and ō (Van Loey 1968: 2), thus coalescing with the short mid vowels ĕ and ŏ that underwent the same process. Some examples from standard Dutch illustrating this are listed in (1) for the front vowels and in (2) for the back vowels.

(1) a. *nemen* /ˈneːmən/ < OS *nĕman* 'to take'
     b. *schepen* /ˈsxeːpən/ < MD *scĭp* 'ships'

(2) a. *geboden* /ɣə'boːdən/ < OS *gibŏdan*
'commandments'
b. *zoon* /zoːn/ < Goth. *sŭnus*
'son'

The lowering of high short vowels in open syllables also took place in the dialects of Weert and Baexem. For instance, the long mid vowels in the words [s(ʃ)meːt] 'smith', [zoːn] 'son' and ['vøːɣəlkə] 'little bird' (Appendix 2, #54, 55, 66) derive from the short high vowels ĭ, ŭ and ŭ (through umlaut), respectively.

Correpondences between Baexem Accent I and Weert short vocalic elements could, for different reasons, not be established in the class of words with West Germanic non-high long vowels (4.2.5.) and with the products of OSL (4.2.3.). Given that high OSL vowels apparently do not exist in the dialects under investigation, it is not clear why OSL and West Germanic non-high long vowels should be considered as two independent conditions that prohibit Weert long vowels to be shortened when Accent I occurs in its Baexem cognate. One category in which the two are collapsed suffices to catch all the non-corresponding cases: non-high long vowels (whether resulting from OSL or originally long) remain unchanged for vowel length. In this respect, non-high long vowels behave differently from high long vowels (which never result from OSL), in that the latter become short in Weert words that have Accent I cognates in the Baexem dialect (4.2.4.).

In order to show that vowel length is retained in OSL products independently of vowel height, we would have to find a word pair with a high lengthened vowel in its Weert member and Accent I in its Baexem counterpart. Words with high OSL vowels are hard to find in the Weert variety spoken just outside the city center and in the surrounding parishes on which the present investigation is based, but not in the variety spoken in the city center, also called 'Stadsweerts'. In 'Stadsweerts', the long mid vowels of the more rural variety correspond to high centring diphthongs, as in [sxeːm, sxiəm] (< MD scēme < OS skĭmo) 'shadow' and [stoːf, stuəf] (< MD stōve < OHG stŭba) 'stove'. In these examples, the original high vowel is retained (or has been restored) in the 'Stadsweerts' OSL products, a rather common development in Limburgian dialects according to Van Loey (1968: 41). Since a schwa was apocopated in a syllable with a voiced onset, Accent I occurs in the corresponding words of Baexem: [ʃeːm]^I 'shadow', [ʃtɔːf]^I 'stove'. Also the high OSL vowels (as opposed to the originally long high vowels) would therefore appear to be long in the current 'Stadsweerts' forms, regardless of which word tone they have in their Baexem cognates. As a result, OSL products and the class of words with West Germanic non-high long vowels are as yet to be considered as two independent categories in which correspondences with the tonal accents of Baexem cannot always be observed.

4.3. The art of mimicking tonal dialects

Inspection of the data presented in the preceding paragraphs seems to warrant the conclusion that vowel length and word tone in the dialects of Weert and Baexem, respectively, link together in the following way: a word with Accent II in Baexem has a long vocalic element in its Weert counterpart, and conversely, a short vocalic element occurs when corresponding to Accent I (although long vocalic elements showed up despite Accent I either with the products of OSL or with the non-high modern reflexes of the West Germanic non-high long vowels).

The question arises as to how the Weert vowel length contrast, whose distribution can in large part be predicted from the Baexem word tones, came about. One possibility is that Weert at some point reanalyzed a prior tonal opposition as a quantity contrast, as suggested by Schmidt: "Aus vokalischen Dauer- und Qualitätsunterschieden, die der diachronischen Besetzung der Tonakzente entsprechen, läßt sich ehemals oder noch heute vorhandene RhA [Rheinische Akzentuierung] (…) erschließen" [One could trace back the differences in vowel quantity and quality that reflect the diachronic distribution of the tonal accents to a former or still existing tonal opposition] (1986: 138-39). Nevertheless, this does not tell us why Accent II words should show up with a long vowel in the Weert cognates instead of with a short vowel (the reverse applies to Accent I). It is a well-known fact, however, that vowel duration differences co-occur concomitantly with the lexical tone contrast, Accent II vowels being usually longer than Accent I vowels (*e.g.* Jongen 1972, Schmidt 1986, Gooskens and Rietveld 1995). In this view then, these durational differences that came with the tonal accents may have been reinterpreted as a vowel quantity contrast in the Weert dialect. This linguistic change has in fact been attested in the Huldingen dialect spoken in Northern Luxembourg, where younger dialect speakers have replaced the tonal opposition used by older speakers with a phonological vowel length contrast (Goudaillier 1987).

Alternatively, Weert may never have been tonal at all. Instead, the use of contrasting vowel length in this dialect might have been socially motivated. It could have sprung from the desire to sound like speakers of the neighboring tonal dialects. This might have been achieved by phonologizing one very salient acoustic property of the word tones: vowel duration. In this view, the phonetically longer Accent II vowels of the nearby dialects were interpreted as phonologically long in Weert while the somewhat shorter Accent I vowels of the same phonological length were perceived as phonologically short by the Weert language users.

At this point, we have no indications whatsoever that the Weert dialect had a lexical tone contrast in the past, nor that it did not have tone. At the very least, both accounts offered here explain why the correspondences are the way they are and not the other way around: short vocalic elements in Weert are closely linked to Accent I, long vocalic elements to Accent II. Whether the contrastive use of vowel length in Weert arose as a purely linguistic reinterpretation of a lexical tone contrast or as a socially-induced imitation of it, it was the intrinsically longer vowel duration of Accent II in comparison with Accent I that triggered this change.

5. Conclusion

Although Weert has usually been grouped with the tonal dialects of the Limburgian-Rhenish region, it should in fact not be considered one. Its non-tonal status was demonstrated by comparing pitch contours of minimal pairs with those of their Baexem counterparts. Clearly, in Baexem, members of a minimal pair were tonally distinct, but segmentally identical. By contrast, vowel length turned out to be the only contrastive feature in the Weert word pairs. Spectacularly, short vowels followed by a glide in the coda are used as short versions of diphthongs in the Weert dialect.

The findings further inspired us to investigate on a larger scale whether the distribution of vowel length in Weert is somehow connected to the word tones of the Baexem dialect. To this end, we searched a large word corpus for correspondences between on the one hand Accent I and short vocalic elements, and between Accent II and long vocalic elements on the other. These could easily be established. To be more precise, they applied to 75 per cent of the words in the corpus. Strangely enough, the exceptional cases were all instances of words, which in Weert have long vowels or diphthongs, while their counterparts in the Baexem dialect are realized with Accent I and have long vowels or diphthongs as well. A closer look at these exceptions revealed that they either belong to the class of words where open syllable lengthening took place or where West Germanic non-high long vowels occur, which in contrast with the West Germanic high long vowels were never shortened. Due to these interfering developments, the picture may seem less straightforward than it in fact is: the occurrence of long vocalic elements in Weert closely corresponds to that of Accent II in Baexem; in principle, Accent I and short vocalic elements are similarly interrelated.

Since the distributions of vowel length and word tone in the dialects of Weert and Baexem, respectively, are inextricably intertwined, the question was raised whether the Weert vowel quantity opposition could have arisen by reanalyzing a prior lexical tone contrast (a longer vowel duration has often been claimed to cooccur with Accent II) or by merely imitating these durational differences that come with the word tones. As yet no evidence could be provided to support either one of these explanations. In other words, "the art of mimicking tonal dialects" can either be interpreted diachronically, in which case the "tonal dialect" is Weert, or synchronically if referring to the more easterly tonal dialects, among which Baexem.

36 *Linda Heijmans*

Appendices

Appendix 1. The Limburgian-Rhenish lexical tone area (adapted from Gussenhoven and Bruce 1999, which was drawn on the basis of reports in the literature)

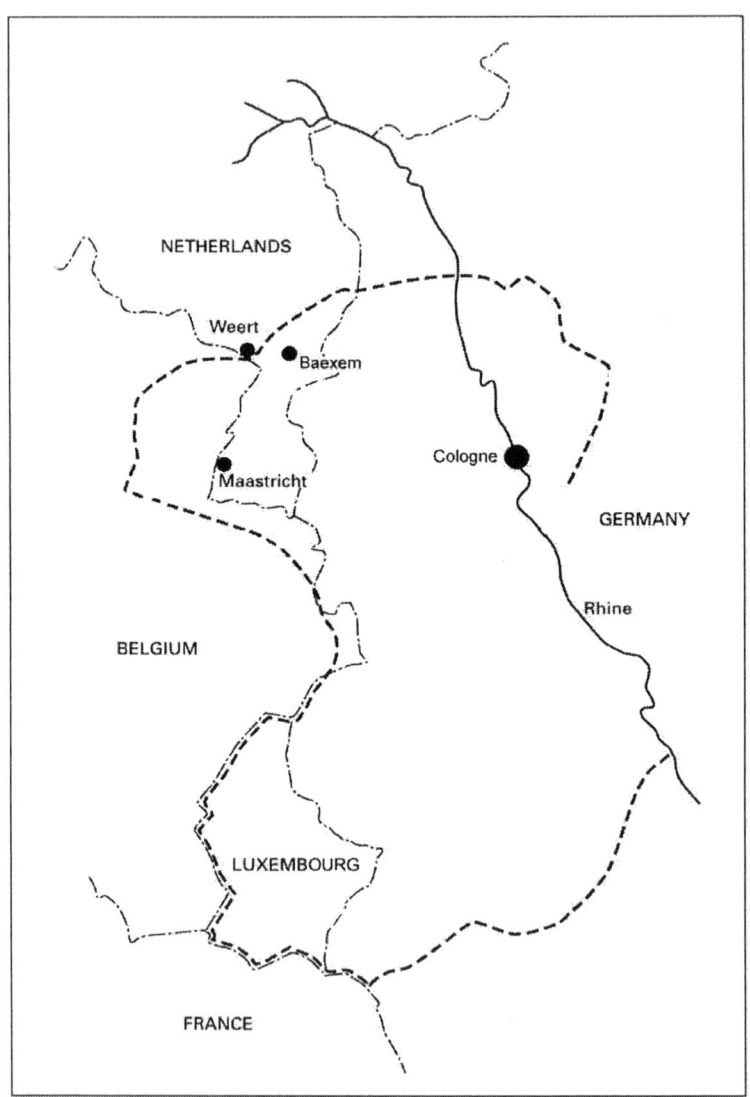

Appendix 2. Word corpus (non-correspondent cases are indicated in bold figures).

#	Weert	Baexem	gloss
1	zɑk	zɑk	'bag'
2	bɛt	bɛt	'bed'
3	hɪtst	hɪts	'heat'
4	pœt	pœt	'pots'
5	vɛs	vɛs	'fish'
6	ˈsɔkəʀ	ˈsʊkəʀ	'sugar'
7	ˈkʀɔlə	ˈkʀɔlə	'curls'
8	ˈkɑlə	ˈkɑlə	'to talk'
9	ˈlækə	ˈlækə	'to lick'
10	bɑːŋk	bɑŋk ᴵᴵ	'bank'
11	bæːŋk	bæŋk ᴵᴵ	'banks'
12	mæːlk	mɛlk ᴵᴵ	'milk'
13	hɑːnt	hɑɲc ᴵᴵ	'hand'
14	kloːmp	klʊmp ᴵᴵ	'wooden shoe'
15	ɣæːlc	ɣælc ᴵᴵ	'money'
16	bæːʀx	bæʀx ᴵᴵ	'mountain'
17	ʀeːŋk	ʀɪŋ ᴵᴵ	'ring'
18	hoːnt	hʊɲc ᴵᴵ	'dog'
19	sxœːlc	ʃɣlc ᴵᴵ	'debt, fault'
20	kæʀs	kɛːʀs ᴵᴵ	'candle'
21	zɔːt	zɔːt ᴵᴵ	'salt'
22	hʌut	hʌut ᴵᴵ	'wood'
23	ɔːt	ɔːt ᴵᴵ	'old'
24	bɑːl	bɑl ᴵᴵ	'ball'
25	æːʀm	æʀm ᴵᴵ	'arm'
26	hɑːmpəl	ˈhɑmpəl ᴵᴵ	'handfull'
27	ˈæːʀmoːj	ˈæʀmoːj ᴵᴵ	'poverty'
28	ˈβ̥eːʀə	ˈβ̥eːʀə ᴵᴵ	'to become'
29	ˈmæːʀɣə	ˈmœʀɣə ᴵᴵ	'tomorrow'
30	ˈbœʀstəl	ˈbœʀstəl ᴵᴵ	'brush'
31	ˈkløːmpkə	ˈklɣmkə ᴵᴵ	'wooden shoe + DIM'
32	ˈkɛːʀcə	ˈkɛːʀcə ᴵᴵ	'card + DIM'
33	ˈeːŋkəl	ˈɪŋkəl ᴵᴵ	'ankle'
34	ˈdœːʀpəl	ˈdœʀpəl ᴵᴵ	'treshold'

35	ˈkæːʀməs	ˈkɪʀməs ᴵᴵ	'fun fair'
36	væːʀkə	ˈvæʀkə ᴵᴵ	'pig'
37	ˈplæːɲcə	ˈplæɲcə ᴵᴵ	'plant + DIM'
38	ˈveːnstəʀ	ˈvɪnstəʀ ᴵ	'window'
39	mɪns	mɪns ᴵ	'human'
40	æʀm	æʀm ᴵ	'arms'
41	stʏm	ʃtʏm ᴵ	'voice'
42	bæʀx	bæʀx ᴵ	'mountains'
43	ɛːʀt	ɛːʀt ᴵ	'earth'
44	ˈhøːmə	heːmc ᴵ	'shirt'
45	haŋ	hæŋ ᴵ	'hands'
46	ˈhæɲcə	ˈhæɲcə ᴵ	'hand + DIM'
47	ˈdɪŋske	ˈdɪŋskə ᴵ	'thing + DIM'
48	ˈhʏɲcə	ˈhʏɲcə ᴵ	'dog + DIM'
49	ˈzoːndəx	ˈzʏɲɪx ᴵ	'Sunday'
50	zaːt	zaːt ᴵᴵ	'drunk'
51	daːx	daːx ᴵᴵ	'day'
52	βeːx	βeːx ᴵᴵ	'road'
53	beːk	beːk ᴵᴵ	'brook'
54	smeːt	ʃmeːt ᴵᴵ	'smith'
55	zuən	zoːn ᴵᴵ	'son'
56	ˈɛːpkə	ˈɛːpkə ᴵᴵ	'monkey + DIM'
57	ˈɛːtə	ˈɛːtə ᴵᴵ	'to eat'
58	ˈlaːjə	ˈlaːjə ᴵᴵ	'to load'
59	ˈhɛːməʀkə	ˈhɛːməʀkə ᴵᴵ	'hammer + DIM'
60	ˈlɛːvəʀ	ˈlɛːvəʀ ᴵᴵ	'liver'
61	ˈʀɛiɣən	ˈʀɛːɣən ᴵᴵ	'rain'
62	ˈvɛːɣə	ˈvɛːɣə ᴵᴵ	'to sweep'
63	ˈvaːdəʀ	ˈvaːdəʀ ᴵᴵ	'father'
64	ˈeːzəl	ˈɛːzəl ᴵᴵ	'donkey'
65	ˈkɔːkə	ˈkɔːkə ᴵᴵ	'to cook'
66	ˈvøːɣəlkə	ˈvøːɣəlkə ᴵᴵ	'bird + DIM'
67	daːx	daːx ᴵ	'days'
68	βeːx	βeːx ᴵ	'roads
69	zaːl	zaːl ᴵ	'saddle'
70	zɛːx	zɛːx ᴵ	'saw'

71	vlaːj	flaːj ¹	'flan'
72	ˈzɛːlkə	ˈzɛːlkə ¹	'saddle + DIM'
73	bɛːʀ	bɛːʀ ¹	'bear'
74	beːj	bɛːj ¹	'(I) pray'
75	kβiːt	kβiːt ᴵᴵ	'lost'
76	stʀuːk	ʃtʀuːk ᴵᴵ	'shrub'
77	stʀyːk	ʃtʀyːk ᴵᴵ	'shrubs'
78	vlɛis	vlɛis ᴵᴵ	'meat'
79	knʌup	knʌup ᴵᴵ	'button'
80	ˈzβɛitə	ˈʒβɛitə ᴵᴵ	'to sweat'
81	ˈzuːpə	ˈzuːpə ᴵᴵ	'to drink'
82	ˈʀʌukə	ˈʀʌukə ᴵᴵ	'to smoke'
83	knœyp	knœyp ᴵᴵ	'buttons'
84	ˈʀyːkə	ˈʀyːkə ᴵᴵ	'to smell'
85	ˈbliːvə	ˈbliːvə ᴵᴵ	'to stay'
86	kniːn	kniːn ᴵᴵ	'rabbit'
87	iːs	iːs ᴵᴵ	'ice'
88	beːj	biː ᴵᴵ	'with'
89	huːs	huːs ᴵᴵ	'house'
90	noːβ̞	nuə ᴵᴵ	'now'
91	boːʀ	buːʀ ᴵᴵ	'farmer'
92	bɛin	bɛin ᴵᴵ	'leg'
93	klɛit	klɛit ᴵᴵ	'dress'
94	stɛin	ʃtɛin ᴵᴵ	'stone'
95	bʌum	bʌum ᴵᴵ	'tree'
96	vøːʀ	vøːʀ ᴵᴵ	'fire'
97	moːʀ	moːʀ ᴵᴵ	'wall'
98	ˈiːzəʀ	ˈiːzəʀ ᴵᴵ	'iron'
99	ˈdʀuːvə	ˈdʀuːvə ᴵᴵ	'grapes'
100	ˈbʀyːcə	ˈbʀyːcə ᴵᴵ	'bride + DIM'
101	ˈzɛivəʀ	ˈzɛivəʀ ᴵᴵ	'drivel'
102	ˈʌuɣə	ˈʌuɣə ᴵᴵ	'eyes'
103	knin	kniːn ¹	'rabbits'
104	mul	muːl ¹	'mouth'
105	yl	yːl ¹	'owl'
106	stæjn	ʃtɛin ¹	'stones'

107	bœjm	bœym ^{I}	'trees'
108	bæjn	bɛin ^{I}	'legs'
109	ʀæjs	ʀɛis ^{I}	'journey'
110	hæj	hɛj ^{I}	'moorland'
111	vʀɑβ	vʀɔβ ^{I}	'woman'
112	blɪj	bli ^{I}	'happy'
113	dœjts	dœyts ^{I}	'German (adj.)'
114	'œjxskə	'œyxskə ^{I}	'eye + DIM'
115	slɔːp	ʃlɔːp ^{I}	'sleep'
116	sxœːp	ʃœːp ^{I}	'sheep'
117	pɔːl	pɔːl ^{I}	'pole'
118	vøːt	vøːt ^{I}	'feet'
119	bloːt	bloːt ^{I}	'blood'
120	stoːl	ʃtoːl ^{I}	'chair'
121	støːl	ʃtøːl ^{I}	'chairs'
122	boːk	boːk ^{I}	'book'
123	zeːk	zeːk ^{I}	'ill'
124	beːʀ	beːʀ ^{I}	'beer'
125	kiəs	kiəs ^{I}	'cheese'
126	blɑβ	blɔβ ^{I}	'blue'
127	kʀæj	kʀɔːn ^{I}	'crow'
128	βæjc	βæjc ^{I}	'(wind) blows'
129	kɔβ	ku ^{I}	'cow'
130	kʏj	kyj ^{I}	'cows'
131	bɪj	bij ^{I}	'bee'
132	ziə	ziə ^{I}	'sea'
133	duət	duət ^{I}	'dead'
134	vluːj	vluə ^{I}	'flea'
135	liːβ	liəβ ^{I}	'lion'
136	pyːj	pyət ^{I}	'paws'
137	dʀyəx	dʀyəx ^{I}	'dry'
138	uːʀ	uəʀ ^{I}	'ear'
139	'yːʀkə	'yəʀkə ^{I}	'ear + DIM'
140	'duːjə	'duəjə ^{I}	'to thaw'
141	'byənkəs	'byənkəs ^{I}	'beans + DIM'
142	'neːstə	'neːsə ^{I}	'to sneeze'

143	ˈmæjə	ˈmæjə ᴵ	'to mow'
144	pəˈstuːʀ	pəˈʃtuəʀ ᴵ	'priest'
145	zɔːxt	zɔːxt ᴵᴵ	'soft'
146	ˈʀøːʀə	ˈʀøːʀə ᴵᴵ	'to stir'
147	ˈbʀøːjə	ˈbʀøːjə ᴵᴵ	'to brood'

Notes

1. These were, going from Weert to Roermond: Swartbroek, Ell, Kelpen-Oler, Grathem, Baexem, Heythuysen, Haelen, Horn, Beegden, Buggenum, Herten.
2. In tonal dialects, it is also not uncommon to find a more open vowel in the first component of the Accent I diphthong [ɛi] when compared to the Accent II diphthong (Goossens 1998b). In the dialect of Baexem, however, the vowel qualities are approximately the same.
3. This part was already published in Heijmans and Gussenhoven (1998), where a full overview is given of the consonantal part of the Weert dialect.
4. The Weert dialect thus strengthens the case for the existence of five-vowel height systems made earlier on the basis of the Bavarian dialect of Amstetten (Austria) by Traunmüller (1982), cited in Ladefoged and Maddieson (1996: 289).
5. The term 'short vocalic elements' is used to refer to short vowels and to short vowel plus glide combinations. By 'long vocalic elements', I mean both long vowels and diphthongs.
6. I have used the following language abbreviations: WGmc (West Germanic), OS (Old Saxon), MD (Middle Dutch), Goth. (Gothic).
7. Among them, only the long vowel in [ɛːʀt] 'earth' can be readily explained. A development that was completed by the time we reach Middle Dutch was the lengthening of a number of short vowels in closed syllables before /ʀ/ when followed by a dental (Schönfeld 1921: 44-49). But what about the Weert forms [ˈbœʀstəl] 'brush' and [kæʀs] 'candle' which kept their short vowels? Lengthening might not take place before a dental fricative. Admittedly, there is not enough evidence here to support this.
8. The long vowels that appear in the words [zɔːt]ᴵᴵ 'salt' (#11), [hʌut]ᴵᴵ 'wood' (#20), and [ɔːt]ᴵᴵ 'old' (#25) are the relics of an ancient /l/ that vocalized.
9. According to Goossens (1959: 149), the words with vowels stemming from the primary umlaut of WGmc *a*, WGmc *i*, *o*, *u* and its umlaut have 'spontaneous Accent II' ("spontane sleeptoon"), although he lists hardly any examples of potential Accent I bearers, *i.e.* words with an apocopated schwa in a syllable beginning with a voiced consonant. One of the few exceptions is [zoːn]ᴵᴵ, number 55 in Appendix 2. The other instances of Accent II that Goossens

counts among the cases of 'spontaneous Accent II' are the items 68 through 74.

10. Exceptions are [daːx]^{II} 'day' and [βeːx]^{II} 'road', where the vowels were lengthened analogously to the plural forms [ˈdaːɣə] 'days' and [ˈβeːɣə] 'roads' that had undergone Open Syllable Lengthening. See also Gussenhoven (2000b), who argues that the lexical tone contrast originated from these stems. This analogical lengthening might also be socially motivated. In the neighboring German dialects, but not in standard Dutch, these stems are long in all forms of the paradigm (see among others, Lahiri and Dresher, 1999).

11. Accent II occurs in [ˈʀøːʀə]^{II} 'to stir' and [ˈbʀøːjə]^{II} 'to brood' (Appendix 2, #146, 147). Paul Boersma suggested to me that these might have Accent II by analogy with forms like [ˈdʀuːvə]^{II} 'grapes' (Appendix 2, #99) with a high long vowel.

12. WGmc short vowels that appeared in a closed syllable with an obstruent in the coda will not be considered here, since a tonal contrast in excluded on these syllables.

References

Catford, J.C.
    1977   *Fundamental Problems in Phonetics*. Edinburgh: Edinburgh University Press.

Gooskens, Charlotte and Toni Rietveld
    1995   Een akoestisch-perceptief onderzoek naar de Maastrichtse tonen [An acoustic-perceptual investigation of the tones in the Maastricht dialect]. *Gramma* 4(1): 17-33.

Goossens, Jan
    1959   Historisch onderzoek van sleeptoon en stoottoon in het dialect van Genk. [Diachronic investigation of dragtone and pushtone in the dialect of Genk]. In: *Handelingen van de Koninklijke Commissie voor Toponymie & Dialectologie*, XXXIII: 141-212. Tongeren: George Michiels.

    1968   Proeve van een typologische kaart van de Zuidnederlandse vocaalsystemen [Attempt to draw a typological chart of the southern Dutch vocalic systems]. *Taal en Tongval* 20: 9-20.

    1977   *Inleiding tot de Nederlandse Dialectologie [Introduction to Dutch Dialectology]*. Groningen: Wolters-Noordhoff.

    1998   Schärfung und Diphthongierung von î, ü, û. Moselfränkisch-limburgische Parallelen. In: P. Ernst and F. Patocka (eds.), *Deutsche Sprache in Raum und Zeit, Festschrift für Peter Wiesinger zum 60. Geburtstag*. Vienna: Edition Praesens.

Goudaillier, Jean-Pierre
1987   Einige Spracheigentümlichkeiten der Lëtzebuergeschen Mundarten im Licht der instrumentellen Phonetik. In J.-P. Goudaillier (ed.), *Aspekte des Lëtzebuergeschen*, 197-230. Hamburg: Buske.
Gussenhoven, Carlos
2000a The lexical tone contrast of Roermond Dutch in Optimality Theory. In: M. Horne (ed.), *Prosody: Theory and Experiment. Studies presented to Gösta Bruce.* Dordrecht: Kluwer Academic Publishers.
2000b On the origin and development of the Central Franconian tone contrast. In A. Lahiri (ed.), *Analogy, Levelling, Markedness: Principles of Change in Phonology and Morphology.* Berlin: Mouton de Gruyter.
2000c The boundary tones are coming: on the nonperipheral realisation of boundary tones. In: J. Pierrehumbert and M. Broe (eds.), *Papers in Laboratory Phonology 5.*
Gussenhoven, Carlos and Gösta Bruce
1999   Word prosody and intonation. In H. van der Hulst (ed.), *Word Prosodic Systems in the Languages of Europe*, 233-271. Berlin: Mouton de Gruyter.
Gussenhoven, Carlos and Peter van der Vliet
1998   The phonology of tone and intonation in the Dutch dialect of Venlo. *Journal of Linguistics* 35: 99135.
Gussenhoven, Carlos and Flor Aarts
1999   The dialect of Maastricht. *Journal of the International Phonetic Association (JIPA)* 29 (2): 155-166.
Heijmans, Linda and Carlos Gussenhoven
1998   The Dutch dialect of Weert. *Journal of the International Phonetic Association (JIPA)* 28: 107-112.
Jongen, René
1972   *Rheinische Akzentuierung und Sonstige Prosodische Erscheinungen.* Bonn: Ludwig Röhrscheid Verlag.
Hermans, Ben
1985   Het Limburgs en het Litouws als metrisch gebonden toontalen[Limburgian and Lithuanian as metrically bound tone languages]. *Spektator* 14: 48-70.
1994   *The Composite Nature of Accent: with Case Studies of the Limburgian and Serbo-Croatian Pitch Accent.* PhD dissertation Katholieke Universiteit Brabant, the Netherlands.
Kats, J.
1939   *Het Phonologisch en Morphonologisch Systeem van het Roermonsch Dialect* [*The Phonological and Morphonological System of the Roermond Dialect*]. Roermond: Romen.
Ladefoged, Peter and Ian Maddieson
1996   *The Sounds of the World's Languages.* London: Blackwell.

Lahiri, Aditi and Dresher, Elan
1999   Open syllable lengthening in Westgermanic. Ms., University of Konstanz and University of Toronto.

Laver, John
1994   *Principles of Phonetics*. Cambridge: Cambridge University Press.

Loey, A. van
1968   *Middelnederlandse Spraakkunst. II. Klankleer* [*Grammar of Middle Dutch. II. Phonology*]. Fifth revised edition. Groningen: Wolters-Noordhoff.

Moorsel, A.A. van
1996   *'t Wieërts Umgespaadj* [*Digging into the Weert dialect*]. Weert: Maes.

Peeters, Wim and Bert Schouten
1989   Die Diphthongierung der Westgermanischen î- und û- Laute in Limburgischen. *Zeitschrift für Dialektologie und Linguistik* 56 (3): 309-318.

Peters, P.
1936   De geslachtsvormen van het adjectief in de Nederlandsche dialecten [Adjectival gender in Dutch dialects]. *Onze Taaltuin* 5: 357-379.

Rietveld, Toni and Carlos Gussenhoven
1995   Aligning pitch targets in speech synthesis: effects of syllable structure. *Journal of Phonetics* 23: 375-385.

Santen, Jan P. H. van and Julia Hirschberg
1994   Segmental effects on timing and height of pitch contours. *Proceedings of the International Conference on Spoken Language Processing* 94: 719-722.

Schmidt, J.E.
1986   *Die Mittelfränkischen Tonakzente (Rheinische Akzentuierung)*. Stuttgart: Franz Steiner Verlag Wiesbaden.

Schouten, Bert and Wim Peeters
1996   The Middle High German vowel shift, measured acoustically in Dutch and Belgian Limburg: diphthongization of short vowels. *Zeitschrift für Dialektologie und Linguistik* 63 (1): 30-48.

Schönfeld, M.
1921   *Historiese Grammatika van het Nederlands* [*Historical Grammar of Dutch*]. Zutphen: Thieme.

Traunmüller, H.
1982   Vokalismus in der westniederösterreichisches Mundart. *Zeitschrift für Dialektologie und Linguistik*, 2: 289-333.

Verhoeven, Jo
1992   Fonetische kenmerken van sleep- en stoottoon in het dialect van Weert [Phonetic properties of drag- and pushtone in the dialect of Weert]. *Taal en Tongval*, 140-155.

Verhoeven, Jo and Bruce Connell
    1992   Tonal accents in a Limburg dialect: an acoustic-phonetic investigation. *Progress Report fromOxford Phonetics (PROPH)* 5: 60-72.

Prosodic change in progress: from quantity language to accent language

Ilse Lehiste

1. Introduction

The general topic of the paper is the possibility of observing and documenting a structural change while it is taking place in a language. The specific topic is the prosody of Estonian. In my opinion, Estonian is undergoing a change of the kind referred to in the title: a change from a quantity language to an accent language. By quantity language I mean a language whose phonology is characterized by a short-long opposition; in other words, a language in which the duration of vowels and consonants is contrastive at the lexical level. Finnish could serve as an example of a quantity language: vowels can be contrastively short or long in every position, and consonants can be short or long in every intervocalic position. I use the term "accent language" to refer to a language in whose prosody stress, duration, and pitch all play a part. Serbo-Croatian might be quoted as a representative accent language: vowels can be contrastively long or short in any position, accented syllables carry contrastive tone, and while syllables with falling tone are restricted to stressed word-initial position, accented syllables with rising tone can occur on any syllable except the last. I claim that Estonian in fact has already become an accent language, but that the system is not stable: a further change is taking place at the present time, which can be documented by observing ongoing changes in inflectional morphology.

2. Development of the prosodic system of Estonian

Historically, the prosodic structure of Estonian can be assumed to have been almost identical with the current prosodic structure of Finnish – its closest living relative. In Finnish, vowels can be contrastively long or short in any position, and consonants can be contrastively long and short in medial position. There is a syllabification rule in Finnish that requires that every non-first syllable begin with a single consonant (initial syllables can also begin with a vowel). When a syllable is open, the next syllable starts with a consonant that constitutes the short member of the opposition, and when a syllable is closed, it is closed by the first part of a geminate or consonant cluster, while the following syllable starts with the second part of the geminate or consonant cluster. The geminate is considered the long member of the short-long opposition in consonants.

When Estonian diverged from Finnish, certain sound changes took place in addition to various other changes. Important in this context is the occurrence of apocope and syncope of short vowels after long syllables. Kask (1972) puts apocope in the thirteenth century and syncope between the fourteenth and sixteenth centuries. Both processes affected short vowels of an open succeeding syllable after a long preceding syllable. For example, the word *laulma* 'to sing' had an earlier form *laulamahan*; the /a/ of the open second syllable was lost through syncope. An earlier form **jalka* became *jalg* 'foot' through apocope. The first syllable of *laulma* is now overlong; *jalg* is an overlong monosyllabic word. Incidentally, both *laulamahan* and *jalka* are standard forms in contemporary Finnish, with the same meanings, but without overlength.

Syncope has not spread into all dialects to the same extent; in the north-eastern coastal dialect, the older system is more or less preserved.

The result of the loss of unstressed short vowels was the emergence of a three-way system of oppositions, which will be referred to as Quantity 1, Quantity 2, and Quantity 3 (Q1, Q2, Q3). Q1 and Q2 are short and long respectively; Q3, the overlong quantity, developed as a result of compensatory lengthening. Now if Estonian were still a quantity language like Finnish, one would expect that vowels have three contrastive quantities in all positions, and consonants have three contrastive quantities in every intervocalic position. This is clearly not the case; the system is much more complicated and follows numerous language-specific rules. I am very well aware of theoretical objections to the possibility that a ternary system might exist, as well as of attempts to reduce the three-way oppositions to a system involving successive application of binary rules. The existence of three contrastive quantities is, however, a phonetic fact, regardless of how the phonetic data are interpreted.

3. Estonian prosody – present state

Finnish prosody can be described by stating the duration of successive vowels and consonants. Estonian prosody has to be described at several levels – levels that constitute a phonological hierarchy: segments, syllables, metric feet, phonological words and phonological phrases. Ternary oppositions are present in the first three of these levels; the quantity of a phonological word is determined by the quantity of the first foot, although the word may consist of more than one foot, which all have their own contrastive quantity structure.

I am using the term "metric foot" in its classical sense, without explicit commitment to any theoretical standpoint. In some earlier work I employed the term "disyllabic sequence"; but while most metric feet in Estonian are disyllabic, not all disyllabic sequences constitute metric feet, and there are also monosyllabic and trisyllabic feet. The following description of metric feet is based on my experimental phonetic research since 1960 (summarized in Lehiste 1997), involving both measurements made from productions by native speakers and listening tests based on natural as well as synthesized stimuli.

The basic phonological unit is the disyllabic sequence, with primary or secondary stress on the first syllable. There are three contrastive patterns that are phonetically manifested through interaction of segmental and syllabic quantity. To simplify the description, let us consider word types where the contrast is realized in vowels: word types that could be symbolized as CVCV (Q1), CVVCV (Q2), and CVVVCV (Q3). There is no durational contrast in consonants in initial position, and the syllable boundary in these words is before the short initial consonant of the second syllable (the syllabification rule in Estonian is basically the same as in Finnish); thus the prosodic structure of the words is manifested by means of vowel duration.

The duration of the second syllable vowel is not independently contrastive, but is dependent on the quantity of the first syllable, which in these word types is realized by means of the duration of the vowel. The first syllables of these disyllabic sequences are also referred to as being in Q1, Q2, and Q3 respectively. It is my considered opinion that this is appropriate only for syllables in Q3, which can also occur as monosyllabic words. Syllables in Q1 and Q2 do not occur outside of the metric feet. In particular, the presence of the half-long vowel of the second syllable in disyllabic sequences in Q1 is just as much a part of the identifying characteristics of Q1 as the short open vowel of the first syllable.

What determines the quantity of the whole disyllabic sequence is the temporal relationship between the durations of V1 and V2. This relationship can be expressed as simple ratios: 2/3 for Q1, 3/2 for Q2, and 2/1 for Q3. An example of actual measured values is given in Table 1, which contains average measurements of words produced by five speakers (Lehiste 1960):

Table 1. Average durations, in milliseconds, of V1 and V2 in Estonian words in three quantities.

	V1	V2	V1/V2
Q1	106	151	0.702
Q2	295	187	1.578
Q3	435	195	2.231

These durational relationships have been confirmed in numerous subsequent studies. For example, Krull (1993) found statistically significant differences between Q1-Q2 and Q2-Q3, both for the durations of V1 and V2 and for the V1/V2 ratios. For all cases, $p<.001$ (Krull 1993, p. 47).

The claim that for the manifestation of the opposition between Q1, Q2 and Q3 more than one syllable is required is supported by the fact that no syllable-level quantity opposition is found in monosyllabic words – monosyllabic words are either in Q3, or they are fused with neighboring words to constitute part of a larger phonological word or phrase. In other words, syllables in contrastive quantities are not freely concatenated into words. There are, however, segmental quantity oppositions within monosyllabic words – minimal triples like *saag, saak, sakk* abound in the language (the spellings with *g*, *k*, and *kk* refer to the three quantity degrees of /k/; the spelling system does not distinguish between long and overlong degrees of vowels and diphthongs). This means that the segmental level cannot be ignored in the description.

I would like to emphasize here that my description of Estonian is based on extensive spectrographic studies and perceptual tests that I have carried out over several decades (summarized in Lehiste 1997). One of these experiments will be described later in some detail.

The complexity of the system is illustrated on Figure 1, which is based on some material published in 1977. The figure represents the average duration of segments in seven disyllabic words that consist of identical segmental sounds. The contrasts are manifested by differences in the durational patterns associated with each word. Each word type represents a numerous class, but I doubt whether there exist many minimal septuples of this kind. Minimal triples, on the other hand, are abundant in the language.

The words are presented in groups of three where the first word is identical. In the first set, the contrast is based on the duration of vowels: *kodi – koodi(2) – koodi(3)* (long and overlong vowels are not distinguished in the orthography). The duration of the intervocalic short consonant remains constant; the duration of the second vowel decreases while the duration of the first vowel increases. Both changes contribute to establishing the difference in the ratio between the syllables.

In the second set, the contrast is based on the duration of the intervocalic consonant: *kodi – koti – kotti*. (The spelling system distinguishes between the segmental durations of plosives by using the letter for the voiced counterpart for Q1, a single letter for the voiceless plosive for Q2, and two letters for Q3.) The duration of the first vowel remains constant, while the duration of the intervocalic consonant increases. The duration of the vowels of the second syllable behaves in the same way as in the first set.

The third set is *kodi – gooti – kooti*. In many respects, this is the most interesting one. Here both the first vowel and the intervocalic consonant are involved in the opposition (after an overlong syllable nucleus, the overlong plosive is spelled with a single voiceless letter). Both are lengthened, but not to the same degree as in the word types where the opposition is based on vowel duration alone or intervocalic consonant duration alone. The second vowel shows the same pattern of reduction in duration as the duration of the first syllable increases.

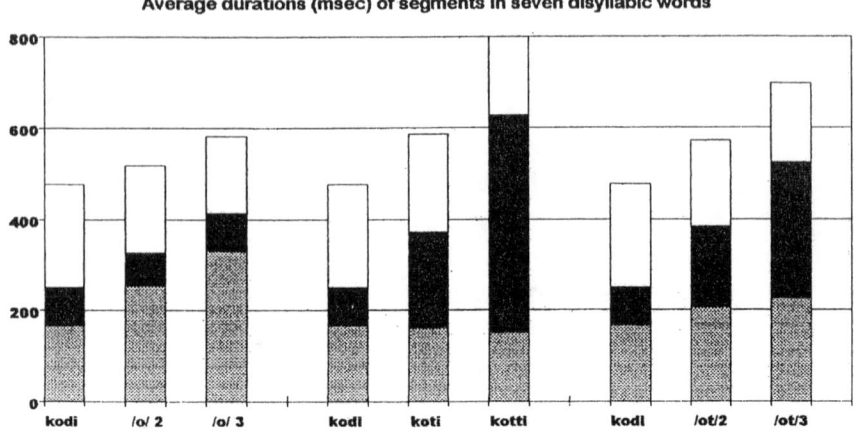

Fig. 1. Average durations, in milliseconds, of first syllable vowel, intervocalic consonant, and final vowel in seven disyllabic words. The first three columns represent the triplet *kodi-koodi(2)-koodi(3)*, the second set of three columns – *kodi-koti-kotti,* and the third set – *kodi-gooti-kooti.*

The long and overlong quantities are phonologically the same across the three sets: *koodi(2) – koti – gooti* are all in Q2, and *koodi(3) – kotti – kooti* are all equivalently Q3. Furthermore, one can observe a tendency toward metric foot isochrony achieved partly by adjustments in the duration of the vowel of the second syllable.

In addition to the differences in duration, there is a pitch difference associated with Q2 and Q3: *koodi(2), koti, gooti* all have a relatively high and level pitch on the first syllable, with low pitch on the second syllable, while the Q3 words *koodi(3)* and *kooti* have a pitch fall on the first syllable, followed by a low-pitched second syllable (in words like *kotti*, the first syllable vowel is too short to display a falling pitch). The Q1 word, *kodi*, has the same pitch pattern as the Q2 words *koodi* and *gooti*.

There had been suggestions in literature that pitch might be at least a factor, if not the decisive characteristic in distinguishing between long and overlong quantities. In my first extensive study involving listening tests I had found a certain amount of variation: words with different pitch patterns could be assigned to the same category by listeners, and words with the same pitch patterns could be assigned to different categories. Nevertheless, there was a tendency to prefer certain contours for each of the quantities. Preferred pitch for Q1 and Q2 was what I called then "rising-returning" pitch on the first syllable and falling pitch on the second syllable (the fundamental frequency curve ended at approximately the same value on the first syllable as it had started). For Q3 words, the pitch fall took place during the first syllable (which ended at a considerably lower value than its beginning), while the second syllable was level at the low end of the speaker's range.

To anticipate further results, both the characteristic syllable ratios and the preferred pitch contours have been confirmed by myself and others in later studies.

Having established the phonetic characteristics of disyllabic words, I moved on to analyzing a larger corpus of 500 sentences. The sentences were constructed to contain a large number of polysyllabic words. The spectrographic analysis of this corpus confirmed the previous observations regarding disyllabic words. The polysyllabic words turned out to consist of successive disyllabic sequences, each of them having characteristic S1/S2 ratios. For example, a word of four short syllables, like *segamini* 'in disorder', contained two Q1 metric feet, both having a short first syllable and a half-long second syllable.

The three quantity contrasts are only possible in a syllable that carries primary or secondary stress. In Estonian, a word carries primary stress on the first syllable, and has secondary stresses on succeeding odd-numbered syllables. These syllables constitute first syllables of metric feet. A three-way contrast can occur between the two syllables of a metric foot, but not across a metric foot boundary; in that position, only a two-way contrast can occur (the second syllable of a metric foot can be open, in which case the next metrical foot starts with a short consonant; the second syllable can also be closed by the first component of a consonant cluster or a geminate, but in the position between two metric feet, there is no opposition between a long and an overlong consonant) A special constraint is placed on the occurrence of vowel-based contrasts: these can occur only in the first metric foot of a word. Nowhere else in a polysyllabic word is there a quantity opposition based on vowel duration. (Overlong diphthongs can occur in non-first syllables; when they occur in the final syllable, they must be followed by a consonant.) Three quantities can occur between odd- and even-numbered syllables beyond the first metric foot, but the three-way opposition can only be manifested through consonant duration.

I developed a general formula for describing the quantity structure of a possible Estonian word, which is shown in Figure 2 (Lehiste 1965).

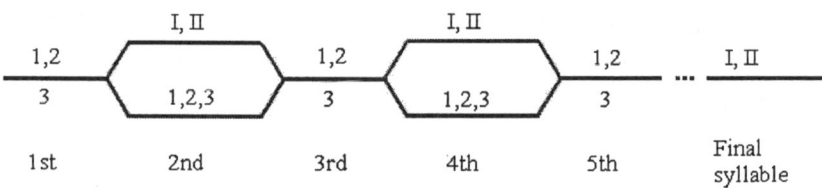

Fig. 2. Formula representing the quantity structure of an Estonian word. 1, 2 and 3 refer to positions in which three contrasts occur. I and II refer to positions in which two contrasts occur.

The graph is to be read as follows. Arabic numerals indicate contrastive syllabic quantities in those positions where three contrasts are possible; Roman numerals indicate contrastive quantities where only two contrasts occur. The graph indicates that if the odd-numbered syllable is in contrastive quantities 1 and 2, the following even-numbered syllable can have two contrastive quantities. If the odd-numbered syllable is in quantity 3, it may be followed by all three contrastive quantities in the even-numbered syllable. In other words, if the first syllable is in Q1 or Q2, then the second syllable can be short or long; if the first syllable is in Q3, the second syllable can be short, long, or overlong. The third syllable can in turn have three quantities; if it is in Q1 or Q2, then the fourth syllable can be short or long, but if the third syllable is in Q3, then the fourth can have three quantities etc., etc. Estonian words can be quite long; people – not necessarily linguists – amuse themselves by inventing long words. The longest I have recently seen had twelve syllables with 28 segmental sounds, and it was not invented by a linguist, but by a professor of sociology. (For the record, the word is *kirjanduslikustatamatuselegi*, occurring in the sentence "Popular songs can be made literary with various methods, but in some cases one has to admit the basic *impossibility of turning them into literature*" (Taagepera 1987).)

It is possible to explain this distribution of potential contrasts by reference to phonetics or to history. Phonetically, a ternary opposition can only occur in the stressed first syllable of a metric foot. A Q3 syllable always carries stress – either primary stress as the first syllable of a word, or secondary stress. The Q3 syllable can be followed by an unstressed second syllable, or by a syllable bearing secondary stress. If it is followed by an unstressed syllable, the two syllables constitute a disyllabic Q3 metric foot. If it is followed by a syllable with secondary stress, that second syllable constitutes the first syllable of the next metric foot. That metric foot can in turn be monosyllabic or disyllabic. If it is monosyllabic and carries secondary stress, it must be in Q3; a Q1 or Q2 syllable cannot carry secondary stress without having another syllable following it (in other words, without being the first syllable of a disyllabic foot). It is possible to have disyllabic words with both syllables in Q3, as, for example, *kindlaid* 'firm' part.pl., or *kaugust* 'distance', part. sg.

As was mentioned already, a Q3 syllable developed from a disyllabic sequence through syncope or apocope. Its synchronic behavior derives from its historical status of having been a disyllabic sequence. Within a word, it behaves as if it were still disyllabic. Another characteristic of a Q3 syllable that supports its status as a formerly disyllabic foot is its falling pitch contour. I have proposed that the falling pitch curve associated with a Q3 syllable can be explained by assuming that the single overlong syllable (its overlength having arisen through compensatory lengthening) now carries the pitch contour of what was formerly a disyllabic sequence (Lehiste 1978). Disyllabic words in Q1 and Q2 still have a high-low pitch pattern on their two syllables, while a Q3 syllable has the high-low pattern on the overlong syllable itself.

This is what I meant when I suggested that Estonian has changed from a quantity language to an accent language. The durational contrasts are still present, but their occurrence is dependent on stress, and their manifestation employs contrastive pitch patterns in addition to contrastive duration.

4. Interaction between pitch, duration, and stress

I tried to disentangle the separate roles of pitch and duration in a series of listening tests employing synthesized stimuli (Lehiste 1970-75). A few illustrations are offered below.

The synthesis was performed at the Bell Telephone Laboratories at Murray Hill in 1968, using the Digital Data Processor synthesizer then available at the Bell Laboratories. The structure of the stimuli is described on Figure 3. There were two sets of stimuli, one testing the perception of variation in intervocalic consonant duration – the *taba-tapa-tappa* set. The stimuli in this set were produced on a monotone, and the first vowel was kept constant at 120 msec. The primary variable was the duration of the intervocalic /p/, which ranged in 21 ten-millisecond steps from 40 to 240 msec. All consonant durations were combined with three V2 durations – 180, 120, and 90 msec. The randomized list of 252 stimuli was presented to 26 listeners (in Estonia), for a total of 6552 individual judgments.

The second set of synthesized stimuli contained three variables: duration of the vowel of the first syllable, duration of the vowel of the second syllable, and the fundamental frequency pattern distributed over the two syllables. The words were *sada-saada(2)-saada(3)*. The vowel durations ranged in 20 msec steps from 120 to 240 msec. The second syllable durations were the same as in the *taba-tapa-tappa* set. Each word was provided with three pitch contours: monotone on both syllables, high on the first syllable and low on the second syllable, and falling high-low on the first syllable, followed by a low second syllable. The randomized list of 252 stimuli was again presented to 26 listeners, who provided a total of 6552 responses. The grand total of responses for both sets was 13,104.

TABA – TAPA – TAPPA set

[p] durations ranging in 21 ten-millisecond steps from 40 to 240 msec.

V1 duration 120 msec, V2 duration either 180, 120, or 90 msec

Constant Fo at 120 Hz

Randomized list of 252 stimuli presented to 26 listeners for a total of 6552 individual judgments

SADA – SAADA! – SAADA set

V1 duration ranging in 20 msec steps from 120 to 240 msec

/t/ constant at 60 msec

V2 duration either 180, 120, or 90 msec

Fundamental frequency patterns applied to the test words:

120-120/120 (monotone), 120-120/80 (step-down), 120-80/80 (falling)

Randomized list of 252 stimuli presented to 26 listeners making a total of 6552 responses (grand total for both sets: 13,104)

PROTOTYPICAL S1/S2 RATIOS:

Q1: 120/180 (2/3)   Q2: 180/120 (3/2)   Q3: 240/90 (2.67/1)

PROTOTYPICAL Fo PATTERNS:

Q1: 120-120/80   Q2: 120-120-/80   Q3:120-80/80

Fig. 3. Structure of stimuli used in listening tests (Lehiste 1970-1975)

Figure 4 shows listener responses to the *taba-tapa-tappa* set, synthesized with a second syllable duration of 90 msec. (That duration characterizes Q3 words.) There are clear crossover patterns indicating categorical perception of Q1, Q2, and Q3.

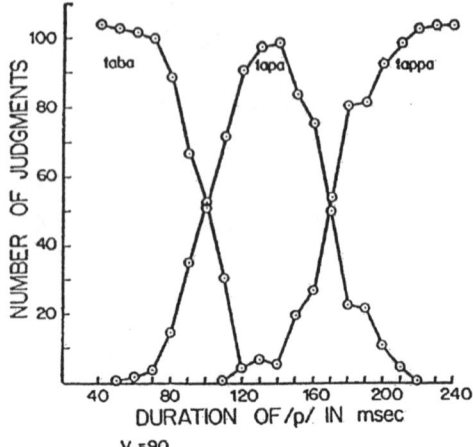

Fig. 4. Number of judgments as *taba, tapa* or *tappa*, expressed as a function of the duration of intervocalic /p/. Duration of the second syllable was constant at 90 msec.

Figure 5 shows a comparable result; here the V2 duration was 120 msec.

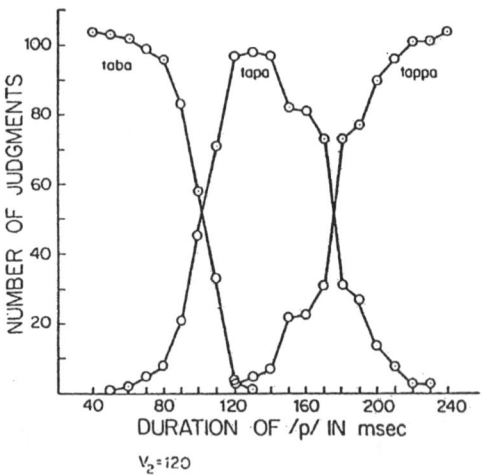

Fig. 5. Number of judgments as *taba, tapa* or *tappa*, expressed as a function of the duration of intervocalic /p/. Duration of the second syllable was constant at 120 msec.

Figure 6 shows the result of providing the stimuli with a half-long second syllable that normally characterizes words in Q1. Now the domain of Q2 judgments has expanded very considerably, while the number of Q3 judgments has decreased until even the longest /p/ duration did not produce a higher level of identification than 70%.

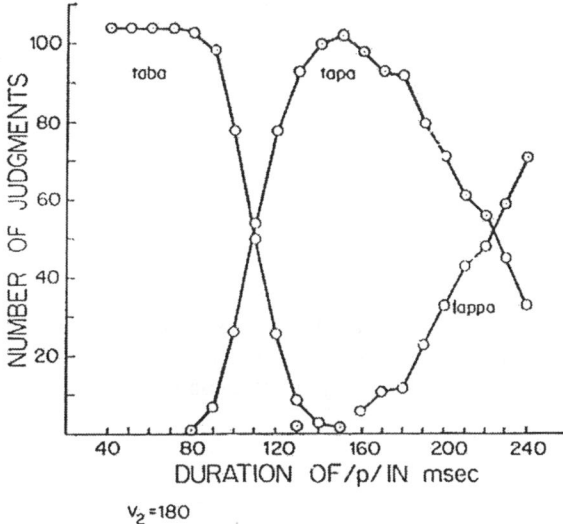

Fig. 6. Number of judgments as *taba, tapa* or *tappa*, expressed as a function of the duration of intervocalic /p/. Duration of the second syllable was constant at 180 msec.

I believe that these results constitute sufficient evidence for the importance of durational patterns of metric feet in the phonological system of Estonian.

The next set of figures illustrates the role of fundamental frequency. Figure 7 shows identifications of *sada, saada(!)(2)*, and *saada(3)* as a function of the duration of first syllable vowel, under the monotone condition (same as in the *taba-tapa-tappa* set), with a half-long second vowel that favors identification as Q1. The responses show indeed a preponderance of Q1 responses.

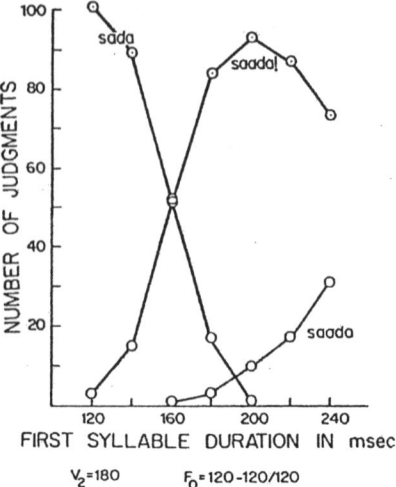

Fig. 7. Number of judgments as *sada, saada(!)(Q2)* or *saada(Q3)*, expressed as a function of the duration of the first syllable. The duration of the second syllable was 180 msec, the fundamental frequency pattern was level at 120 Hz.

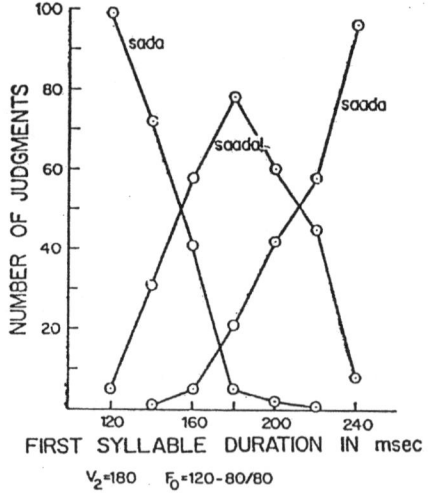

Fig. 8. Number of judgments as *sada, saada(!) (Q2)* or *saada(Q3)* expressed as a function of the duration of the first syllable. The duration of the second syllable was 180 msec, the fundamental frequency pattern was falling during the first syllable.

Identification of Q3 does not rise higher than 30% even with the longest first vowel duration. There are two factors here that disfavor Q3: the half-long second syllable, and the monotone fundamental frequency.

Figure 8 demonstrates the effect of the F0 pattern. The second syllable is still 180 msec, but the stimuli have been provided with the falling F0 contour that characterizes Q3, and the identification of Q3 jumps from 30% to 100%.

Figure 9 shows the results when the pitch and the ratio between syllables are maximally favorable for Q3 identification; the second syllable is short, the first vowel carries a falling F0 contour, and the assignment of stimuli to Q3 is greatly increased. Interestingly, the increase of Q3 responses has been mainly at the expense of Q2 responses: even at optimal V1 duration for Q2, the identifications do not reach 70%.

I believe these experiments demonstrate what I mean by talking about Estonian having become an accent language: for the identification of an Estonian word, segmental duration, relationship between the durations of the stressed syllable and the succeeding syllable, and the F0 contour are all necessary; each one plays a part in establishing the identity of the word.

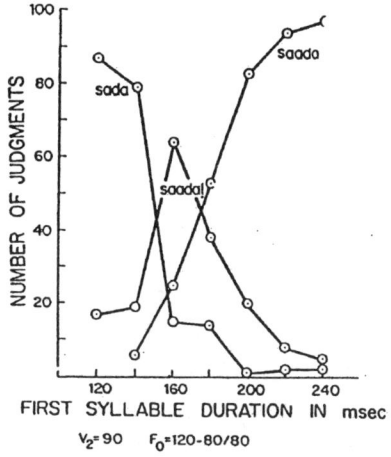

Fig. 9. Number of judgments as *sada, saada(!)(Q2)* or *saada(Q3)*, expressed as a function of the duration of the first syllable. The duration of the second syllable was 90 msec, the fundamental frequency pattern was falling during the first syllable.

But there are certain special problems connected with the opposition between long and overlong quantities. The phonetic correlates of overlength are not completely stable. In a series of studies (reviewed in Lehiste 1997), I found that the ratio between syllables was not always a sufficient cue for separating long quantity from overlong quantity. These studies involved listening tests with pairs of noise signals that were synthesized to represent durational ratios that do actually occur in spoken language. In the experiment, Estonian and English subjects were asked to state whether two pairs of noise signals were the same or different (for example, sh – sh vs. sh – shhh). Both groups of listeners could distinguish the stimuli mimicking Q1 from stimuli mimicking either Q2 or Q3, but they could not tell Q2 and Q3 apart. In other words, they could only tell whether the first or the second member of the pair was longer; they grouped together S1/S2 ratios of 3/2 and 2/1.

The signals had the expected durations, but no fundamental frequency; one might then conclude that the presence of F0 is a necessary condition for the perception of the difference, and that durational patterns alone do not provide a sufficient amount of information. On the other hand, Krull (Krull 1993), analyzing about ninety minutes' worth of free conversation, found that the most stable characteristic of the three quantities was the S1/S2 ratio. Sentence intonation could completely override the fundamental frequency patterns that are found in controlled productions, but the durational patterns remained intact.

5. Interaction between phonological patterns and morphology

There is a further development that suggests that, metaphorically speaking, Q3 is beginning to forget that it should play the part of a disyllabic sequence. This can be observed in everyday speech in the form of deviations from so-called correct usage.

Correct usage is codified in authoritative dictionaries, representing the standard of literary language at the time of the compilation of the dictionary. The dictionaries also assign each word to an inflectional paradigm. Estonian is a morphologically complex language, and the number of paradigms is considerably larger than in most Indo-

European languages: the 1960 dictionary (Nurm, Raiet, and Kindlam, 1960) lists ninety paradigms for nouns and adjectives, and twenty-five paradigms for verbs. Schoolteachers are supposed to correct forms that do not correspond to what is expected according to correct usage.

Mati Hint has studied the so-called mistakes made by highschool students, and has observed that these mistakes reflect an ongoing phonological process (Hint 1980, pp. 221-223). As was mentioned already, Estonian words are made up of metric feet that are basically disyllabic. A four-syllable word like *inimene* 'human being' consists of two Q1 metric feet, and forms its partitive plural with the ending –*i*: *inimesi*. A three-syllable word like *tuline* 'hot, fiery' forms its partitive plural with the ending –*eid: tuliseid*. Now there are trisyllabic words in the language with a first syllable in Q3, like *endine* 'previous', with secondary stress on the second syllable, -*dine* forming a Q1 metric foot. The 'correct usage' partitive plural of words of this type is *endisi*: the first syllable functions as if it were still a separate metric foot, and *endisi* corresponds to *inimesi*.

The contemporary incorrect usage of schoolchildren treats words of this type as if they were simply trisyllabic: the partitive plural form is *endiseid*, parallel to the partitive plural of *tuliseid*.

Since a word like *endiseid* is still in Q3, this means that the secondary stress on the syllable following the overlong first syllable has disappeared. If the overlong first syllable were still equivalent to a metric foot, the word forms *endine* and *endisi* would be divided into metric feet as *en-dine* and *en-disi*, with secondary stress on –*di*. A form like **en-diseid*, with secondary stress on –*di*, is impossible. The word *endiseid* has to be divided into metric feet as *endi-seid* rather than **en-diseid*.

But if the syllable following the overlong first syllable does not carry secondary stress, then the overlong syllable does not constitute a monosyllabic metric foot. The reassignment of words of this type (which are numerous) to a different inflectional paradigm constitutes evidence of ongoing phonological change. This is also witnessed by entries in dictionaries of correct usage: while the 1960 dictionary provides only the ending –*si* for the example used here, the 1999 dictionary (Erelt, 1999) lists both –*si* and –*seid* as possible partitive plural endings.

The language still has plenty of words in which there is no question that an overlong first syllable is followed by secondary stress. For example, the illative case of the word *kindel* 'firm' is *kindlasse*, where the first syllable is overlong, and the second syllable is overlong as well – which is possible only if that syllable carries stress. These forms continue to exist in the language and show no tendency to become restructured. In other words, the sound change has not been completed. The observed changes in morphology reflect an ongoing phonological change.

6. Conclusion

I started out trying to show how Estonian has changed from a quantity language to an accent language. Due to certain historical processes, the binary quantity system of the language changed into a ternary one. Metric feet became the basic constituents of phonological words. Overlong syllables retained some characteristics of their previous status as disyllabic long-short sequences; these features consisted of extra length due to compensatory lengthening, a falling F0 contour otherwise associated with disyllabic words, and the property that in a polysyllabic word, an overlong syllable could be followed by a syllable with secondary stress. There are numerous restrictions on the occurrence of overlength. If the phonetic properties of overlength have ever been unambiguous, they are not unambiguous at the present time. The language is in the process of changing, and it is indeed possible to document ongoing change – in the Estonian case, by observing the effect of phonological change on morphology.

References

Erelt, Tiiu (Ed.)
    1999   *Eesti keele sõnaraamat.* Eesti Keele Instituut. Tallinn: Eesti Keele Sihtasutus.

Hint, Mati
1980   Minevikuline ja tulevikuline aines keelesüsteemis. Prosoodiatüübi nihked ja selle tagajärjed. *Keel ja Kirjandus* 23: 215-23, 270-78, 349-55.

Kask, Arnold
1972   *Eesti keele ajalooline grammatika.* Tartu: Tartu Riiklik Ülikool.

Krull, Diana
1993   Word-prosodic features of Estonian conversational speech: Some preliminary results. *PERILUS* XVII: 45-54. Stockholm: Department of Linguistics.

Lehiste, Ilse
1960   Segmental and syllabic quantity in Estonian. *American Studies in Uralic Linguistics* Vol. I., 21-82. Bloomington: Indiana University.
1965   The function of quantity in Finnish and Estonian. *Language* 41, 3: 447-456.
1970-75 Experiments with synthetic speech concerning quantity in Estonian. *Congressus Tertius Internationalis Fenno-Ugristarum, Tallinn 1970.* Part I, 254-269. Ed. by Valmen Hallap. Tallinn: Valgus.
1977   Variability in the production of suprasegmental features. *Studies in Finno-Ugric Linguistics In Honor of Alo Raun:* 131-139. Ed. by Denis Sinor. Indiana University Uralic and Altaic Series Volume 131. Bloomington: Indiana University.
1978   Polytonicity in the area surrounding the Baltic Sea. *Nordic prosody: Papers from a Symposium:* 237-47. Ed. by Eva Gårding, Gösta Bruce, and Robert Bannert. Lund: Department of Linguistics, Lund University.
1997   Search for phonetic correlates in Estonian prosody. *Estonian Prosody: Papers from a Symposium:* 11-35. Ed. by Ilse Lehiste and Jaan Ross. Tallinn: Institute of Estonian Language.

Nurm, E., E. Raiet, and M. Kindlam (editors)
1960   *Õigekeelsuse sõnaraamat.* Eesti NSV Teaduste Akadeemia Keele ja Kirjanduse Instituut. Tallinn: Eesti Riiklik Kirjastus.

Taagepera, Rein
1987   Kui pikk on pikim eestikeelne sõna? *Keel ja Kirjandus* XXX, 12: 738.

Prosodic change from tone to vowel length in Korean

Kyung-Keun Kwon

0. Introduction

This paper discusses the relationship among tone, syllable cut, and vowel length in the prosodic change from Middle Korean to Modern Standard Korean (hereafter, Modern Korean). Middle Korean was a tone language, but Modern Korean has a length opposition without a tonal opposition. Regarding this prosodic change in Korean, it has been said that the long vowels in Modern Korean came from the syllables with a rising tone in Middle Korean.[1] However, there are many exceptions: for example, from the syllables with a rising tone, short vowels have developed, and long vowels have come from the syllables without a rising tone. The explanations about these exceptions need to consider other phonological features, in addition to tones.

This paper will show that tone, syllable cut, initial strengthening, and compensatory lengthening are involved in the prosodic change from tone to length in Korean. The first section of the paper deals with the prosodic features of Middle Korean and Modern Korean. The section discusses the existence and the functions of tone, syllable cut, stress, and length in Korean. In the second section, various cases of prosodic change from tone to length are shown. The third section focuses on the relationship between syllable cut and vowel length. The fourth section is devoted to compensatory lengthening at the phonological level.

1. Phonological oppositions in Korean

1.1. Middle Korean

Middle Korean was a tone language and had three tones: a low tone, a high tone, and a rising tone. Tonal oppositions are shown in (1).

(1)   low tone (L):   *nun* 'eye'
       high tone (H):   ·*nat* 'sickle'
       rising tone (R): :*nun* 'snow'
                        :*nat* 'grain'

Middle Korean had a particular marking system for tones in which dots are used. The dots are on the left side of syllables. The low tone has no dots, as in *nun*; the high tone has one dot, as in ·*nat*; the rising tone has two dots, as in :*nun* and :*nat*.

It is not clear, however, whether or not Middle Korean had a length opposition in addition to a tonal opposition. It has been assumed that in Middle Korean only syllables with a rising tone had a long vowel because of the historical development of these syllables, from which came the long vowel in Modern Korean.[2] However, it is thought that diachronic changes are of secondary importance in understanding synchronic phenomena. Therefore, this study will attempt to investigate the existence and the role of vowel length in Middle Korean by studying the language's contemporary phenomena in relation to vowel length.

About the existence of vowel length in Middle Korean, it has been stated in old texts that if a syllable has a rising tone, the sound of the syllable is pulled out long and later raised.[3] However, there has been no description of the phonological function of vowel length, and it remains controversial. To scrutinize the phonological function of vowel length in Middle Korean, the following questions are raised: Is vowel length predictable based on tone? Can syllables with tones other than a rising tone have a long vowel? Can both vowel length and tone have a phonological function in Middle Korean? Consider the following examples from Middle Korean texts (the dots indicate a syllable boundary).

(2) a. *cu.ljə* (RH) 'hungry'; *cu.ɯ.ljə* (LHH)
       pu.tʰjəj (LR) 'Buddha';
       pu.tʰjə (LL) + *i* (H) 'nominative ending'
    b. *cɯk.caj* (HL) 'soon'; *cɯk.ca.hi* (HLH)
       kol.pʰom (LH) 'hungriness';
       kol.pʰʌ- (LL) 'hungry' + *om* (H) 'nominalizing suffix'
    c. *s'a.hwa* (LH) 'fight'; *s'a.ho.a* (LHH)
       sul (L) 'liquor'; *su.ɯl* (LL)

The examples in (2) suggest the possible occurrence of compensatory lengthening through syllable contractions. If it is accepted that only those syllables with a rising tone can have a long vowel, then the occurrence of compensatory lengthening can be predicted by simply observing the tone resulting from a syllable contraction.

The rising tone consists of a low tone followed by a high tone. Therefore, a rising tone can come from the combination of a low tone and a high tone. Or, it can be decomposed into a low tone and a high tone. The examples in (2a) show that a syllable with a rising tone results from the contraction of two successive syllables, and thus has a long vowel. However, in the cases shown in (2b), in which a syllable contraction takes place as in (2a) and the resultant syllable is expected to have a long vowel, a compensatory lengthening cannot be said to occur, because the resultant tone from the syllable contraction is not a rising tone.

Compensatory lengthening is not a tonal phenomenon. It is not correct to accept the occurrence of a compensatory lengthening according to the tone resulting from a syllable contraction. If the compensatory lengthening as shown in (2a) is accepted, then it is expected that it also occurs in (2b), even if the resultant tone is high or low, because the syllable contraction in (2a) and (2b) are the same.

In (2c), a syllable results from the contraction of two syllables, which have two identical low or high tones, not a sequence of a low tone followed by a high tone. The contracted syllable does not have a rising tone. However, it seems that compensatory lengthening occurs even in this case because of the same syllable contraction as in (2a) and (2b). Therefore, in Middle Korean, there is a possibility that a syllable has a long vowel regardless of its tone. Thus, this possibility should be discussed in more detail.

In Middle Korean texts, there are passages where a word is written both in a normal form and in the so-called lengthened form in which one syllable of a normal form is considered to be lengthened as two syllables. The first syllable of the wordform *cu.ljə* in (2a) has a rising tone, but it is often lengthened into two syllables *cu.ɯ.-* with a low tone and a high tone. It has been claimed that long vowels in Modern Korean have come from syllables with a rising tone in Middle Korean.[4] In fact, most syllables with a long vowel in Modern Korean correspond to syllables with a rising tone in Middle Korean. The examples in (2a) indicate this correspondence. They show that long vowels appear in the Modern Korean reflexes of syllables with a rising tone, as in *cu:lita*. Based on this correspondence, it has also been said that syllables with a rising tone in Middle Korean have a long vowel, and Middle Korean has a length opposition.[5] However, I think this is questionable. Length in Middle Korean is not a relevant feature. The wordform *sul* in (2c) is also written as *su.ɯl*, which can be considered as its lengthened form. If Middle Korean has a length opposition, then the vowel in *sul* is probably long, as in the case of *cu.ljə*. In other words, *sul* comes from the contraction of two syllables *su.ɯl*. Here, compensatory lengthening occurs to restore the quantity of the lost syllable, and the resultant syllable has a long vowel, despite the fact that it has a low tone. It would be incorrect to accept a compensatory lengthening only in *cu.ljə*, but not in *sul*, on the basis of diachronic change (i.e. the historical development of long vowels from syllables with a rising tone). If length of Middle Korean as a synchronic phenomenon is interpreted by means of a diachronic change, it is not adequately observed nor explained. It is expected that the first syllables of *cu.ljə* and *sul* all have long vowels because of compensatory lengthening through syllable contraction. Therefore, it can be concluded that even a syllable with a low or a high tone in Middle Korean can have a long vowel.

Further, in examining whether or not the vowel length in Middle Korean also had a phonological function in addition to a tone, the phonological phenomena that are generally related to vowel length can be considered. If vowel length functions phonologically, it may make a difference in the syllable weight that plays a role in the assignment of an accent. Besides, if a segment is deleted or a contraction of two syllables takes place, a compensatory lengthening occurs at the phonological level to keep the length of the lost segment or syllable. Middle Korean has rhythm patterns based on tones, and vowel length does not affect the assignment of an accent.[6]

Therefore, it must be investigated how compensatory lengthening occurs, in order to ascertain whether or not vowel length in Middle Korean has a phonological function. In Middle Korean, there can be six types of syllables, according to differences in tone and length, as follows:

(3) a. L- toned syllable with a short or long vowel
     b. H-toned syllable with a short or long vowel
     c. R-toned syllable with a short or long vowel

Let us consider how the syllables in (3) are distinguished from each other and what phonological functions they have. In Middle Korean, compensatory lengthening can only occur through syllable contractions, as seen in (2). Low or high toned syllables with a long vowel, as shown in (3), can be predicted from syllable contractions or by the presence of the syllables' lengthened form. In other words, they are predictable from other corresponding word forms. In Middle Korean, syllables with a rising tone generally have long vowels. However, it is also possible that a syllable with a rising tone has a short vowel,[7] if the syllable carries an abrupt syllable cut, which will be explained later in detail. In brief, the short vowel in a syllable with a rising tone can be predicted by its syllable cut. If vowel length has a phonological function, it may not be predicted from other phonological phenomena. But vowel length in Middle Korean is predictable from compensatory lengthening and syllable cut. Moreover, the accent assignment in Middle Korean does not show that there is any difference between the syllables as shown in (3) regarding syllable weight. Thus, it follows that vowel length does not function phonologically.

So far various phenomena have been observed that seem to be related to vowel length in Middle Korean. In most cases, vowel length can be predicted from tone, syllable cut, and syllable contraction. It has not been shown that vowel length has a phonological function independently of tone. In Middle Korean, while the function of tones has been clearly observed, the phonologically distinctive role of length cannot be determined. All the available evidence indicates that length was not relevant in Middle Korean. So, it can be concluded that vowel length in Middle Korean exists not at the phonological level, but at the phonetic level.

In addition to tone, the prosodic feaure of syllable cuts exists in Middle Korean. According to the text *Hunminchŏngŭm*,[8] Middle Korean has a contrast between syllables with *Ipsŏng* and those without *Ipsŏng*. The property of *Ipsŏng* is explained in *Hunminchŏngŭm* and *Hunminchŏngŭm-ŏnhae*[9], as follows:[10]

(4) *Ipsŏng* is a hurried yet blocked syllable.
     Ipsŏng is an abruptly ended syllable.

Middle Korean syllables can be distinguished from each other, depending on whether or not they have *Ipsŏng*, as seen in (5).

(5)   non-*Ipsŏng*   *Ipsŏng*
      nun 'eye'   -   *kit* 'pillar'
      ·*nal* 'day'   -   ·*ip* 'mouth'
      :*nun* 'snow'   -   :*nat* 'grain'

However, it has not been clear to what phonological feature *Ipsŏng* is related, even though *Ipsŏng* plays an important role in the prosodic changes from Middle Korean to Modern Korean. In section 3, the feature of *Ipsŏng* and how it plays a part in prosodic changes will be discussed.

1.2. Modern Korean

Modern Korean has no tone. It has a length opposition between short and long vowels, as can be seen in (6).

(6) *nun* 'eye'
 nu:n 'snow'

Unlike Modern Korean, some dialects still have tones. In general, correspondences exist between Middle Korean, Modern Korean, and the *Kyungsang* dialect, as shown in (7).[11]

(7) Middle Korean   Modern Korean   *Kyungsang* dialect
    mal (L) 'horse'   *mal*   *mal* (H)
    mal (H) 'a unit of measure' *mal*   *mal* (M)
    mal (R) 'word'   *ma:l*   *mal* (L)

The low tone in Middle Korean corresponds to a short vowel in Modern Korean and to a high tone in the *Kyungsang* dialect. There is also a correspondence between the high tone of Middle Korean, the short vowel of Modern Korean, and the middle tone of the *Kyungsang* dialect. The rising tone of Middle Korean corresponds to the long vowel of Modern Korean and to the low tone of the *Kyungsang* dialect. These examples show the tonal shift from Middle Korean to the *Kyungsang* dialect. They also indicate that in the historical development from Middle Korean to Modern Korean, the phonological opposition was changed from tone to vowel length.

In Modern Korean, the accent is usually on the word-initial syllable.[12] This implies that accent does not have a phonologically distinctive function in Modern Korean. Examples in (8) show the tendency to place an accent on the initial syllable in Modern Korean, regardless of the syllable structure.

(8) '*nɛ.nɛ* 'always'
    '*paŋ.soŋ.kuk* 'a broadcasting station'
    '*pun.mjəŋ.ha.ta* 'clear'

I think that the tendency to the word-initial accent in Modern Korean results from the initial strengthening by which the initial syllable in a word is stressed or has a long vowel. In Modern Korean, the domain of the initial strengthening is even expanded from a word to a breath group. In (9), it is shown that in Modern Korean, long vowels remain only in the initial position in a breath group. The long vowel in *ma:l* is shortened if it is no longer in the initial position in a breath group, as seen in (9b).

(9) a. *ma:l* 'word' + *i* 'nominative ending' => *ma:.li*
    b. *kə:.cis* 'falsehood' + *ma:l* => *kə:.cin.mal* 'a lie'
       tɯt.ki 'to hear' + *co:.hɯm* 'pleasant' + *ma:l*
       => *tɯt.k'i.co.ɯm.mal* 'a pleasant thing to the ear'

2. Change from tone to length

From the comparison between the phonological oppositions of Middle Korean and Modern Korean, it can be seen that a prosodic change from tone to length occurred in the historical development of the Korean language. It has generally been said that long vowels in Modern Korean have come from syllables with a rising tone in Middle Korean.[13] Examples in (10) show such a historical change.

(10) *nun* (R) 'snow' > *nu:n*
     mal (R) 'word' > *ma:l*

However, there are many exceptions. First, there are cases where syllables with a rising tone in Middle Korean do not have long vowels in Modern Korean. In (11), it is shown that the second syllable with a rising tone in Middle Korean has a short vowel in Modern Korean, even if it has a diphthong, as in (11b).[14]

(11) a. *tu.tʰəp.ta* (Wŏrsŏk 2:56) 'thick'
        han.sum (Sŏk 19:14) 'sigh'
     b. *naj.naj* (Yong 16) > *nɛ.nɛ* 'always'
        mot.naj (Sŏk 9:37) > *mot.nɛ* 'constantly'

The changes in (11) are related to the position of the syllable in a word. As seen in (8) and (9), Modern Korean has an initial accent. This means that the initial syllable of a word was strengthened during the development from Middle Korean to Modern Korean. I will call this phenomenon the word-initial strengthening in Korean. Because of this word-initial strengthening, the second syllables in (11) have no long vowels in Modern Korean, in spite of their rising tone.

If the domain of word-initial strengthening is expanded to the phonological word, examples can be found where the word-initial syllable has a short vowel in Modern Korean, in spite of the presence of a rising tone in Middle Korean.

(12) *ma.ta* (Hun) 'every'
      pun (Yong 37) 'person'
      spun (Wŏr 166) > *p'un* 'only'

Words in (12) cannot be used alone. They can only be used when preceded by other words, as seen in (13).

(13) *kjə.ŋu* + *ma.ta* => *kjə.ŋu.ma.ta* 'every case'
      'case'   'every'
      cə + *pun*   => *cə.pun* 'that person'
      'that' 'person'

This means that the initial syllables of the words in (12) are never in the initial position of a phonological word. So, with the expansion of the domain of initial strengthening to the phonological word, the short vowels in the examples of (12) can be explained.

However, examples in (14) show that, even if Middle Korean syllables with a rising tone are in the initial position of a prosodic domain, short vowels appear in Modern Korean.

(14) *əs.tə.ha.ta* (Wŏr 146) > *ə.t'ə.ha.ta* 'how'
      mut.kɯ.li (Sŏk 9:36) > *mu.k'u.li* 'a shamanistic divination'
      cams.kan (Sŏk 13:41) > *cam.k'an* 'moment'

These examples are thought to be concerned with *Ipsŏng*. All the initial syllables in (14) end with a voiceless consonant, therefore have *Ipsŏng* according to *Hunminchŏngŭm*.[15] Examples in (14) indicate that *Ipsŏng* prevents syllables from having long vowels, thus plays a role in the historical development from tone to length. Above all, the *cams.kan* example shows that *Ipsŏng* in the initial syllable is realized through ambisyllabicity. *cams.kan* is also written as *cam.skan* in Middle Korean texts. According to Middle Korean orthography in which a word is written as pronounced, it means that *s* is an ambisyllabic consonant and causes the preceding syllable to have *Ipsŏng*. Because of *Ipsŏng*, the initial syllable with a rising tone, as in *cams.kan*, has a short vowel in Modern Korean. So it follows that *Ipsŏng* has a characteristic of preventing a syllable from having a long vowel.

In addition, there are cases in which long vowels in Modern Korean have come from syllables without a rising tone in Middle Korean, if the syllables had no *Ipsŏng*. As shown in (15), long vowels in Modern Korean have been able to come from word-initial syllables with a low tone in Middle Korean.

(15)   *kam.ta* (Wŏr 76) 'wind'
       kol (Wŏr 141) 'valley'
       mʌj.ta (Wŏr 76) > *mɛ.ta* 'bind'
       mo.tʌn (Sŏk 6:30) > *mo.tɯm* 'all'
       pʌj.ta (Sŏk 13:10) > *pɛ.ta* 'conceive'

Examples in (16) show that word-initial syllables with a high tone in Middle Korean have long vowels in Modern Korean, if they had no *Ipsŏng*.

(16)   *kʌl.ta* (Wŏrsŏk 1:29) > *kal.ta* 'grind'
       kʌm.ta (Wŏrsŏk 8:8) > *kam.ta* 'close'
       kɨ.li.ta (Yong 46) 'draw'
       mo.kʌj (Sŏk 9:9) > *mo.ki* 'mosquito'
       sum.ta (Wŏrsŏk 2:33) 'hide'

The examples in (15) und (16) indicate that if a long vowel in Modern Korean came from a syllable without a rising tone in Middle Korean, it is generally the case that the syllable had no *Ipsŏng*. This means that in Korean, there is a relationship between *Ipsŏng* and vowel length in prosodic changes. The following section discusses what phonological features *Ipsŏng* has and how *Ipsŏng* is related to vowel length.

3. Relationship between *Ipsŏng* and vowel length

As shown earlier, *Ipsŏng* plays an important role in prosodic changes in Korean. However, the phonological feature of *Ipsŏng* is not clear as yet. In this section, it will be discussed and the relationship between *Ipsŏng* and vowel length will be described.

3.1. Phonological feature of Ipsŏng

As seen earlier in (4), *Ipsŏng* is described as a hurried yet blocked syllable or an abruptly ended syllable in *Hunminchŏngŭm*. According to this text, *Ipsŏng* is a feature that a syllable has in relation to its ending.

It has been said that there is a phonological opposition according to how a syllable ends. In (17), different terms that indicate this opposition are given.

(17) Sievers (1976: 222-223): Silbenaccent:
schwach geschnittener Accent
stark geschnittener Accent
Jespersen (1904: 202): Anschluß: loser Anschluß
fester Anschluß
Trubetzkoy (1989: 196): Silbenschnitt:
ungeschnitten (loser Anschluß)
geschnitten (fester Anschluß)
Vennemann (1991: 218-219): syllable cut: smooth syllables
abrupt syllables

Based on Sievers, Jespersen, and Trubetzkoy, Vennemann (1991) interprets syllable cut phonologically. He suggests that there is a phonological opposition between an abrupt syllable cut and a smooth syllable cut, as shown in (18).

(18) smooth syllable; a smoothly ended syllable
abrupt syllable; an abruptly ended syllable

Syllable cut is well described in the nuclear phonology of Vennemann (1994). In nuclear phonology, a syllable consists of a decrescendo and a crescendo, which are associated with segments on a time arrow. In abrupt syllables, the nucleus ends on a crescendo. In smooth syllables, the decrescendo begins in the nucleus itself. Syllable cuts are represented in nuclear phonology as follows:

(19) smooth cut   abrupt cut

In an abrupt cut, a speech sound following the nucleus is required to be connected with a decrescendo. This means that an abrupt cut occurs in a closed syllable.

In relation to these properties of a syllable cut, the phonological feature of *Ipsŏng* is regarded as an abrupt syllable cut. The description of *Ipsŏng* as an abruptly ended syllable in old texts indicates that *Ipsŏng* is a feature that a syllable has in relation to its abrupt ending. This means that the property of *Ipsŏng* is related to an abrupt syllable cut.

The conditions under which syllable cut occurs support the interpretation of *Ipsŏng* as an abrupt syllable cut. In contrast to a smooth cut, which exists both in open and in closed syllables, an abrupt cut occurs only in closed syllables. According to *Hunmin-chŏngŭm*, *Ipsŏng* occurs in closed syllables that end with a voiceless consonant. This means that both *Ipsŏng* and an abrupt cut can only occur equally in closed syllables. It is therefore possible that *Ipsŏng* in Korean shares the prosodic feature of an abrupt syllable cut as described by Vennemann. This interpretation is also supported by the role that *Ipsŏng* plays in the historical changes in Korean, which will be discussed in the following section.

3.2. Syllable cut and vowel length

In (14), (15), and (16), it was shown that in the historical development of Korean, *Ipsŏng* prevents syllables with a rising tone from having long vowels. Long vowels in Modern Korean can come from syllables without *Ipsŏng*, even if the syllables do not have a rising tone. These cases can be properly explained on the basis of the relationship between syllable cut and vowel length.

First, consider examples from other languages that also have a relationship between syllable cut and vowel length. The opposition between abrupt and smooth syllable cut also exists in Modern German,[16] as seen in (20). The examples in (20) show that, while only short vowels appear in abrupt syllables, long vowels occur in smooth syllables, if they are accented.

(20) smooth syllable cut   abrupt syllable cut
     Wahn ['va:n] 'delusion'   *wann* ['van] 'when'
     Koma ['ko:ma] 'coma'   *Komma* ['koma] 'comma'

In Hopi, vowel length has a distinctive function in addition to syllable cut, as shown in (21).[17] However, there are no abrupt syllables with a long vowel.

(21) *pas* 'very'; with a short vowel and an abrupt syllable cut
     pas 'field'; with a short vowel and a smooth syllable cut
     pas 'still'; with a long vowel and a smooth syllable cut

The historical development in German also shows this relationship between vowel length and syllable cut. According to Vennemann (1994: 26, Ms: 11-13), a prosodic change from length to syllable cut occurred in the historical development from Middle High German to Modern German. The prosodic change is represented in (22), using the notation of syllable cuts.

(22) Middle High German > Modern German
a. open syllables with a short vowel   syllables with a smooth cut
        loben 'praise'   *loben*

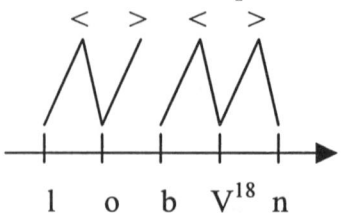 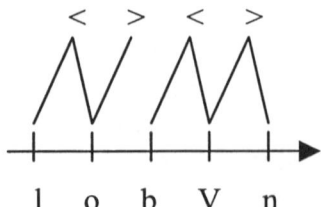

b. closed syllables with a short vowel   syllables with an abrupt cut
        kunde 'customer'   *Kunde*

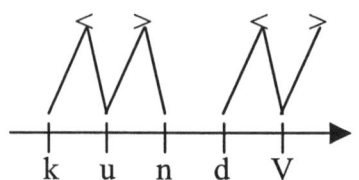 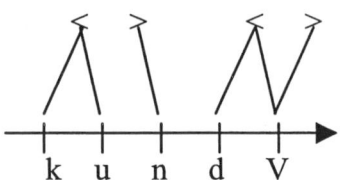

c. syllables with a long vowel   syllables with a smooth cut
        sat 'sowing'   *Saat*

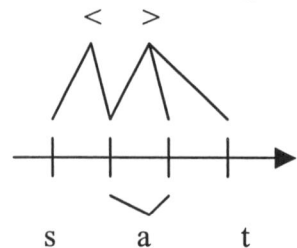 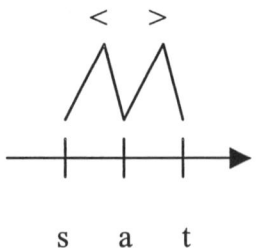

The change from open syllables with a short vowel to smooth syllables is illustrated in (22a); the change from closed syllables with a short vowel to abrupt syllables is shown in (22b); the change from syllables with a long vowel to smooth syllables is shown in (22c). These changes indicate that an abrupt syllable cut is preferred in closed syllables and that long vowels are not preferred in abrupt syllables.

   The synchronic or diachronic examples in (20), (21), and (22) show the relationship between syllable cut and vowel length that short vowels are preferred in abrupt syllables.[19]

The fact that *Ipsŏng* prevented syllables from having long vowels, as seen earlier in (14), (15), and (16), shows this relationship, i.e., long vowels are not preferred in abrupt syllables, implying that *Ipsŏng* is a form of an abrupt syllable cut.

According to the notation of nuclear phonology, prosodic changes in relation to syllable cuts in Korean are represented in (23); the change from syllables with a smooth cut and a rising tone to syllables with a long vowel is shown in (23a); the change from syllables with an abrupt cut and a rising tone to syllables with a short vowel is shown in (23b).

It is interesting to note that, in Middle Korean, an abrupt syllable cut can occur with ambisyllabicity, as in Modern German. Prosodic changes in relation to an abrupt syllable cut with ambisyllabicity are comparable in both languages. With the loss of length opposition, geminates in Middle High German have become ambisyllabic in Modern German, as seen in (24).[20]

(23) a   Middle Korean;   Modern Korean;
          syllables with a smooth cut   syllables with a long vowel
          and a rising tone
                mal 'word'   *ma:l*

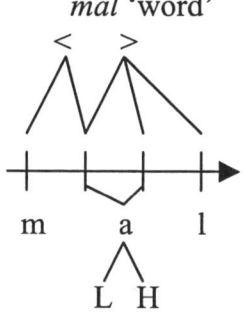   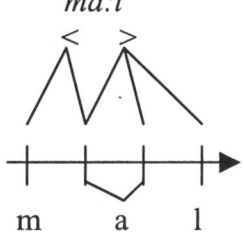

b.   Middle Korean;   Modern Korean;
     syllables with an abrupt cut syllables with a short vowel
     and a rising tone
         əs.tə 'how'   ə.t'ə

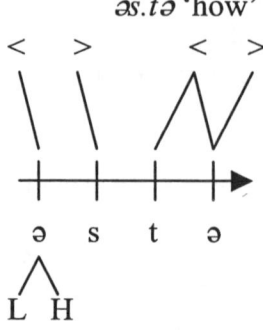

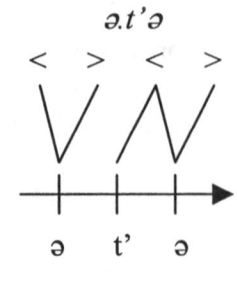

(24) Middle High German;   Modern German;
      geminates   ambisyllabicity
         mitte 'middle'   Mitte

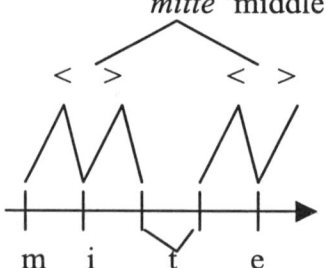

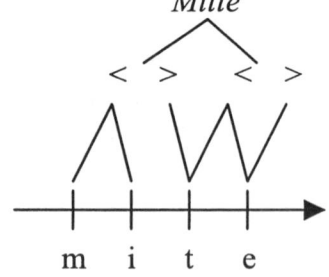

Abrupt syllables with ambisyllabicity in Middle Korean have developed differently according to the disappearing period of an ambisyllabic consonant, which can cause the obstruent following it to be glottalized. If an ambisyllabic consonant disappeared after the glottalization of the following consonant, the reflex form in Modern Korean has a glottalized consonant. In this case, even a vowel with a rising tone became short, because the abrupt syllable cut kept the vowel from becoming long. The entire process is illustrated in (25).

(25) Middle Korean; ambisyllabicity;   from tone to length;
     abrupt cut with a rising tone   short vowel
              camskan 'moment'

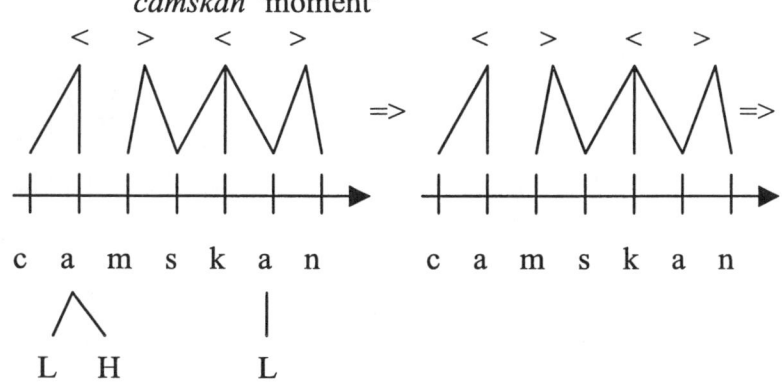

glottalization and   Modern Korean; smooth cut
loss of an ambisyllabic consonant
                                          camk'an

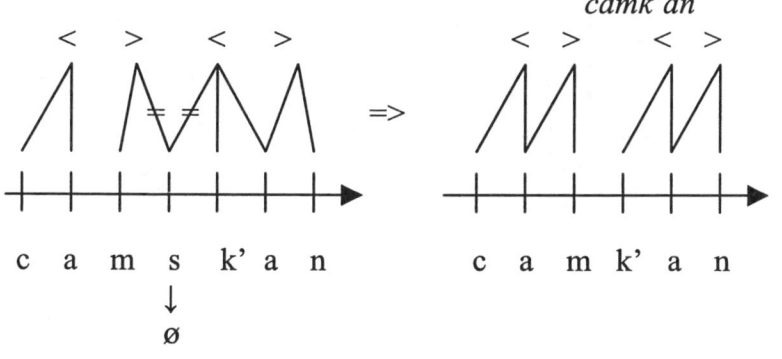

However, when the ambisyllabic consonant was lost before the glottalization of the following consonant, the reflex form in Modern Korean has no glottalized consonant. At the same time, with the disappearance of the ambisyllabic consonant, the syllable cut became smooth. The smooth syllable cut and the initial strengthening enabled a vowel to become long, as illustrated in (26).

(26) Middle Korean; ambisyllabicity;   loss of an ambisyllabic
     abrupt cut with a low tone   consonant; smooth cut
     kamstol- 'curve around'

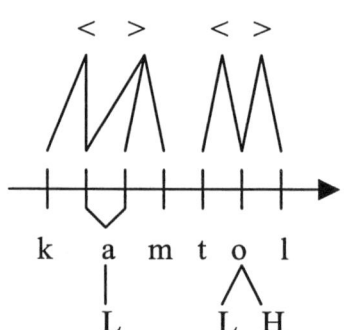

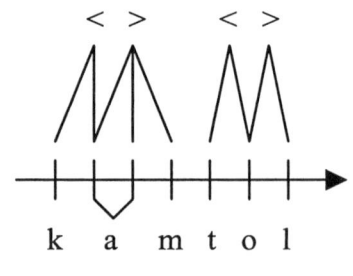

4. Compensatory lengthening

With tonal perturbation, length became a relevant feature in Korean. It is to be expected that, after the distinctive function was changed from tone to length, compensatory lengthening can take place at the phonological level, because compensatory lengthening presupposes the existence of a length. It is very interesting that, in Korean, compensatory lengthening does not occur through the loss of a coda consonant, but rather because of syllable contraction or the loss of a syllable.[21] It is illustrated in (27) that vowels of word-initial syllables were thus lengthened.

(27) a.   caj.hi- (LH) > ca.i- > cɛ:- 'measure'
          ka.hi (LH) > ka.i > kɛ: 'dog'
     b.   kaj.ja.mi (LL) > kɛ:.mi 'ant'
          pʌj.jam (HL) > pɛ:m 'snake'

From the examples in (27a), it could be supposed that the long vowel in the word-initial syllable in Modern Korean was caused by a rising tone, because two successive syllables have a low and a high tone, the combination of which can result in a rising tone. However, the monophthongization from *ai* to *ɛ* took place only after tonal perturbation.[22] Therefore, it can be concluded that the word-initial vowels in (27a) were lengthened to compensate for the loss of a syllable. In contrast, in (27b), the role of the rising tone cannot be considered, because two successive syllables have low tones or a high and a low tone, the combination of which never results in a rising tone. So, it follows that the long vowels of word-initial syllables in (27b) resulted from compensatory lengthening through syllable contraction or syllable loss.

As seen earlier in (2), it is possible that, in Middle Korean, compensatory lengthening occurred at the phonetic level. Only after the change of the phonological opposition from tone to length did the compensatory lengthening come to play a role at the phonological level. In Modern Korean, in which vowel length takes a distinctive function, compensatory lengthening through syllable contraction occurs often, as seen in (28).

(28) ka.ɯl; ka:l 'autumn'
      chə.ɯm; chə:m 'beginning'
      po.a; pwa: 'seeing'

5. Conclusion

This paper discussed how vowel length in Modern Korean developed from Middle Korean. From this investigation, it can be concluded that four factors are involved in the prosodic change from tone to length in Korean: tone, word-initial strengthening, abrupt syllable cut, and compensatory lengthening.

Long vowels in Modern Korean have generally come from syllables with a rising tone in Middle Korean. However, if a syllable with a rising tone is not in the initial position in a word or a breath group, a long vowel did not develop from it. This change is attributed to word-initial strengthening.

An abrupt syllable cut, called *Ipsŏng*, prevented syllables from having long vowels in Modern Korean. If a syllable with a rising tone has an abrupt syllable cut, a short vowel can appear in Modern Korean. From syllables without a rising tone, if they have a smooth syllable cut, long vowels can be developed.

After the phonological opposition was changed from tone to length, compensatory lengthening through syllable contractions took place at the phonological level. From compensatory lengthening, long vowels also came into being in Modern Korean.

The results from the prosodic changes in Korean should not be confined to language-specific phenomena. Such results can contribute to the understanding of the prosodic properties of syllable cuts and the relations among prosodic features, especially those between syllable cuts and length.

Notes

1. See Heo (1991: 506) and Kim (1973: 3).
2. S. Lee (1978: 71-72), based on the fact that the reflexes of the same words in Modern Korean show long vowels, assumes that Middle Korean syllables with a rising tone had long vowels in the underlying representations.
3. Cf. the English translation by S. Lee (1978: 20).
4. See Heo (1991: 506).
5. See S. Lee (1978: 71-72).
6. The rhythm patterns in Middle Korean consist of tones. See, for example, Kim (1973: 77-91) and Gim (1993: 132-134).
7. Goldsmith (1976) has shown the possibility of a short vowel having a contour tone.
8. *Hunminchŏngŭm* is the first text written about the formation of the Korean alphabetic system, which was invented in the fifteenth century by King *Sejong*.

9. *Hunminchŏngŭm-ŏnhae* is an abridged edition of *Hunminchŏngŭm* translated into Korean.
10. See the English translation by S. Lee (1978: 20).
11. Heo (1955: 95-164) suggests tonal correspondences between Middle Korean and the *Kyungsang* dialect. In Heo(1955), the words of Middle Korean are compared with those of the *Kyungsang* dialect, according to the word class and the number of syllables.
12. See H. Lee (1996: 199).
13. See Heo (1991: 506).
14. For this paper, the following texts served as major sources for Middle Korean data:
    a. *Hunminchŏngŭm* (1446, hereafter Hun) [Correct sounds for the people]
    b. *Yongbiŏch'ŏnga* (1447, hereafter Yong) [Songs of flying dragons]
    c. *Sŏkposangjŏl* (1447, hereafter Sŏk) [A biography of Buddha]
    d. *Wŏrinch'ŏngangchigok* (1449, hereafter Wŏr) [Songs of moon's reflection on thousand rivers]
    e. *Wŏrinsŏkpo* (1459, hereafter Wŏrsŏk) [A combined edition of *Sŏkposangjŏl* and *Wŏrinch'ŏngangchigok*]
15. See section 3.1 about the condition of *Ipsŏng*.
16. See Vennemann (1991: 216-220).
17. See Trubetzkoy (1939: 176-179) and Vennemann (1994: 47).
18. V means an indistinctive vocality in reduced syllables.
19. In comparison, Vennemann (Ms: 11) suggests that there is a "correlation default" between syllable structure and syllable cut as follows: everything else being equal, a smooth cut is preferred in open syllables and an abrupt cut in closed syllables.
20. See Vennemann (1994: 26-27).
21. Ko (1991: 4-5) suggests that the compensatory lengthening in Korean is involved not in the loss of a coda consonant, but in the loss of syllabicity in a neighboring syllable.
22. According to Heo (1991: 512-514), in Korean, tonal perturbation occurred in the sixteenth century and the monophthongization from *ai* to *ε* in the nineteenth century.

References

Becker, Thomas
    1996   Zur Repräsentation der Vokallänge in der deutschen Standardsprache. *Zeitschrift für Sprachwissenschaft* 15: 3-21.
de Chene, Brent
    1985   *The Historical Phonology of Vowel Length*. Ph.D. dissertation, The Ohio State University. New York: Garland.

Donegan, Patricia
1985 On the Natural Phonology of Vowels. Ph.D. dissertation, The Ohio State University. New York: Garland.
Gim, Cha-Gyun
1993 Urimal-ŭi sŏngcho [On tones in Korean]. Seoul: Taehaksa.
Goldsmith, John
1976 Autosegmental Phonology. Ph.D. dissertation, Massaachusetts Institute of Technology. Reproduced by the Indiana University Linguistics Club.
Heo, Ung
1955 Pangjŏm yŏngu [A study on tonal marks]. Tongbanghakchi 2: 38-194.
1991 Kugŏ ŭmunhak [Korean phonology]. Seoul: Saemmunhwasa.
Jespersen, Otto
1904 Lehrbuch der Phonetik. Leipzig: Teubner.
Kim, Wan-Jin
1973 Chungsegugŏ sŏngcho-ŭi yŏngu [A study on the tone of Middle Korean]. Seoul: Tap.
Ko, Kwang-Mo
1991 Kugŏ-ŭi posangchŏk changŭmhwa-e taehayŏ [A study on compensatory lengthening in Korean]. Ph.D. dissertation, Seoul National University.
Kwon, Kyung-Keun
1997a Phonologische Entwicklungen im Koreanischen und Deutschen. Ph.D. dissertation, Ludwig-Maximilians-Universität zu München.
1997b Chungsegugŏ Ipsŏng-e taehayŏ [On Ipsŏng in Middle Korean]. Ŏnŏhak 20: 39-57.
Lee, Ho-Young
1996 Kugŏ ŭmsŏnghak [Korean phonetics]. Seoul: Taehaksa.
Lee, Ki-Moon
1977 Geschichte der koreanischen Sprache. German translation by Bruno Lewin. Wiesbaden: Reichert.
Lee, Pyonggeun
1978 Kugŏ-ŭi changmoŭmhwa-wa posangsŏng [Lengthening and the compensable possibility in Korean]. Kugŏhak 6: 1-28.
Lee, Sang-Oak
1978 Middle Korean Tonology. Ph.D. dissertation, University of Illinois. Seoul: Hanshin.
Lutz, Angelika
1991 Phonotaktisch gesteuerte Konsonantenveränderungen in der Geschichte des Englischen. Tübingen: Niemeyer.
Sievers, Eduard
1976 Grundzüge der Phonetik. Hildesheim/New York: Georg Olms. First published Leipzig: Breitkopf & Härtel [1901].

Trubetzkoy, Nikolai Sergejewitsch
1989   *Grundzüge der Phonologie.* Göttingen: Vandenkoeck & Ruprecht [1939].
Vennemann, Theo
1991   Syllable structure and syllable cut prosodies in Modern Standard German. In P. Bertinetto, M. Kenstowicz, and M. Leporcaro (eds.), *Certamen Phonologicum II: Papers from the Cortona Phonology Meeting 1990*, 211-243. Turin: Rosenberg & Sellier.
1994   Universelle Nuklearphonologie mit epiphänomenaler Silbenstruktur. In K. H. Ramers, H. Vater, and H. Wode (eds.), *Universale phonologische Strukturen und Prozesse*, 7-54. Tübingen: Niemeyer.
Ms.   From quantity to syllable cuts: On so-called lengthening in the Germanic languages, Manuscript from Krems Phonology Meeting 1992.

Diachrony of the Scandinavian accent typology

Tomas Riad

1. Introduction[1]

The diachrony of Scandinavian tone accent involves several questions. Three famous ones are (a) the origin of the lexical tones, (b) the development of a phonological distinction (Kock 1878, 1901; Oftedal 1952; Öhman 1967; Elstad 1980; d'Alquen & Brown 1992; Riad 1998a), and (c) the relationship between the tonal accent system of Swedish and Norwegian dialects, on the one hand, and the stød system of Danish, on the other (Kroman 1947; Liberman 1982; Ringgaard 1983; Riad 2000ab). A fourth question, which has not received much attention so far, but which will be the concern here, is (d) the diachronic development of the tone accent system into a finer typology of tonal grammars.

Approaching the diachrony of the accent typology amounts to filling the space between two hypotheses, one regarding the origin of tonal accent, the other regarding the nature of the present-day tonal typology. The proposal for the origin of tonal accent in Riad (1998a) singles out one of the so-called "two-peaked" realizations of accent 2 as the most conservative type, namely the central Swedish (Stockholm) accent variety. This raises some questions and makes some predictions regarding the routes of development into the extant typology, where we find variation along several parameters (Bruce & Gårding 1978; Bruce 1998; Lorentz 1995; Riad 1996, 1998b). The specific goal of this article is to find out to what extent a view of central Swedish as the relatively oldest accent variety makes for a reasonable reconstruction of the diachrony of the typology. Differently put, what can the internal synchronic properties of the typology itself tell us about the diachrony of the typology?

The paper is organized as follows. After going over a few basic facts and assumptions in this section, the parameters of variation making up the typology are presented (section 2). We then discuss tone shifts (section 3) and the sub-typology of connective accent 2 (section 4). In section 5, we will have a look at the isoglosses resulting from two individual typological features. In section 6, the diachronic predictions of the typology will be discussed. Section 7 then shows how a specific pattern of stress in compounds can provide evidence for the diachrony of the typology. Section 8 concludes the paper.

1.1. The accents

The Scandinavian tone accents are usually referred to as "accent 1" and "accent 2" (also called "toneme 1" or "acute" and "toneme 2" or "grave", respectively), which are in fact cover terms for a contour consisting of three or four different tones in accent 2 and one less in accent 1. The opposition is always a privative one, where accent 2 contains a lexically specified tone and accent 1 lacks such a specification (Sweet 1877, 155; Haugen & Joos 1952; Haugen 1967). Such a privative opposition is also at the basis of tonal Dutch Limburgian dialects (Heijmans, this volume). Accent 1, then, is pure intonation, while accent 2 is a lexical tone plus intonation. Thus, we can always predict the shape of accent 1 from the shape of accent 2, simply by subtracting the lexical tone, which is invariably associated to the primary stressed syllable. There is maximally one lexical tone to a word (simplex or compound).

Functionally, the pitch accent opposition is more or less superfluous, at least in Swedish (Elert 1972). Several dialects lack the distinction, and truly (lexically and syntactically) minimal pairs are hard to come by. Nevertheless, lexical tones are phonologically real (Haugen 1963, 1967; Bruce 1977; Kristoffersen 1990, 254ff.; Ladd 1996, 159; Lorentz 1995; Engstrand 1997).

The lexical tone (T*) is followed by two tones, which will here be referred to as the prominence tone ($\underline{T}$) and the boundary tone (T]), intended as fairly neutral terms with regard to function. The specific functions of these tones may vary between dialects. In particular, they seem to interact differently in different dialects with regard to focus (Gösta Bruce and Gjert Kristoffersen p.c.). A reservation is therefore in place here. We shall abstract away from complications relating to the actual functions of individual tones, and we will only be concerned with the limited context of citation forms. Accent will be described in all dialects as constituted by the same three functions in the same order.[2] This is necessary in order to keep the typology and its predictions in check, given the still limited number of in-depth studies of individual dialects. At a general empirical level, however, it is perfectly reasonable to expect and assume that the accentual typology is not very widely varied. While dialects may *sound* radically different, it is striking how similar they are with regard to the lexical distribution of accent 2 and the general tonal behaviour (cf. Gårding, Bruce & Willstedt 1978; Lorentz 1995; Riad 1998b). Thus, we are trying here to focus on some structural properties, without being overly concerned with how these structural properties are linked to functional tasks.

Accent 2 in fact occurs in two roles in most Swedish and some Norwegian dialects. We speak of the *lexical* accent 2 when a lexical tone is stored together with a root or, more often, a suffix. Then there is *connective* accent 2, which occurs in words containing two stresses or more (Elert 1970, 44ff., 111f.; Linell 1972,14). In this case, accent 2 is postlexically assigned, not only to all regular compounds, but also to several derivational forms, where the derivational suffix is stressed.[3]

(1) Central Swedish accents

| *lexical tone* | *prominence tone* | *boundary tone* | *stylized tracings* |

Accent 1. simplex. 'tobacco'

	LH	LH L]	
	|	|	
'tobak	'tobak	'tobak	'tobak

Accent 2. simplex. 'nun'

```
    H*              H*LH           H*LHL]
    |                |              |              ⋁⋀
  'nunna           'nunna         'nunna          'nunna
```

Connective accent 2. compound. 'snack'

```
    H*              H*  LH         H*   LHL]
    |                |   |          |    |
 'mellan͵målet   'mellan͵målet  'mellan͵målet  'mellan͵målet
```

Accent 2 has two peaks in this dialect, the lexical tone being H* and the prominence tone being LH. Below, it will be argued that the "two-peaked" accent variety of central Swedish is archaic relative to the others.

1.2. Origin of tone accent

In Riad (1998a), it was argued that accent 2 originated in the context of stress clash. Thus, the two peaks would originate as two unmarked stress peaks. In clash situations, resulting from syncope and other prosodic developments in the late Old Norse period, the secondary stress reduced, but the pitch part was retained. Where stress reduction became permanent (such as in inflectional and some derivational suffixes), tonal information was directly encoded as lexical. There are several arguments to support this theory. One is the lexical correlation between suffixes inducing accent 2 today and suffixes, which carried secondary stress in late Old Norse. Other arguments are of a null-hypothetical character, like the very fact that there are two ways of getting accent 2 (lexical and connective). Under the stress clash hypothesis, it makes sense to connect the two synchronic sources of accent 2. Dialectological evidence also points to a diachronic flow from connective accent 2 to lexical accent 2.

(2) The flow from connective to lexical accent.

	Old Norse two stresses	Modern Swedish two stresses	Modern Swedish one stress	Gloss
compound	¹Hlewa-ˌgastiz	²¹Eva-ˌKarin		names
	¹sol-ˌhvarf	²¹sol-ˌvarv		'sun loop, year'
derivation	¹sjúk-ˌdómr	²¹sjuk-ˌdom		'illness'
	¹klók-ˌskapr	²¹klok-ˌskap		'wisdom'
	¹hofð-ˌingi		²¹hövd-ing	'chief'
	*¹tung-ˌoːn		²¹tung-a	'tongue'
	*¹mann-ˌliːka		²¹man-lig	'manly'
inflection	*¹herði-ˌoːz		²¹herd-ar	'shepherds'
	*¹doːmi-ˌdeː		²¹döm-de	'deemed'

The table shows that many suffixes that were stressed in Old Norse are no longer stressed, but induce accent 2 in the forms they attach to. Inflectional suffixes are all unstressed today, while some derivational suffixes remain stressed, and others do not. The thrust of the argument is that the process of replacing stress with a lexical tone is productive in the same way today as it was a good millennium ago. Further arguments and a fuller discussion is given in Riad (1998a), where other proposals are also reviewed (Kock 1901; Öhman 1967; Elstad 1980; Liberman 1982).

Under the hypothesis that accent 2 originated from stress clash, there is a set of arguments that demonstrate the archaic character of the two-peaked accent type relative to the one-peaked accent types. There are also a few arguments for the general conservativeness of central Swedish (CSw) dialects.

First, since the same two-peaked variety also occurs in the archaic dialect of Älvdalen, which is spoken in an isolated area more or less enclosed by other accent systems (Dala and Göta), CSw can be said to be archaic as well.

Second, compared to most other dialects to the south and west, CSw shows relatively little weakening in the final syllable of disyllabic words with accent 2. This is manifest both in richer vowel quality distinctions in unstressed syllables, and in the inhibition of vowel deletion in forms where comparable vowels in accent 1 forms get deleted (Wessén 1969, 80ff.). This relative absence of weakening in CSw could be connected with the second peak of accent 2.

Third, Älvdalska has not yet implemented the quantity shift (Hesselman 1901, 1902). The same relatively archaic pre-quantity shift stage is found in a dialect in eastern Uppland, close to the heartland of central Swedish.

Fourth, a more indirect argument for the conservativeness of CSw is the fact that the tonal system preceding the development of stød in Danish seems to have been like the present-day CSw one (Kroman 1947, 183, passim). This argument relies on the credibility of the general theory of the origin of stød from a tonal system. It is argued in Riad (2000ab) that there are great similarities in the tonal dynamics of Zealand in Denmark and Uppland/Sörmland in central Sweden. There are also other southern relic areas along the Swedish coast, around Kalmar on the east coast and in Halland on the west coast.

In the rest of the paper, we shall look at typological facts, grammatical as well as geographical, to see if we can find further clues to the diachrony of Scandinavian accent.

1.3. Map

Pitch accent dialects occur all over Scandinavia, except the northernmost parts of Norway and Sweden, most Swedish dialects in Finland, and most Danish dialects. In addition, there are a few smaller areas, which lack distinctive accent, such as eastern Uppland and the area surrounding Bergen. There is no accent distinction in Iceland or the Faroe Islands. These facts are indicated in the map in (3), which is based on the map in Gårding (1977, 47). The typology indicated is based on the shape of the accents in disyllabic simplex words, and the locus of peaks. The legend in the upper right corner indicates which dialects have two and which ones have one peak for accent 2. The map includes a number of place-names, which occur in the typology in (4), below, and elsewhere in the article.

Diachrony of the Scandinavian accent typology 97

(3) Overview of the tone accent dialects

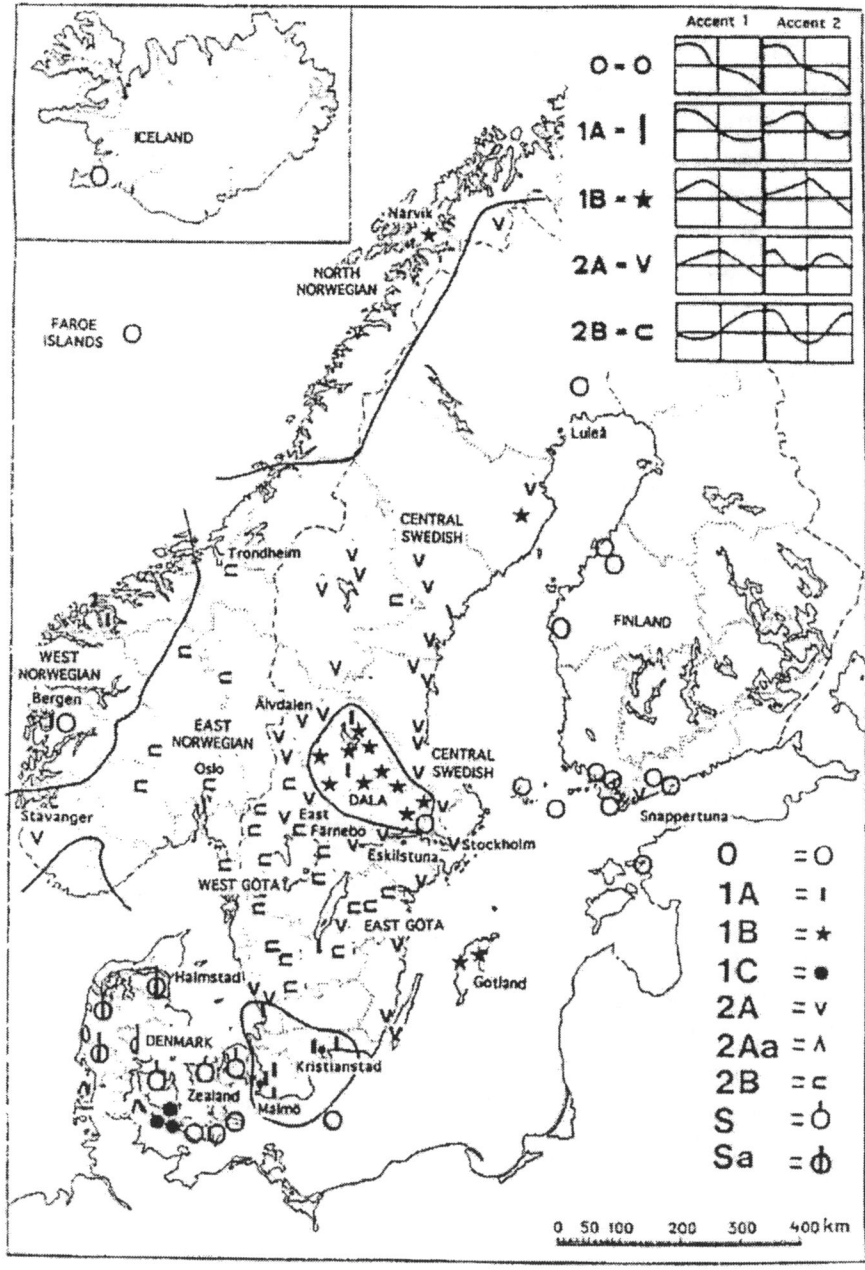

Work on the accent typology, at least in the Swedish tradition, starts with Meyer (1937, 1954) and his data is registered on the map, which primarily shows the Swedish accent varieties. It has here been complemented with a few more symbols based on information on Norwegian taken from Fintoft et al. (1978), Mjaavatn (1978) and Lorentz (1995). Symbols added here, as well as isoglosses given later (cf. 22), etc. should be considered as tentative, not least because the work carried out on Norwegian in the 70s was cast in a different model than the one used for Swedish by Gårding, Bruce and others around the same time.

2. The typology

Many of the claims made here regarding the typology of Scandinavian accent are based on previous typological work by Meyer (1937, 1954), Öhman (1967), Gårding (1977), Bruce & Gårding (1978), Gårding, Bruce & Willstedt (1978), Lorentz (1995) and Riad (1996, 1998b), and on synchronic work on the best studied Swedish dialects by Bruce (1977, 1987) and Engstrand (1995, 1997). The empirical base has been broadened here and there by information available from a number of dialect descriptions of varying degrees of sophistication and depth (e.g. Klintberg 1885 for Gotland and Kallstenius 1902 for East Färnebo).

There are different opinions of what the functions of the different tones are, and in order to keep variation under control, the strategy here has been to segment the tones in each dialect according to a single set of functions in a single order: lexical, prominence and boundary tone. Ultimately, this might require some adjustments, but there appears to be consensus about the most important fact, namely that the first tone is the lexical tone. What the other functions are is largely theory dependent, but this needs not affect the typology as such. The important part is that a) enough is similar for it to be meaningful to talk about one typology, and b) the tonal string is segmented in three parts in a similar way for all dialects.

In the description given, stylized tracings and autosegmental representations will be used and the variation will be discussed along several parameters. A more technical analysis of the typology is given in Riad (1998b) in terms of optimality theory (Prince & Smolensky 1993). The present analysis is updated on a couple of points. The main parameters of variation between dialects can all be connected to the prominence tone: its value, whether or not it is associated and what direction it is oriented towards (right/left/both).

2.1. Value of the prominence tone

The value of a tone is largely predictable from the value of the others in a given dialect, since the obligatory contour principle is everywhere obeyed. The segmentation of tones into the functions used singles out the prominence tone as the least predictable, since it can be complex.[4]

(4) Tones and dialect types[5]

accent 1	lexical tone accent 2	promi- nence tone	boun- dary tone	dialect
Ø	H*	LH	L]	central Swedish /Stockholm, Älvdalen, Stavanger, Snappertuna
Ø	H*	L	H]	Göta, East Färnebo (south), east Norwegian /Oslo
Ø	L*	H	L]	Malmö, Dala/Nås, East Färnebo (north), Gotland, Bergen, north Norwegian /Narvik

There is some variation with regard to how many tones (3 or 4) are present in a citation form, but the variation is limited. Under the assumption that the CSw two-peaked variety is archaic, the presence of four tones only in this type could be seen as another archaic feature.

2.2. Association and orientation of the prominence tone

In order to study the behaviour of the prominence tone, we should look at long compounds, since they make available more than one stressed syllable. In accent 2 simplex words, there is only one stress and the lexical tone has precedence to it. In these words, then, the prominence tone floats (but gets interpreted). In accent 1 words, when there is no lexical tone present, the prominence tone associates to the stressed syllable, cf. (1). It is therefore interesting to see whether a prominence tone can associate to some other stressed syllable than the primary stressed syllable. It turns out that whether or not the prominence tone associates in compounds is a major parameter of variation between dialects, in fact forming an isogloss (cf. 5.1). Long compounds with more than two stresses will also show to which of several secondary stresses, if any, a prominence tone associates, in a given dialect. This is required to establish the fact that there are independent grammatical constraints pulling the prominence tone both to the right and to the left. Furthermore, long compounds also allow for variation in internal morphological structure, which in fact seems to guide the association of the prominence tone in at least one dialect (Snappertuna, 4.2.3). Earlier typological work has been overly concerned with the shape of the tonal contour (in disyllabic simplex words), which rather limits the empirical scope and conceals important phonological variation.

Below is an overview of the various dialect realizations of connective accent 2 in compounds. The example word used is *midsommardansen* 'the midsummer dance', which is a compound consisting of three stressed roots. It will be given in standard Swedish form throughout. The stylized tracings give an idea of what the dialects sound like and the autosegmental representations to the right illustrate the assumed grammar. In particular, one can see here whether the prominence tone is associated (the first three dialects) or not (the rest). One can also see that all dialects except the last three have a right oriented prominence tone, which spreads to the left in some dialects. The last three have a left oriented prominence tone, which never spreads. Spreading is marked by an arrow, while an interrupted line marks interpolation.[6]

(5) Accent 2 in compounds in various dialects
    (Riad 1998b modified)

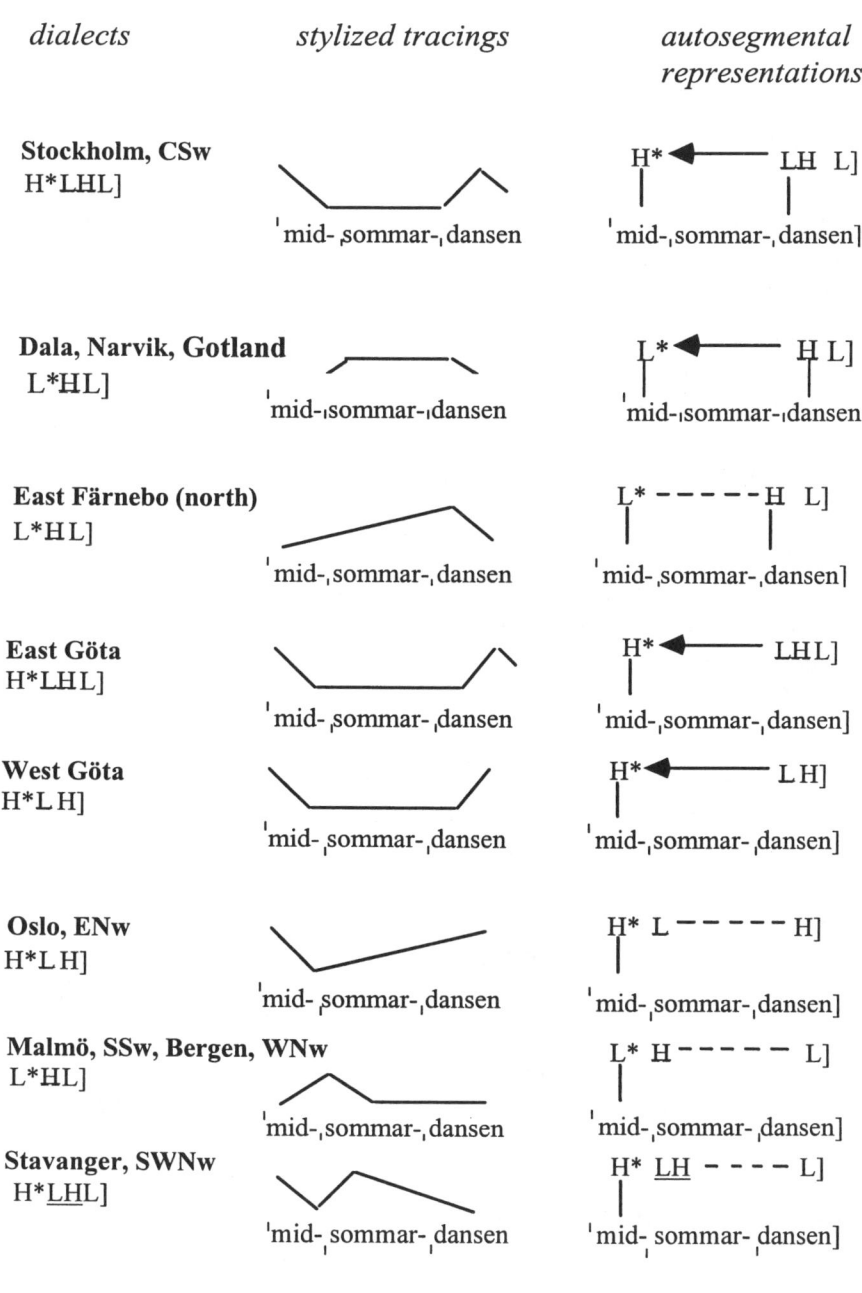

What all dialects have in common is the association of the lexical tone to the primary stress, and the alignment of the boundary tone with the right edge of the word. Tones are sequenced on one tonal tier and are therefore always adjacent on that tier. However, when we look at how tones are realized in relation to the segmental string, there seem to be three types of transition. First, tones may be realized (in full) on adjacent syllables or moras, giving rise to fairly abrupt transitions.[7] The transition between the lexical and prominence tones in e.g. Oslo, Malmö and Stavanger is of this type. Second, spreading occurs when a tone is wanted in two places at the same time.[8] In CSw, Dala and the Göta varieties, the transition between the lexical tone and the prominence tone, which spreads, is of this type. Finally, there is interpolation, that is, when tones are at a distance, but there is no spreading of either tone. In Oslo, which has the same set of tones as the west Göta variety, the transition between the prominence tone and the boundary tone is a gradual rise, hence interpolatory in our interpretation.[9] The same type of transition occurs between the lexical and prominence tones in East Färnebo.

In the data available, interpolation is more readily ascertained in rises from L to H, than in falls from H to L, which seem to be more varied (cf. Malmö and Stavanger). Presumably, this has to do with the difference in articulatory effort, but it also allows for a different analysis, where the boundary tone spreads. In this typology, however, it has been assumed that there is no spreading of boundary tones, in part to constrain the model, in part because firm evidence, such as a clear target for spreading, is lacking. There is at least one dialect, Eskilstuna (cf. 3.1), which could be interpreted as having a spreading boundary tone with a highly abrupt transition from the prominence tone as consequence. Nevertheless, an alternative interpretation where the boundary tone actually associates (rather than just spreads) to the last stress will be proposed.

One complicating factor here is the variable quality of the data. Data for Malmö, Bergen and Oslo are readily available from modern work by Bruce (1979, 1998), Kristoffersen (2000), and Lorentz (1995), along with auditory impressions. The data for Stavanger is taken from the graphs of Selmer (1927). The data for East Färnebo (north) are from Kallstenius (1902) and given in musical notation, and are thus based on auditory impression only, rather than registered fundamental frequency.[10]

3. Diachronic tone shifts

The most direct kind of support for the relative age of two accentual systems is when it can be directly and empirically demonstrated that one type developed from the other. We therefore should study transitional areas between CSw and its neighbours, and look for evidence for the direction of the transition.

3.1. From CSw to Dala

Fortunately, there are several concrete factors that provide us with insight into the dialect transition from central Swedish to Dala (Bergslagen), situated to its west. These two dialects have the same tonal grammar, but different values for the lexical and prominence tones. The area around Eskilstuna in Sörmland provides a transitional variety, famous for its so-called curl (Bleckert 1987). The curl is a pragmatically induced speech habit, which is characterized by a sharp tonal drop, often accompanied by creaky voice. In Riad (2000ac), this is analyzed as a leftward shift of the final L boundary tone into the last stressed syllable. Curl typically happens under emphasis in phrase-final position (for F0 tracings, cf. Bleckert 1987, 116 ff.). It is interesting to see here that the compression of the tonal contour caused by the boundary tone in turn forces the LH prominence tone to shift leftwards. Instead of the LH rise, we get a HL] fall in the primary stressed syllable of accent 1 and in the secondary stressed syllable of connective accent 2. This is illustrated on the next page.

(6) Pragmatic accent variation within central Swedish

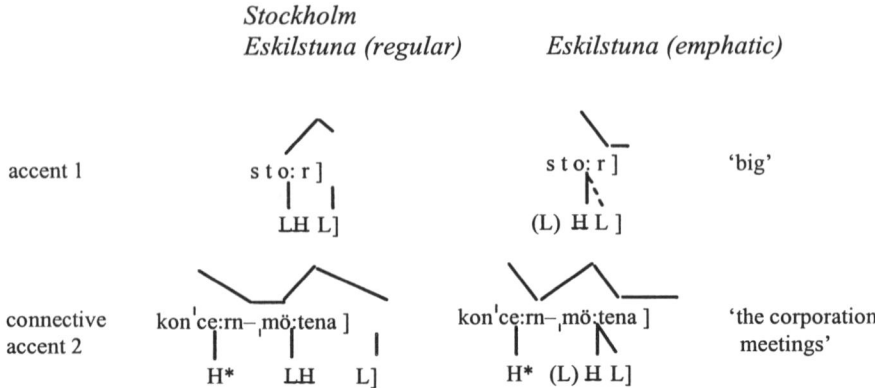

From this situation, changes in two further directions can be observed to take place. One leads to the loss of the accent distinction, yielding the so-called generalized accent 2 and Danish stød. This suggests similar developments in central Sweden and in Denmark (cf. Riad 2000ab). The other direction of change leads to the Dala system, which is our central concern here. Here, the curl causes the lexical tone, too, to shift leftwards.

(7) Effect of curl on the overall accent contours

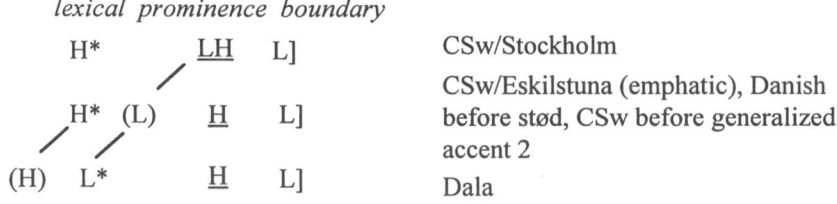

(8) Transition from CSw to Dala in compounds

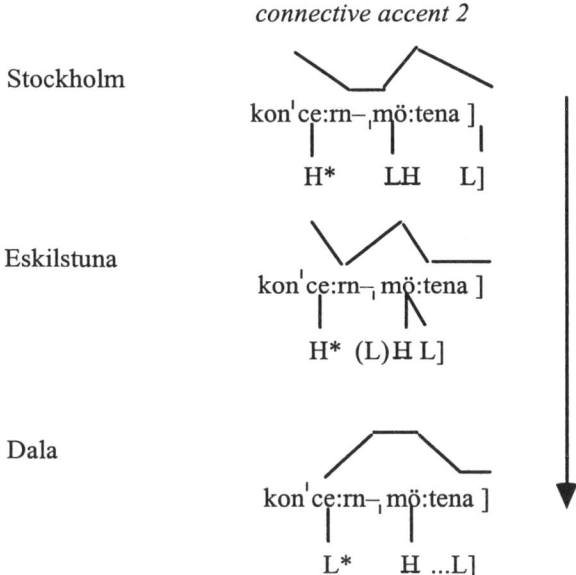

All that changes here is the shifting of tones to the left, whereby these tones come to be matched with new functions. The grammar remains exactly as it is.

This shift is easy to study in dialect geography, the Eskilstuna dialect representing an intermediate stage between CSw and Dala, and it establishes the central Swedish tonal variety as older than the Dala variety. A change in the opposite direction would require a complication from three to four tones, an assumption that is hard to motivate. As we have already seen before, there are also other dialect geographic reasons for assuming the conservativeness of the CSw variety. The previously mentioned Älvdalska dialect is a relic area with a CSw accent type bording on the Dala dialects, but which has little in common with them. This speaks for the relative conservativeness of this accent type.

The tonal composition of the Dala type occurs in several dialects, as indicated in (4) above. Some of these have the same grammar as Dala, viz. Narvik in northern Norway and the dialects spoken on the island of Gotland, east of the Swedish mainland. Others have lost connectivity, e.g. south Swedish and Bergen (west Norwegian). The central Swedish variety occurs chiefly in the area around Stockholm and northward, but also in other places scattered around Scandinavia. This can be seen in the map in (3).

3.2. From CSw to Göta

The shift from CSw to Dala involved the shift of both prominence and lexical tones to the left. In the shift from CSw to Göta, however, the prominence tone moves to the right. The chief reason to assume that the direction of the diachronic shift is from CSw to Göta, rather than the other way around, is the origin of tone as summarized in section 1.2. If that hypothesis is right, an associated prominence tone represents an older stage than an unassociated one, everything else being equal. As previously mentioned, there are also other reasons to assume that CSw is archaic relative to its immediate neighbours and beyond.

Göta is a large and clearly circumscribed dialect area, which borders central Swedish and Dala in the north and south Swedish (Malmö, etc.) in the south. To the west, it borders east Norwegian, with which it has many things in common (cf. 4.2.2). It seems that we can tentatively divide Göta into two varieties based on the degree to which a final boundary L is realized. This is illustrated in (9).

(9) Comparing CSw with the Göta dialects

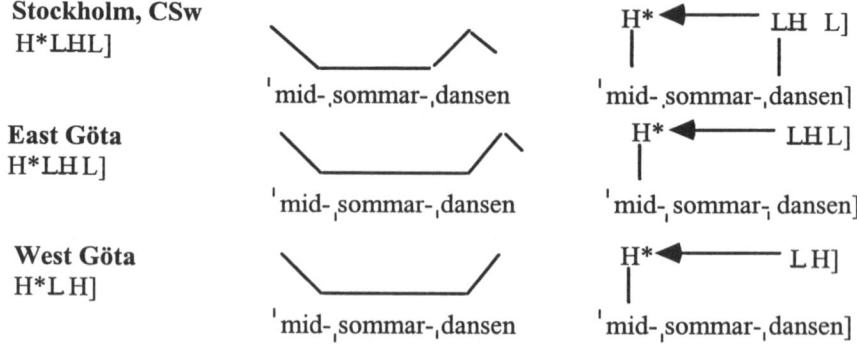

The difference in grammar between east Göta and CSw is small but precise and concerns the association of the prominence tone. In east Göta, the prominence tone is no longer associated to the rightmost stressed syllable in compounds, and the tone sequence extends to the right edge of the word. Right-edge orientation is a property of the Göta dialects, as well as of the CSw dialect, where it is manifest as the preference to associate to the rightmost free stressed syllable, regardless of how long the compound is (Riad 1998b, 87). The step from east to west Göta amounts to a rematching of functions, where the H is reinterpreted as boundary tone, and L alone becomes the prominence tone.[11]

The distinction between associated and unassociated prominence tones is easy to observe in the empirical data. When associated, the rise from L to H takes place in the final stressed syllable of the compound, whereas if the prominence tone is unassociated, the rise takes place in the unstressed final syllable. Clearer cases than the one given are the plural ˈmidˌsommarˌdanserna 'the midsummer dances' and a quadrisyllabic accent 1 simplex like ˈsyfilisen 'the syphilis'. These examples are illustrated in (10). The TBU for lexical and prominence tones in Scandinavian dialects always appears to be a stressed syllable, the variation being whether both primary and secondary stresses may function as anchor points, or only the primary stressed syllable.[12] In Göta, only the primary stressed syllable is a legitimate TBU.

(10) Unassociated prominence tone in Göta
    East Göta
    H*LH L]

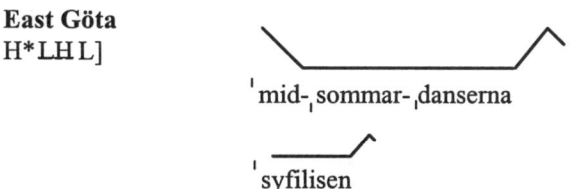

There are some further and direct indications of the rightward orientation in CSw trisyllabic simplex words, which might be worth mentioning. In accent 2 simplex words, it will be recalled, the prominence tone is never associated, for lack of TBUs. The default is for the prominence tone to be realized directly after the lexical tone, by virtue of the constraint implementing leftward orientation. In disyllables, the floating second peak will be realized somewhere in the second syllable, but in trisyllables there are two options, crudely speaking, the second or the third syllable. Both syllables are possible realization sites for the prominence tone, at least in some varieties of CSw.[13]

(11) Variable realization of prominence tone in trisyllabic simplex words (Stockholm).

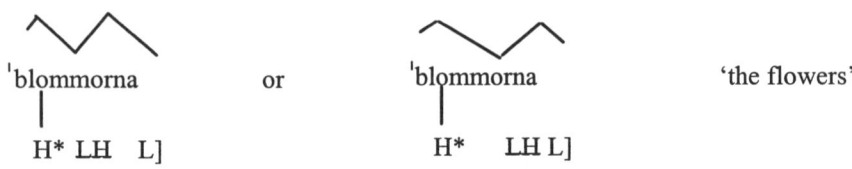

This variation suggests that the rightward orientation, which is clearly visible in compounds, might have some influence in simplex forms as well. These opposite constraints are taken to be unranked with respect to each other in CSw (Riad 1998b). We also see that the direction of orientation is a separate parameter of variation from the association/no association of the prominence tone parameter. In Göta, the rightward orientation is fully generalized, as the association of prominence tone no longer hampers it. Like in CSw, however, leftward orientation remains important in Göta, since the prominence tone spreads to the left. Leftward orientation is thus taken to be the cause of spreading, whether or not the prominence tone is associated. To complete the picture, leftward orientation of the prominence tone with no signs of rightward orientation also occurs, e.g. in Oslo, Malmö and Stavanger, cf. (5).

In the model underlying the typology, the leftward/rightward orientation parameter is not tied to either value on the association of prominence tone parameter. It is by virtue of the rightward orientation that the association of the prominence tone selects the final stress as anchor point in a long compound in CSw. If rightward orientation is weak in some dialect, leftward orientation could, in principle, select the stress nearest to the primary stress as anchor point.[14]

We have now looked at two tonal shifts. In the Dala case, there was no change of grammar, only of the tonal specifications. In the Göta case there was a small change in grammar (CSw > east Göta), perhaps coupled with a change of the tonal specifications of tones (east Göta > west Göta). In what follows, we shall look at some dialects where delinking of the prominence tone results in a *leftward* shift. This has dramatic consequences for the assignment of accent in compounds, as it puts connective accent 2 at stake.

4. Loss and acquisition of connective accent

The notion of connective accent is assumed here to be an archaic feature. It invariably has the same contour as lexical accent 2, and this identity must have an explanation. As mentioned in 1.2, there are several good indications that lexical accent 2 developed from connective accent 2 via a regular secondary split (Riad 1998a). Now, there are many dialects which do not have a particular *connective* accent 2 in compounds. In these dialects, accent is realized in the same way in compounds as in simplex words, and since accent is no longer predictable from the number of stresses, we expect to find compounds with accent 1 as well as with accent 2. This expectation is borne out in southern Swedish, Oslo Norwegian and elsewhere.

Our task is to make likely that the absence of connective accent 2 in a dialect is indeed a case where connective accent has been *lost*, rather than the other way around. The issue is tricky, since in systems with lexical assignment of accent in compounds, prosodic factors too are involved, which interact with the lexical factors (cf. Bruce 1973, 1974; Ström 1998). As we shall see, there is evidence that these mixed systems gradually move towards postlexical connective accent, i.e. they generalize the prosodic factors, rather than the lexical factors. The loss of connective accent, however, would be a more drastic and abrupt event, as it seems highly unlikely that lexical factors would be able to sneak into the totally general postlexical process of connective accent 2 assignment. Our hypothesis will be that a change from connective (e.g. west Göta) to non-connective accent (e.g. Oslo) is abrupt, while the way back, manifest in the Malmö-Kristianstad-Halmstad-Stockholm typology (4.1.2), is gradual. If this can be substantiated, then we can establish connective dialects as relatively archaic, and the two-peaked realization of accent 2 as the original one.

We shall first look at the typology of accent assignment in compounds in southern Sweden to establish the historical direction of the change from non-connective accent to connective accent in compounds. Then, to get indications of an abrupt change in the other direction, we shall look at Stavanger and Snappertuna, both of which have lost the general rightward orientation of the prominence tone, which is characteristic of CSw and Dala. In section 5, we shall take a bird's view of the Scandinavian map and see what the dialect geographical isoglosses can tell us about connectivity.

4.1. From non-connective to connective accent in compounds

In a superb study, Bruce (1973, 1974) showed that accent assignment in compounds in southern dialects of Swedish (Malmö, Kristianstad, Halmstad) is influenced by both lexical and prosodic factors in mixed but principled ways. In central Swedish, accent assignment in compounds is completely prosodic (viz. connective). Bruce presented nonsense compounds like *blod-prins* 'blood prince', *banan-kust* 'banana coast', *skog-s-hals* 'forest neck', etc. to his informants, and varied the properties of the components in order to determine the factors influencing the choice of accent. It turned out that lexical accent 2 of the first member is a dominant lexical feature, whereas clashing stresses is a strong prosodic feature, favouring accent 2 in the compound. A linking-*s* in the compound favours accent 1, as does non-initial stress in the first member of the compound (*banán* 'banana').

Regarding the general conditions for accent assignment, recall that there is an asymmetry between accent 1 and accent 2 in that only accent 2 can be lexically specified (privativity). In addition, putative conflicts between factors favouring accent 1 and accent 2 are limited in that accent 2 can only be realized in disyllabic forms or longer. This might seem to make for a reasonably happy cohabitation of different accent assignment procedures. Nevertheless, there are clear points of conflict. Compounds consisting of two monosyllabic elements provide the most spectacular case. Such compounds do not invariably get the same accent, although one might have thought that they would get either accent 1 because of the monosyllabicity of the first element, or accent 2 because of the stress clash. The issue is well illustrated in east Norwegian (Oslo), where accent variation in compounds is common (Withgott & Halvorsen 1984, 1988; Kristoffersen 1992). We find accent alternations in compounds consisting of monosyllables, e.g. ²*lys-fest* 'light party', ¹*fest-lys* 'party light'. Withgott & Halvorsen's approach was to assume that monosyllables can be lexically specified for either accent even if they are just monosyllabic, and therefore are unable to realize their accent in simplex forms. This "latent" accent 2 would be brought out in compounds. Kristoffersen's less abstract, and therefore more convincing analysis is based on the fact that segmental linking elements may contain tonal information (*sans* 'mind', but ²*sans-e-brand* 'mind fire'). His proposal is that linking elements may also consist of just tonal information. Such segmentally invisible linking elements yield ²*lys-fest* 'light party'. The distribution of linking elements is controlled by both diachronic and synchronic generalizations.

When we put the Norwegian data together with Bruce's south Swedish data, it becomes clear that Oslo typologically places itself at the lexical extreme with regard to accent assignment in compounds, cf. (12).

(12) Tone accent assignment in compounds

lexical accent ◄──────────────────────► *prosodic accent*
assignment   *assignment*

Oslo   Malmö   Kristianstad   Halmstad   Stockholm

Oslo is not part of a dialect continuum with the south Swedish dialects (cf. the maps in (3) and (22)). Even if Malmö and Oslo appear to be typologically close, it should be noted that the descriptions given for Norwegian and south Swedish are not fully compatible. Bruce makes no assumptions about the tonal information contained in, or constituting, linking elements, and Kristoffersen does not take prosodic factors (stress clash) into account. It is therefore the task of future research to establish how consistent the typology found in southern Swedish is when extended to other (e.g. Norwegian) dialects without connective accent 2. Let us now take a closer look at how accent assignment comes about in compounds in Oslo and the south Swedish dialects.

4.1.1. Oslo

In Oslo, the grammar would appear to work in the following way. Accent 2 is assigned if there is lexical tonal information present in the first root or in the linking element following the first root, otherwise no accent is assigned (i.e. accent 1). This is illustrated in (13), where 'H' marks the lexical tone of accent 2 in east Norwegian.

(13) East Norwegian sources for accent in compounds

compound	root accent	link accent	default accent	gloss
^{H}sommer-Ø-sko	2			'summer shoe'
^{H}glede-s-rus	2			'elation'
sans-^{H}e-brand		2		'mind fire'
hassel-^{H}-nøtt		2		'hazel nut'
lys-^{H}-fest		2		'light party'
verden-s-del			1	'continent'
dåp-s-handling			1	'baptism'
fest-Ø-lys			1	'party light'
taxi-bil			1	'taxi car'
taxi-^{H}säte			1	'taxi seat'

None of the southern Swedish dialects that Bruce studied has a categorical lexical system like this.

4.1.2. Southern Sweden

In Malmö, there are a couple of contexts in which accent 2 is assigned for prosodic reasons, namely in case of stress clash (²blód-prìns 'blood prince') unless there is some overriding lexical factor like the linking-*s* in ¹skóg-s-hàls 'forest neck'. The important part here is that, unlike Oslo, prosodic factors have at least a say. The influence of prosodic factors becomes greater as one moves to the other dialects, in turn Kristianstad, Halmstad and Stockholm. An overview of the state of affairs in southern Sweden in 1974 is given in (14) below. CSw is included to mark the prosodic extreme of the typology.

(14) South Swedish compounds (Bruce 1974)[15]

examples	Malmö	Kristian-stad	Halmstad	Stock-holm
táxi-grìs	1	1	1	2
skóg-s-hàls	1	1	1 (48%)	
skóg-s-hàls			2 (52%)	2
ín-kl`äckt	1	1	2	2
banán-kùst	1	1 (35%)		
banán-kùst		2 (65%)	2	2
láx-choklàd	1	2	2	2
klót-²[árm-bànd]	1 (68%)			
klót-²[árm-bànd]	2 (32%)	2	2	2
c'ykel-plànk	1 (43%)			
c'ykel-plànk	2 (57%)	2	2	2
blód-prìns	2	2	2	2
²[másk-ròs]-brànd	2	2	2	2
²sómmar-tr`äsk	2	2	2	2

The table is organized according to the relative influence of lexical and prosodic factors on accent assignment, which are as follows:[16] *táxi-grìs* 'taxi pig' contains a disyllabic root with accent 1 as first element; *skóg-s-hàls* 'forest neck' exhibits a linking-*s* and stress clash; *in-kl`äckt* 'in-hatched' is a past participle and contains a stress clash; *banán-kùst* 'banana coast' has non-initial stress and a clash; *láx-chokläd* 'salmon chocolate' has an initial monosyllable but no stress clash; In *klót-²[arm-bànd]* 'ball bracelet', the second member is an accent 2 compound, *arm* is destressed; *c´ykel-plànk* 'bicycle board' represents words in *-el, -er, -en*, which often behave like monosyllables in Swedish morphophonology (e.g. Teleman 1969); *blód-prìns* 'blood prince' contains a stress clash and has no segmental linking element; In ²[*másk-ròs*]-*brànd* 'dandelion fire', the first member is an accent 2 compound, *ros* is destressed; ²*sómmar-tr`äsk* 'summer marsh' has lexical accent 2 in the first member.

The "stairs" pattern in (14) indicates that the nearer to Stockholm one gets, the more general accent 2 becomes, in compounds.[17] The very fact that there is a pattern to this sub-typology may mean that there are underlying principles guiding it. To get a better grasp of the internal dynamics, Ström (1998) closely repeated Bruce's 1974 investigation. It turned out that time has left a mark on the distribution of accent in compounds. In (15) on the next page, the two stages of each dialect are represented next to one another.

The picture is quite telling: Kristianstad and Halmstad have each taken a step in the direction of generalizing connective accent 2. This means that the general direction of change here is from lexical to increasingly prosodic assignment of accent. Interestingly, both dialects have taken this step where they are expected to, as it were. This faithfulness to the stairs pattern might mean that the change follows a common path.

The dialect geography can teach us a couple of things. The south-north dimension within Sweden could be interpreted as a historical dynamic, where either prosodic or lexical factors become increasingly dominant, depending on the direction in which one travels. It seems natural to assume that this pattern has a common background, such as the loss of connective accent. The fact that Oslo has a fully lexical pattern (and a non-prosodic default) might mean that a dialect can acquire a lexical pattern without language contact. To say that Oslo and Malmö are part of the same historical change makes little immediate geographic sense, but could be couched within a broader hypothesis where Denmark is the centre of innovations (cf. 6.1).

(15) Twenty-five years of south Swedish compounds (Bruce 1974; Ström 1998)

examples	Malmö		Kristianstad		Halmstad		Stock-holm
	73	98	73	98	73	98	73/98
táxi-grìs	1	1	1	1	1	1 (53%)	
táxi-grìs						2 (47%)	2
skóg-s-hàls	1	1	1	1	1 (48%)		
skóg-s-hàls					2 (52%)	2	2
ín-kl`äckt	1	1	1	1	2	2	2
banán-kùst	1	1	1 (35%)				
banán-kùst			2 (65%)	2	2	2	2
láx-choklàd	1	1	2	2	2	2	2
klót-²[árm-bànd]	1 (68%)	1					
klót-²[árm-bànd]	2 (32%)		2	2	2	2	2
c´ykel-plànk	1 (43%)	1 (40%)					
c´ykel-plànk	2 (57%)	2 (60%)	2	2	2	2	2
blód-prìns	2	2	2	2	2	2	2
²[másk-ròs]-brànd	2	2	2	2	2	2	2
²sómmar-tr`äsk	2	2	2	2	2	2	2

For now, if we hang on to the hypothesis that connective accent is original, we might just as well assume it has been lost separately in at least two areas. It seems that most Norwegian dialects south of Nordland share the property of lacking connective accent 2 (cf. 5.2).

The change from non-connective to connective (lexical to prosodic) accent is gradual. In the following, the opposite change, from connective to non-connective accent will be discussed. We hypothesized earlier that this is a rather abrupt shift. To see how this works in theory, we must first consider which changes are predicted by the accentual grammar (section 4.2). We turn to the abruptness of the change in section 4.3.

4.2. *From connective to non-connective accent in compounds*

In discussing the typology, we talked about the rightward and leftward orientation of the prominence tone. The phonological interpretation given in Riad (1998b) is that, in the absence of association, a tone will either align with other tones or with edges. The comparison of citation forms in different dialects reveals that the prominence tone may be oriented towards the lexical tone (the common case in simplex words), or towards the final edge, or towards both, if tone spreading is permitted, as in CSw (Stockholm).

(16) Stockholm, CSw

H*LHL]

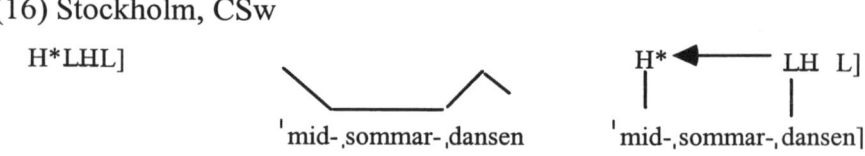

'mid-,sommar-,dansen   'mid-,sommar-,dansen]

However, not all dialects permit spreading. If that is the case, the prominence tone is normally realized right after the lexical tone.[18] This means that leftward orientation is important, and if it is overriding, connective accent will be precluded. The delinking of the prominence tone in a dialect exhibiting connective accent may therefore have far-reaching consequences for the assignment of accent in compounds. The prosodic basis – association to two stresses – is cut and accent in compounds is assigned in the same way as in simplex words. Lexical information at the beginning of the compound becomes available, and in addition, prosodic factors such as clash and rhythm come to influence the assignment of accent.[19] This then is the proposed dramatic effect of the delinking of the prominence tone. Let

4.2.1. From Stockholm to Stavanger

Starting from a two-peaked dialect like central Swedish, we should in principle be able to find a sister dialect which is similar in all respects except for connectivity. We find the dialect we are looking for in southwest Norway, where Stavanger is situated.

(17) Stavanger, southwest Norway

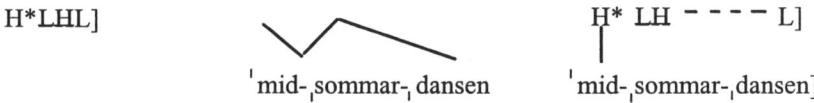

Selmer (1927, 51ff.) provides F0 tracings for some longer compounds which, although of poor quality, still clearly indicate that accent 2 in compounds is not sensitive to the last secondary stress of the domain. A rendering of two of Selmer's tracings is given in (18), with contrastive data from Stockholm.

(18) Comparing Stavanger and Stockholm

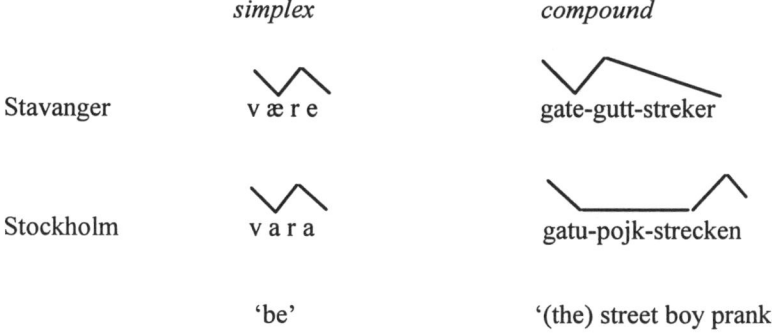

Other examples provided by Selmer are ²vår-dag 'spring day', ²sølv-bryllup 'silver wedding', ²stue-pike-kappe 'house girl jacket'. Now, if tone accent were assigned in the same way in compounds as in simplex words, then we would expect to find compounds exhibiting accent 1 in Stavanger. These can indeed easily be found: ¹rød-vin 'red wine', ¹gård-s-gutt 'street boy', ¹gård-s-gutt-plass 'street boy place'.

In typological terms, the difference between Stockholm and Stavanger is that the former has an associated prominence tone, which is oriented to the right as well as the left (spreading), whereas the latter has an unassociated prominence tone which is oriented to the left only (no spreading). The hypothesis is that the way in which tone accent is assigned in Stavanger results from the delinking of the prominence tone. As a consequence, accent is realized in the same manner in compounds as in simplex words. The tonal contrast available in simplex words should then also be able to exist in compounds, everything else being equal. This prediction is indeed borne out, as illustrated by the Stavanger dialect, as well as the other dialects with a left-oriented prominence tone (e.g. Malmö and Oslo). Geographically, Stavanger is far away from Stockholm or in fact any CSw dialect. If there is a connection, it has to be historical and earlier than dialect splits, because there are no grounds for assuming specific dialect contact with the CSw area. The situation is similar with Danish stød, which seems to have originated from a tonal system of the CSw type (Kroman 1947; Riad 2000abc), yet in an area which is far away from where the CSw tonal type occurs today. It is possible to at least entertain the hypothesis that there was a historical stage when the CSw tonal type had a much wider spread. It would then become broken up by tonal shifts, changes in tonal grammar and development of stød. One alternative is of course to look for separate origins for these phenomena, despite the similarities they exhibit with the CSw tonal system.

We will now consider a similar typological situation as that of CSw and Stavanger, but where two dialects are geographically adjacent.

4.2.2. From west Göta to east Norwegian

The typological difference between west Göta and east Norwegian (Oslo) is minimal. They have the same tonal make-up. Neither dialect has an associated prominence tone, and in both dialects the prominence L tone is left-oriented, directly following the lexical H*. The only difference appears to be whether or not the prominence tone is right-oriented (and spreads leftward). In Göta, the prominence tone spreads between the two H tones at both ends of the word, while in Oslo, the prominence L̲ immediately begins to rise gradually until the very end.

(19) Comparing west Göta and Oslo

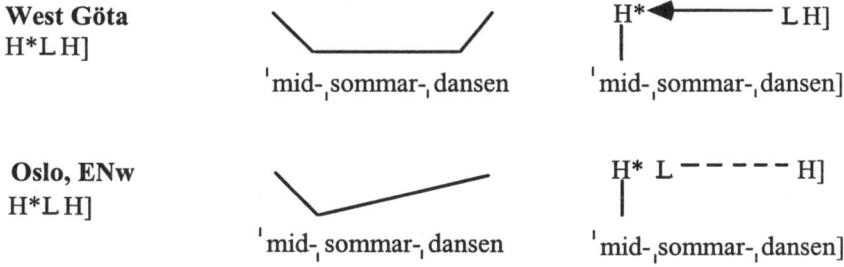

Again, Oslo can be easily derived from Göta by simply dropping the condition on rightward orientation of the prominence tone. This is in part an interpretation provided by the theory, but whatever functions one attributes to the individual tones, the phonetic similarity is quite clear. The predicted consequence is the same as in the case of Stavanger: loss of connective accent and therefore variation between accent 1 and 2 in compounds.

4.2.3. Snappertuna

Stavanger exhibits a phonetic similarity to Stockholm, but has grammatical differences. Another dialect of the two-peaked CSw kind at the other geographic extreme of the accent area is Snappertuna, thoroughly described by Selenius (1972). The village of Snappertuna is situated in the region of west Nyland in west Finland (cf. (3)), and is one of few dialects in Finland, which exhibits the accent distinction. In the Snappertuna dialect, we encounter a variant of connective accent 2, which is sensitive to morphology. While the prosodic right-edge requirement has here been weakened, the prominence tone is still associated, although not necessarily to the final stressed syllable. Rather, the morphological structure of the compound may influence to which stressed syllable the prominence tone goes. In addition, there is a rhythmic effect in some compounds (and in simplex loans), by which stress tends to go to the initial syllable. Selenius found that the two stresses used in connective accent 2 always occur in separate morphological domains within the compound. However, to which stress within the second domain the prominence tone is associated is not entirely predictable. According to Selenius, there are several patterns. We will limit ourselves here to some examples to give an idea of the situation. The data are organized according to the number of syllables and grouped in two columns called 'morphological connectivity' and 'prosodic connectivity'. '=' indicates that there is no difference between the two in a given form. Stresses which have a tone associated to them (and therefore remain unreduced) are indicated with accent marks.

(20) Snappertuna compounds (Selenius 1972)

morphological connectivity	prosodic connectivity	gloss
[dágs-verks]-hjòn	=	'day worker'
[kvínn-folks]-kàrl	=	'womanizer'
[mál-ört]s-kvìst (cf. mal-'ört)	=	'worm wood twig'
[tvílling]s-làmm (cf. tvillíngi)	=	'twin lamb'
kálas-màt (cf. kalás)	=	'party food'
úgns-[pànn-kaka]	úgns-[pann-kàka]	'ovenbaked pancake'
v´år-[skrìft-skolan]	v´år-[skrift-skòlan]	'spring writing school'

[áll-helgon]-dàgen	=	'Allhallows'
píngst-[ànder-dagen]	píngst-[ander-dàgen]	'Whit-Monday'
kápell-m`ästare (cf. kapéll)	=	'band leader'
—	[físk-rom]s-[in-g`ången]	'fish roe entrance'
[gámmel-man]s-b`yggn-ing	=	'old man's building'
[för-ró-skulls]-g`öra	=	'pleasure pasttime '
[för-ró-skull]s-[àr-bete]	—	'pleasure work'
—	p´äron-[upp-tàgare]	'potato picker'

Thus, the dialect retains connective accent 2, which is conditioned by morphology, presumably in interaction with prosodic factors (rhythmic stress shift). In the broader perspective of language use, these conflicts between morphology and prosody are rare, since they only occur in compounds of some complexity.

A similar tendency toward morphological control, manifest in the stress pattern of compounds, occurs in other Swedish dialects spoken in Finland, most of which lack a tonal accent. A connection beween these dialects and Snappertuna is not unthinkable, but it remains to be investigated whether the morphological hierarchical structure of compounds can also influence non-connective accent varieties, or whether it is only a property of dialects having connective accent 2.

It also remains an open question if a system like Snappertuna can be understood as a first step toward losing connectivity. Thus, it might be worthwhile to look for traces of morphological control in Stavanger, for instance. Also, the analysis given here, which assumes that Snappertuna developed from a system of the CSw type (with prosodic connectivity only), predicts that there should not be an organic relationship between morphological connectivity and the non-prosodic factors influencing accent assignment in Malmö and Kristianstad.

4.3. Conclusions

We have now looked at some dialect situations relating to changes in the behaviour of the prominence tone. We found diachronic evidence that dialects with mixed systems in compounds tend to move towards generalizing prosodic accent assignment. Stavanger fulfilled the predictions made by combining a proposed archaic accent type (two-peaked) with the loss of prosodic connectivity. Snappertuna, a partly morphologically driven connective accent variety, might be typologically closer to Stockholm, although we do not know in which direction such a dialect would develop, or indeed, if it belongs to the rest of the picture suggested here. Our general hypothesis regarding the dynamics of losing and acquiring connective accent 2 is as depicted below, where the different dialects represent stages of development relative to one another.

(21) Diachrony of connective accent 2

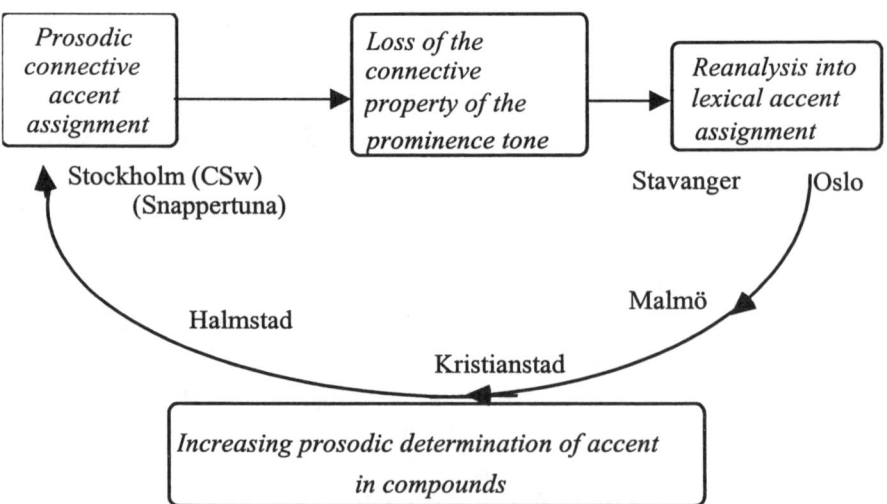

This scenario indicates that the change from a connective to a non-connective accent is swift and dramatic. All it takes to change from the CSw system to Stavanger is the dissociation of the prominence tone. By this change, compounds will behave like simplex words do (in CSw), i.e. the prominence tone will default to the left edge and occur right after the lexical tone.[20] It is thus the question of a single change in the grammar, which opens up for the variation in accent among compounds that we see in Stavanger, Oslo and Malmö. In these dialects, the lexical properties of the first compound element determine the resulting accent to a great extent. Once the grammatical change has taken place, prosodic factors (viz. stress clash and rhythmic structure of the initial element) can again begin to exert their influence on accent assignment and begin the slow and gradual change from non-connective to connective accent.[21]

We have seen two cases of the loss of connectivity: CSw > Stavanger and west Göta > east Norwegian. In both cases the change is minimal, in the one case involving dissociation of the prominence tone (CSw > Stavanger), in the other the loss of rightward orientation (west Göta > east Norwegian). We saw in section 3.2 that the change from CSw to Göta is also simply the dissociation of the prominence tone. Unlike Stavanger, however, the prominence tone there defaulted to the right edge. Furthermore, we have seen that Dala developed from CSw by tone shift (section 3.1), but with no change of grammar. A similar system to that of Dala can be found in Narvik (northern Norway) and in Gotland. These changes can all be traced in minimal steps to the CSw system and this strengthens the hypothesis that CSw represents a relatively archaic stage, and that these dialects have developed rather directly from a CSw system. The tonal type represented by Malmö in southern Sweden and Bergen in western Norway is much like Dala, but with the prominence tone dissociated, i.e. without connectivity. Thus, Malmö is to Dala what Stavanger is to CSw. However, I am not aware of any dialect geographic indication of the transition from a Dala/Narvik type system to a Malmö/Bergen type system.[22] Geographic adjacency would be such an indication. In Sweden, the tonal type of Malmö (and southern Sweden generally) borders the Göta type. In the context of the typology proposed here, these two types are not closely related. They differ in tonal values as Göta has a H lexical tone, connectivity and a spreading L prominence tone, whereas Malmö has a L lexical tone, no connectivity and no spreading of the H prominence tone. In view of these facts, it seems a good idea to look for historical indications that the Malmö system is the result of influences from the south, i.e. Denmark, whereas Göta has developed under influences from the north, as discussed above. This historical scenario is discussed in section 6.1.

5. Three isoglosses

It might now be a good idea to look at the dialects in a broader perspective and discuss the parameters of variation within the accent typology. Three isoglosses, which we will call Siv, Liv and Viv, can be drawn. Let us begin with the isogloss Siv, which separates connective from non-connective accent varieties.

5.1. Isogloss Siv

A careful study closer to the ground, as it were, will eventually be required to do this properly, but nevertheless, enough is known for us to see that the exercise of separating prosodic connectivity from its absence amounts to drawing an isogloss, rather than marking dots and spots here and there. This indicates that there is something principled and general going on. As seen in (22), Siv runs westward from eastern Småland to the Swedish west coast. Below this line we find Malmö, Kristianstad and Halmstad. The isogloss then runs northward more or less along the coast. Variable accent in compounds is known from Halland (Halmstad), but has not been investigated further to the north along the west coast, that is in the region of Bohuslän, which is known as a transition area between Norwegian and Swedish dialects (Janzén 1936, 1f.). Siv then separates the west Göta from the east Norwegian dialects. This means that it runs roughly along the national border. From here the trajectory of the isogloss is more or less straight northbound until it reaches the North Sea between Trøndelag and Nordland. Narvik in the north of Norway has connective accent 2 (Lorentz 1995).

(22) Isoglosses

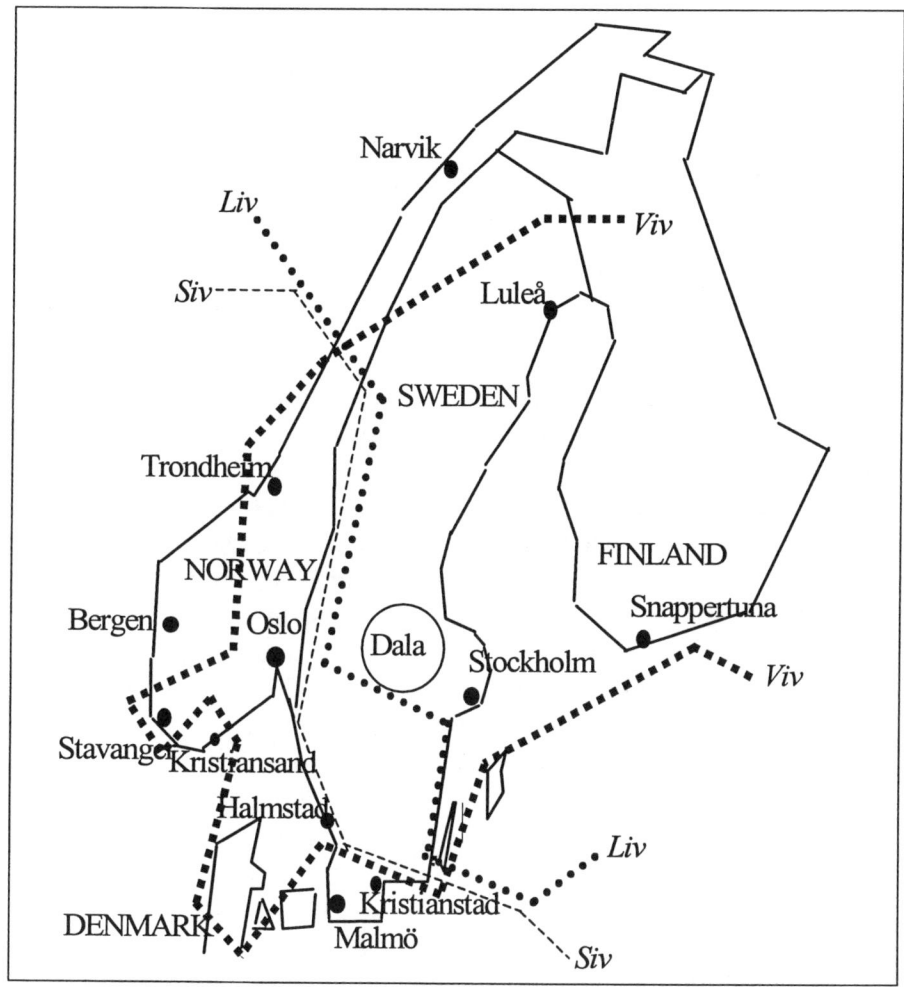

One could ask whether all of southern and western Norway lacks connective accent. We have seen that Stavanger does. The west Norwegian (Bergen) and south Norwegian (Kristiansand) dialect type, as well as the east Norwegian (Oslo) type, all have their tonal contour located around the primary stress. This means that there is no association of the prominence tone, and no connective accent either.

The diachronic implication of the isogloss can go both ways. The loss of connective accent 2 in most Norwegian and in southern

Swedish dialects could be an innovation. If this is the case, it can hardly be expanding any longer, at least not in southern Sweden, since the trend was shown to go in the other direction (cf. 4.1.2). The other possibility is that loss of connective accent was more widespread and that connective accent 2 is now expanding again. However, in view of the fact that the absence of connective accent 2 seems to go together with three-tone systems, a relatively recent development, this scenario does not seem very likely.[23]

5.2. Isogloss Liv

The map in (22) also contains Liv, an isogloss, which refers to whether the prominence tone is associated or not. Liv runs in parallel with Siv or somewhat further to the east. The trajectory is again highly tentative in its details, but the general pattern is sufficiently clear. The area lacking connective accent 2 is contained within the area with an unassociated prominence tone. The invited diachronic interpretation is that at least for a large area, the two are interconnected. First the prominence tone delinks but stays at the right edge. In a later stage, it moves to the left, thereby losing connectivity. This does not account for Stavanger, but that might be a relic area anyway. Alternatively, the non-connective pattern could also spread as an innovation in its own right.

5.3. Isogloss Viv

The last isogloss on the map indicates the areas which have a H prominence tone, that is north, west and south Norwegian, south Swedish, Gotland and Dala. According to the hypothesis, these dialects have undergone a tone shift like the one described in section 3.1. As can be seen, this parameter is insensitive to the other two isoglosses, and it should be, since it has nothing specifically to do with compounds, but rather with the general composition of the tonal contour. Thus, we find the Dala dialects, which have the same grammar as Stockholm (CSw), hence exhibiting connective accent 2, and the west Norwegian grammars without connective accent 2, within the same group.

The diachronic implication that follows from isogloss Viv is that the shift from LH (CSw) to H (Narvik, Bergen, Kristiansand, Malmö, Gotland, Dala) independently took place in different areas. Tone shifts seem inevitable. As discussed above, the shift in Eskilstuna and further north into Dala is conditioned by a pragmatic speech habit (curl), which involves pulling the boundary tone into the stressed syllable. This in turn causes the lexical tones to shift. It is argued in Riad (2000abc) that the same thing has happened in Denmark too, as a precursor to stød. If these two geographically distant areas have both developed this innovation, then it might also occur elsewhere. The shift preserves the accent distinction (in Dala), and might therefore be a grammatical reaction to curl.

6. Geographic and typological distance

The tradition in dialect geography that focussed on the tone accent melody alone (Öhman 1967; Fintoft et al. 1978; Bruce & Gårding 1978) is not going to solve the question of which dialect types are relatively old. In fact, it seems doubtful that even more sophisticated dialect geography will provide answers. The reason is that the spread of dialect types allows for conflicting interpretations. Looking at the map in (3), we could interpret the fact that the central Swedish accent type has a centre in central Scandinavia and northward, and satellites in Stavanger, Snappertuna, Älvdalen and Denmark (according to Kroman 1947) as support for an earlier general spread, with new dialects forming in various places. We know there are tonal innovation centres outside central Sweden, Zealand in Denmark being one. However, a look at the same map also allows for a different interpretation, namely that the Bergen-Dala-Malmö type is archaic. Bergen and Malmö are in the outer regions, and Dala could be a relic area. This interpretation would favour a view that the two-peaked type has spread as an innovation.

This illustrates that there are limits to what we can do with melody and dialect geography alone. Adding the compound data and a phonological model for the accent grammar makes the accent history easier to trace. These tools help us interpret the typology as the result of a diachronic process. For one thing, the two isoglosses Siv and Liv divide the accent area in a quite different way than the purely melodic data would. It seems reasonable that these isoglosses should be taken into account in a discussion of what is an innovation area and what is an archaic area. Also, hypotheses regarding the origin of accent obviously play a role in determining, for instance, whether two-peaked vs. one-peaked or connective vs. non-connective accent varieties are a priori most likely to be original. The same goes for other facts that independently establish a local order of events, such as the Stockholm to Dala pattern and the final stress pattern to be discussed in section 7.

Another principled, if theory-dependent tool for reconstructing the diachrony of accent are the predictions made by the model itself. Under the usual "fewer differences" = "historically closer" equation, we may compare the accentual grammars and see which types are relatively similar and which ones are relatively distant, typologically speaking, and investigate whether such a reconstruction makes sense in other respects. Consider the picture in (23).

This diagram shows the six major types and the predictions in terms of typological relationships of the model used here. When relating it to our hypothesis regarding the diachronic routes, the relationship between CSw and Dala is clear, as is presumably the relationship between CSw and Göta, although more work is needed to precisely pinpoint how the latter transition takes place. These dialects occur next to one another within the connectivity area. Given what we know of the CSw to Dala transition, we may extrapolate this understanding to other dialects which resemble Dala, viz. Gotland (to the east of the Swedish mainland) and Narvik in northern Norway. These dialects have the same tonal make-up and grammar as Dala, and are hence typologically equally near to CSw, even if they are geographically far away.

(23) Dialect transitions in terms of the typology

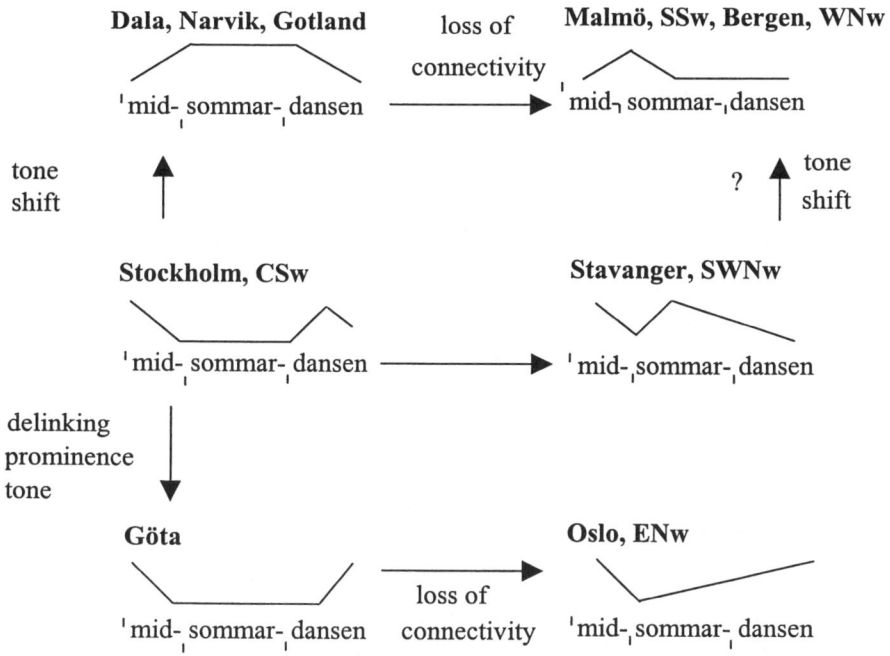

Interestingly, the west Göta and Dala dialects also border on each other, although their melodies (LHL vs. HLH) and grammars (association of the prominence tone only occurs in Dala) are quite different. The typology in (23) predicts that a direct transition between Göta and Dala is not likely. The transition between CSw and Stavanger is typologically minimal, however, in that it amounts to losing connectivity in compounds. Geography does not provide direct support here. In fact, this is one of the questions that the reconstruction is supposed to answer. All of western Norway appears to lack connectivity and it is impossible to know at present at what point it was lost, and whether the melodic differences between the dialects had already developed by then. The important fact is that this feature (Siv and Liv) seems to cut right through the melodic typology. Thus, it seems that connectivity is a free agent in reconstructing the diachrony. The relationship between Stavanger and Bergen is similar to that between CSw and Dala. The difference is that CSw and Dala both have connective accent 2, whereas Stavanger and Bergen both lack connectivity. A tone shift like the one in Eskilstuna may therefore also be at the basis of the transition from Stavanger to west Norwegian. A question mark signals this putative transition in (23) above, independent arguments lacking at present. Moreover, a general thing to look for is whether there are any relic areas in Norway south of Trondheim where connectivity would still be manifest. This would help answer the question whether any parts other than northern Norway ever had connective accent (as we have predicted by assuming that CSw represents the most an archaic tonal type).

According to the typology, the Oslo dialect should be a natural extension of the Göta variety (cf. 4.2.2). By contrast, the relationship between Oslo (east Nw) and the western and southern Norwegian dialects is by no means as close. By the same token, the relationship between the Göta and Malmö types is also not close, according to the typology presented here. This is expressed in (23), but more evidence is needed to substantiate or refute the interpretation. Next we take a brief look at the political and linguistic influence of Denmark on southern Sweden, which might shed some light on why there is such a major typological boundary beween the Göta system and the Malmö system (spoken in Skåne and Blekinge).

6.1 Influences from Denmark

The lexical distinction expressed by tone accents came about ca 1000–1200 A.D. The process of epenthesis before certain sonorants and, above all, the suffixation of the definite article led to a number of minimal pairs. While the lexical tones might already have existed as such for quite a while, this is the birth date of the lexical distinction. Let us assume that the predominant accent type around 1200 A.D. was of the CSw type. In particular, this was the accent type used in the political centres of Zealand in Denmark and Uppland in Sweden.

During all of the Middle Ages, Denmark was the leading state in Scandinavia. Around the year 1200, it had about twice the population of Sweden and Norway together, and also had a strategic position in both military and cultural respects. Importantly, the southern regions of Sweden (Blekinge and Skåne) were part ot Denmark until the middle of the 17th century. Much of the time, the southwestern coastal regions (Halland and Bohuslän), as well as all of Norway belonged to Denmark. Skåne and Blekinge were not just outskirts of the Danish empire, but very much integrated, especially the city of Lund, which was an archbishopric as well as a trade centre. In the middle of the 17th century, Sweden regained the southern and southwestern regions, and the cultural and political impulses would instead come from the north.

These facts carry some implications for dialectology. The area below the present-day isogloss Siv (in Sweden at least) should exhibit basically Danish features for those traits that developed before, say, 1650, everything else being equal. And indeed, we find many shared features between the central dialects of Denmark and those of its earlier dominions. The best-known shared feature between Denmark, southern Sweden and southern and southwestern Norway (to the exclusion of most other areas in the vicinity) is the lenition of voiceless stops (Sandøy 1987, 79). The uvular /R/ has a general southern distribution in both Norway and Sweden. There are also similar isoglosses for dental /l/, secondary diphthongs, retained final /n/ in the definite form of feminines (*solen* 'the sun' as opposed to *sola* or *soli*). These isoglosses which largely coincide with each other, all run along at least parts of the isogloss Siv, sometimes slightly to the north or slightly more inland (at least with regard to its trajectory within Sweden).

The political and cultural influences of Denmark and Sweden, respectively, thus meet roughly where Siv traverses Sweden, and this influence can be traced in the dialectology. It seems, then, that we can add the typological boundary between the Malmö and Göta accent types to the set of dialect isoglosses. The relative typological distance between the Göta and Malmö accentual types can thus be understood as the corollary of political and cultural influences from two different directions during different periods of time. Concretely, this would mean that the starting point for the southern influence was a CSw accent system, used in Zealand in Denmark. At some point, there was a tone shift into the Dala accent type in Skåne and Blekinge in southern Sweden. In Zealand, however, there was no tone shift, but rather a development of stød and the concomitant loss of lexical tone.[24] Sometime after these changes, connectivity (a feature of both the original CSw and subsequent Dala systems) was lost and this yielded the Malmö system. Looking at the influences from the north, the starting point is again a CSw type of accent system. In the area south of Uppland and Sörmland, the prominence tone was dissociated, under retained rightward orientation, yielding the Göta system. This change happened over the large Göta area, but did not spread into the very south of Sweden, that is Skåne and Blekinge, since the Malmö system had already developed there, under the previous Danish rule. The timing here dictates that the southernmost accentual variety developed during the Middle ages, when Denmark was politically dominant, and the Göta variety somewhat later. The fact that Siv often runs slightly more to the south indicates that a couple of the segmental Danish features have continued to spread northward even after the period of Danish dominance.

The postulated Dala type stage in southern Sweden might have lasted for a long time.[25] When the prominence tone was dissociated and shifted to the left, connective accent 2 was lost. This would have yielded a lexical system of accent assignment, presumably like the one we find in Oslo today. The present-day Malmö system already has a mixture of lexical and prosodic factors determining the accent in compounds (section 4). The other cities studied in Bruce's 1974 investigation were all located within the previously Danish area (Malmö, Kristianstad in Skåne and Halmstad in Halland).[26]

7. Final tonal mark only

Let us now turn to a final source of support for the hypothesis that the two-peaked accent of the CSw type is archaic relative to the other ones. The argument presupposes the connection between two peaks and connective accent and is based on a particular prosodic pattern in compounds. This pattern is best known from northern Swedish dialects (e.g. Luleå), where compounds may end up with a tonal mark on the last stressed syllable only, turning that syllable into the primary stressed one. The phenomenon has no impact on the accent typology as such, it seems. It is a surface rule, always applying with some degree of optionality.

Crucially, compounds, which undergo this process invariably, get accent 1. Other compounds exhibit the regular connective pattern with accent 2. The structure of the argument is that this so-called "final element stress" pattern (here called "final tonal mark only" to avoid confusion) makes sense only if it developed from a connective accent 2 pattern of the central Swedish type. Therefore, dialects that exhibit it bear evidence of an earlier stage of (general) connective accent 2 of the CSw type, which thus establishes the CSw variety as relatively archaic.

Although it is typically associated with the northern Swedish dialects (Bruce 1982), final tonal mark only in compounds is, or was, in fact a geographically quite widespread phenomenon. Selenius (1972) provides a thorough review, both from a historical and dialectological perspective. Below is a list of Swedish-speaking regions where this pattern or similar variants have been reported.

(24) Geographic spread of final tonal mark in compounds (Selenius 1972, 202ff.)
    north: Lappland, Norrbotten, Västerbotten, Ångermanland, east Jämtland, Medelpad
    central: Uppland, Sörmland
    west: Värmland, Västergötland, Bohuslän
    south: Halland, Skåne, Blekinge
    east: Gotland, west Nyland (Finland)

Final tonal mark only in compounds is also known to exist in some Norwegian and Danish dialects. It is not completely general anywhere, and its distribution in particular dialects is far from clear with the exception of the Luleå dialect, where it has been systematically investigated (Bruce 1982). Factors that influence the distribution are the number of syllables of the compound elements (few in the first element and many in the last), the quantity of the first element in older language stages (light), lexical category, semantic opacity, segmental edge of first compound element (vocalic). However, at the moment it is not clear if these conditioning factors also apply in other dialects than Luleå.

7.1. The pattern

The following description of final tonal mark only in compounds is based on Bruce's analysis of Luleå.

(25) Comparing Stockholm and Luleå

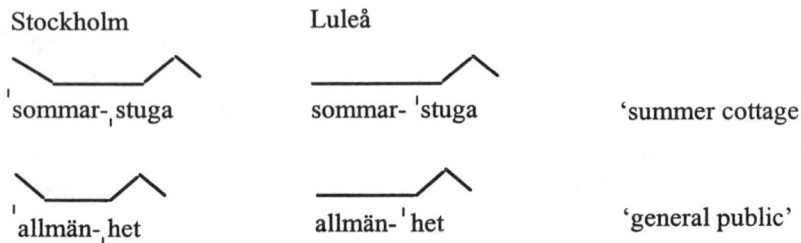

Although the phenomenon has usually been associated with stress, it seems more likely that we should understand it as the suppression of the lexical tone in connective accent 2. In regular connective accent 2, the lexical tone goes to the primary stress and the prominence tone goes to the final secondary stress. This makes those two syllables particularly prominent. Other stressed syllables do not receive a tonal mark, but properties like vowel duration and vowel quality are retained. Thus, the first and final stressed syllables are particularly salient, because they are also marked tonally. By suppressing the lexical (in compounds actually post-lexical) tone that associates to the first stressed syllable, the tonally marked final stressed syllable will become the phonetically most salient one. Since this syllable carries the prominence tone, it is predicted that these compounds always have accent 1, which can indeed be observed.

7.2. The distribution

In Luleå, the pattern with a final tonal mark only competes with connective accent 2 of the CSw type (Bruce 1982, 1998). Final tonal mark only occurs when the two stresses do not clash, preferably in structures where the first compound element is disyllabic and does not end in a stressed syllable.

(26) Some nonsense words

a. Typical context: unstressed post-tonic syllable in the first compound element

ˈsommar+ˌträsk	> sommar+ˈträsk	'summer marsh'
ˈtaxi+ˌgris	> taxi+ˈgris	'taxi pig'
kaˈdaver+ˌkål	> kadaver+ˈkål	'corpse coal'

b. Less often in prosodically similar, but morphologically different structures

ˈtand+kaˌnal	> tand+kaˈnal	'tooth canal'
sigˈnal+garˌdin	> signal+garˈdin	'signal curtain'
ˈklot+[arm+ˌband]	> klot+[arm+ˈband]	'ball bracelet'

c. Clash blocks final tonal mark only and the CSw pattern is retained

ˈblod+ˌprins	= ˈblod+ˌprins	'blood prince'
baˈnan+ˌkust	= baˈnan+ˌkust	'banana coast'

Since the pattern is obviously sensitive to rhythm, we might try to understand it as rhythmically motivated.

7.3. The analysis

Just as in Malmö and Kristianstad (cf. 4.1.2), stress clash is the most favourable context for accent 2. In such structures, the regular CSw response is to reduce the second stress and this is also what happens here. If the final stress is preceded by at least one unstressed syllable, however, all stresses except the final one are reduced. Since tones cannot remain associated to reduced syllables, the lexical tone is deleted.

136 Tomas Riad

(27) Tonal suppression and delinking

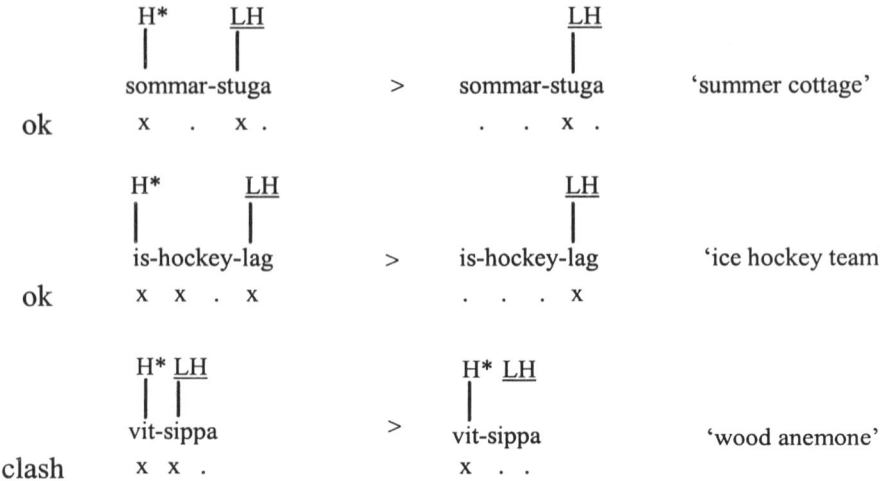

Delinking normally occurs in clash contexts, in CSw as well, and leads to the prosodic neutralization between simplex words and compounds. Incidentally, this is what allows the reanalysis of connective accent 2 as lexical accent 2, described in (2). Another sign of delinking is the shift of the prominence tone to an unstressed syllable in some compounds containing a clash (Bruce 1998, 88). This is illustrated in (28).

(28) Delinking in clash contexts

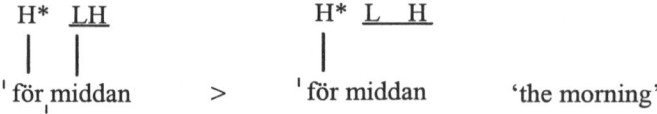

The point of this exercise was to show that final tone marking only in compounds is best analyzed as resulting from the CSw connective accent 2 variety. The connection is obvious in the case of northern Swedish, because the pattern there alternates with the central Swedish accent type. The occurrence of this pattern in dialects, which do not have connective accent 2 to the same extent as CSw is telling since it would bear witness of an earlier stage when connective accent 2 was present. Dialects with a different tonal make-up from that of CSw are also of interest, since they raise the question of whether delinking can take place if the lexical tone is L^*.[27] If not, then that could provide a source of information on an earlier stage with a two-peaked tonal contour.

8. General conclusions

The basic hypothesis has been that connective accent 2 of the central Swedish kind is relatively archaic. The initial impetus for this comes from the hypothesis regarding the origin of tonal accent in Scandinavian, as presented in Riad (1998a). Assuming the tones originate from stress clash, connective accent 2 is the most archaic feature of the accent system, the lexical use for it being a later consequence (cf. (2)). Here, we have tried to find support for the archaic character of the CSw accent variety, both as regards tonal values and the presence of connectivity, by looking at the accent typology itself and the dialect geography of tonal accent. In order to understand to what extent dialects are related to one another, we have looked at several parameters of variation, viz. the tonal make-up of the contour, the association status of the prominence tone and its directional orientation. The latter two features provide information on the notion of connective accent 2.

Summing up, we have found some support for the hypothesis that CSw is archaic in all respects. It can be seen to develop into the Dala system, while there is no evidence for the reverse change. The transition of the CSw to the other adjacent dialect type, Göta, could easily be described in terms of the typological model (delinking of the prominence tone), while the dialects of the Bergen-Malmö type are geographically as well as typologically more distant (different tonal values, no connectivity). An accent system of the CSw kind is further required to understand the pattern of final stress in compounds, which used to have a wide spread in Scandinavia. The geographic spread of the CSw accent type does not contradict a scenario where it is archaic, since we find this melody in the far West (Stavanger) and the far East (Snappertuna) as well as in the North (Luleå) of the tonal accent area.

We also found two isoglosses cutting diagonally through the accent area, which must ultimately be understood in diachronic terms, although at present it is not fully clear how. Their primary interest at the present stage is the very fact that there are isoglosses. One interpretation, which is substantiated by the typological distance between dialects, is that the isogloss Siv marks the front-line of the loss of connective accent 2. The west and south Norwegian dialects as well as the south Swedish dialects have the same accent system, and it might be that the common denominator is their closeness to Denmark, a well-known innovation centre, prosodically and otherwise.

Notes

1. I would like to thank Gösta Bruce, Staffan Hellberg, Gjert Kristoffersen and Arne Torp for valuable input and discussions. I am most grateful to the anonymous reviewer for highly useful comments and suggestions on content as well as language. Mistakes are my own. This work was in part carried out within the research project called Prosody in Swedish Morphology, funded by The Bank of Sweden Tercentenary Foundation.
2. Initial boundary tones have been ignored. While such tones are likely to often be present, they are not very visible in the most common type of data available (viz. disyllabic simplex words).
3. In connective accent 2, the initial tone is not lexical in the strict sense, but we shall nevertheless refer to it as the lexical tone.
4. In the Norwegian tradition, one talks of high-tone and low-tone dialects, with reference to what we here call the prominence tone (Fretheim & Nilsen 1989; Nilsen 1992, 84).
5. This tonal typology involves a simplification from Riad (1998b). The Malmö variety was earlier kept apart from the Dala and Bergen type, but Gösta Bruce has pointed out (p.c.) that it is more reasonable to treat them as belonging to the same group.
6. Note that we can predict the shapes of accent 1 and accent 2 in simplex words from the compound data given in (5). Accent 2 in simplex words will have the prominence tone floating directly after the lexical tone (which is associated to the stressed syllable), while accent 1 only has a prominence tone associated to the stressed syllable.
7. This does not amount to a claim that either moras or syllables are tone bearing units in Scandinavian languages. In view of the strong dependence on stress, it seems more natural to assume that the foot or the prosodic word are TBUs in these languages (cf. Bruce 1987; Riad 1998b).

8. In Riad (1998b), spreading is analyzed as the joint satisfaction of two constraints, which implement rightward and leftward orientation, respectively.
9. The intonation varies some between speakers. In fact, in Kristoffersen's (2000, 249) analysis, the speakers of the Oslo dialect are assumed to have a speading (prominence) L, rather like west Göta, while I analyze this as a rising contour. It remains to be established whether this is a difference of interpretation or a real difference among speakers.
10. East Färnebo (north) is the only dialect among those included here, which exhibits interpolation between the lexical tone and the prominence tone, all other interpolations occurring between the prominence and boundary tones. Clearly, we need to find out more about this accent variety before we make too much of its grammatical properties. It has been included here since Kallstenius is so clear about the shape of the curve, and because it bears out a prediction of the model in Riad (1998b). In the discussion about dialect transitions, however, it will be left to the side.
11. As Gjert Kristoffersen has pointed out (p.c.), other theories will express these circumstances differently. The issue of which potential combinations of tones and functions are possible is partly theory dependent and as mentioned at the outset, I have stayed with the one-to-one matching of tones and functions in order to keep the typology homogeneous and its predictions in check. Regarding diachronic transitions, the issue is important but not crucial in the present context. Our main concern is with the overall shape of the contour, but simplicity of description is also a concern, since we are dealing with many dialects at the same time. For now, then, we say that the transition from central Swedish to Göta is simply the delinking of the prominence tone.
12. We may conceive of the TBU as a set of constraints referring to the categories of the prosodic hierarchy. If only the primary stressed syllable is an anchor point, the TBU is the prosodic word, while if another stress can be used, the TBU is the prosodic foot. Realization of an associated tone in the stressed syllable follows from headedness of prosodic categories. Tonal languages in Africa or South-East Asia often presuppose the syllable or mora as the TBU, and thereby predict (and exhibit) types of tonal behaviour that are unheard of in Scandinavia.
13. The phenomenon is not sufficiently studied regarding synchronic phonology and spread among dialects.
14. No good example of this state of affairs has been found, but some dialects (cf. 4.2.3) may select another stress than the last on the basis of the morphological make-up of the compound (rather like stress in English compounds).
15. Bruce had several different compounds of each type and 10 informants for each dialect. When there is 70% consensus of more, it is here assumed that the choice is categorical. When the outcome is more balanced, values are indicated in the table.
16. Because of the variation between dialects, the presence of a lexical tone is

marked with the neutral digit '2'. In Malmö this corresponds to a L tone, while in Stockholm it is a H tone.

17. Connective accent 2 is general already in the Göta dialects. Bruce (1974) uses Stockholm as a reference point simply because it is the best studied tonal dialect.
18. East Färnebo (north) is the exception. In this dialect, pitch rises gradually from the first to the final stress, suggesting interpolation rather than spreading between lexical tone and prominence tone.
19. Why these prosodic factors should favour accent 2 is a different issue. The empirical fact that clash favours accent 2 is consistent with the basic hypothesis regarding the origin of accent proposed in Riad (1998a).
20. They could of course default to the right edge, too. This is what happens in the transition from CSw to Göta. What happens in a specific change has to do with how the other constraints which influence the typology hold themselves, in particular the constraint against spreading vis-à-vis the constraint on association of the prominence tone (cf. Riad 1998b).
21. I have not been able to find a case where the prominence tone in compounds would regularly associate to the *leftmost* available secondary stress directly following the primary stress. A dialect fulfilling this theoretical possiblity would have prosodically conditioned connective accent 2 but without the connective embrace of the compound. In view of what we have seen above, such a dialect seems unexpected, however. It seems that the weakening of right-edge orientation or the delinking of the prominence tone immediately make available lexical and morphological information, leading to other strategies than prosodic ones for assigning accent in compounds.
22. One should perhaps look for one in Norway, at the southern boundary of the Narvik type area.
23. The geographically limited Stavanger system is an exception to this pattern.
24. This amounts to postulating a tonal shift in southern Sweden for which we have no direct evidence. But there is plenty of indirect evidence, which I will briefly mention here, discussion occurring elsewhere: First, the extant accent type in Malmö is like Dala minus connectivity. Second, Eskilstuna and its neighbours exhibit two connected features otherwise known primarily from Zealand in Denmark, namely stød and generalized accent 2. The third factor, tone shift, is so far only known from Dala, but is here assumed for southern Swedish. These features are discussed extensively in Riad (2000abc).
25. It remains a possibility that some remote dialect still retains this system, crucially with the prominence tone associated in compounds.
26. It is uncertain whether we can infer anything about the time depth from the extent of prosodic and/or lexical influence on accent assignment in compounds. If we do, however, our analysis would suggest that, everything else being equal, the purely lexical accent system of Oslo should be relatively younger than the south Swedish system, which has several systematic pro-

sodic influences on accent assignment in compounds. Careful further study of several Norwegian dialects is required to advance our understanding of this aspect of the typology.
27. I am grateful to the anonymous reviewer for raising this point. Empirical work is needed to find out just what the ramifications for the rule of final tonal marking only is.

References

Bleckert, Lars
    1987   *Centralsvensk diftongering som satsfonetiskt problem.* (Skrifter utgivna av institutionen för nordiska språk vid Uppsala universitet 21) Nordiska språk, Uppsala.
Bruce, Gösta
    1973   Tonal accent rules for compound stressed words in the Malmö dialect, *Working papers* 7, Phonetics laboratory, Lund University.
    1974   Tonaccentregler för sammansatta ord i några sydsvenska stadsmål. In Platzack, C. (ed.): *Svenskans beskrivning* 8, 62–75.
    1977   *Swedish word accents in sentence perspective.* CWK Gleerup, Lund.
    1982   Reglerna för slutledsbetoning i sammansatta ord i nordsvenskan. In Elert & Fries (eds.) *Nordsvenska.* University of Umeå.
    1987   How floating is focal accent? In Kirsten Gregersen & Hans Basbøll (eds.) *Nordic Prosody* 4, 41–49. Odense University Press, Odense.
    1998   *Allmän och svensk prosodi.* (Praktisk lingvistik 16) Department of Linguistics, Lund University.
Bruce, Gösta & Eva Gårding
    1978   A prosodic typology for Swedish dialects. In Gårding et al., 219–228.
d'Alquen, Richard & Kevin Brown
    1992   The Origin of Scandinavian Accents I and II. In Irmengard Rauch, Gerald Carr & Robert Kyes (eds.) *On Germanic Linguistics: Issues and methods,* 61–79. Berlin: Mouton de Gruyter.
Elert, Claes-Christian
    1970   *Ljud och ord* i svenskan. Almqvist & Wiksell: Uppsala.
    1972   Tonality in Swedish: Rules and a list of minimal pairs. *Studies for Einar Haugen* ed. by Evelyn S. Firchow, Kaaren Grimstad, Nils Hasselmo & Wayne O'Neil, 151–173. Mouton, The Hague.
Elstad, Kåre
    1980   Some Remarks on Scandinavian Tonogenesis. *Nordlyd: Tromsø University Working Papers on Language & Linguistics* 3, 62–77. (Repr. in Jahr & Lorentz 1983. 388–398.)

Engstrand, Olle
    1995   Phonetic interpretation of the word accent contrast in Swedish, *Phonetica* 52, 171–179.
    1997   Phonetic interpretation of the word accent contrast in Swedish: Evidence from spontaneous speech *Phonetica* 54, 61–75.
Fintoft, Knut, Per Egil Mjaavatn, Einar Møllergård & Brit Ulseth
    1978   Toneme patterns in Norwegian dialects. In Gårding et al., 197–206.
Fretheim, Thorstein & Randi A. Nilsen
    1989   Terminal rise and rise-fall tunes in east Norwegian intonation. *Nordic journal of linguistics* 12, 155–181.
Gårding, Eva
    1977   *The Scandinavian word accents*. (Travaux de l'institut de linguistique de Lund 11) CWK Gleerup, Lund.
Gårding, Eva, Gösta Bruce & Robert Bannert (eds.)
    1978   *Nordic prosody. Papers from a symposium* (Travaux de l'Institut de Linguistique de Lund 13). Lund University.
Gårding, Eva, Gösta Bruce & Ursula Willstedt
    1978   Transitional forms and their position in a prosodic typology for Swedish dialects. In Gårding et al., 197–206.
Haugen, Einar
    1963   Pitch accent and tonemic juncture in Scandinavian. *Monatshefte für deutschen Unterricht* 55, 157–161.
    1967   On the rules of Norwegian tonality. *Language* 43, 185–202.
Haugen, Einar & Martin Joos
    1952   Tone and Intonation in east Norwegian. *Acta Philologica Scandinavica* 22, 41–64. (Repr. in Jahr & Lorentz 1983. 178–202.)
Hesselman, Bengt
    1901   Skiss öfver nysvensk kvantitetsutveckling. *Språk och stil* 1, 10–25.
    1902   *Stafvelseförlängning och vokalkvalitet. Undersökningar i nordisk ljudhistoria* 1. Uppsala.
Jahr, Ernst Håkon & Ove Lorentz (eds.)
    1983   *Prosodi/Prosody*. (Studies in Norwegian Linguistics 2) Novus, Oslo.
Janzén, Assar
    1936   *Studier över substantivet i bohuslänskan*. Elanders boktryckeri, Göteborg.
Kallstenius, Gottfrid
    1902   *Värmländska Bärgslagsmålets ljudlära*. Norstedt & Söner, Stockholm.
Klintberg, Mathias
    1885   *Laumålets kvantitet ock aksent*. (Svenska landsmål ock svenskt folklif VI.1), Norstedt & Söner, Stockholm.
Kock, Axel
    1878,   *Språkhistoriska undersökningar om svensk akcent*. 2 vols. CWK
    1884-85 Gleerup, Lund.
    1901   *Die alt- und neuschwedische Accentuierung*. Karl J. Trübner, Strassburg.

Kristoffersen, Gjert
 1990   *East Norwegian prosody and the level stress problem.* ms. University of Tromsø.
 1992   Tonelag i sammensatte ord i østnorsk, *Norsk lingvistisk tidsskrift* 10, 39–65.
Kroman, Erik
 1947   *Musikalsk akcent i dansk.* Einar Munksgaard, København.
Ladd, D. Robert
 1996   *Intonational Phonology.* Cambridge University Press, Cambridge.
Liberman, Anatoly
 1982   *Germanic Accentology.* Vol.I: *The Scandinavian languages.* University of Minnesota Press, Minneapolis.
Linell, Per
 1972   Remarks on Swedish Morphology. *RUUL* 1, Department of Linguistics, Uppsala University.
Lorentz, Ove
 1995   Tonal prominence and alignment, *Phonology at Santa Cruz* 4, 39–56.
Meyer, Ernst A.
 1937   *Die Intonation im Schwedischen I. Die Sveamundarten.* Fritzes bokförlags AB, Mercators tryckeri, Helsingfors.
 1954   *Die Intonation im Schwedischen II. Die norrländischen Mundarten* (Stockholm studies in Scandinavian Philology 11). Almqvist & Wiksell, Uppsala.
Mjaavatn, Per Egil
 1978   Isoglosses of toneme categories compared with isoglosses of traditional dialect geography. In Gårding et al., 207–216.
Nilsen, Randi A.
 1992   *Intonasjon i interaksjon. Sentrale spørsmål i norsk intonologi.* Diss. Department of linguistics, University of Trondheim.
Oftedal, Magne
 1952   On the origin of the Scandinavian tone distinction. *Norsk tidsskrift for sprogvidenskap* 16, 201-225. [Reprinted in Jahr, Ernst Håkon & Lorentz, Ove, eds. 1983. *Prosodi/Prosody.* (Studies in Norwegian Linguistics 2). Oslo. 154–177.]
Öhman, Sven
 1967   Word and Sentence Intonation: A quantitative model. *Speech Transmission Laboratory Quarterly Progress and Status Report* (STL-QPSR) 2–3.20–54. Dept. of Speech Transmission, Royal Institute of Technology, Stockholm.
Prince, Alan & Paul Smolensky
 1993   *Optimality theory: Constraint interaction in generative grammar.* ms, Rutgers University and University of Colorado, Boulder.
Riad, Tomas
 1996   Remarks on the Scandinavian Tone Accent Typology. *Nordlyd* 24, 129–156. Univ. of Tromsø, Tromsø.

1998a The origin of Scandinavian tone accents, *Diachronica* XV:1, 63–98.
1998b Towards a Scandinavian accent typology. In Wolfgang Kehrein & Richard Wiese (eds.) *Phonology and Morphology of the Germanic Languages,* 77–109. (Linguistische Arbeiten 386) Niemeyer, Tübingen.
2000a The origin of Danish stød. In Aditi Lahiri (ed.) *Analogy, Levelling and Markedness. Principles of change in phonology and morphology.* Berlin/New York: Mouton de Gruyter. 261–300.
2000b The rise and fall of Scandinavian accent. *The Nordic Languages and Modern Linguistics* 10. Proceedings of The Tenth International Conference of Nordic and General Linguistics. University of Iceland, June 6-8, 1998. Edited by Gudrún Thórhallsdóttir. Institute of Linguistics, University of Iceland. 2000. 15–33.
2000c Stöten som aldrig blev av – generaliserad accent 2 i Östra Mälardalen. *Folkmålsstudier* 39, 319–344.

Ringgaard, Kristian
1983 Review of Liberman 1982. *Phonetica* 40, 342–344.

Sandøy, Helge
1987 *Norsk dialektkunnskap.* Oslo.

Selenius, Ebba
1972 *Västnyländsk ordaccent.* (Studier i nordisk filologi 59). Helsingfors

Selmer, Ernst W.
1927 *Den musikalske aksent i Stavangermålet.* (avhandlinger utgitt av Det Norske Videnskaps-Akademi i Oslo. Hist.-filos. II:3) Brøggers boktrykkeri, Oslo.

Ström, Anna
1998 Tonaccent i sydsvenska sammansättningar. ms Stockholm University.

Sweet, Henry
1877 Sounds and Forms of Spoken Swedish. *Transactions of the Philological Society* 1877, 478–543.

Teleman, Ulf
1969 Böjningssuffixets form i nusvenskan. *Arkiv för nordisk filologi* 84, 163–208.

Wessén, Elias
1969 *Svensk språkhistoria I. Ljudlära och ordböjningslära.* 8th edition (Reprinted as Nytryck i nordiska språk 4, 1992). Lund.

Withgott, Meg & Per-Kristian Halvorsen
1984 Morphological constraints on Scandinavian tone accent, *Report no. CSLI-84-11,* Stanford University.
1988 Phonetic and phonological considerations bearing on the representation of east Norwegian accent. In van der Hulst, Harry & Norval Smith (eds.): *Autosegmental studies on pitch accent,* 279–294. Foris, Dordrecht.

Kaluza's Law and the progress of Old English metrics

Thomas Cable

1. Introduction

When Pope (1942) surveyed the state of scholarship on Old English meter, he identified three metrists of the past half century as having presented serious theories. Of these only Sievers (1885, 1893) continues to command attention, and Pope's system itself has no current followers, though his book remains useful for its detailed catalogue of verses, and his sense of Old English verse structure must always be respected. Bliss (1958) restated certain key elements of Sievers' system that in Bliss's view had been ignored by temporal metrists such as Pope. Bliss also called attention to discoveries in Kaluza (1896, 1909) that had generally been forgotten by Old English metrists. In the second half of the twentieth century, no fewer than twelve books on the subject were published, culminating in the twin peaks of Fulk (1992) and Suzuki (1996), arguably the most important works since Sievers.[1]

If there is a common theme running through this burst of scholarship, it is that Old English meter is much less free than the traditional handbooks describe it. From separate studies that find metrical constraints on anacrusis, secondary stress, the count of syllables, and the weight of syllables, Old English poetry begins to look extremely regulated. While these newly discovered constraints do not necessarily tell us directly what Old English poetry sounded like, they do at least tell us what it did not sound like. The familiar comparisons of Old English meter to folk meters, nursery rhymes, the incantatory styles of Serbo-Croatian and Zulu recitation, rap, nonce sequences with thudding beats, and Gregorian chant (this by the present author in the 1970s) cannot be maintained.

Instead, it is more plausible to assume that Old English poetry conformed to normal patterns in the language, patterns slightly stylized and sometimes already described in the grammars without specific metrical reference. The inferred mode of recitation then would be ordinary careful speech. What separated metrical from nonmetrical discourse would be the length of the frame within which these normal linguistic patterns operated. That length was basically four syllables or syllable-equivalents with the allowance of one expansion.

A good example of this slight stylization of normal linguistic patterns is the process of resolution known as Kaluza's Law (see Kaluza 1896). Both Dresher and Lahiri (1991) and Suzuki (1995, 1996) relate resolution in Old English poetry to high vowel deletion that produced the plural variants *scēap* 'sheep' and *scipu* 'ships'. Such connections are helpful in reminding the modern reader that Old English poetic resolution is not some strange and unlikely borrowing from classical meter, where two short syllables equal one long syllable.

What resolution involves is the well-known tendency of metrical ictus to occur on a stressed, heavy syllable. "Stressed" means primary or secondary stress, but the important point is that ictus is relational. Icus in Old English meter occurs on a syllable (or a resolved syllable-equivalent) bearing metrically significant greater stress than an adjacent syllable (see Cable 1974: 84-93). Thus, in (1) there are five syllables bearing ictus, marked by / or \. Both *drēor-* and *fāg* have metrically significant greater stress than *–e*:

(1)   / x x x / x   / \ x /
        wæter under wolcnum   *wældrēore fāg*[2]
        'water under skies   slaughter-blood stained'

For reasons that will become clear later, each verse that is scanned in this essay with the traditional notation is also scanned with a grid. The construction of the grid follows Suzuki 1996, which is a summary, revision, and consolidation of studies of relative stress in Old English poetry by various metrists over many years. Because it would be impossible within the limits of the present study to rehearse the issues involved, the contours of stress will simply be taken from

Suzuki as given—plausible representations of relative stress (with which the present author agrees). Thus:

(2)
```
                                x
     x                          x       x
     x            x             x   x   x
     x x x x   x  x             x   x x x
     wæter under wolcnum        wældrēore fāg
```

If the ictus-bearing syllable is short (an open syllable with a short vowel), as is the first syllable of *wæter*, it is scanned metrically with the next syllable, as shown in (1). The two syllables are resolved into a single metrical position — still two syllables, not to be confused with phonetic elision. (A note on graphics. The long connecting curve over *wæter* in (1) indicates resolution. The shorter curve, or breve, directly beneath a scansion mark, as in (3) below, indicates a short unresolved syllable.) The first syllable of the function word *under* bears greater stress than the second syllable of that word but not greater stress that is metrically significant. Each syllable is scanned with a single x in the grid.

The second syllable of the resolved pair of syllables will always have phonological weak stress, as does the *–er* in *wæter*, and because there are no stressed short syllables word-finally in Old English, that second syllable will occur in the same word as the stressed short syllable. However, the second syllable might itself be long or short, and this is where Kaluza's Law comes in.

One way of stating Kaluza's Law is to say that the stressed short syllable in need of resolution can take any following short syllable, but it can take a following long syllable only if its own stress is sufficient. (See, for example, Fulk 1992: 153-235.) Cable (1994) argued that the idea of "sufficient stress" as used in this context can be given precise definitions using a combination of metrical grid and moraic count. The present essay repeats and clarifies this claim. It is useful to see the overall picture first.

2. Overall picture

The main determinant of stress, of course, is grammatical category. In Old English poetry the stressed syllables of nouns, adjectives, infinitives, participles, and lexical adverbs always bear metrical ictus. Finite verbs and nonlexical adverbs are variably stressed, depending on the context. Function words are seldom stressed. One of the most obvious features of Old English poetic style is the compound word. Because the second element of a compound bears less stress than the first element, the question is whether that second element bears sufficient stress for resolution. This is the main question that has concerned all studies of phenomena related to Kaluza's Law. It has always been recognized that the answer involves the quantity of the unstressed syllable following the syllable with secondary stress. This, in fact, is the heart of Kaluza's Law, the correlation of secondary stress with the quantity of the following, resolving syllable.

What happens, then, if this secondary stress falls on a short syllable? Do short syllables with secondary stress resolve with the following syllable? For example:

(3)
```
                                      x
                                      x  x
                                      x  x    x
   /   /   ˇ   x                      x  x   x x
   wīs wordcwida                      wīs wordcwida        (1845a)
   'wise of words'
```

(4)
```
                                      x
                                      x          x
                                      x   x      x
   /  ˇ   x  /  x                     x   x x   x x
   brimclifu blīcan                   brimclifu blīcan     (222a)
   'sea-cliffs shine'
```

Anyone familiar with the basic principles of Old English meter would recognize that resolution should not be allowed in (3): the verse would come out too short, with only three syllable-equivalents, or metrical positions, instead of the minimal four (see Cable 1974: 81-93).

What to do about (4) is less obvious, but a survey of occurring and nonoccurring patterns in *Beowulf* shows that / \ x / x, with five metrical positions is a problematic pattern, and resolution should occur, giving / \ / x, with the normal four positions (see Suzuki 1996: 65-76):

(5)   /   \ ‿ x   / x
        brimclifu blīcan

If, then, resolution occurs sometimes on secondary stress and sometimes not, it might seem that it simply depends on the number of syllable-equivalents that is needed in the verse. As with final *-e* in Chaucerian meter, one might wish to say, "Use it or not to get the syllable count right." Both of the vowels forming the unstressed syllables in these examples occur without the macron in modern texts, and so both would normally be considered short.

Kaluza's Law looks to a slightly earlier stage of phonology than that represented by macrons in modern texts. At this stage the *-u* in *brimclifu* was short, but the *-a* in *wordcwida* was long. These verses are representative of two sets of verses in *Beowulf*, one with the historically short vowel that happens to occur in a place where resolution is required for the overall metrical pattern (otherwise the pattern would exceed four positions) and one with the historically long vowel that cannot be resolved for the opposite metrical reason (the pattern would have only three positions). The long and short vowels overwhelmingly occur, with a few exceptions, where the meter needs them. Furthermore, the historically long vowels occur in the same position in the same metrical type (Sievers' type D) as do syllables closed by a consonant and counting as long – and thus unresolvable with a syllable bearing secondary stress, as in *-locen*:

(6)

heard hondlocen (322a, 551a)   heard hondlocen
'hard hand-linked'

With few exceptions in *Beowulf*, then, there is a complementary distribution that establishes the regular metrical use of syllabic length.

"Long syllable" has been given slightly different definitions that have resulted in slightly different though largely overlapping sets of examples in question. If an unstressed syllable ends in a consonant, as the second syllable on *-locen* in (6), all metrists agree that it counts as long for purposes of resolution. If the unstressed syllable ends in a vowel, as the final syllable of *wordcwida* in (3) above, two different interpretations have been used to determine the earlier historical length of the vowel. Kaluza (1896) and Fulk (1992) define long vowels as those that bore the *Schleifton* or circumflex in Proto-Germanic; otherwise, final vowels are short. Bliss (1958) and Suzuki (1996) define short vowels as those that underwent high vowel deletion (*-i and *-u) after a heavy syllable (producing the familiar morphophonemic alternations *scip, scipu*; *scēap, scēap*); other-wise, final vowels are long. It turns out that both sets of criteria identify the final syllable of *wordcwida* as historically long. The ending of the masc. *i*-stem gen. pl. *-cwida* is *-a* (<PGmc. *-ôn*).

These patterns had been noticed and had received a cursory description by Kaluza (1896) and others, but it was not until Bliss (1958) that the data were arranged so that implications could be drawn; even then, metrists did not pay attention to the subject until Fulk (1992) revived Kaluza's and Bliss's observations, called them Kaluza's Law, and used them for positing an early date for *Beowulf*. By linking the latest date of Kaluza's Law to the change of *æ* to *e*, Fulk posits a *terminus ad quem* of ca. 725 for the composition of *Beowulf* if Mercian in origin, or a century later if Northumbrian. Because *Beowulf* is the only long Old English poem to observe Kaluza's Law, Fulk assigns it an early and unique place in the tradition.

3. Grids and moraic count

Suzuki (1996: 211-18) showed that Kaluza's Law applied more regularly to more metrical types in *Beowulf* than had been thought, especially to type C, reviving and extending an observation originally made by Kaluza (1896). When a short stressed syllable and a following long unstressed syllable follow a stress clash, resolution is normally suspended. This is a complicated statement, but essentially, it means that the short syllable *bo-* looks both to the stress level of the preceding syllable and to the quantity of the following syllable:

(7)
```
                                        x
                                        x  x
    x  x   /   ⌣x                 x  x  x  x x
    ne wæs ecg bona (2506a)       ne wæs ecg bona (838b)
    'nor was edge slayer'
```

The present understanding of the phenomena gathered under Kaluza's Law can now be summarized. The context for resolving a short stressed syllable depends not only on the syllable that follows it but also on the syllable that precedes it within the same verse. The preceding syllable is a determinant of the light syllable's relative stress. This relationship is obvious in compounds, as we have seen, where the light syllable bears secondary stress. Curiously, the relationship also holds between separate words, if the short syllable does not have significantly more stress than the preceding syllable, as in (7) above, a type C verse, or in (8), a type A verse:

(8)
```
    x
    x           x
    x   x       x
    x   x       x x
    gūðrinc monig
```

The grid notation evokes obvious visual analogies with mountain ranges, foothills, and tablelands: the peak on *mo-* is less high than if it rose from an unstressed syllable, and it is not high enough to resolve with the heavy syllable that follows. A general principle has been argued in Cable (1994):

(9) *Relative peaks:* A short syllable must have at least two levels of stress above the preceding syllable for resolution with a long syllable to occur.

The peak on *mo-* in (8) rises only one level above the preceding syllable, and so resolution with the following long syllable cannot occur.

A similar metrical pattern occurs in the masc. *n*-stem nom. sg., for which the ending is *-a* (<PGmc. *-ô*). The syllable *–frum-* falls below the peak of the preceding syllable *land-*, and so resolution with historically long *–a* does not occur:

(10) x
      x x
      x x   x
      x x   x x
      lēof landfruma (31a)
      'dear land-prince'

There are twelve type D verses such as this in *Beowulf* (see also 160a, 288a, 554a, 2042a, 2090a, 2112a, 2271a, 2273a, 2315a, 2368a, and 2414a).

Among adjectives the masc. nom. pl. ending *-e* (<PGmc. *-ai*) occurs three times as an unresolved syllable in these type D patterns, twice in the same collocation of words in unresolved *-hwate* in (10):

(11) x
      x x
      x x   x
      x x x   x x
      frome fyrdhwate (1641a, 2476a)
      'bold war-like'

Other type D patterns include verses with the masc. *a*-stem dat. sg. *-e* (<PGmc. *-ai*) as in *Samod ǣrdæge* (1311b) and the fem. *ō*-stem gen. sg. *-e* (<PGmc. *-ôz*) as in *gearo gyrnwræce* (2118a), for a total of twenty-one long vocalic endings by Suzuki's count (p. 210) — Bliss's original list expanded by six. To these may be added twenty-four verses with consonantal endings; for example *Beowulf* 2025a:

(12) x
    x x
    x x x
    x x x x
    geong goldhroden
    'young gold-adorned'

Perhaps the most striking discovery in Suzuki's reconsideration of Kaluza's Law is the regularity with which it applies to type C. Type C verses in which both metrical stresses occur in a compound word conform to Kaluza's Law, by Suzuki's count, in about 91 per cent of the 225 relevant examples in *Beowulf*, slightly lower than the 94 per cent conformity rate of type D verses. Exceptions include, for example, *Beowulf* 2884b, with unresolved *gifu*, the fem. *ō*-stem nom. sg.:

(13)   x
        x x
    x x x x
    ond swyrdgifu
    'and sword-giving'

If the historically short *-u* were resolved, as Kaluza's Law would allow, the verse would have only three positions.

When the type C verses contain two words, Suzuki found the rate of conformity to Kaluza's Law to be even higher, there being only three final short vowels, or just over one per cent exceptions, among the 265 verses in which the second metrical stress is short; 188 of these verses end in a consonant, 74 in a historically long vowel, as in (7) above or in (14), *Beowulf* 1801a:

(14)   x
            x   x
         x x x x x
     oþ þæt hrefn blaca
     'until raven black'

There are other exceptions to the version of Kaluza's Law presented here. For example, *Beowulf* 2430b has the same difficulties for any version of Kaluza's Law as it had for Dresher and Lahiri (1991: 263):

(15)   x
       x   x
     x x   x x
     Hrēðel cyning
     'Hrēðel king'

Fulk (1992: 185) calls this particular pattern "admittedly unique in *Beowulf*."

4. Conclusions

In the past, resolution in Old English meter was often seen as a technical detail with a rather suspect status. The fact that "suspension of resolution" was frequently needed to avoid the deleterious effects of resolution led some metrists to reject the whole idea and to look for another explanation that would not require attention to quantities; however, it is now clear that vowel quantity and syllable weight, at least in *Beowulf*, follow precise patterns. These regular moraic distinctions in *Beowulf* do not mean that *Beowulf* was composed in a quantitative meter. The stylization and metrical incorporation of processes associated with high vowel deletion in Old English produce something quite different from the dactylic hexameter of Greek and Latin poetry.

Similarly, the recently recognized importance of syllable count in Old English meter does not mean that the meter is analogous to the

French decasyllabic. Nor does the "gabble of weaker syllables," which is the feature, along with alliteration, that has always been recognized, mean that Old English meter is strong-stress in the way that handbooks often describe it. These traditional descriptions typically draw analogies with nursery rhymes and with Middle English alliterative meter. It turns out that during the same period when progress was made in understanding Old English meter, similar progress was made in understanding the meter of *Sir Gawain and the Green Knight* and other alliterative poems of the West Midlands. Now the differences between the alliterative meters of the eighth century and the fourteenth century can be seen as more salient than the similarities.

The *Beowulf* meter is none of these alone – quantitative, syllabic, or strong stress – but a mix. There is in *Beowulf* a hierarchy of metrical elements that has as its base a count of four:

    One   Two   Three   Four

At its simplest, the meter of *Beowulf* is a mapping of four syllables onto these four metrical positions without any attention to linguistic stress:

(16)   /   x   /   x
       gomban gyldan (11a)
       'tribute pay'

However, because some syllables receive linguistic stress, and because the assignment of stress is bound up with syllabic length, there is a question whether a word such as *-cwida* in *wīs wordcwida* counts as "Three" or as "Three Four" – hence, the subject of the present essay.

Similarly, the well-known tendency of two or more unstressed syllables in a stress-timed language to occupy something like the perceptual space of a single stressed syllable is the linguistic basis for allowing an expansion in one of the first two positions of the verse. In *Beowulf* 495a the first three syllables count as "One," not as "One Two Three":

(17)   x x x / x /
sē þe on handa bær
'who in hands bore'

Notice, now, how we are backing into the notion of allowed patterns of stress in Old English meter – the most famous positivistic scheme of which is Sievers' Five Types. However, these types actually fall out epiphenomenally, and they do not need to be named. If a stretch of unstressed syllables is allowed in one of the first two positions, then of necessity a stressed syllable will delimit it, bringing it to an end. Working the permutations on a stretch of unstressed syllables in one of the first two positions while observing other independent constraints such as the correlation of stress and moraic length discussed above will produce Sievers' Five Types. Then one does not have to worry whether *Beowulf* 725b has secondary stress on the unlikely medial syllable of *treddode*, a weak verb of class 2:

(18)   /   / x x
fēond treddode
'fiend stepped'

The verse is simply a one-to-one matching of syllable and position, in which the syllables *-dode* occupy separate positions because they do not occur in one of the first two positions, the part of the verse where the gabble of weaker syllables is allowed.

    Once the patterns of stress emerge from these separate considerations, derivative from the basic meter, rules of alliteration serve to make it all more easily perceptible. However, "alliterative" is yet another mode that the *Beowulf* meter is *not*, despite the convenience of the term for identifying an obvious feature of the tradition and for designating the tradition itself – or one of several English traditions. The *Beowulf* meter is perhaps best called a "four-position meter," because the term is not transparent. In being prevented from bringing immediate and inappropriate analogies from other traditions, the metrist is forced to define the meaning of "position" in this mixed mode and thus to organize the relationships of stress, quantity, syllable count, and alliteration.

Notes

1. For a critical survey of theories of Old English prosody, including notes on developments from the eighteenth century to 1995, see Stockwell and Minkova (1997).
2. *Beowulf* 1631. All examples of Old English poetry are from *Beowulf* in the Klaeber (1950) edition. Verses are cited by first half-line (a) and second half-line (b).

References

Bliss, A. J.
   1958   *The Metre of Beowulf.* Revised edition 1967. Oxford: Blackwell.
Cable, Thomas
   1974   *The Meter and Melody of Beowulf.* Urbana: University of Illinois Press.
   1994   Syllable weight in Old English meter: Grids, morae, and Kaluza's Law. *Diachronica* 11: 1-11.
Dresher, B. Elan, and Aditi Lahiri
   1991   The Germanic foot: Metrical coherence in Old English. *Linguistic Inquiry* 22: 251-86.
Fulk, R. D.
   1992   *A History of Old English Meter.* Philadelphia: University of Pennsylvania Press.
Klaeber, Frederick (ed.)
   1950   *Beowulf and the Fight at Finnsburg.* 3rd edition. Boston: Heath.
Kaluza, Max
   1896   Zur Betonungs- und Verslehre des Altenglischen. In: *Festschrift zum siebzigsten Geburtstage von Oskar Schade*, 101-133. Königsberg: Hartung.
   1909   *Englische Metrik in historischer Entwicklung dargestellt.* Berlin: Felber.
Pope, John C.
   1942   *The Rhythm of Beowulf.* 2nd edition 1966. New Haven: Yale University Press.

Sievers, Eduard
    1885   Zur Rhythmik des germanischen Alliterationsverses. *Beiträge zur Geschichte der deutschen Sprache und Literatur* 10: 209-314, 451-545.
    1893   *Altgermanische Metrik*. Halle: Niemeyer.

Stockwell, Robert P., and Donka Minkova
    1997   Prosody. In: Robert E. Bjork and John D. Niles (eds.), *A Beowulf Handbook*, 55-83. Lincoln: University of Nebraska Press.

Suzuki, Seiichi
    1995   Resolution and mora counting in Old English. *American Journal of Germanic Linguistics and Literatures* 7:1-28.
    1996   *The Metrical Organization of Beowulf: Prototype and Isomorphism*. (Trends in Linguistics, Studies and Monographs 95.) Berlin/New York: Mouton de Gruyter.

Middle English stress doubles: New evidence from Chaucer's meter

Michael Redford

1. Introduction

Reconstructing the stress rules of a dead language is rarely, if ever, easy, particularly when the primary data comes from metered verse: assumptions about stress-based meters lead to "conclusions" about stress, which are "substantiated" by evidence from meter. Stress and meter are inexorably intertwined in English, and they can be disentangled without resorting to the solution for the Gordian knot, severing the crucial relationship between meter and stress. For Middle English the difficulties involved are exacerbated by the introduction of Romance loan words, and conflicting views about how these loans were incorporated into the language lead to different conclusions about Middle English stress and meter.

The crucial cases are so-called "stress doubles", or words that appear to have initial stress in certain lines (1a) of Chaucer's *Canterbury Tales* (CT) and final stress in other lines (1b). In (1) "stressed" syllables are marked with *s* and "unstressed" syllables are marked with *w*, assuming that in iambic pentameter syllables alternate *unstressed-stressed-unstressed-stressed...* (Note that *citee* in line (1b) rhymes with degree):

(1) a. w   s w s   w   s   w s w s w   CT 1:4343
        And by assault he wan the <u>citee</u> after
    b.   w   s w   s   w   s w s   w s   CT 1:2191
        Whan he had broght hem into his <u>citee</u>

Alternations such as these are common in Chaucer's poetry and they have often been cited as evidence that the stress rules of Middle English were in flux as a result of the influx of Romance loan words. The first problem is that stress doubles are not always loan words, e.g. *sikness(e)* and *housband* show the same alternations as *citee*. The second problem is that these alternations are not evenly distributed: line-internally, stress tends to be initial (1a); at the end of the line, stress is invariable final (1b). It is therefore conceivable that stress doubles are merely an artifact of end-rhyme; the fact that stress is initial in unrhymed Alliterative verse provides further evidence for the influence of rhyme on stress. Also, consider how valuable (1) is as evidence for the stress of *citee* in light of lines such as those in (2), from Milton's *Paradise Lost*:

(2) a. w s w s w s   w s w s
        O visions ill forseen! Better had I   *PL 10:759*
    b. w   s w s   w   s w   s w s
        In the **visions** of God. It was a hill   *PL 10:377*

While (1) has been taken as evidence for English stress in the fourteenth Century, (2b) cannot be seen as evidence for English stress in the seventeenth Century. Instead (2b) is an example of Milton's idiosyncratic metrical style, which occasionally permits stressed syllables in the "wrong" places, e.g. the word *visions*, which is in Weak-Strong in in (2b), although the word has initial stress.

The central question addressed in this paper is whether Chaucer's stress doubles are providing evidence for Middle English stress or evidence for Chaucer's metrical style, i.e. are the alternations in (1) like those in (2), or are they a reflection of the stress rules of Middle English? In the next section, the theory of Generative Metrics is outlined, in particular with regard to the kinds of deviations given in (2), i.e. what determines and regulates such cases where stressed syllables are in the "wrong" places in Modern English verse. In section 3 Chaucer's iambic pentameter is discussed; new data from the Canterbury Tales shows that final stress in stress doubles may be a result of phrasal structure. In the first part of section 4 previous accounts of Middle English stress are discussed, in particular Halle and Keyser (1966) and a recent critique of their account by Minkova (1997). This paper takes up an idea put forth by Nakao (1977) that stress doubles contain two prominent syllables, an idea that harkens back to concept of *schwebende Betonung* (ten Brink 1881: §274) – with certain refinements. Section 4.1 is dedicated to the phenomenon of "level stress", followed by a general discussion of stress in 4.1 and 4.2. In section 4.3 an Opimality-theoretic account of "prominence mismatches" is given, since the new data points to a conflict between word stress and phrasal stress in Middle English due to diachronic changes. Section 5 contains a discussion of the analysis and the data as well as a conclusion.

2. Generative Metrics

The foundations of Generative Metrics are based on the Structuralist distinction between the metrical pattern (verse design) and the possible individual manifestations of that meter (verse instance) attested in a particular language or tradition (Jakobson 1987). In the Generative framework, each meter has an underlying, invariable abstract pattern and a set of association conventions that map any given line of verse to that pattern. I assume that the abstract pattern of the meter is organized into a strictly hierarchically organized structure of binary constituents: the metrical position, the metrical foot, and the colon.[1] The abstract pattern for iambic pentameter is given below:

(3)
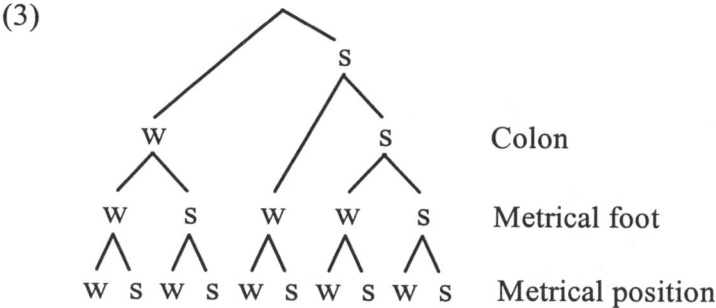

There are many formal accounts of the correspondence rules, which reflect developments/debates within Generative Phonology.[2] It is not the goal of this paper to defend a particular theory of meter, and therefore the formalization of the correspondence rules will not be considered here.

Studies of English meter show that there are often mismatches between the prominence expected from the abstract pattern and the actual distribution of stressed syllables in a line, as shown in (4). (Metrical positions are marked above the line and mismatches are in bold.) Unstressed words, e.g. the closed class of function words, are free to be in Strong position (*on* and *two* in 4a), as are the unstressed syllables of lexical words (4b). We therefore cannot assume that a syllable in a Strong position is stressed. We do know, however, that Modern English poets restrict the occurrence of stressed syllables in Weak, but there are several additional qualifications: (i) Stressed monosyllables regularly occur in Weak, as in (4c), a line from Browning's, *Meeting at Night*, (ii) the stressed syllables of polysyllabic words are generally prohibited in Weak (inversion being a systematic exception (4d)). In addition, disyllabic words with final stress are almost universally restricted to Weak-Strong position, with the notable exceptions from Donne's verse, while disyllabic words with initial stress can sometimes occur in Weak-Strong positions, as in (2) repeated in (4e).

(4) a. w **s** w s w **s** w s w s
      So **on** he fares, and **to** the border comes   *PL 4:131*

b. w s w s w s w s w **s**
      Where he fell flat and shamed his worshi**pers**   *PL 4:461*

c. w s w **s** w s w **s**
      The gray **sea** and the dark **black** land

d. **w s** w s w s w s w s
      Regions of sorrow, **doleful** shades, where peace   *PL 1:65*

e. w s **w s** w s w s w s
      In the **visions** of God, it was a hill,   *PL 10:377*

Finally, certain mismatches are restricted to the right edge of prosodic domains, and the larger the phrasal domain, the more marked the deviation; thus Milton's mismatches of the kind in (2) do not occur at an Intonational Phrase boundary (IP) or an Utterance Boundary (U).[3] Taken together, these observations provide diagnostics for determining the stress pattern of a word based on its occurrence in meter:

(5) a. If a disyllabic word occurs in Strong-Weak but also in Weak-Strong, the word has initial stress.
 b. If a disyllabic word occurs in Weak-Strong at a phrasal boundary (IP or U), it has final stress.
 c. The underlying stress pattern is maintained at phrasal boundaries (IP or U).

These diagnostics show that the location of word and phrase boundaries is crucial for analyses of Modern English poets.

3. Chaucer's meter

3.1 Abstract pattern

Middle English marks the end of Germanic meter and the beginning of the primacy of iambic pentameter in English.[4] In the last five hundred years, a vast amount has been written about Chaucer, his language, and his meter. It is impossible to revisit the entire literature and the reoccurring debates, such as the metrical/phonemic status of orthographic <e>, and uncertainties surrounding the manuscripts. Putting these factors aside, Chaucer's meter differs from later poets in several ways (Cable 1991; Guthrie 1988; Woods 1984; Zonneveld 1998). First, "rising cadences" (Cable 1991) of four syllables are rare. For example, the stress of each syllable increases progressively in the sequence "rembr-*ance ôf things pást.*" Second, headless lines occur, i.e lines with 9 syllables, beginning and ending on a stressed syllable, *Twénty bóokes, clád in bláck or réd (CT 1:294).* Third, Chaucer has less inversion than later poets. The number of lines with initial, disyllabic inversion in Shakespeare's Sonnets is ca. 4.7%, but only ca. 1.4% in an equal sample of the *Canterbury Tales*. Fourth, Chaucer's line is "lighter" than Shakespeare's, i.e. it contains fewer stressed syllables (Guthrie 1988). Fifth, there is a lack of anapestic feet or resolution, which also indicates that Chaucer's meter is more strictly syllabic than Shakespeare's (see Stockwell and Minkova (1998) for a recent discussion). The crucial question is whether these differences indicate that Chaucer's meter is fundamentally different from Shakespeare's, or should these differences be interpreted as poet-specific variation? If the difference is fundamental, then the diagnostics in (5) may not be valid for Chaucer, but if the differences are not a matter of kind, but of degree, then we can use the diagnostics in (5) to examine stress patterns in Chaucer's meter.

Cable (1996) claims that rising cadences are indicative of foot-based meter, such as Shakespeare's, and the absence of such cadences in Chaucer's meter shows that his verse design is not foot-based, but strictly alternating. Youmans (1996), however, argues that the similarities between Chaucer's meter and that of later poets outweighs any of the differences, and the verse design for both Chaucer and Shakespeare is that given in (3). Chaucer is indeed more regular than other English poets and Cable is correct in calling his meter "alternating". However, in Redford (2000) I argue that this is a result of correspondence rules Chaucer employed, and that these rules reflect the distribution of stresses in Middle English.

Rising cadences usually have adjacent lexical stresses, e.g. Cable's example above and lines such as *Than thôse òld níne* (Shakespeare, *Sonnets*, 38) and a stressed monosyllable is in Weak; Beaver (1974) notes that adjective + noun sequences make up 80% of the cases where a monosyllable is in Weak. Therefore there is a relationship between rising cadences, stressed syllables in Weak, and adjective + noun sequences. In German, and to a lesser degree in Dutch, inflectional endings prevent adjacent lexical stresses in adjective+noun sequences: *der álte bláue Stúhl* and *de óude bláuwe stóel* "the old blue chair". Rising cadences as such are rare in these languages and thus rare in the meters of these languages. The inflectional system of Dutch does lead to adjacent lexical stresses in certain cases *een óud bláuw hémd* "an old blue shirt", and the system is similar to, but not identical with, that of Middle English (using on the rules for inflectional <e> given in Cable (1991)). In addition Caon (1999) shows for *old(e)* and *fals(e)* that the disyllabic form predominates in attributive position (88% and 93%, repectively), but that the monosyllabic form is always found in predicative position (100%). A sample of roughly two thousand lines taken from Chaucer's Canterbury Tales and a similar sample from works by the sixteenth Century Dutch poets Hooft and Vondel shows a striking similarity: monosyllables occur in weak metrical positions in only ca. 4% of the lines, compared to 21.3% for Shakespeare (Sonnets) and 12.8% for Milton (Paradise Lost).[5] Thus it appears that the inflectional system of Middle English leads to a more even distribution of lexical stresses, which does not facilitate/mandate rising cadences (on the role of inflection in Middle Dutch verse, see Zonneveld, this volume).

The lack of rising cadences also explains the lightness of Chaucer's line. The number of lexical stresses per line is influenced by their permissible occurrences in the line: each unstressed syllable in Strong decreases the number of stresses per line, while each stressed syllables in Weak increases the number of stresses per line. Chaucer allows unstressed syllables in Strong (e.g. *by* in 1a) but rarely allows stressed monosyllables in Weak, which means that the overall number of stressed syllables per line will be lower than that for a poet such as Shakespeare, who frequently places lexical stresses in Weak. Taken together with the evidence from Youmans (1996), it would appear that the abstract pattern for Chaucer, Shakespeare, and Milton is the same. We can now return to the question of stress doubles and examine them in light of the diagnostics given above, since it appears that the differences between Chaucer and later poets is not a result of a different abstract pattern, but of a difference in the inflectional system of Middle English and Modern English.

3.2 Stress Doubles in CT

Using data from Nakao (1977) and Minkova (1997) a list of some 735 disyllabic word forms was created (alternate spellings are counted individually). There are a total of 4,321 lines, or 18.4% of the text, that contain a stress double from this list.[6]

Before considering the diagnostics presented above, several possible explanations for stress doubles should be considered. Chaucer knew French and one could argue that he often uses *mots savants* or gallicisms/latinisms to a knowledgeable audience. The frequency of these words makes this unlikely, and the argument cannot account for the alternation in native words, such as *siknesse* or in native compounds such as *housbonde*. Alternate pronunciations might also have been intended to convey other meanings as well. Consider the following lines, for example:

(6) a. w s w   s w
        a maner **latyn** was hir speche   *CT 2:519*

    b. w s   w s
        and in **latyn** I speke a wordes few   *CT 6:344*

In (6), is Chaucer trying to tell us exactly how corrupt "her speech" is by having her put the stress on the wrong syllable? Or in (6b) is Chaucer trying to be ironic by having the Pardoner put the stress on the wrong syllable? Or is the Pardoner being pedantic and putting the stress on the "correct" syllable? The joke is lost on — or is on — the modern reader. It appears that the different stress patterns cannot give any indication of the (desired) social standing of the speaker.

A further possible explanation is that stress shift applies in these cases, as in Modern English *thìrteen mén*. Referring to the Rhythm Rule may seem circular, but this hypothesis is easily tested, because there must be a clash and the rule applies within a phonological phrase. Unstressed syllables are allowed in Strong and therefore when a stress double is in Strong-Weak and the following syllable in Strong is unstressed or a non-lexical word, stress shift cannot be used as an explanation, since there is no clash.

(7) a.   s w   s
        thurghout the citee by the maister strete   *CT 1:2902*

    b. s w   s
        in siknesse nor in meschief to visite   *CT 1:493*

    c. s   w   s
        my housbonde is so ful of jalousie   *CT 1:3294*

Some stress doubles may be fixed expressions, such as *blood roial* (1:1546), as in Modern English *Casino Royál* vs. *róyal casino*

(Youmans 1996: 203). Youmans notes that *blood roial* has an equally regular stress pattern, and that putting the adjective in postposition has no metrical motivation. These cases are limited to attributive position and cannot explain other examples, however.[7]

Turning now to the diagnostics (metrically relevant <e> are indicated with diaersis):

(8) *SW line internal*

a.	for *certeyn* oldë dotard by youre leve	*CT 3:331*
b.	in *siknesse* nor in meschief to visite	*CT 1:493*
c.	myn *housbonde* was at londoun al that lente	*CT 3:550*

(9) *WS line internal*

a.	for I wol be *certeyn* a wedded man	*CT 4:1405*
b.	and hath *siknesse* and greet adversitee	*CT 1:1311*
c.	whan myn *housbonde* is fro the world agon	*CT 3:47*

(10) *WS line final (with rhyming lines)*

a.	thou lovëst me I woot it wel *certeyn*	*CT 4:309*
	and al that likëth me I dar wel seyn	*CT 4:311*
b.	that cause is of his mordrë greet *siknesse*	*CT 1:1256*
	som man desirëth for to han richesse	*CT 1:1255*
c.	now wol I spekë of my ferthe *housbonde*	*CT 3:452*
	swiche manere wordes hadde we on honde	*CT 3:451*

The data in (8-10) provide conflicting evidence. First, *certeyn*, *siknesse*, and *housbonde* occur in SW (8) and WS (9), and should therefore have initial stress. On the other hand, the same words occur in WS line-finally, and phrase-finally (10), from which we can conclude that they have final stress.

The doubles in (10) are also in rhyme, which adds another factor, or rather, another unknown variable. In order to avoid, or at least sidestep, the uncertainties of end-rhyme, it is crucial to look at the cases where stress doubles occur in WS line-internally. Restricting the data to the line-internal cases raises the question of whether such examples are instances of mismatches akin to Milton's given in (2). As noted above for Modern English poets, phrasing plays a crucial role in determining when disyllabic words with initial stress can occur in Weak-Strong and phrasing may provide a means of determining whether the placement of stress doubles is a metrical phenomonenon.

For Middle English it would be possible to assume that the phrase-building rules are the same as those for Modern English, but such rules can be subject to diachronic change, and it is therefore conceivable that the rules for these two stages of English are different.[8] Halle and Keyser (1966) note that punctuation serves as an indicator of phrasing, but this practice is rightly questioned by Guthrie (1988), who also questions the use of published editions for metrical analysis, since punctuation, amongst other things, is often modernized. Guthrie's uneasiness is well-founded, but there is in fact something to be said for punctuation, in particular when it is in the manuscript itself. One particular "punctuation mark" or diacritic in the Ellesmere and Hengwrt manuscript is a virgule, a diagonal stroke or slash /.

Obviously, it is impossible to know whether Chaucer or the Hengwrt/Ellesmere scribe is the ultimate source of the virgulae. In fact, Woods (1984: 40, fn 41) notes that virgule placement is inconsistent, in particular when one compares the Ellesmere and the Hengwrt manuscripts. The inconsistency is certainly there, but it does not lessen the importance of the virgule. For example the lines from (9) above appear in the Hengwrt manuscript as follows:

(11) a. for I wol be / *certeyn* / a wedded man *CT 4:1405*
 b. and hath *siknesse* / and greet adversitee *CT 1:1311*
 c. whan myn *housbonde* / is fro the world agon *CT 3:47*

These examples are not a coincidence. The data given below show the occurrence of stress doubles in Weak-Strong line-internally in relation to the placement of a virgule:

Table 1. Stress doubles in WS line internally

	Nr. Lines	WS before virgule	WS after virgule	Others
Hengwrt	95	76(80%)	6 (6.3%)	13 (18.8%)

The data from the Hengwrt Ms. show that there is a clear, and hitherto unnoticed relationship between the distribution of stress doubles in the line and virgule placement: when a stress double is in Weak-Strong line internally, it is either preceeded or followed by a virgule in 86.3% of the lines. (Note it is not the case that a stress double before a virgule must be in WS; rather when a stress double is in WS, a virgule is almost always present.)

We have tacitly assumed that the virgule is a marker for phrasing, but before continuing we should ask what else the virgule could be a diacritic for: irregular punctuation? a caesure? or indeed a phrasal boundary? It seems implausible that the virgule is meant to mark those cases where the stress is "irregular", i.e. where the double is in WS, since we would then expect virgules to be at the end of every line, where "irregular" pronunciation is the norm. This is not the case. As Duffell (1996: 215-6) has shown, Chaucer adopted the mobile caesure of the Italian endecasillabo into English, while restricting himself to duple rhythms. In this context it is irrelevant if the virgule is a caesura or a phrase marker, because a caesure is a phrase boundary.

This new evidence for line-internal phrasing can be interpreted in several ways: (i) the line internal cases are examples of a mismatch similar to Milton's, (ii) Chaucer was trying imitate French meter, (iii) stress doubles reveal something about phrasal stress in Middle English. If Chaucer, like Milton, allowed the stressed syllables of disyllabic words such as *certayn* to be in Weak-Strong at line-internal phrase boundaries, then the occurrence of stress doubles line finally, in particular at IP and U boundaries, cannot be explained without treating such cases as inversion. There are good reasons to doubt this. As for Chaucer trying to imitate French meters, it is unclear why he would fail so miserably, because the meter of the Canterbury Tales is not that of a French decasyllable or an Italian hendecasyllable, as Duffell (1996) clearly shows. In conclusion, it appears that alternations in the placement of stress doubles is not a metrical phenomenon. Otherwise, it remains unexplained why stress doubles can occur in WS line internally, since end-rhyme cannot be a factor.

Scribal diacritics have been shown to be a indicator of phrasing in the bible (Dresher 1994), and making a similar claim for Middle English does not seem overly hasty. Assuming that the virgules are a diacritic for phrasing in the Canterbury Tales, we can conclude that stress doubles can occur in WS at the beginning or the end of "virgule" phrases. Based on this new evidence the distribution of stress doubles in the line is even more regular than stated in the introduction. Stress doubles are in SW line internally; in WS line finally, and in WS line-internally if a virgule is present. What is the connection between line ends and virgules? Guthrie (1988) notes that Chaucer only makes limited use of enjambement (but cf. McCully (1998)), with line ends generally corresponding to some phrase/syntactic boundary, although enjambed lines do of course occur. This further supports the assumption that the virgule corresponds to a phrase marker, because it is then possible to make the following generalization: at line-internal phrase boundaries – as indicated by a virgule – stress doubles may occur in WS, and at the end of lines (which normally coincide with a phrase break) stress doubles are invariably in WS.

There are several phonetic explanations why phrase-final positions may influence the prominence of the final syllable. Domain-final lengthening is well documented in Modern English and due to Open Syllable Lengthening in Middle English, vowel length and stress were interconnected in Middle English. The phonetic lengthening of the vowel may have been an indicator that the final vowel was to a certain degree "stressed", since it was lengthened. This would hold especially for Romance loans with a final long vowel, as word-final vowel length was lost during Old English, with some exceptions, e.g. ī < -iġ Another possibility is the influence of phrasal boundary tones, which would associate with the final syllable in the phrase. Pitch is a strong correlate of stress in Modern English, and this perhaps led Chaucer to hear the final syllable as having a pitch movement on it. These are possible explanations for the distribution of stress doubles in Canterbury Tales. The open question is what this new data concerning phrases implies in terms of the stress rules of Middle English.

4. Middle English Stress

There is general agreement that in Early Middle English native words were stressed according to the rules that applied for Old English: stress usually falls on the initial syllable of the root; certain prefixes are unstressable *licgan* 'lie'; others can be either stressed or unstressed *fórwyrd* 'ruin' vs. *forwiernan* 'to refuse'; compounds have secondary stress on the second root in the compound (Campbell 1959: 71-99; Mitchell and Robinson 1992: §6; Lass 1992: §2.6.2; Hogg 1992:).[9] All non-initial, heavy syllables or their resolved equivalent received secondary stress, except for word-final, closed heavy syllables.[10]

Early borrowings into English, as well as the other West-Germanic languages, were stressed according to the native stress rules (Lahiri et al., 1999); the situation in the Middle English period is less clear. The rules proposed for Middle English stress fall into four broad categories:

(12) a. Romance Stress Rule: "stress the penultimate if heavy, else antepenultimate"
Halle & Keyser (1966, 1971); Lahiri et al. (1999)
b. Initial Stress
Minkova (1997); Lahiri and Fikkert (1999); Morsbach (1896: §25); Learned (1922)
c. Countertonic: "primary stress in Middle English where secondary stress was in French and vice versa"
Dobson (1957: V, §1); Eckhardt (1936: §12, §83-86); Eliason (1939: §78); Jordan (1974: §218); Luick (1921)
d. Hovering Accent: "schwebende Betonung", "even stress", or "level stress"
ten Brink (1881: §274); Dobson (1957: §2-3); Morsbach (1896: §26); Paul (1891: §31); Kaluza (1919: §211)

Halle and Keyser's (1971) extensive analysis of the development of English stress has become the standard view of Middle English stress: "stress doubles" reflect the synchronic state of the grammar, which reflects a conflict between the Germanic Stress Rule (GSR) and Romance Stress Rule (RSR), which entered into Middle English in the wake of Romance loans.[11] In addition to the RSR applying to the loan vocabulary, certain native words shifted to the non-native category, becoming subject to the RSR as well as the GSR. In their account stress doubles arose from two sources. For native words the application of the GSR or the RSR stress rule lead to alternate stresses: (i) /siknesse/ → (síkness) (GSR) or (ii) /siknesse/ → (siknéss) (RSR). For non-native words an optional schwa-deletion rule feeds an optional vowel-shortening rule in Romance words: (i) /manērə/ → manēr → (mánĕr) or (ii) /manēr/ → (manḗr). The segmental rules lead to an alternation in the weight of the final syllables, which in turn leads the weight-sensitive RSR to stress the final syllable *manér* or the initial *máner*. The data presented in the last section show that the distribution is dependent on the placement of virgules/phrasing, which is not incompatible with Halle and Keyser's analysis, because the optionality of the rules can be limited to phrase-specific contexts. However, it remains unexplained why stress double alternations are not encountered in Alliterative verse, if both forms were equally acceptable. In addition, the shift from the native to the non-native category is difficult to motivate, since none of the words in question have final stress in MnE (ignoring noun/verb pairs), which is unexpected if the native/non-native distinctions were optional.

The existence of two, antipodal stress rules in Middle English has recently been questioned by Minkova (1997), who notes that monomorphemic, native words longer than three syllables did not occur in Middle English, and, as a result, the Germanic stress rule and the Romance stress rule show a high degree of correspondence (Lass 1992: §2.6.2). She presents a morphological account of Middle English stress, in which the Romance Stress Rule did not replace the Germanic Stress Rule in Middle English. Based on empirical evidence, she concludes that the stress-shift was not frequent and was limited to certain lexical items. There is therefore no need to postulate that a Middle English phonological rule lead to stress shift: Native words and loans were stressed on the initial syllable and therefore stress doubles in rhyme is a purely metrical phenomenon. The data in Table 1 further supports her conclusion, because aside from the special cases (line ends and virgule positions) stress doubles are normally in SW in the Canterbury Tales and in Alliterative verse.

Summarizing, Halle and Keyser claim word stress is either initial or final, while for Minkova word stress is initial, except in rhyme position. Both conclusions have supporting evidence and problematic exceptions – all of which involve indirect evidence from meter. The data presented in the previous chapter indicates that words such as *citee* do have two prominence patterns, but that the WS-pattern is subject to a specific condition, namely it only occurs at the edge of a phrasal domain (virgule or line end). In the remainder of this section, I present an analysis of stress doubles that assumes that both the initial and the final syllable count as stressed, or rather as prominent, in specific phrasal contexts. A similar proposal is made by Nakao (1977), and much earlier by (ten Brink, 1881) and other scholars (cf. 12d).[12] In other words, stress doubles appear to be a kind of *schwebende Betonung*, or "hovering stress" within well-defined prosodic environments.

4.1 Level stress/stress levels

One of the cornerstones of Metrical Phonology is that stress is relative, which also implies that every word has one, and only one, primary stressed syllable.[13] This view of stress seems to preclude "hovering" or "level" stress, but to do so would be premature. Although the abstract phonological formulation of stress as a function of constituent structure in general excludes level stress, level prominence, in an articulatory, auditory and/or acoustic sense cannot be ruled out.[14] In this sense "level stress" does not mean "equal stress". In addition, prominence may be perceived as level even when actual measurements show that the correlates of stress are not equal, much like stresses are perceived to be isochronous, even when the measured intervals between the stresses may or may not be. Granted, there are several different explanations for level prominence, many of which are not phonological: flawed data collection, failure to control for pitch accents, etc. Nonetheless, there are also several possible linguistic motivations, such as historical change(s) in progress.

Several languages are reported to have level stress: Yidiɲ, Central Alaskan Yupik, Tübatulabal, Kinyambo (Hayes 1995: 25); Campa, Nimboran, Yuma (Hyman 1977: 38); Guugu Yimidhirr, Gamilraay, Gidabal, Yaralde (Goedemans 1998: 235-50). Some of these languages have also been analyzed without level stress, but there are some additional well-documented cases that are clear examples of level prominence: from acquisition data, from Australian languages, from Scandinavian dialects, from Welsh, and, perhaps, from Modern English.

During the acquisition of stress, Dutch children pass through several developmental stages (Fikkert 1994: 202-207). In the initial stages, the child builds words that are maximally two syllables and stress is initial: *konijn* "rabbit" /kōn'ɛin/ → ['kūla] (Tom 1;7.23). At stage 3 the child determines that syllable weight plays a role in stress placement, but in words with two feet the child has level stress, because it has not yet learned the word stress rule: /kōn'ɛin/ → ['kun'ɛi] (Tom 1;8.20). Level stress does not occur in adult speech, because the end rule has been learned.[15] Historical developments may also give rise to level stress, as in certain Australian languages. Stress in Yaralde, a Murray language, can be distributed over the first two syllables in certain cases (Goedemans 1998: 187). A historical process that deleted intial vowels forced stress to shift to the second syllable, but the process was partially blocked, yielding stress on both syllables in words that retained the initial vowel. In both of these examples, level stress is a characteristic of transitory phases in language development, but further examples show that level stress can be persistent in the phonology.

In certain Scandinavian dialects, for example Nord-Gudbrandsdalen and Tinn in Norway, stress has been reported to be "level" in stems with two short vowels, primarily in prepausal position, positions of emphasis, and in citation form, i.e. at an IP boundary.[16] A precise phonetic description of level stress has proven elusive (Kristoffersen 1990), which has fostered different approaches to the problem. Each provides a different description of the phonological structures that lead to level stress: a monopositional, or balanced foot (Riad 1992); a clash at the foot level (Bye 1996); a mismatch between Accent 2 and stress/syllable quality (Kristoffersen 1990; Lorentz 1995).

(13) Level Stress in Scandinavian

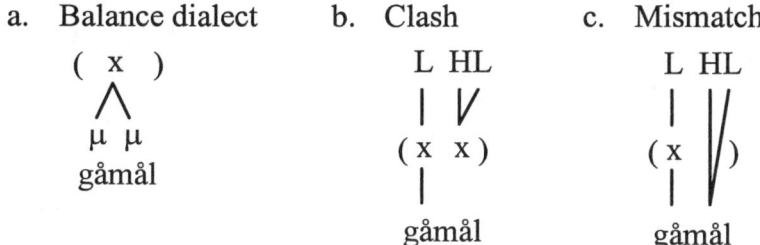

Riad (1992) analyzes level stress in the context of diachronic changes in Scandinavian.[17] In balance dialects, there is a unipositional foot, or the head of the foot is centered over both light syllables (13a). He (Riad 1992: 194) emphasizes that this foot leads to equal stress on both syllables, not to two adjacent stressed syllables.

Other analyses emphasize the synchronic occurrence of level stress and the interaction of stress and Accent 2.[18] Bye (1996) proposes that the branching tone on the second syllable is prominent and thus adds a grid mark, creating a clash at the foot level (13b), and therefore both syllables are stressed. Kristoffersen (1990) provides an extensive overview of the problem and looks at the synchronic status of level stress, including phonetic studies. He argues that "stress" in East Norwegian is purely a function of syllable structure and tonal accent. An initial light syllable cues Accent 1, which is incompatible with the Accent 2 pattern on the second syllable. This incompatibility leads to the perception of stress on both syllables. Lorentz (1995) sees this interaction as a case of split prominence or a mismatch between stress on the initial syllable and a prominence tone on the second syllable (13c).

Analyses of Welsh stress have led several scholars to propose a similar interaction of stress and tone, which is a result of diachronic changes. A rhythmic stress is realized on the penultimate syllable in Welsh with a pitch prominence on the final syllable (Alan, 1993;

Thomas, 1979). This is supported by phonetic studies carried out by Williams in Dogil and Williams (1999).[19] The ultimate syllable is nonetheless prominent, because it is the only syllable in the word that does not undergo the process of vowel mutation – just as the second syllable in the Scandinavian level stress dialects do not reduce (Kristoffersen 1990: 46). Interestingly, final vowels in Welsh poetry can rhyme, indicating that they are perceived by poets as being prominent, although this is not the case for poets writing in level stress dialects (Kristoffersen 1990: 56-7).

The final example of level stress is from Modern English. Halle and Keyser (1966) assume that in British English, stress is level on adjective+noun phrases such as *black bird* and *old man*. Otherwise several lines would incorrectly be declared unmetrical because a stress maximum would be in weak position (Halle and Keyser 1966: fn 2). This may be debatable, but certain compounds can also be realized with level stress, according to Selkirk (1985: 69) and Gussenhoven (1991: 23). See Visch (1999) for a recent discussion.

In conclusion, "level stress" is an empirical and a representational problem; however, "split prominence", or what I would like to call "prominence mismatches" are well-documented in several languages. Accepting the possibility of mismatches does not void the claim that stress is relative, because the relative nature of stress still holds at the abstract level of of the phonology. Rather, there can be a mismatch between the abstract representation of stress and the cues of accent in a word. The examples above provide support for the claim made here that Middle English stress doubles are an example of "hovering stress" similar to that found in Scandinavian dialects and Welsh, with an important difference. Prominence mismatches in Middle English are limited to the right edge of phrasal domains, and were a short-term phenomenon in the history of English. To explain how it arose, a more general discussion of stress is needed, in particular (i) rhythm and intonation and (ii) the formulation of the End-Rule. These topics are complex and therefore the following will only touch upon those issues that are relevant here.

4.1.1 Rhythm and intonation

Although phonologists agree that the stress rules of a language can be formalized, there are theoretical differences on how to formally represent stress. Different views arise, at least in part, from the difficulties in determining how the abstract representation of stress relates to the acoustic manifestation(s) of stress. Broadly speaking, there are the "rhythmical" and the "intonational" schools, a dichotomy that is in many ways reminiscent of the debate between the "timers" and the "stressers" in metrics. Both schools agree that stress and intonation interact, it is a matter of relative autonomy and/or primacy.[20] There has been a strong focus on general rhythmical constraints (No Clash, No Lapse, Eurhythmy, etc.) and on rhythmic phenomena, such as the Rhythm Rule in English (see Kager (1995) and Visch (1999) for an overview). In the literature, there has been a recent shift away from a purely rhythmical approach to the "Rhythm Rule" in English. Gussenhoven (1991), following Bolinger (1986) presents an analysis of stress shift in intonational terms. Although the listener may perceive a shift, this is the result of the deletion of non-peripheral accents. Selkirk (1995) and Visch (1999) note that the shift occurs not only to alleviate clashes and create more even rhythmic alternations, but also to strengthen boundaries. These analyses point to a interaction, or conflict, between word stress and phrasal stress rules in the domain in which stress shift occurs, i.e. right-headed phrasal domains. This conflict is resolved by both a rhythmic shift and an intonational one. It is possible to conceive of a system where only one prominence shifts, yielding a mismatch similar to that found in the Scandinavian dialects with "level stress".

4.1.2 End Rule

In the theory of Metrical Phonology most analyses begin by parsing moras and syllables into feet and then structure is built up level for level, with the structure of one level influencing the structures built upon it, exemplified by Halle and Vergnaud (1987) and Hayes' (1995) extensive analyses. An alternative approach is to place primary accent first, and then build structure around it. Stress in this approach is a kind of stamp, superimposed on a specific position in the word (van der Hulst, 1984). Whether stress-building rules are like bricklaying, i.e. "bottom up", or like setting up a tepee, i.e. "top down", may be moot, or depend on the language in question.[21]

Stress placement in Optimality Theory (Prince and Smolensky 1993; McCarthy and Prince 1993a) has much in common with the top-down approach, as van der Hulst (1996: 5-6) points out. In Optimality Theory (OT), an Alignment constraint defines which edge of a domain should be prominent, and in essence states that stress has a demarcative function, either indicating the beginning of a domain, or signalling the end of it. The End rule for English is Align (PrWd,R,Head(PrWd),R) or "align the right edge of the Prosodic-word with the right edge of the head of the P-word" (Pater 1995: 17; Prince and Smolensky 1993). This is not the same as the traditional formulation of End rule in earlier accounts (Prince 1983), because it places the word head to the right edge, not on the rightmost grid mark. That is, the traditional rule is bottom-up and the OT constraint is top-down. As we just noted, the difference is often — outside of the context of theory-specific debate — irrelevant. Given the appropriate ranking, however, the OT constraint can lead to some complications. In the tableau below the Alignment version of the End Rule (ALIGN) is ranked above the constraint requiring feet to be trochaic (TROCH):[22]

(14)　　End Rule in OT

			Align	Troch
☞	ω	(. x)		
	Σ	(x .)		
	ω	(x .)	*!	
	Σ	(x .)		
	ω	(. x)		*!
	Σ	(. x)		

The winning candidate places word stress on the rightmost syllable, and satisfies the edge requirement of the End-Rule, but violates the Continuous Column Constraint (Prince 1983: 33), since the word-level grid mark does not have a gird mark under it. But is this constraint a constraint in the OT sense of the word, i.e. a ranked, violable constraint? If inviolable, what is its place in the grammar? These broader questions cannot be addressed here, but we will assume that the Continuous Column Constraint is not a violable constraint.

This does not resolve the issue, however, because in a top-down system it is possible to project grid marks downward in order to place stress at an edge. This does lead to a clash at the foot level, in violation of the markedness constraint *CLASH:

(15) *Top-down system*

		Align	Troch	*Clash
ω (. x) Σ (x .)			*!	
☞ ω (. x) Σ (x [x])				
ω (. x) Σ (. x)		*!		

Here the Continuous Column Constraint is not violated and the winning candidate inserts a grid mark at the lower level to provide a base for the word stress. Note that the winning candidate has a clash at the foot level, thereby violating *CLASH and it also violates DEP-X, which prevents the insertion of grid marks. Such an analysis resembles level stress in Scandinavian given in Bye (1996) for level stress in Norwegian. In the traditional, bottom-up formulation of the End-Rule this analysis is impossible, because a particular grid mark is elevated to the status of primary stress near the edge of the word, and it is impossible to insert grid marks downward at the word level. In order to prevent the second candidate from being the optimal form, the constraint NONFIN must be ranked higher. (This is also possible by ranking TROCH higher, but NONFIN will become relevant in the next section.) NONFIN, prevents word stress from being final. Since this constraint plays a role in Old and Modern English, it is safe to assume that it was similarly high-ranked in Middle English, to which we know return.

4.2 Analysis

In the last section the OT formulation of the Modern English End-Rule at the word level was discussed in the general context of traditional bottom-up frameworks, and in top-down oriented OT. At the phrasal level, however, it is well-known that phrasal stress is top-down and may impose structure downward in Modern English (Hayes, 1995: 376-381). In OT a constraint similar to the Align-ω rule above aligns the head of the phrase with the right edge of the phonological phrase: Align(φ,R,Head(φ),R). A further constraint ALIGN-HD (McCarthy and Prince, 1993b) requires that the head of one domain associate to the heads of larger domains (see van Oostendorp (1995) for a discussion of head-alignment in terms of projection).[23] A top-down approach — in either a constraint-based or a derivational system — permits mismatches between levels. This is either a drawback or an advantage. Here it proves advantageous to assume that the Alignment rule at the phrase level and the Alignment rule at the word level were out of phase. The following tableau shows the interaction of these constraints in phrase-medial position:

(16) *Phrase-medial*

			NONFIN	END-φ	END-ω	ALIGN-HD
	ω	(. x)	*!			
	Σ	(. x)				
	ω	(x)			*	*!
	Σ	(x [x])				
☞	ω	(x .)			*	
	Σ	(x .)				

The constraint End-ϕ is irrelevant in this tableau, because phrasal stress is not assigned to the word. Note that there is no evidence for ranking here, and the constraint DEP-X has not been included in the tableau. The second candidate violates ALIGN-HEAD because the head of the phrase is not aligned with the head of the word, but rather with the inserted grid mark (x). Similarly, the second candidate does not violate NONFIN since the head of the word is not final. Thus I assume there is a fundamental distinction between heads of domains and epenthetic grid marks. In the next tableau, the same candidates are evaluated in phrase-final position:

(17) *Mismatch in phrase-final position*

	NONFIN	END-ϕ	END-ω	ALIGN-HD
ω (. x) Σ (. x)	*!			
ω (x) Σ (x [x])			*	*
ω (x .) Σ (x .)		*	*	

There is no winning candidate in the tableau, although the second candidate has additional violations, namely of DEP-X and *CLASH, and therefore the third candidate should be optional in this tableau as well. The data presented here suggest however that there is a mismatch at phrase-final domains, and that the second candidate should win, or at least tie, in phrase-final positions. Thus it appears that END-ϕ is ranked above END-ω.

(18) *Phrase-final position*

		NONFIN	END-φ	END-ω	ALIGN-HD
ω (. x) Σ (. x)		*!			
☞ ω (x) Σ (x [x])				*	*
ω (x .) Σ (x .)			*!	*	

This ranking would provide a grammar that would show "split prominence" or a "prominence mismatch" at the right edge of phrasal domains due the interaction of NONFIN, END-φ, and END-ω. In non-final domains, as in (16) we see the emergence of the unmarked, initial word stress.

5. Discussion and conclusions

The somewhat abbreviated analysis in the last section makes several predictions and raises important questions. First, the Romance Stress Rule did enter into Middle English, but this phrasal rule only influenced stress placement at the right edge of phrases. The Middle English End-Rule at the word level was Left, as in Old English, i.e. word stress was initial. This explains why initial stress is always observed in Alliterative meter; in strong-stress meters in general it is only the lexical stress that is relevant for the meter. Due to the influence of the Romance Stress Rule at the phrasal level, a prominence mismatch developed at the right-edge of phrasal domains. This explains why so-called stress doubles can occur in Weak-Strong at the end of phrases. Second, the ranking predicts that Middle English, unlike Modern English, should have rightward stress shift, as found in other Germanic languages such as Danish, Dutch, and German (Visch, 1999). Further research is needed to discover whether rightward shift is a reflex of the shift from initial to final stress in Germanic (Lahiri et al. 1999; Zonneveld et al. 1999). The fact that these languages tended not to shift the stress of Romance loans to the initial syllable (as English did) and that these languages have rightward stress shift points to a connection between the two.

The shift from initial stress to a three-syllable window has occurred in the history of English as well as Romance (Lahiri et al., 1999: 6.9.2). The chronology differs, but what is interesting is that there are several parallels: Pre-Classical Latin had initial stress; "stress doubles" occurred in the metrical works of Plautus and Terence, with stress shifting rightward at the edge of syntactic domains (Fraenkel, 1928: 21, 346-8); by the end of the 17th Century, French also had a kind of "level" word-stress (Pope, 1956 §223) before ultimately became phrasal. There appears to have been a shift in Latin phrasal stress stress, from initial and falling in Latin to rising and final in Old French (Lahiri et al., 1999: 3.8.1; Jacobs, 1993). A shift in phrasal stress as a result of language contact may have ultimately led to End-Rule Right in Germanic as well.

The OT analysis presented here has several drawbacks. First and foremost, nothing prevents each successive level of the Prosodic Hierarchy from projecting downward, leading to multiple clashes at multiple levels. This however is a result of the freedom of constraint ranking as such and top-down analysis in general. One thing seems to restrict these possibilities, however, and that is the desire to reestablish Head-Alignment, since it is essential to delimit domains. If this is correct, it appears then that certain constraint *rankings* are also marked. Third, given the proposed ranking, all Middle English words should be possible stress doubles, but words such as *brother* are not stress doubles, while *citee*, etc are. One could mark stress doubles as such in the lexicon, and then rank a FAITHFULNESS constraint in the tableau to account for these cases. Or there may be segmental reasons why certain words are stress doubles, as Nakao (1977) claims.

Summing up: In this paper we have seen that meter can give important clues for reconstructing stress rules and scribal diacritics should not be discarded as mere doodles. The new data presented here shows that there is an interaction of virgule placement and the occurrence of stress doubles in Weak-Strong position line-internally. With this new data it is possible to address Minkova's 1997 objections to the assumption that the Romance Stress Rule entered into Middle English. By looking at line-internal cases it is possible to avoid the problems associated with end-rhyme, which are indeed problematic (Minkova 1997: 151, fn 26) and to supplement Nakao's (1977) analysis by distinguishing between line-internal and line-final occurrences (cf. Minkova 1997: 136, fn 3).

Level stress is not desirable on theoretic grounds, but there are enough cases to show that split prominence or prominence mismatches can occur in natural languages. The interaction of tone and stress in the synchronic grammar of certain Scandinavian dialects shows that there can be a mismatch between stress and tone. Similarly, the top-down phrasal stress rule that was borrowed into Middle English from French led to a kind of prominence mismatch.

The problem of stress doubles did not end with Chaucer. As Halle and Keyser (1971: 123) catalogue, there was uncertainty in the 18th Century over the correct stress placement in "learned" words such as *academy* and *refractory*. It is difficult to know whether these were in part prescriptive rules or reflected a general uncertainty in native speakers. The analysis presented here may also be relevant for these cases but also for an analysis of the development of "stress doubles" such as *récord* and *recórd* or *ádult* and *adúlt* in Modern English. If prominence mismatches are limited to the right edge of phrases, this would be common on verbs in SOV constructions. In other words, we would expect split prominence more often in verbs, with the potential context-based stress difference between nouns and verbs. After the shift from SOV to SVO, this context is lost, but the stress distinction between nouns and verbs could have become lexicalized.

Finally, interpreting the data has been the greatest problem in this paper, and the proposed analysis is quite simple: word stress in Middle English was initial, except at the end of phrases, where both syllables were prominent.

Acknowledgments

I would like to thank the following in reverse alphabetical order for their comments on this paper, or on specific portions of the material:

Wim Zonneveld, Curt Rice, Chris McCully, Aditi Lahiri, Geert Kristoffersen, Astrid Kraehenmann, Jan Kooij, Harry van der Hulst, Jennifer Fitzpatrik, Martin Duffell. The comments from two anonymous reviewers and from the editors helped me to clarify many points. Many thanks.

I would also like to thank the audiences in Konstanz, Leiden, Manchester, and Nijmegen for their questions and comments on presentations of this material. Finaly, I would like to thank Wim Zonneveld and Chris McCully for stimulating conversations on Middle English, Chaucer in particular, and just in general.

Notes

1. See Piera (1980), Youmans (1983), Nespor and Vogel (1986), Hayes (1988) and articles in Youmans and Kiparsky (1989). Halle & Keyser do not represent the abstract pattern as given in (3), but rather as a strictly linear one WSWSWSWSWS. Duffell (1991) argues that the nodes should best be labeled with language-neutral numbers, i.e. 0 and 1, but since I am only discussing English, I will stick to Weak and Strong here.
2. See Kiparsky (1975, 1977), Hayes (1983, 1989), Hammond (1991), Hanson (1992), Hanson and Kiparsky (1996).
3. See Kiparsky (1977), Hayes (1989), following Smith (1968). A further diagnostic is used by Youmans in a series of articles (Youmans 1983, 1989, 1996). He assumes that syntactic inversions are often motivated by metrical restrictions, and by undoing the inversions, it is possible to determine what the poet wanted to avoid. He controls for stylistic inversion by studying prose texts written by the same author to compare the overall frequency of inversion in the poets style. If a inversion systematically moves a word from WS to SW, the word must have initial stress.
4. This new meter did not immediately overwhelm the native tradition, however, and almost paradoxically, the so-called Alliterative Revival took place after Chaucer introduced iambic pentameter. Alliterative verse in Middle English appears to be truly a Revival and not the continuation of the Old English tradition, cf. Cable (1991) and articles in McCully and Anderson (1996).
5. See Redford (1999) for an analysis of Chaucer's meter in the Hanson and Kiparsky (1996) framework, in which I claim that the parameter settings for these three poets are the same. Chaucer differs from Milton and Shakespeare in that he has few examples of disyllabic inversion and of monosyllables in weak, which falls out from the parameter settings Prominence Type=stress and Position size=syllable. Stockwell and Minkova (1998) note that resolution

generally does not occur in Chaucer and therefore independently point to Position size=syllable in Chaucer's meter.
6. The word list has since grown to 980. There are at most three alternate spellings for each word at the moment, but I am in the process of adding all alternate spellings to the list.
7. Youmans (1996: 188) offers two potential explanations for compounds such as *housbonde*. In rhyme position, *bond(e)* may be promoted, i.e. metrical requirements overwhelm the linguistic stress. These lines are not a problem for Stress Maximum Position since stressed syllables are allowed in Weak if the adjacent syllable is stressed, but are a problem if one assumes that rhyme must contain main-stressed syllables. Modern poets such as Frost often put disyllabic compounds in the same position, and therefore these examples may or may not be a problem.
8. I am unaware of any documented examples of diachronic change in phonological phrase construction rules, but since they are subject to parameter setting/constraint reranking, historical changes are in fact predicted. One factor leads me to believe that the Middle English and Modern English rules may be similar. Hanson (1999) has most recently noted that of the two influences on English iambic pentameter, the Italian model was more readily adapted into English than the French one. Duffell (1996: 216-7) argues that the Italian endecasillablo, because of its variable caesura, was incorporated into English by Gower. Another contributing factor may have been the difference in the phrasing algorithms used in these languages. The rules for Italian and English are almost identical (Nespor and Vogel 1986; Ghini 1993) and differ from the French rules. The similar phrasing rules in the two languages may have further facilitated the use of Italian models in English meter. Using the Modern English phrase rules to determine the phonological phrasing for the four-thousand-plus-and-growing lines in the sample is beyond the scope of this study, although it would provide evidence for (or against) the virgule as a phrase marker.
9. Whether these stress rules are phonologically or morphologically defined has been debated: Minkova and Stockwell (1994) and Minkova (1997) assume that Old English stress was morphologically, not phonologically, based, contrary to others (McCully and Hogg 1990; Dresher and Lahiri, 1991; McCully 1992; Idsardi 1994, Bermúdez-Otero, 1996). This fundamental question will not be considered here, and I will follow traditional descriptions and assume that stress is phonologically governed.
10. The existence of secondary stress has been debated, cf. Keyser and O'Neil (1985) and Dresher and Lahiri (1991) for discussion.
11. The analysis of stress doubles in Halle and Keyser (1971) is different than that in Halle and Keyser (1966), as the authors note Halle and Keyser (1971: 105, fn. 11). In the original article they had claimed that the combination of final <e> and changes in vowel quality led to the creation of stress doubles. As they further note, there should be no examples of trisyllabic forms with initial

stress in this account, and they provide counterexamples, including the following:

ful weel she soong the service dyvyne (1:122)

I am youre doghter custance quod she (2:1107)

These lines provide some evidence that schwa can occur in Strong, unlike in Middle Dutch meter; see Zonneveld, this volume.

12. It is important to note that ten Brink used 'hovering stress' to describe cases of inversion (ten Brink 1881: §301), which is not the position adopted here, although he uses the term primarily to describe the placement of secondary accents (Nebenton) in rhyme position (ten Brink, 1881: §323).

13. These assumptions are built on Structuralist theories of phonology, and have been termed Culminativity (Liberman and Prince, 1977: 262): each word or phrase has a single strongest syllable bearing main stress: *the domain (Σ, ω, φ, IP) of validity is language dependent* (Hayes, 1995: 24-5) (my emphasis). We are particularly interested in the qualifications, which in essence say that within a language, culminativity may not be valid at a domain of the Prosodic Hierarchy. Therefore it is possible that prosodic prominence at a certain level may be non-cumulative, or level. Culminativity is reinforced by the faithfulness constraint (not to be confused with the OT constraint FAITH), since each domain should have a unique head, (see Hayes 1995: 380).

14. In general these properties work in concert, but as Ladd (1995: 59) points out, "the theory does not preclude the occurrence of systematic disassociations".

15. Zvi Penner (p.c.) has reported that level stress also occurs in the acquisition of Bern German. On a personal note, my daughter at one point pronounced German *sauber* [zaube] "clean" as if it were *Sau Bär* [zau bɛːɐ] "sow bear". One could question whether there is not some distinction made between the two stresses, however.

16. Level stress appears to coincide with bisyllable words, in particular when both are light. This is true for the Scandinavian dialects as well as for Southeast Ambryan, where an initial heavy is stressed, but stress is even otherwise Parker (1968).

17. In Riad's analysis there is a crucial interrelation between balance and the quantity shifts that took place in Scandinavian (Prokosch's Law). Historical changes, e.g. vowel elision, led to the creation of heavy syllables, and there are no longer stems with two short syllables standard Scandinavian dialects, and therefore no level stress. There are parallels with Middle English, which, as we argue below, has level stress and which underwent Open Syllable Lengthening.

18. This analysis assumes that level stress and Accent 2 are interrelated. (Riad, 1992: 196-8) concurs that there is a one-to-one relation synchronically, but gives two examples of dialects that have level stress, although they do not have Accent 2. Kristofferson (p.c.) points out that the literature on these dialects is not clear about what is meant by level stress. The facts remain elusive.

19. The vowel of the stressed penult may be shorter than the ultimate vowel, but F_0 and segmental cues signal stress on the ultimate vowel (Dogil and Williams, 1999: 5.2.4.2)
20. The rhythmic view is stated in Hayes (1995: 1): "The central claim of the theory [of Metrical Phonology, MR] is, in my view, the linguistic manifestation of rhythmic structure". The intonational view is stated by Bolinger (1986: 477-8) "Rhythm...appears to play a secondary role, supporting (and sometimes replacing) other parts of prosody...[m]uch more needs to be known about rhythm before it can be discussed in the context of linguistic universals."
21. In certain cases "bottom up" stressing is the only possible analysis according to Hayes (1995: 116-118), e.g. Cairene Arabic, while top-down stressing is required for other languages, e.g. English phrasal stress. Van der Hulst (1996) claims that primary stress assignment can precede footing even in languages such as Cairene Arabic.
22. An alternative would be to formulate the constraint Align(FT',R,ω,R) or "align the right edge of the stressed foot at the right edge of the word". This would be a problem for words such as *agenda* in Pater (1995: 17), since the ranking NONFIN >> ALIGN-FT >> PARSE-σ would make *(ágen)da* the winning candidate over *a(gén)da* because the candidates violate all of the higher ranked constraints equally, but differ with regard to the number of syllables parsed. Moreover, the "stressed foot" is an ad hoc stipulation, which if used, creates the possibility of specifying "the secondary stressed foot" or "a non-primary, non-secondary stressed foot" in some other context.
23. Since the grid marks correspond to the heads of levels of the Prosodic Hierarchy, this constraint overlaps with the Continuous Column Constraint, given Faithfulness (cf. note 13). I leave open whether a unified application of the CCC might make this align constraint redundant. This constraint is underspecified, in that the edge of association is not given, i.e. it applies to both left and right edges. A similar underspecified constraint could be used to reformulate Riad's account of balance in Scandinavian dialects, since an underspecified foot alignment constraint leads to a foot aligned to both edges, i.e. a unipositional foot.

References

Beaver, Joseph
    1974   Generative Metrics: The Present outlook. *Poetics* 12: 7-28.
Bermúdez-Otero, Ricardo.
    1996   Stress and quantity in Old and early Middle English: Evidence for an optimality-theoretic model of langauge change. ROA-136-0996.

Bolinger, Dwight
1986 *Intonation and its parts: Melody in spoken English.* Edward Arnold, London.

Bye, Patrik
1996 Scandinavian "level stress" and the theory of prosodic overlay. *Nordlyd*, 24:23-62.

Cable, Thomas
1991 *The English Alliterative Tradition.* Philadelphia: University of Pennsylvania Press.

1996 Clashing stress in the metres of Old, Middle, and Renaissance English. In: C. B. McCully and J.J. Anderson (eds), *English Historical Metrics*, 7-29. Cambridge: Cambridge University Press.

Campbell, Alistar.
1959 *Old English Grammar.* Oxford: Clarendon.

Caon, Luigina
1999 Final -e in the *Wife of Bath's Prologue*: A study of adjectives in the fifteenth-century versions of he text. MA Thesis, University of Leiden, The Netherlands.

Dobson, E. J.
1957 *English Pronunciation 1500-1700.* Oxford: Clarendon.

Dogil, Greg and Briony Williams
1999 The phonetic manifestation of word stress. In: H. van der Hulst, H. (ed), *Word Prosodic Systems in the languages of Europe*, 273-334. Berlin and New York: Mouton de Gruyter.

Dresher, B. Elan
1994 The prosodic basis of the Tiberian Hebrew system of accents. *Language* 32: 1-52.

Dresher, B. Elan and Aditi Lahiri
1991 The Germanic foot: Metrical coherence in Old English. *Linguistic Inquiry* 22: 251-286.

Duffell, Martin
1991 The Romance hendecasyllable: an exercise in comparative metrics. PhD thesis, Queen Mary and Westfield College, University of London.

1996 Chaucer, Gower, and the history of the hendecasyllable. In: C. B. McCully and J.J. Anderson (eds), *English Historical Metrics*, 210-18. Cambridge: Cambridge University Press.

Eckhardt, Eduard
1936 Die Quantität Einfacher Tonvokale in offener Silbe bei zwei- oder dreisilbigen Wörtern französischer Herkunft im heutigen Englisch.[The quantity of simple stress vowels in open syllables of two or three syllable words of French origin in Modern English]. *Anglia* 60: 49-116.

Eliason, Norman
1939 The short vowels in French loan words like *city*, etc. *Anglia* 63: 73-87.

Fikkert, Paula
1994 *On the acquisition of prosodic structure.* (HIL Dissertation 6, University of Leiden.) The Hague: Holland Academic Graphics.

Fraenkel, E.
1928 *Iktus und Akzent im lateinischen Sprechvers.* [Ictus and Accent in Latin Spoken Verse]. Berlin: Weidmannsche Buchhandlung.

Ghini, Mirco
1993 φ formation in Italian: a new proposal. *Toronto Working Papers in Phonology* 12: 41-78.

Goedemans, Rob
1998 *Weightless Segments.* (LOT Dissertation 9, HIL/Unversity of Leiden.) The Hague: Holland Academic Graphics.

Gussenhoven, Carlos
1991 The English rhythm rule as an accent deletion rule. *Phonology* 8: 1-35.

Guthrie, Steven
1988 Prosody and the study of Chaucer: A generative reply to Halle-Keyser. *The Chaucer Review* 23.1: 30-49.

Halle, Morris and Samuel J. Keyser
1966 Chaucer and the study of prosody. *College English* 28: 187-219.
1971 *English Stress: Its form, its growth, and its role in verse.* New York: Harper and Row.

Halle, Morris and Jean-Roger Vergnaud
1987 *An Essay on Stress.* Cambridge: MIT Press.

Hammond, Michael
1991 Poetic meter and the arboreal grid. *Language* 67: 240-259.

Hanson, Kristin
1992 Resolution in modern meters. PhD thesis, Stanford University.
1999 From Dante to Pinsky: a theoretical perspective on the history of the Modern English iambic pentameter. *Rivista di Linguistica*, special issue edited by I. Vogel.

Hanson, Kristin and Paul Kiparsky
1996 A parametric theory of poetic meter. *Language* 72(2): 287-335.

Hayes, Bruce
1988 Metrics and phonological theory. In: F. Newmeyer (ed), *Linguistics: The Cambridge survey. Linguistic theory, volume 2. Extensions and implications*, 220-49. Cambridge: Cambridge University Press.

1989 The prosodic hierarchy in meter. In: P. Kiparsky and G. Youmans (eds), *Phonetics and Phonology, volume 1: Rhythm and meter*, 201-60. San Diego: Academic Press.
1995 *Metrical Stress Theory: Principles and case studies*. Chicago: Chicago University Press.

Hogg, Richard
1992 *A Grammar of Old English, volume 1: Phonology*. Oxford: Basil Blackwell.

Hyman, Larry
1977 On the nature of linguistic stress. In: L. Hyman (ed), *Studies in Stess and Accent*, Southern California Occassional Papers in Linguistics 4, Dept. of Linguisitcs, 37-52. Los Angeles: University of Southern California.

Idsardi, William
1994 Open and closed feet in Old English. *Linguistic Inquiry* 25: 522-533.

Jacobs, Haike
1993 The phonology of enclisis and proclisis in Gallo-Romance and Old French. In: W. Ashby (ed), *Linguistic Perspectives on the Romance Languages*. Amsterdam: John Benjamins.

Jakobson, Roman
1987 *Language in Literature*. Cambridge, MA.: Harvard University Press,

Jordan, Richard
1974 *Handbook of Middle English*. (Janua Linguarum, Series practica 218). Translated by E.J. Cook. The Hague: Mouton.

Kager, René
1995 The metrical theory of word stress. In: J. Goldsmith (ed), *Handbook of Phonology*, 366-402. Oxford: Basil Blackwell.

Kaluza, Max
1919 *Chaucer-Handbuch für Studierende*. [Chaucer Handbook for Students]. Leipzig: von Bernhard Tauchnitz.

Keyser, Samuel and William O'Neil
1985 *Rule Generalization and Optionality in Language Change*. Dordrecht: Foris.

Kiparsky, Paul
1977 The rhythmic structure of English verse. *Linguistic Inquiry* 8: 189-247.

Kristoffersen, Geert
1990 East Norwegian prosody and level stress problems. Ms. University of Tromsø.

Ladd, D. Robert
1995 *Intonational Phonology*. Cambridge: Cambridge University Press.

Lahiri, Aditi and Paula Fikkert
  1999   Trisyllabic shortening. *English Language and Linguistics* 3.2: 229-267.
Lahiri, Aditi, Thomas Riad and Haike Jacobs
  1999   Diachrony. In: H. van der Hulst (ed), *Word Prosodic Systems in the Languages of Europe*, 335-422. Berlin: Mouton de Gruyter.
Lass, Roger
  1992   Phonology and morphology. In: N. Blake (ed), *The Cambridge History of the English Language, volume II 1066-1476*, 23-155. Cambridge: Cambridge University Press.
Learned, Henry
  1922   The accentuation of Old French loanwords in English. *Publications of the Modern Language Association* 37: 707-21.
Liberman, Mark and Alan Prince
  1977   On stress and linguistic rhythm. *Linguistic Inquiry* 8: 249-336.
Lorentz, Ove
  1995   Tonal prominence and alignment. In: R. Walker, O. Lorentz and H. Kubozono (eds), *Phonology at Santa Cruz*, volume 4, 39-56. Santa Cruz: Linguistic Research Center.
Luick, Karl
  1921   Über die Betongung der französischen Lehnwörter im Mittelenglischen.[On the stress of French loan words in Middle English]. *Germanische und romanische Mitteilungen*, 9:14-19.
McCarthy, John and Alan Prince
  1993a   Prosodic morphology I: constraint interaction and satisfaction. Ms. University of Massachusetts, Amherst and Rutger Univervity, New Burnswick.
  1993b   Generalized alignment. In: G. Booij and J. van Marle (eds), *Yearbook of Morphology 1993*, 79-153. Dordrecht: Kluver.
McCully, Christopher B.
  1992   The phonology of resolution in Old English word-stress and metre. In F. Colman (ed), *Evidence for Old English*. Edinburgh: John Donald.
  1998   Reading between the lines: the quality of Chaucer's silence. Ms., University of Manchester.
McCully, Christopher B. and Richard Hogg
  1990   An account of Old English stress. *Journal of Linguistics* 26: 315-339.
McCully, Christopher and John J. Anderson (eds)
  1996   *English Historical Metrics: Prosody from Old English to the Renaissance*. Cambridge: Cambridge University Press.

Minkova, Donka
 1997 Constraint ranking in Middle English stress-shifting. *English Language and Linguistics* 1: 135-175.
Minkova, Donka and Robert Stockwell
 1994 Syllable weight, prosody, and meter in Old English. *Diachronica* 11.1: 35-64.
Mitchell, Bruce and Fred Robinson
 1992 *A Guide to Old English*. 5th edition. Oxford: Blackwell.
Morsbach, Lorentz
 1896 *Mittelenglische Grammatik*. [Middle English Grammar]. Halle: Max Niemeyer.
Nakao, T.
 1977 *The Prosodic Phonology of Late Middle English*. Tokyo: Shinoyaki Shorin.
Nespor, Marina and Irene Vogel
 1986 *Prosodic Phonology*. Dordrecht: Foris.
Parker, G. J.
 1968 Southeast Ambrym phonology. *Oceanic Linguistics* 7: 24-37.
Pater, Joe
 1995 On the nonuniformity of weight-to-stress and stress preservation effects in English. ROA-107-0000.
Paul, Herman
 1891 *Grundriss der germanischen Philiologie*, Band 2.[Overview of German Philology, volume 2]. Strassburg: Karl J. Trübner.
Piera, Carlos
 1980 Spanish Verse and the Theory of Meter. PhD thesis, University of California, Los Angeles, California.
Pope, Mildred
 1956 *From Latin to Modern French*. Manchester: Manchester University Press.
Prince, Alan
 1983 Relating to the grid. *Linguistic Inquiry* 14: 19-100.
Prince, Alan and Paul Smolensky
 1993 Optimality theory: Constraint interaction in generative grammar. Ms. Rutgers University, New Brunswick and University of Colorado, Boulder.
Redford, Michael
 1999 The monosyllable rule and metrical inversion. *Talk presented at the Conference on Formal Approaches to Poetry*, University of Toronto, October 8-10.

Riad, Thomas
    1992   Structures in Germanic prosody. A diachronic study with special reference to the Nordic languages. PhD thesis, Stockholm University.

Rice, Curt
    2000   Stress clash and metricality. Ms University of Tromsø.

Selkirk, Elizabeth
    1985   *Phonology and Syntax: The Relation between Sound and Structure*. Cambridge, MA: MIT Press.
    1995   Sentence prosody: Intonation, stress, and phrasing. In: J. Goldsmith (ed), *Handbook of Phonology*, 550-569. Oxford: Blackwell.

Smith, Barbara
    1968   *Poetic Closure: A study of how poems end*. Harmondsworth: Penguin.

Stockwell, Robert and Donka Minkova
    1998   The partial-contact origins of English pentameter verse: the Anglicization of an Italian model. Ms. University of California, Los Angeles.

ten Brink, Bernhardt
    1881   *Chaucers Sprache und Verskunst*. Leipzig: T.O. Weigel.

Thomas, Alan
    1979   A lowering rule for vowels and its ramification in a dialect of North Welsh. In: *Papers in Celtic Phonology*, volume 6 of Occasional papers in linguistics and language learning. Ulster: The New University of Ulster.

van der Hulst, Harry
    1984   *Syllable Structure and Stress in Dutch*. Dordrecht: Foris.
    1996   Separating primary and secondary accent. In R. Goedemans, H. van der Hulst and E. Visch (eds), *Stress Patterns of the World. Part 1: Background*, 1-25. The Hague: Holland Academic Graphics.

van Oostendorp, Marc
    1995   Vowel Quality and Syllable Projection. PhD thesis, Katholieke Universiteit Tilburg.

Visch, Ellis
    1999   The rhythmic organization of compounds and phrases. In: H. van der Hulst (ed), *Word Prosodic Systems in the Languages of Europe*, 161-231. Berlin: Mouton de Gruyter.

Watkins, T. Arwyn
    1993   Welsh. In: M.J. Ball (ed), *The Celtic languages*. Routledge: Routledge Language Family Descriptions.

Woods, Susan
    1984   *Natural Emphasis: English Versification from Chaucer to Dryden*. San Marino: The Huntington Library.

Youmans, Gilbert
    1983   Generative tests for generative meter. *Language* 59: 67-92.
    1996   Reconsidering Chaucer's prosody. In: C. B.McCully and J.J. Anderson (eds), *English Historical Metrics*, 185-209. Cambridge: Cambridge University Press.

Youmans, Gilbert and Kiparsky, Paul editors
    1989   *Rhythm and Meter*, (Volume 1 of Phonetics and Phonology.) San Diego: Academic Press.

Zonneveld, Wim
    1998   Lutgart, Willem and Geoffrey: A study of 13th Century Dutch metre. Ms. University of Utrecht.

Zonneveld, Wim, Mieke Trommelen, Michael Jesen, Curt Rice, Gosta Bruce and Kristian Árnason.
    1999   Wordstress in West-Germanic and North-Germanic languages. In: H. van der Hulst (ed), *Word Prosodic Systems in the languages of Europe*, 273-334. Berlin and New York: Mouton de Gruyter.

Constraining S and satisfying fit

Wim Zonneveld

1. Introduction[1]

Lines of poetry such as those below are specimens of the *iambic pentameter* (the major English poetic tradition of the second millennium), but are not typical of it:

(1) *Will praise a hand, a foot, a face, an eye*
    A gait, a state, a brow, a breast, a waist
        (Shakespeare, *Love's Labour's Lost*, 4.3.184-185)
    And sinks or swims, or wades, or creeps, or flyes
        (Milton, *Paradise Lost*, 2.950)
    Behind, before, above, between, below
        (Donne, "Elegie: to his Mistress going to Bed)"

Each of these lines is decasyllabic by virtue of five consecutive units consisting of one monosyllabic function word (auxiliary, article, conjunction) followed by one monosyllabic content word (first three examples), or of five bisyllabic adverbs (final example). Their perfect iambic rhythm is caused by a choice of words which fruitfully invokes two stress rules of English: in a sequence of a function word and a content word the latter counts as relatively prominent, and in prefixed adverbs the stem is prominent relative to the affix.

Although naive expectations about metrics might lead one to expect otherwise, lines such as those in (1) are extremely infrequent, and more adventurous ones completely commonplace. The latter's characteristics may reside in a variety of properties:

(2) Mismatches between positioned word and bisyllabic iambic unit:
- The spinsters, carders, fullers, weavers, who
  (Shakespeare, *Henry VIII*, 1.2.33)

More than 10 syllables:
- Of *perilous* seas, in faery lands forlorn
  (Keats, "Ode to a Nightingale")

More than 10 syllables by 'feminine ending':
- So that the wolf ne made it nat *myscarie*
  (Chaucer, *General Prologue*, 513)

Fewer than 10 syllables (in 'headless' lines):
- Bootless home, and weather-beaten back
  (Shakespeare, *1 King Henry IV*, 3.1.68)

Non-prominent syllables in 'even' positions:
- A dupe and *a* deceiver, - *a* decay
  (Shelley, *Prometheus Unbound*, 4.550)
- Yet *impotent* of mind, and uncontrol'd
  (Pope, *Odyssey*)

Prominent syllables in line- or phrase-initial position ('initial inversion'):
- *Sermons* in stones, and good in every thing
  (Shakespeare, *As you like it*, 2.1.17)
- *Swift to* their several quarters hasted then
  (Milton, *Paradise Lost*, 3.14)
- And peace proclaims *olives* of endless age
  (Shakespare, *Sonnet 107*, line 8)

Prominent syllables in (line-internal non-phrase initial) 'odd' positions:
- In the *visions* of God: It was a hill
  (Milton, *Paradise Lost*, 11.377)

The formal investigation of adventurous lines was initiated by Halle and Keyser (1966, 1971), and one of the most recent contributions is Hanson and Kiparsky (1996)[2]: these authors present a *parametric theory* of metre, with illustrations from English and Finnish metrics. These parameters define properties of weak and strong positions in lines of verse, and the authors propose that their settings essentially define a metrical style. But importantly the parameters do so in close cooperation with a small number of "functional principles". The two functional principles they put forward are:

(3) INTEREST: The parameters are set so as to maximize the esthetic interest of the verse.
    FIT: Languages select metres in which their entire vocabularies are usable in the greatest variety of ways.

Clearly the collection of lines in (2) is "esthetically much more interesting", in the relevant sense, than the ones in (1). Although obviously important, this INTEREST principle is not subjected to further investigation in Hanson and Kiparsky's contribution, and neither will it be here. Conversely, the FIT principle is a pivotal feature of these authors' exposition, in view of lines of reasoning such as these. In the standard variety of the iambic pentameter, the strong (*i.e.* even) positions are "unconstrained" in that they may contain both prominent and non-prominent syllables. The collection in (2) contains examples of this phenomenon, of a type quite commonly encountered in the work of many poets. The iamb becomes just that, then, by constraints on the weak (odd) position, which is allowed to contain a prominent syllable only under highly limited conditions (Kiparsky 1977, Hayes 1983). Hanson and Kiparsky point out that this parameter setting is utterly reasonable because it enables the poet to considerably boost the lexicon through FIT: run-of-the-mill English language material will have many sequences of unstressed syllables (especially in content words), and "unconstrained strong" will contribute no end to the fulfilment of this principle. The other way around, suppose that a poet has selected a (less frequent) style in which "strong" is limited to or must contain prominent syllables; then one way of resolving the ensuing conflict with FIT is to choose a second parameter setting that allows metrical positions to contain more than one syllable by *"resolution"*, in fact: to contain a "minimal (English) foot", *i.e.* a trochee. The authors point out that this latter style is employed by G.M. Hopkins in his *sprung rhythm*. Consider the first four lines of his "The Windhover" (Kiparsky 1989: 309, intended prominent positions italicized):

(4) I *caught* this *mor*ning *mor*ning's *min*ion, *king*-
    dom of *day*light's *dau*phin, dapple-*dawn*-drawn *Fal*con, in his
    // *ri*ding
    Of the *rol*ling level *under*neath him steady *air*, and *stri*ding
    High there, how he *rung* upon the *rein* of a *wim*pling *wing*

They conclude their discussion of English poetic styles as follows:

(5) In sum, then, our theory predicts that English has one optimal syllable-based meter, where W is constrained by strength, and two optimal Φ_{min}-based meters, one where S is constrained by stress (sprung rhythm), and the other where W is constrained by strength (Shakespearean iambic verse with resolution). Other syllable-based and Φ_{min}-based metres, including all those which restrict both W and S, would violate Fit. (p.300)
    [Legend: W = odd/weak, S = even/strong, Φ_{min} = more than one syllable per metrical position allowed.]

In other words: the restriction that W not contain prominent syllables must conincide, in order to boost the lexicon, with unrestricted S, where a metrical position is a syllable in one style ("isosyllabic" iambic pentameter) and a foot in another (Shakespearean iambic pentameter); the restriction that S contain stress must coincide, for the same reason, with the metrical position being a foot.

The aim of the present paper is threefold. Its principal goal is to comment on the idea (the last-mentioned one immediately above) that metrical constraints on the contents of S must cooccur with a liberal setting of the parameter for metrical position (frequent *resolution*), in order for the vocabulary of the language, promoted by FIT, to find a way out in something like sprung rhythm. This paper presents a case of Middle Dutch poetry which implies a constraint on the contents of S, but at the same time does not invoke resolution to boost the lexicon, but rather more straightforward means of matching linguistic material and the abstract iambic pattern: invoking a distinction drawn by Kiparsky (1977), these means will be identified as "prosodic" (*i.e.*, "paraphonological") rather than "metrical". This Dutch case is the thirteenth century *Het Leven van St.Lutgart* [The Life of St.Lutgart], a completely isolated but solidly iambic Tristan da Cunha in an ocean of contemporary accentual verse. The second aim of this paper is to use part of its empirical material to shed more light on some (hitherto underexplored) properties of the Middle Dutch pronoun system. And third, a contribution is made to the study of the Dutch metrical tradition by pointing out that the observed prosodic constraint defines a formal difference between the thirteenth century Dutch iamb and the later Renaissance iamb (with which it otherwise shares many of the usual characteristics).

Section 2 of this paper will provide a brief summary of the history of Dutch metrics up to and including the Renaissance, ranging from the late twelfth to the early seventeenth century. It will also set the scene for an investigation of *Het Leven van St. Lutgart*. Section 3 delves more deeply into the *Lutgart*'s iambic character. Section 4 elaborates on this, and provisionally formulates the "No Schwa in S" (*[ə]$_S$) constraint that is the focus of the second half of this paper. Section 5 briefly looks into the status of this constraint *vis-à-vis* the English and Modern Dutch traditions. Section 6 gives the evidence for it from the *Lutgart*. Section 7 contains the conclusions, returning to the Hanson and Kiparsky issue of properties of poetic metre interacting with the FIT principle.

2. Dutch metrics and The Life of St.Lutgart

In the Dutch poetic tradition, native accentual verse was replaced with iambic metre in the final few decades of the sixteenth century. There is no early alliterative tradition in Dutch, and the entire period of four centuries from the late twelfth to the late sixteenth century is covered by accentual verse (in Dutch: *heffingenvers*). The earliest texts are mostly translations or adaptations of French originals from the *chanson de geste* and *troubadour* traditions. The French *Floire et Blancheflor* (*ca*.1150) is solidly octosyllabic, but its Dutch counterpart *Floris ende Blanchefloer* (*ca*.1260) looks as in (6):

(6)   *Floris ende Blanchefloer*, Middle Dutch *ca*.1260

>   Dat moestese ghedoghen algader   152
>   Ende nochtan vele meer daer toe,
>   Want si namen haer selven doe
>   Ende voerdense wenende ende claghende sere   155
>   Voor den coninc haren here,
>   Die hem so willecome was.
>   Doe hise sach, ghedacht hem das
>   Doe hie vander coninginne sciet
>   In sijn lant, daer hise liet   160
>   Dat si seide hoe gherne si name [...]

In this passage, line 160 has seven syllables, line 155 has fifteen. The characteristics of the metre are these. Rhyming lines have an equal number of strong syllables, which can be found in content words or "upgraded" (metrically ambiguous) function words; most often there are four strong syllables in a line, occasionally three. The late twelfth century poetry of Hendrik van Veldeke was written in a variant of this metre, as is Jacob van Maerlant's (second half of the thirteenth century), and the famous *Reynaert the Fox* (idem) by a sadly unknown poet. The tradition culminated in the *Chambers of Rhetoric* movement of the fifteenth and sixteenth centuries, of which the *Elckerlijc* [Everyman] (*ca*.1475) is the most famous product.[3]

When the Renaissance reached the Low Countries in the 16th century, a new syllable counting metre came into existence, under the influence of the study of the classics and of the French *Pléiade* movement. Poetry such as that by the Flemings Lucas d'Heere and Jan van der Noot is part of the "rhythmic" French tradition, but others like the Leyden classical scholar Jan van Hout, Willem of Orange's personal secretary Marnix van St. Aldegonde, and the Amsterdam burgomaster's son and national historiographer Pieter Corneliszoon Hooft, wrote poetry in which the crucial step towards "alternation" was an integral part of their innovation. Consider the following *iambic alexandrine* by Hooft (S-positions are in italics when they contain stressed syllables of content words, and underscored if they contain monosyllabic function words or unstressed syllables):

(7)   Pieter Corneliszoon Hooft, *Letter from Florence, ca.*1600

Die *stadt*, wiens *vrý*heit is in *vórst*lijk<u>heit</u> ver*kéert*,   [1]
En die zich *éind*lijk van haar *búr*gers *ziet* ver*heert*,
Van *búr*gers, die door *list* en *kóop*ge<u>luk</u>, haer *zee*gen,
's Groot *Hár*tog<u>hdom</u> en *eer* en *héer*lijk<u>heit</u> ver*kréeg*en,
Flo*rénce*, 't *schóon*ste dat mijn *oogh* ooit <u>heeft</u> ont*móet*,
Wiens *vrúcht*baa<u>re</u> land*óuw* van d'*Ár*no <u>werd</u> ge*vóedt*,
Doet <u>om</u> haar *héer*lijk<u>heit</u> van *taal* my <u>in</u> haar *blíj*ven.   [7]

Hooft is the first major poet of the Dutch cultural and economico-political Golden Age, in which the *alexandrine* became the standard metre in the work of poets such as Bredero and Vondel. Up until the present age their successors use the iamb in eight-, ten-, and twelve-syllabled variants (see also section 5 below).

In this picture, the thirteenth century *Life of St. Lutgart* poem has a completely unique position. It dates from around 1270, and is an octosyllabic, consistently iambic poem. It antedates the Dutch Renaissance iambic tradition by three centuries. Trying to get an idea of its contents, the sample passage in (8) explains the notion of "Love of God".

The *Lutgart* is a hagiography or Saint's Life. Born in Tongeren in Limburg, the poem's protagonist, Lutgart, is a mid-thirteenth century Benedictine nun who spent most of her life in the Aywires convent just south of Brussels in Brabant. The poem's author is Willem van Afflighem, from the renowned monastery of the same name in the Flanders-Brabant border area to the west of Brussels. The sole extant manuscript was discovered in 1897 in the Royal Library in Copenhagen by the Flemish philologist Frans van Veerdeghem. It is probably a first generation copy of the original, in very good condition, with extremely few scribal errors.[4] The manuscript contains two out of the

(8)　　*Lutgart* (±1270), from book II

  Die van Lutgarden gerne ontfaen
7770 *Die tale mijn, hir sitten gaen*
  Bi mi; ic sal hen noch vertrekken
  En schone exempel, ende onttekken
  Hoe mechtech es die Godes minne
  Dar menre wale werdt in inne.
7775 *Ic sal u seggen wis si pleget;*
  Si geft dengenen, die is dreget
  In herte binnen goeden spoet
  Te comene in dat Gods gemoet;
  Si doet hen allen, dire plin,
7780 *Afstaen der sonden ende onttin;*
  Oc plegt si geven vol aflaet
  Van alre noseliker dat
  Der herten, daer si toe geraket
  Si es die van din dulen maket
7785 *Den wel gesedden, ende van*
  Den dommen knecht den vroeden man.
  Noch heft die minne meerre macht:
  Din si beverdt met harre cracht
  Ne can die viant nit gederen
7790 *Die minne makt die mareleren;*
  Oc makt die minne die propheten,
  Want si hen doet die dinge weten
  Die al dengenen sijn verholen
  Die nit ne gaen te haren scholen;
7795 *Die minne sterket dat geloeve;*
  Bi harre cracht so hort die doeve;
  Den blenden doet die minnen schowen;
  Beide onder heren ende vrowen.

'Everyone who wants to hear my story about Lutgart must come and sit near me. I will tell another educating story, and explain how strong God's Love is, when experienced. Let me tell you how it works. To those bearing it in their heart Love offers an excellent opportunity of meeting God. All who cherish it, will keep sin at bay. Love also offers compete relief of all sins to those hearts it can reach. She turns a fool into a decent man, and a stupid servant into a sage. Love is even stronger: those protected by her are shielded from the devil. This Love creates martyrs and prophets, because it shows them the things that are kept hidden from all who fail to heed her teachings. She strengthens faith, makes the deaf hear, the blind see, both among men and women.'

original poem's three "books" (*i.e.*, chapters); book I is missing from it, but even so the current version has 20,406 rhyming lines, which is longer than either the *Iliad* or *Odyssey*, longer than Chaucer's unfinished *Canterbury Tales* and considerably longer than Dante's *Divina*

Commedia. Van Veerdeghem's 1899 edition contains detailed philological observations, two of which currently stand out. First, the *Lutgart* is a highly creative Middle Dutch *verse* adaptation of a Latin *prose* original by the Brabantic minor scholar Thomas van Cantimpré, Lutgart's confidant and "soul mate". Second, Van Veerdeghem claims that completely un-expectedly and uniquely for this period of Dutch, the *Lutgart* has a thoroughly iambic (alternating) metre. An analysis of the first ten lines of the passage in (8) (using the same notation as in the Hooft example) shows that there is little reason to doubt the accuracy of Van Veerdeghem's claim:

(9)		1	2	3	4	5	6	7	8	fem
		Die	van	Lut	gár	den	gér	ne⌢ont	fáen	
	7770	Die	tá	le	mijn,	hir	sit	ten	gaen	
		Bi	mi;	ic	sal	hen	noch	ver	trék	ken
		En	schó	ne⌢ex	ém	pel,	en	de⌢ont	ték	ken
		Hoe	méch	tech	es	die	Gó	des	mín	ne
		Dar	mén	re	wá	le	werdt	in	ín	ne.
	7775	Ic	sal	u	ség	gen	wis	si	plé	get;
		Si	geft	den	gé	nen,	die	is	dré	get
		In	hér	te	bín	nen	góe	den	spoet	
		Te	có	me	ne⌢in	dat	Gods	ge	móet;	

The poem's metre has an isosyllabic octosyllabic basis (in parametric terms, there is no reason to think the metrical position is not a syllable). Its lines can be overlong by two well-known conventions: the feminine ending, and contraction or *synalepha* (indicated here by a ⌢-symbol) when two vowels (the first here always a schwa) are immediately adjacent and "count as the metrical equivalent of a single syllable" (Halle and Keyser 1971: 141).

3. The *Lutgart*'s iambicity

The *Lutgart*'s iambic metre, conceived three full centuries before the introduction of the Renaissance iamb, has continued to stand out as one of the great unsolved puzzles of Dutch metrics. Zonneveld

(1992/2000, 1993, 1999) supports and expands Van Veerdeghem's original claim.[5] In view of the fact that the poem's iambicity is absolutely central to this paper's principal points, this section provides a necessarily brief indication of the extreme regularity and tightness of its metre.

The analysis in (9) shows that stressed syllables (including monosyllabic content words) well-behavedly occupy the strong positions of the lines (always taking synalepha into account). However, we are dealing with relatively old language material, and it would be methodologically less than completely sound to assume that the word stress patterns of such a stage will be identical to the current ones, or that our modern intuitions can be fully trusted to tell us where thirteenth century main stresses are. In the first line of (9), for instance, the stress pattern of the prefixed verb form *ontfáen* is not really open to doubt; but that of the inflected proper name *Lutgárden* ís, seriously so: the modern Dutch pronunciation of the name is *Lútgart* (according to a pattern also illustrated by *Ádolf*, *Árnold*, *Bérnard*, and *Máurits*), and, from that point of view, the addition of stress-neutral inflection should give **Lútgarden*. In English, iambic pentameter lines such as those in (10a) indicate that the noun *language* changed its stresscontour somewhere between Chaucer (late fourteenth century) and Shakespeare (late sixteenth century), and those in (10b) show that the noun *aspect* changed its contour after Shakespeare:

(10)a.: the nouns *langage* in Chaucer, and *language* in Shakespeare
- In hir *langage* mercy she bisoghte
    The Man of Law's Tale, 516
  Allas! I ne have no *langage* to telle
    The Knight's Tale, 2227
  So muchel of daliaunce and fair *langage*
    General Prologue, 211
- The *language* I have learn'd these forty years
    Richard II, I.3.159
  You taught me *language*; and my profit on 't
    The Tempest, 1.2.363
  If they do speak our *language*, 't is our will
    Love's Labour's Lost, 5.2.176

They say, our French lack *language* to deny
All's Well that Ends Well, 2.1.20
Let me entreat you speak the former *language*
Measure for Measure, 2.4.141

(10)b.: the noun *aspect* in Shakespeare (cf. Kiparsky 1975: 594-595)
- Save in *aspect*, have all offence seal'd up
King John, 2.1.250
Corrects the ill *aspects* of planets evil
Troilus and Cressida, 1.3.92
I tell thee, lady, this *aspect* of mine
Merchant of Venice, 2.1.8

Thus, a criterion for iambicity independently of stress should be welcomed. Fortunately, this is available because the following holds: in iambic poetry, polysyllabic words necessarily occupy a limited number of fixed positions in lines. In order to see what this means, consider the use of the frequent nouns *treason* and *traitor* in Shakespeare's *Richard II*:

(11) - V.3.49   The *treason* that my haste forbids me show
      I.1.57   These terms of *treason* doubled down his throat
      V.3.43   Shall I for love speak *treason* to thy face
      I.1.27   Namely, to appeal each other of high *treason*
    - V.3.72   The *traitor* lives, the true man's put to death
      II.3.88   I am no *traitor*'s uncle; and that word "grace"
      V.3.54   I tore it from the *traitor*'s bosom, king
      I.1.102   And consequently like a *traitor* coward
      II.3.30   Because your lordship was proclaimed *traitor*

Throughout the play these words are exceptionlessly found in sequences of *even-odd* (*s-w*) in the line. In accentual verse, on the other hand, the situation is crucially different. The unknown poet of the 2530 line 14th century *Sir Gawain and the Green Knight*, for instance, writes in an alliterative variant of this metre. The result for word positioning is as if from a decidely different metrical world - in (12) below the word *lady* is "all over the place" in the line:

(12) *Sir Gawain and the Green Knight* (alliterative accentual verse, Gollancz ed., 1940)
    1757   þe *lady* luflych com laðande swete
    1733   Bot þe *lady* for luf let not to slepe
    947   An oþer *lady* hir lad bi þe lyft honde
    2497   þe luf of þe *ladi*, þe lace at þe last
    1212   Al laðande þe *lady* lauced þo bourdeð
    933   þe lorde loutes þerto, & þe *lady* als
    1248   "In god fayth, sir Gawayn", quoþ þe gay *lady*

The conclusion we draw from these examples is this one: an assessment of the iambic character of a given poem (as opposed to, for instance, accentual verse) can be given simply and literally by "looking at the words on the page". If these words pattern as in (10) and (11) (as opposed to (12)), the poem is iambic. (Next, it becomes possible to extract from the text information about the stress patterns of words for that stage, as illustrated above.[6] An analysis of the stress systems of three stages of English, using Chaucerian versification for the late fourteenth century, can be found in Halle and Keyser (1971)).

The lines of the *Lutgart* have exactly this latter property. As an example, consider the following collection of lines containing the frequently occurring noun *abdesse* (occasionally *abdisse*) 'abess', Modern Dutch *abdis*:

(13) *abdesse* 'abess' in the *Lutgart*
    starting in:
    1   *Dabdesse*, die groet ongemac   4814
            Abdisse wart gekoren daer   9751
    3   Dat sise *abdesse* souden maken   0242
            Dat eene *abdesse*, maget fijn   0427
    5   Dat si aldaer *abdesse* worde   0278
            Dat ic en werde *abdesse* nit   0351
    7   Dat si in enen worde *abdesse*   0249
            Dat wart gelevert dire *abdessen*   4745(3)[7]

Bearing in mind the effects of synalepha, this word's first syllable is always in a W position, and simply never in S. It patterns like Chaucer's *langage* in (10a). In the first example the noun is preceded by the prevocalically reduced form of the definite article *die* [di]; such forms will be returned to later.

The name of the poem's protagonist is one of its most frequently used words: it has 746 entries in the Index to the 1985 Gysseling edition. Here is a small selection:

(14)   *Lutgart* in the *Lutgart*
    1   *Lutgart*, die magt van groten prise   0198
        Lutgarden sijn gegaen in hant   4881
    3   Mar doe *Lutgart*, die maget fijn   1357
        Al dat *Lutgarden* it te vromen   3805(3)
    5   Do sijt vernam, *Lutgart*, die vrowe   0806
        Dat provic bi *Lutgarden* wale   1231
    7   Daertoe so mote mi *Lutgart*   0192
        Hort hir noch wonder van *Lutgarden*   0897

Although the principal interest of this discussion is not in Middle Dutch word stress but in word patterning in lines, the obvious conclusion is that, *pace* modern intuitions, this name is consistently used as if it has second syllable rather than initial stress.

The most severe restrictions are those on the longest words. Consider the examples in (15), in which the italicized words have an increasing number of syllables:

(15)   polysyllabic words in the *Lutgart*

    two syllables
    - Die *gracie*, die hem was verleent   0789 'grace'
      Die meeste *gracie* hevet worden   2929
      Die so volmakde *gracie* hevet   2922
    - *Masschin* dan hi verleende somen   10402 'perhaps'
      Hem welt *maschin* met selken dingen   6323
      Al hevet hi *masschijn* gelogen   9042
      Ende in meswende. Also *maschin*   9021

three syllables
- *Sententie* heft also gegeven — 1871 'verdict'
  Dat die *sententie* was gegeven — 12669
  Also Got die *sentencie* gaf — 8856
- Die *losengir*, die dese ghile — 3178 'traitor'
  Dat gi, fel *losengir* verwaten — 5033
  Nu, segt mi, valsche *losengir* — 5009
- Dat *sacrament* also ontfane — 4617 'sacrament'
  Ende ons sijn *sacrament* beval — 4628
  Dit es dat werde *sacrament* — 4553

four syllables
- Van *disciplinen*, noch fineren — 1122 'discipline'
  Verloet met *disciplinen* hare — 0826
  Met eiseliken *disciplinen* — 0808
- Mijn *purgatorie* es gedaen — 4277 'purgatory'
  Die in dat *purgatorie* sijn — 2935
- In d*ewangelie* noch gescreven — 3152 'gospel'
  Al daer men d*ewangelie* las — 1061(3)
- Die *consciëncie* dar si mede — 5463 'conscience'
  Dat u die *conciëntie* late — 5810

five syllables
- Die *onderschedechheit*, ic meene — 6351 'distinction'
  Kinnesse ende *onderschedechheit* — 3137

The *Lutgart*'s iambicity also shines through in the way grammatical aspects of Middle Dutch manifest themselves in it. Reconsider the first example of (13). This example actually illustrates a more general phenomenon typical of the left edge of the line. There, vowel-initial words fall out into two classes: those that are systematically preceded by a consonantal form *d-* of the definite article *die* [di], and those that are just as systematically preceded by the full form, cf. (16). It is not the case that the words in (16) cannot for some reason be preceded by, respectively, the full and reduced article forms: line-internally, the effect is absent, and the same word can occur with either *die* or *d-*, cf. (17) (the accents indicated will be explained shortly):

(16) Article-noun combinations at the beginning of a line:
a.
	Dabdésse, die groet ongemac	4814	'abess'
	Dapóstelen, die marteleren	2635(3)	'apostles'
	Dimaginácie die men vurt	0172(3)	'imagination'
	Dewangelísten songen na	4025(3)	'evangelists'
b.	Die *órdne* sent dat sijs beginnen	8087	'order'
	Die *ógen* hem begonden sapen	12080	'eyes'
	Die *óverdaet*. Mar des began	3122(3)	'excess'
	Die *abstinéntie* mogen comen	9560	'abstinence'
	Die *institúcie* hebbe ontfaen	0931(3)	'right of entrance'
	Die *ewangélie*, die tracteert	1120(3)	'gospel'

(17a) in 2:

In *dórdne* van den kordeliren	12427	cf. 8087
Want *díngle* van din paradise	11031	'angel'
Daer *dewangélie* op ghelach	4378(3)	cf. 1120(3)

in 3:

Began *donwíllege* Yolent	3840	'stubborn'
Dat was *dolénde* van ambachte	0272	'misery'

in 4:

Die boven *díngele* es verheven	0453	
Der silen *déewelike* leven	1678	'eternal'

in 5:

Oc seggen ons *dewangelísten*	2227	cf. 4025(3)

in 6:

Nochtan al waren *dógen* blent	0158(3)	cf. 0158(3)
Van sinen sonden *dóverdaet*	0547(3)	cf. 3122(3)
Meest speciael mar *doppenbáren*	4592(3)	'overt'

in 7:

Al daer Taiwires in *dabdië*	7383	'abbey'

in 8:
Want hi begraven lach in *dérde*   4774(3)   'soil'

(17b)   in 2:
Sprac *die elíjt*, nu es algader   11642   'bishop elect'

in 3:
Daer gi *die órdne* houden moett   9643   cf. 12427
Daer hen *die íngele* in besin   1970(3)   cf. 11031
Dat Got, *die éwelike* vader   4265   cf. 1678
Als si *die ógen* hadde ontdaen   3966(3)   cf. 0158(3)

in 7:
Noch worme crupende in *die érde*   5069   cf. 4774(3)

The generalisation underlying this distribution is clear once the (presumed) main stresses in these words are taken into consideration. When stress is on an even syllable of the noun counting from the *left* wordedge, the reduced consonantal form of the article is found (the (16a)-cases). When stress is on an odd syllable of the word, the full form is found (the (16b)-cases). Standard Middle Dutch accentual verse would be at a loss to explain such facts. However, if the basic pattern is the iamb, the facts *are* explained: neither *[dórdne... nor *[die abdésse... can be a correct beginning of a line.

Consonant-initial nouns do not have a line-initial form with a consonantal definite article. Nevertheless, they can occur in line-initial position, typically without an article whatsoever. This is the prerogative, however, of nouns with an appropriate stress pattern, such as *pitánce* and *senténtie*, of which the first two syllables are iambic. If main stress is on the third syllable from the left, the noun cannot be used line-initially.

(18)   *Prióer*, was comen tire onleden   1729(3)   'prior'
Pitánce quam ochte een prosent   0716   'gift'
Senténtie heft also gegeven   1871   'verdict'
Devócie heden desen dage   1355(3   'devotion'
Matérie, sent dat si verschit   4368(3)   'matter'

- Was din *prióer*, mar van der dinge	1794(3)	
Dis alt *convént* hadde it te bat	0703	'convent'
Na die *senténtie*, daer af seide	1670(3)	
Dat si *devócie* hem verbade	1262(3)	
Op die *matérie* so verstart	7887	
Na die *natúre* die hi hevet	0104	'nature'
- Dit *parlemént* om ons te derne	5215	'parliament'
Die *consciéncie*, dar si mede	5463	'conscience'
Die *abstinéntie*, die gemeene	9454	'abstinence'
Want *absolútie* ende afflaet	0245(3)	'absolution'

It cannot be sufficiently emphasized that these are not deliberately selected patterns: they are, per individual word and per word class, the *only* patterns on offer in the *Lutgart*. Not a single line starts with **Die sententie...*, no line with **[Dat dit parlement...* The iamb is the perfect explanation for these distributional facts. Given this conclusion, we can now go on and compare the nature of the *Lutgart*'s iamb with that of the variants of the English iambic pentameter discussed by Hanson and Kiparsky (1996).

4. Introductory remarks about the contents of W and S

The examples of the previous section make it clear that the *Lutgart*'s W-position has two natural states: it can be occupied by the weak vowel schwa; and, one step up on the strength scale, by an unstressed full vowel: configurations such as *grác[ie]*$_W$, *[na]*$_W$*tú[re]*$_W$ and *ab[so]*$_W$*lú[tie]*$_W$ are far from infrequent. Next, vowels can be stressed without carrying the main stress of the word. In "Shakespearean iambic verse with resolution", in which W is constrained, long words with sequences of unstressed syllables can be used because of the Φ_{min} setting of the metrical position parameter. Thus, both situations of (19) can be found in this type of verse (the stresses are partly determined by morphological embedding, as indicated; cf. Kiparsky 1977: 196-198; Hanson and Kiparsky 1996: 295):

(19)

```
                    x              main stress
    .   x   .   x   .              stressed syllables
    σ   σ   σ   σ   σ              syllables
```

a: con si de ra tion
    W   S   W   S   W
    [consíder]-átion

```
                    x              main stress
    x   .   .   x   .              stressed syllables
    σ   σ   σ   σ   σ              syllables
```

b: for ti fi ca tion
        S   W   S   W
    [fórtify-c]-átion

a. Albeit / [con]_W[si]_S / [de]_W[ra]_S / tions infinite
    1 Henry IV, 5.1.102
    That the / preci / pita / tion might down stretch
    Coreolanus, 3.2.4
    My strong / ima / gina / tion sees a crown
    The Tempest, 2.1.208

b. This [forti]_S / [fi]_W[ca]_S / tion, gentlemen, shall we see 't?
    Othello, 3.2.5
    And are upon / the [medi]_S / [ter]_W [ra]_S / nean float
    The Tempest, 1.2.234

In this metre strict isosyllabicity gives way to resolution. The *Lutgart* poet, on the other hand, strongly prefers isosyllabicity, as shown (again) by lines such as those in (20):

(20) -   Een vrai *experimént* gegeven   5562(3) 'experiment'
         Een din gebrekt *experimént*   2022(3)
     -   Op sine grote *auctoritéit*   1837   'authority'

In Modern Dutch, these nouns have the stresscontours *èxperimént* and *àutoritéit*, respectively, with secondary stress on the first syllable for two reasons: because it is initial and undergoes "beat addition", and because it is heavy (closed or diphthongic). It is difficult to say anything with certainty about Middle Dutch secondary wordstress. If absent, these examples are uneventful; if present, it can reasonably be expected to occur either two syllables away from the main stress, or on the initial syllable. In the former case, these examples are uneventful again; in the latter, it follows that secondary word stresses can occupy W in the *Lutgart*: this seems the most likely state of affairs.

Function words appear in the *Lutgart* in both W and S. This can be illustrated by the scanning possibilities of the definite article *die* [di], the personal pronoun *ic* 'I', and the adverb *oc* 'also', which simply occur in any metrical position of the line:

(21) *die* in all metrical positions
    in 1: *Die viant pijnde mi te derne*   2366
          'enemy'
         Die consciencie dar si mede   5463
          'conscience'
    in 2: *Na die nature die hi hevet*   0104
          'nature'
         In die possessie sijn gedaen   3594(3)
          'possession'
    in 3: *Daer gi die ordne houden moett*   9643
          'ordrer'
         Dos bleef die maget noch in vare   1386
          'virgin'
    in 4: *Doe ginge die ijonfrowen lesen*   2476
          'ladies'
         Gelijc dat die scrifture ons seget   8840
          'scripture'
    in 5: *Dat parlement, die ijongelinc*   1512
          'young man'
         Daer boven wert die gheest van hare   2579
          'Spirit'
    in 6: *Van ijongen lieden die mesdaden*   0981
          'crimes'

	Die boese mensche die tiran 'tirant'	0549(3)
in 7:	*Die wilen clarre dan die dach* 'day'	0561
	Van din viant die u die pine 'pain'	13577

(22) *ic* in all metrical positions

in 1:	*Ic sal u seggen hoe gedaen* 'I will you say ...'	1278
in 2:	*So ic dat cortelingest mach* 'So I that briefly can'	0019
in 3:	*Nu hort ic sal u seggen hoe* 'Now hear I'll you say how'	0624
in 4:	*Mijn dicht dat ic hir nu bedide* '... I here now clarify'	0173
in 5:	*Mar wonder sie ic ende merke* '... see I and notice'	0036
in 6:	*So we mi dan dat ic hir quam* '... that I here came'	0333
in 7:	*Van din gelove dat ic dede* '... that I did'	0033

(23) *oc* in all metrical positions

in 1:	*Oc was ten tiden in dat lant* 'Also was in that time ...'	0749
in 2:	*Es oc en ander rike nu* 'Is also another person ...'	4023
in 3:	*Dat hi oc beeste si genamt* '... also beast is called'	0142
in 4:	*Die saken oc te seggene u* 'Those things also to say ...'	2062
in 5:	*Die meester Yan oc was genamet* '... John also was called'	2175
in 6:	*Dar toe so willic oc dat gi* '... want I also that you'	2740

in 7: *Welt si ontbeiden ende ⌒ oc saen*   9935
       '... and also soon'
in 8: *Dis Walsches, noch gesproken oc*   0483
       '..., nor spoken also'

Finally, monosyllabic content words are virtually absent, and primary stressed syllables of polysyllabic words are completely absent, from W. In the English iambic pentameter, especially that of Shakespeare, "rising sequences" such as those below can have content words in W both in pre- and post-S positions (Kiparsky 1977: 208-209, among others):

(24) a.   *Pronounce thee a [gross$_W$ lout$_S$], a mindless slave*
            (Shakespeare, *The Winter's Tale*, 1.2.301)
       Nor shall [death$_W$ brag$_S$] thou wander's in his shade
            (Shakespare, *Sonnet 18*, line 11)
       His knowledge of [good$_W$ lost$_S$], and evil got
            (Milton, *Paradise Lost*, 11.87)
   b.   *But, like a [sad$_S$ slave$_W$], stay and think of nought*
            (Shakespare, *Sonnet 57*, line 11)
       Above the [broad$_S$ sweep$_W$] of the breathless bay
            (Swinburne, "In the Bay")
       With breed and chese, and [good$_S$ ale$_W$] in a jubbe
            (Chaucer, *The Miller's Tale*, 3628)

And some pentameter poets (but emphatically not Shakespeare) occasionally allow primary wordstresses in W:

(25)   *Created thee, in the [í$_W$mage$_S$] of God*
            (Milton, *Paradise Lost*, 7.527)
       By that [wín$_W$dow$_S$] what task what fingers ply
            (Hopkins, *The Candle Indoors*)
       Who yet remain [stúb$_W$born$_S$]. I overrule
            (Shelley, *The Cenci*, 5.2.185)

Types (25) and (24b) are absent from the *Lutgart*; type (24a) occurs just sporadically:

(26) in 1: [Hit_W mees$_S$]ter Yacob van Vitry   0753
'Is called Jacob ...'
[$Magt_W$ ut$_S$]vercoren ende wert   2024
'Virgin chosen ...'
[$Groet_W$ won$_S$]der dat er na geschide   0456
'Big miracle ..'
in 3: Dat si [$best_W$ vu$_S$]get, want hi weet   7306
'... she best agree'
Noch een [$lanc_W$ stuk$_S$]ke, vrië maget   12851
'... a long bit'
in 5: Den genen die [$meest_W$ hei$_S$]lech es   3018
'... who most holy'
Oc weset hir [$groet_W$ wil$_S$]lecome   8699
'... here big welcome'
in 7: Oc moten hebben din [$Gods_W$ hat$_S$]   4960
'... the God's hate'
Dat si begerde. Nu [$hort_W$ dan$_S$]   11839
'... Now hear then'
Ic bleef er sider een [$goet_W$ stic$_S$]   11980
'... a good bit'

As shown monosyllabic content words in W are often semantically weak specifiers such as *goet*, *best*, *meest*, and so on.

Interestingly, a ban on content words in W explains a seemingly independent *Lutgart* phenomenon: compounds never consist of two adjacent monosyllabic content words, but always have an internal schwa syllable. If Hanson and Kiparsky (1996: 291) are right in assuming that metrically the members of compounds are separate words, we can understand why (27a) below is the exclusive compound type of the *Lutgart*, even though the simpler one is readily available in Middle Dutch, as shown by those in (27b) taken from Verdam (1932).

(27a) *Lutgart* compound nouns: always an internal schwa syllable

- *Van [somer-tide] schinen plach*   0562
'summer (-time)'

	In [hemel-rike] spannen crone	1068
	'heaven (-realm)'	
	Nochtan dat [sonne-schijn] al dar	10448
	'sunshine'	
	Van [hovet-sonden], sonder waen	2275(3)
	'cardinal sins' (head-sins)	
	Daer si in [knie-gebede] lach	0292
	'knee-prayer'	
	Want wildic u dat [hant-geslach]	12788
	'desperate wringing' (hand-clap)	
-	*Ten inde van din [schak-e-spele]*	8995
	'chess-game'	
	Dat ic des menschen [scherm-e-schilt]	3156(3)
	'patron saint (shade-shield)'	

(27b) range of Middle Dutch compound nouns (from Verdam 1932)

(i) *somer-tide ... hant-geslach*

(ii) *schaec-spel*   'chess-game'   cf. 8995 above
    scherm-schilt   'shield, patron saint' cf.3156(3) above

(iii) *dienst-knecht*   'valet'   (service-hand)
    erf-deel   'inheritance'   (inherit-part)
    clein-broot   'marzipan'   (small-bread)
    croon-brief   'letter of complaint' (appeal-letter)
    roey-schip   'galley'   (row-vessel)
    and so on.

We see that an internal schwa is added even when the regular Middle Dutch compound word (as appearing in Verdam) lacks one, into the two examples in (ii).[8]

The content of *Lutgart* metrical S can be: primary or secondary stress of a polysyllabic word, a monosyllabic content or function word (see (21) and (22)), or an unstressed full vowel ((20), perhaps). It shares these possibilities with the English iambic pentameter, in which, too, "S is unconstrained" (as explained in the introduction: in order to comply with FIT). The single remaining case is this one, then: can the weakest vowel, schwa [ə], occur in *Lutgart* metrical S position? In other words, is there reason to think that the matching of the linguistic material and the abstract metrical pattern in this poem is subject to the following condition:

(28)   *[ə]s

> 'A schwa syllable cannot be dominated by a strong metrical unit'

We will see that the answer to this question is, interestingly, 'yes'.

5. [ə]s in English and Dutch iambic poetry

For English, the uncertain status of schwa syllables in the 14th century work of Geoffrey Chaucer, the initiator of the English iambic pentameter, is well-documented (see Minkova 1991 and references discussed and cited there). There are in fact two stumbleblocks for well-supported statements about the behaviour of Chaucerian schwa: the often virtually inextricable manuscript variation, and the phonological phenomenon of *final schwa loss* in Middle English, which took place between 1150 and 1450, and which had its peak between 1250 and 1350.

In (29) is a passage from Chaucer's pre-pentameter *Book of the Duchess* in two versions: the text of the "Bodleian Fairfax 16" manuscript is compared to the emended version appearing in the authoritative *Riverside Chaucer* (Benson 1987), the successor to F.N. Robinson's (1957/1966) standard edition:

(29) *Robinson/Riverside*   *Manuscript*

825 For al the worlde so had she   For al the world so hadde she
    Surmonted hem al of beaute   Surmounted hem alle of beaute,
    Of maner and of comelynesse   Of maner, and of comlynesse,
    Of stature and of so well sette   Of stature, and of wel set
        /gladnesse,   /gladnesse,

Of godelyhede and so wel be sey Of goodlyhede so wel beseye -
Shortly what shal y sey   Shortly, what shall y more seye?
831 By god and by halwes twelve   By God and by his halwes
                                  /twelve

This is more or less typical of the differences between a given manuscript and the text appearing in a responsible edition. In a similar vein, consider the line from *Troilus and Criseyde* in (30a) below, given in the version appearing in *The Riverside Chaucer*; this line can be scanned as an iambic pentameter. The comment on this line in (30b) is taken from Southworth (1962: 45), the principal detractor of the iambic pentameter hypothesis of Chaucer's poetry, who summarizes the versions appearing in the manuscripts:

(30) a.   *Nor under cloude blak so bright a sterre*
          (*Troilus and Criseyde*, I, 175)
     b.   In Campsall, there is no *-e* in *cloud* or *blak*; in Harleian 2280 and St.John's College, Cambridge, we have *cloude* and *blake*, both with final *[-]e;* in Cambridge 427 and MS. 61 Corpus Christi College, Camb., we have *cloude* with a final *-e* and *blak* without it; in Harleian 1239, *cloud* with no final -e, but *blake* with one.

Suspecting that the situation "is even worse than Southworth puts it", Conner (1974: 44, 59) gives all variants of a single line from the *Six-Text Print* of The Chaucer Society (1868-1877). Notice that not a single one of them actually *is* the Riverside version:

(31) a.   *Hire gretteste ooth was but by Seinte Loy*
          (*General Prologue*, 120)
     b.   El   *Hire gretteste ooth was but by seint Loy*
          Hg   *Hir gretteste ooth was but by Seint Loy*
          Ca   *Here gretteste oth was bu by seint Loy*
          Co   *Hir grettest oþ was but by seint loy*
          Pt   *Hire grettest ooth was but by seyte loy*
          La   *Her grettest oþe was bot be seint Loye*

In this situation the status of lines such as those in (32), originally quoted by Halle and Keyser (1966/1970: 384-5) to illustrate that weak syllables may occur in S, is not *a priori* clear (they also appear in this form in both Robinson and the *Riverside Chaucer*):

(32) And weddede the queene Ypolita
       The Knight's Tale, 868
  And whan he cam, hym happede, per chaunce
       The Pardoner's Tale, 606

In fact each potential such case should be carefully checked against the manuscript or manuscripts. This reveals in this particular case that the (comparatively reliable) Hengwrt manuscript has schwa-less *wedded* and *happed*, respectively.[9]

One can also think of having a look at the behaviour of words like *pardoner* or *carpenter*, both of which are frequent in specific *Tales*. Some examples are in (33)-(34):

33) - This Pardoner answerde nat a word
       The Pardoner's Tale, 956
    Thou beel amy, thou Pardoner, he sayde
       Intr. to the Pardoner's Tale, 318
  - This carpenter to blessen hym bigan
       The Miller's Tale, 3448
    Bothe of a carpenter and of his wyfe
       The Miller's Tale, 3142
    For what so that this carpenter answerde
       The Miller's Tale, 3843

(34) - Ne was ther swich another pardoner
    For in his male he hadde a pilwe-beer
       General Prologue, 693-694
  - It is an honour to everich that is heer
    That ye mowe have a suffisant pardoneer
       The Pardoner's Tale, 932

- Upon the mynour or the carpenter
  I slow Sampsoun, shakynge the piler
    The Knight's Tale, 2465-6
- This dronke millere hath ytoold us heer
  How that bigyled was a carpenteer
    The Reeve's Prologue, 3913-4

At the line edge, in metrical positions 8-10 (cf. (34)), they rhyme to a variety of words in a manner suggesting a full vowel pronunciation of the *-er* ending.

In Shakespeare metrical S can be occupied by weak material; (35) below contains cases illustrating the possibility of inflectional schwa in S position:

(35) Cases of [-əs] and [-əd] in S in Shakespeare
- In golden palaces, as it becomes
    1 Henry VI, 5.3.169
  Though palaces and pyramids do slope
    Macbeth, 4.1.57
- These lords are visited; you are not free
    Love's Labour's Lost, 5.2.423
  Thy sins are visited in this poor child
    King John, 2.1.179
- I am solicited, not by a few
    Henry VIII, 1.2.18
  Which have solicited - The rest is silence
    Hamlet, 5.2.372

Words such as *minister, murderer,* and *messenger* also appear with their final syllable in S, and so do the definite and indefinite article:

(36) Cases of [-ər] in S in Shakespeare
- Are ministers of fate: the elements
    The Tempest, 3.3.61
  How sweetly do you minister to love
    Much ado about nothing, 1.1.322

- Of Edward's heirs the murderer shall be
    Richard III, 1.1.40
  Out on thee, murderer! thou kill'st my heart
    Titus Andronicus, 3.2.54
- Thou baleful messenger, out of my sight!
    2 Henry VI, 3.2.48
  Whose watery arch and messenger am I
    The Tempest, 4.1.71

(37)(a) "*the* in S" in Shakespeare:
  And *the* great care of goods at random left
    The Comedy of Errors, 1.1.42
  For blunting *the* fine point of seldom pleasure
    Sonnet 52
  A kneaded clod; and *the* delighted spirit
    Measure for Measure, 3.1.121
  How will she love, when *the* rich golden shaft
    Twelfth Night, 1.1.35

(37)(b) "*a* in S" in Shakespeare:
  With *a* disdainful youth: anoint his eyes
    Mids. Night's Dream, 2.1.261
  A bump as big as *a* young cockerel's stone
    Romeo and Juliet, 1.3.54
  Not half so big as *a* round little worm
    Romeo and Juliet, 3.4.66

In Renaissance and Modern Dutch poetry schwa in S is extremely common. One example is in line 6 of the Hooft passage in the previous section. Numerous similar cases can be cited,[10] such as those in (38):

(38) "[ə] in S" in Dutch poetry

  Word-final schwa syllable in octosyllabic verse
  - Verschrómpelden tot púin en doken
            Diels (1897-1956), *Het oude huis*

- *Toen door een hémelse vergíssing*
    Alberts (1893-1967), *Vincent*

Word-final schwa syllable in a pentameter (10 syllables)
- *Het flúisteren der goddelijke stem*
    De Mérode (1887-1939), *Ganymedes*
- *En vóór mij krónkelen de dúistre wegen*
    Van Nijlen (1884-1965), *Zwerver*
- *Wanneer mijn stemklank prévelend en bítter*
    Bloem (1887-1966), *Zwerver*
- *Klinkt helder op, gebéeldhouwde sonnétten*
    Perk (1859-1881), *Aan de Sonetten*

Word-final schwa syllable in an alexandrine (12 syllables)
- *En héftiger. Zo stórt de stenen galerij*
    Vondel (1587-1679), *Hofvliet*
- *Want d'ópperste beléit zijn zaeken wonderbaer*
    Vondel, *Gysbrecht van Aemstel*
- *Gij zijt een réiziger en niemand kent uw naam*
    Van Nijlen, *Bericht aan de reizigers*
- *Kabau in Hofvliet riep: "Oubóllige kabóuter!"*
    Vondel, *Hofvliet*

Word-internal schwa syllable
- *Met píjnigende slág zijn bevend hart*
    De Mérode, *Ganymedes*
- *En aan de húiverende zúiverheid*
    De Mérode, *Ganymedes*
- *En om de schijn der tíntelende stérren*
    Bloem, *Zwerver*
- *En vóór de zwáluwen en 't bíbberende groen*
    Gericke, *De tuinman*

Indefinite article "een" [ən]
- *Op Géysbeek een berijmd vervolg te wezen.*
    Ten Kate (1819-1889), *Sonnet*

- *Wat rubbertúinen, een fabríek*
   Ter Gast, *De nacht brak*
- *En streed en víel voor een verlóren zaak*
   Boutens (1870-1943), *De nalatenschap van Andries de Hoghe*
- *Toen dit kristal weer. Dán in een onstúimig noorden*
   Roland Holst (1888-1976), *Bij het kristal*

Definite article *"de"* [də]
- *Aan de gelíjken schijnbaar zeer gelijk*
   Bloem, *Grafschrift*
- *De dóodsvlam, de vertérende, de smálle*
   Werumeus Buning, *Gods molens*
- *En machtig wúiven de geplúimde toppen*
   Perk, *Lied der storm*
- *Maar goed. Terúgkomend op de bekóring*
   Burssen (1896-1965), *Zelfportret*

6. "No Schwa in S" (*[ə]$_S$) in the *Lutgart*

6.1. Introduction

This section's aim is to support the idea that the condition formulated at the end of section 4, proclaiming a ban on schwa syllables in metrical S position, is a genuine constraint on the Middle Dutch thirteenth century *Lutgart*'s metre. Recall that it was shown in sections 2 and 3 that this 20,406 line poem is consistently (octosyllabically) iambic, with optional feminine endings. Let us consider the strongest evidence first, namely that involving the definite article forms *die* [di] vs. *de* [də]; after that, further evidence will be presented as support.

The Modern Standard Dutch gender-dependent system of two definite articles, *de* [də] for non-neutral (*de tafel* 'the table', *de letter* 'the letter') and *het* [ət] (often spelled *'t*) for neutral (*het boek* 'the book', *het cijfer* 'the number')[11] historically evolved, just as the currently even simpler situation in English, out of a more elaborate system of (inflected) demonstrative pronouns.

(39)

	Middle Dutch	*Modern Dutch*	
		articles	demonstratives
non-neuter	die	də	die
neuter	dat	ət	dat

Most historical grammars give this picture, but are otherwise relatively uninformative. In its most recent edition, Schönfeld's *Historische Grammatica van het Nederlands* (Van Loey 1970: 145-146) simply talks about "a less sharp distinction" between definite articles and demonstrative pronouns in Middle Dutch, with no further details or temporal qualifications. The passage quoted in (40) is from Van der Horst and Marschall (1989: 51) (translation by W.Z.):

(40) Early Middle Dutch did not have separate articles. The current distinction between *die* and *dat* on the one hand, and *de* and *het* on the other, was absent. [...] Perhaps in the thirteenth century there was a difference between emphatically pronounced *die* and *dat*, and *de* and *'t* without emphasis. In any case, in the fourteenth and fifteenth centuries the distinction is introduced between *die* and *dat* (with emphasis) and *de* and *'t* (no emphasis).

Another handbook of Middle Dutch, Overdiep & Van Es's 1946 *Vormleer van het Middelnederlandsch der XIIIe Eeuw*, points out (pp. 46-47) that it is difficult to distinguish between definite articles and demonstrative pronouns, assumes that even the definite article has a full vowel most of the time, and mentions that the weak form *de* "is not excluded", giving two examples from the well-known thirteenth century *Walewein* and *Moriaen* poems, both written in accentual verse. The *Lutgart* is part of the empirical underpinning of this handbook, but not referred to in this passage. In fact, a close look at the *ca.* 1270 *Lutgart* situation shows two things: this poem gives clear insight into the thirteenth century situation regarding full and

reduced versions of the demonstrative pronouns/articles, and into the
"No Schwa in S" phenomenon. Focusing on (non-neutral) *die*, this is
what the *Lutgart* reveals:

- the full form *die* occurs freely in all metrical positions;
- the form *de* occurs only in W, never in S;
- before vowel-initial words, a consonantal variant can be found.

The behaviour of the full-vowel form (*die* in all metrical positions)
was illustrated in (21) of section 4. (41) below exemplifies the second observation, about *de*; contrastively it is also shown that the
choice between *die* and *de* is not governed by individual nouns:

(41) The form *de* occurs just in W (never in S)

in 1:	
[De hogste coninc] van den trone	3564
'the highest king'	
[Die hogste coninc] van den trone	1330
[De kracht] van din scrifturen tonen	0756
'the strength'	
Iegen [die cracht] van din viande	2547
[De vriheit] van gerechter minnen	0080
'the freedom'	
Lutgart [die vriheit] van der kerken	5315(3)
[De gracie] van der Godes hulden	2001
'the grace'	
[*Die gracie*] *weder, dat si binnen*	0877
in 3:	
Hadde in [de werelt] hir gestaen	2289
'the world'	
Got die [die werelt] al geboet	1163(3)
Alse ons [de vite] segt van hare	2880
'the Life'	
Alse in [die vite] staet gescreven	7412

in 5:
So wart gevurt [de gheest] van hare 0800(3)
   'the spirit'
Daer boven wert [die gheest] van hare 2579

in 7:
Af danken soude haddics [de macht] 1301(3)
   'the power'
Dat hi [die macht] hare heft verleent 6700

The use of the prevocalic consonantal form *d-* ([*D-abdesse die groet ongemac*]) was illustrated earlier and elaborately in (17).

The analysis suggesting itself for these facts is this one. Semantically and pragmatically, and from a modern point of view, the forms in these examples strike one as articles, not as full demonstrative pronouns. Furthermore, in the thirteenth century language underlying the *Lutgart* the forms *die* and *de* appear to have been in free variation. The form *de* has a schwa ([də]), and it is prohibited from occurring in S by "No Schwa syllable in S". The distribution of *die* and *de* strongly supports this condition. There may be two sources of the prevocalic consonantal form: there could be a true grammatical rule of optional procliticization of *die* involved, independently of the metrical requirements; or these are simply cases of obligatory metrical synalepha of *de*, directly displayed in the spelling. In any case, this subsection has made three contributions to our discussion. First, a clearer picture has emerged of the status of the variants *die* and *de* in thirteenth century Middle Dutch. Second, their distribution in the *Lutgart* can be taken as evidence for the authenticity of the "No Schwa in S" constraint operating in that poem. And third, comparing the findings of this subsection with that of section 5, we observe a formal discontinuity in Dutch metrics to the extent that "No Schwa in S" is absent from the iamb introduced in the Renaissance era.

6.2. Word-final schwa syllables and [ə]s

In spite of what has just been said, the *Lutgart* definitely contains lines in which a schwa syllable occurs in a metrically strong position. (43) below contains a complete list of lines in which a word-final schwa syllable occurs in S, in all cases immediately after another unstressed (schwa or full vowel) syllable:

(43) "Schwa in S" in the *Lutgart*

(a) Schwa-final words (5)

in 4:	*Ontfarmede* sere utermaten	3417	'pitied'
	Al *suchtende* met groten sere	0812	'sighing'
	Al *suchtende* met groten tranen	1282	
	So *seghende* die maget hare	5156	'blessed'
in 6:	So verre *ontdekkede* sijn spel	3645	'discovered'

(b) Schwa in the word-final syllable after a schwa syllable (12)

in 4:	*Dapostelen*, die marteleren	2635(3)	'th'apostles'
	Dis *predekens* ende omme wat saken	0785[12]	'preaching'
	Van *mageden* schone ende groet	2662	'virgins'
	Daer *heveten* ontboden lise	3341	'has-him'
	Al *heveten* mi ondergaen	9002	
	Tin *dogeden*, dat hi besat	3466	'virtues'
	Ten *dogeden*, ende uten wegen	3792	
in 6:	Die alle *loveden* wel schone	2629	'praised'
	Die beide *lachterden* wel sere	3378	'condemned'
	Dat si *beschiweden* wel schire	5187	'abhorred'
	Ende oc met *hemelscher* musiken	5393	'heavenly'
	Mettin tween *hemelschen* gesellen	13765	

(c) Schwa in the word-final syllable after an unstressed full-vowel syllable (18)

in 4:	*In graciën wart op verheven*	1237 'graces'
	Wat graciën gi hebbet vonden	10530
	Oc hebbikker meer af vernomen	8089 'have-I-there'
	Noch hebbikker meer af verhoert	1552(3)
	Die bedingen, die ic u noeme	4142 'pleas'
	Der nodingen van din gelage	1073(3) 'invitations'
	Van koringen no groet no cleene	13629[13] 'tests' [12x]

This list's 35 lines constitute a very low figure, which in itself can be considered indicative of the poem's strategy of "avoiding Schwa in S". Two additional considerations make the figure even more impressive, however. First, there is a very strong bias in (43) towards a prohibition against absolutely word-final (open syllable) schwa: just five cases have schwa word-finally, the remaining thirty have schwa in a closed syllable.[14] If *[ə]$_S$ refers to an open syllable, there are just five exceptional lines *vis-à-vis* this constraint. We will see below that there is independent evidence for this reinterpretation of the constraint. Second, the figures for schwa in S are not just low in some intuitive sense, but also in comparison to the stunning amount of lines which actually have sequences of schwa syllables in them. How can there be many lines with sequences of schwa syllables but vanishingly few with [ə]$_S$? The (*Lutgart* poet's) answer is: *synalepha*.

6.3. Synalepha

"Schwa in S" can be avoided by having a schwa-final word immediately followed by a vowel-initial word, as in the frequent examples in (44):

(44) *Want hem ontfarmede ⌒ onser schaden* 12801 [cf. 42a))]
 Al suchtende ⌒ af beclaget u 1384(3)
 Dat icse sechhende ⌒ altehant 5119

	Want si din man ontdekkede ⌒ al	13245	
in 4:	*Si vastede ⌒ al die dage lanc*	0663	'fastened'
	So kriepende ⌒ alse conen wel	11215	'complaining'
	Verloessede ⌒ ende weder gaf	14437	'saved'
	Kanoneke ⌒ ende regulire	1439(3)	'canons'
	Te leggene ⌒ op in tresoriën	4751(3)	'to put'
in 6:	*Die tirst volmakede ⌒ in Latijn*	2068	'completed'
	Van haren ijammere ⌒ al genas	2529	'misery'
	So wie dat dogede ⌒ ongemac	3580	'suffered'
	Van langen suchtene ⌒ also mat	7592	'sighing (N.)'
	Des goedes dankende ⌒ onsen here	10046	'thanking'
in 8:	*Die saken oc te seggene ⌒ u*	2062	'to say'
	So datter Got oc restede ⌒ in	2202	'rested'
	Dat enech mensche levende ⌒ es	4014	'living'
	Want vele bat dan imene ⌒ el	4448	'someone (else)'
	Om dat convent te wekkene ⌒ op	7158	'to raise'

The first 1,000 lines contain twenty-five of such cases. It would be wrong to suggest, though, that it is the *deliberate function* of synalepha to alleviate the *[ə]$_S$ situation. Synalepha is simply obligatory *as soon as* a schwa-vowel sequence arises, anywhere:

(45) Obligatory synalepha[15]

	in 1:	*Taiwires, daer si lange sent*	0021
		Tabdessen noch te priorinnen	0367
		Tontcommerne (⌒) u van allen dingen	3993
	in 2:	*Tote ⌒ op den ijoncsten doemesdach*	2029
		Gode ⌒ onsen vader dis vernamen	3164
		Schone, ⌒ amoreus, ende (⌒) achemant	3604
	in 3:	*Te borge ⌒ u mine trowe gaf*	2358
		Die here ⌒ antwerde gaf met sinne	3353
		Hort hare ⌒ in welkerhande wise	8801
	in 4:	*Dat si hadde ⌒ eenen vrint verloren*	2449
	in 5:	*Of houden wilde ⌒, of houden conste*	11421
		Mar over mate ⌒ alteenen dede	12229

	Van Denremonde ⌒ in ene (⌒) abdije	12329
in 6:	*Die selve wart ere ⌒ andre vrowen*	2519
	Dat evel ware (⌒) ochte ⌒ arch gedaen	3172
in 7:	*Die ic beschowet hebbe ⌒ al bloet*	1796
	Die hem verwegt of clene ⌒ of groet	2968
	Der vriër maget Sente ⌒ Agneesen	7361
in 8:	*Ende (⌒) also willech, dar sire ⌒ af*	5291

The device of synalepha, however, does have the fortunate consequence of enabling the poet to use schwa syllable sequences, with ə#V in S.[16] It implies that *[ə]$_S$ must be interpreted as "S cannot exclusively contain (open syllable) ə".

The semantically weak function word *oc* 'also' (cf. (23)) is occasionally used as a filler word to avoid "Schwa in S", it being a useful synalepha trigger; see (46):

(46) *oc* in synalepha

in 4:	*Dat togede ⌒ oc wel har abijt*	0523
	'That showed (also) well her clothes'	
	Wart pensende ⌒ oc hoe grote pine	7866
	'Contemplated (also) what fierce pain'	
	Daer blikkede ⌒ oc dat rode gout	10465
	'There glittered (also) the red gold'	
in 6:	*Hi es te wrekene ⌒ oc gereet*	4875
	'He is to revenge (also) ready'	
	Die puls tekrankene ⌒ oc begonste	12575
	'The pulse weaken (also) began'	
	Van hem te helpene ⌒ oc met beden	12923
	'Him to help (also) with prayers'	
in 8:	*Agnese (⌒) ende (⌒) andre menege ⌒ oc*	7095
	'Agnese and others many (also)'	

It is not always easy to distinguish between a semantically empty filler use of *oc* and a meaningful one; the cases mentioned here seem to qualify.

6.4. The morphemes ge- and te, and the Principle of Closure

The "No Schwa in S" constraint makes a prediction about the behaviour of morphemes such as the past tense prefix *ge-* [ɣə-], the infinitival marker *te* [tə], the personal pronoun *se* [sə] 'she, they', and the negation element *ne* [nə], namely that they will not occur in S position. This subsection discusses this prediction, using the behaviour of the first two as an illustration.

So far cases were considered in which a word-final schwa syllable occupies an S-position at the right wordedge. The past participle prefix *ge-* represents the mirror image situation: at the left edge. Normally this prefix simply occurs in W, and the stress pattern of the verbal stem determines the position of the word in the line. Consider the examples in (47), which are just a very small list out of many examples. Over and above this, the examples in (48) constitute the full list of forms in which this prefix occurs in S.

(47) The regular behaviour of past participle *ge-*
    in 1: *Geblóedet* meer dan int gevoch   7202
            'bled'
            Gedisputéert tin selven stonden   1943(3)
            'argued, disputed'
    in 3: Sijs heft *gedánkt* Gode onsen Here   2670
            'thanked'
            Daer dos *geprofetéert* af es   3508(3)
            'predicted'
    in 5: Daer gi nu met *gecléedet* sijt   2402
            'dressed'
            So vaste ende oc *geconfirméert*   2227
            'confirmed'
    in 7: Dat si so wale was *geráect*   0238
            'hit'
            Nu hebbic u die noet *gecláget*   0355
            'complained'

(48) Och *gekastijt* van haren pape   0688   'chastised'
      Want *gejugéert* het es van Gode   12689   'judged'
      Want *gejugiert* het was van Gode   12579
      Wel *gewarnéert* met enen stave   5302(3)   'equipped'
      Dar was hi *gewalóppet* schire   12591   'galopped'
      Neen, sprac dat wijf, hets *gejugéert*   3944

The usual behaviour of this prefix, in (47), can be taken as support for the "No Schwa in S" constraint. Four of the six counterexamples in (48) have the prefix in the second position of the line. This bias deserves commenting upon, but let us first have a look at another schwa morpheme.

The infinitival marker *te* [tə] is extremely frequent in the *Lutgart* but, as expected, occupies S only in a very small handful of cases. The facts are these. Infinitival *te* is used across-the-board when the verb starts with a consonant, but only when stress is on an odd syllable of the verbstem, counting from the left. This is true both line-initially and line-internally.

(49) The behaviour of infinitival *te* (before consonants)
      in 1: *[Te bréngene] over, maget goet*   0627
            'to bring'
            [Te plégene] in die Godes eere   2268
            'to act'
            [Te dárvene] alles dis men ett   2769
            'to miss'
            [Te líggene], ende bi costume   3826
            'to lie down'
            [Te hélpene] allen goeden lieden   5613
            'to help'
            [Te sermonéerne] din ijonfrowen   1689(3)
            'to preach (to)'
      in 3: *Dat bloet [te léttene], of si conde*   7119
            'to let blood'
            Began [te dánkene] onsen Here   7252
            'to thank'

Die meest [te ghéecelne] es gewone	9504
'to whip, chastise'	
Die magt [te visitéerne] comen	0199(3)
'to visit'	
in 5: *Die alle dinc [te rékkene] hevet*	1531
'to treat'	
Dat het wel goet [te hóerne] ware	7532
'to hear'	
In dat beghin [te dóene] wesen	11627
'to do'	
Der Tatren van [te cómene] hir	1627(3)
'to come'	
in 7: *Mar si die was gereet [te stáne]*	7190
'to stand'	

Thus, easily imaginable lines are excluded starting with *Te* followed by verb of which the first syllable is unstressed: *[Te failliren...* ('to fail'). The list below contains the complete collection of cases in which infinitival *te* occurs in S.

(50) Infinitival *te* in S (complete list)

Al *te* volbrengene dat gi meenet	1790	'to complete'
Al *te* vertrekkene in Latine	5118	'to relate'
Dat *te* volbrengene over macht	5331	
Dis *te* volcomene an din tide	5333	'to arrive'
Voert *te* tormentene oc gegeven	7012	'to torment'
Don *te*verstáne dat het si	12160	'to grasp'
Hem *te*bekírne ende af testane	12489	'to turn'
Daer sise vonden *te*geléden	11492	'to lead'

Notice that seven of these eight lines have *te* in their second metrical position.

Before vowel-initial verbstems the reduced consonantal form *T-* appears line-initially before unstressed vowels (just as the consonantal form *D-* of *die/de*). Thus, lines are excluded starting with *Te* followed by a vowel-initial verb of which the first syllable is stressed: *[Téeren..* ('to honour'). Line-internally any type of verb can be used, simply with *t-* appearing before vowels, independently of the stress pattern of that verb (so *t-éeren* is possible here, for instance):

(51) Infinitival *te* before vowels:
    in 1: *[Tonfáne] uwe eewelike miede*   2386(3)
           'to receive'
    in 2: *Hem [takointéerne] metter vrowen*   8168
           'to familarize'
           Mi [téeren], ende vilt al mede   11105
           'to honour'
    in 3: *Om raet [tontfáene] ende omme leeren*   12985
           'to receive'
    in 4: *Der silen [téeren] van der nonnen*   4003(3)
           'to revere'
    in 5: *Dat sacrament [tontfángene] hare*   4649
           'to receive'
           Die mate gnoch [tonthóudene] es   11158
           'to remember'
    in 6: *Din men din dage [téeren] dede*   7488
           Ende oc den genen [tondergáne]   9890
           'to undergo'
    in 7: *Ontbere, al staet mi dis [tontbérne]*   9608
           'to manage without'
           Dat mi dat lijf began [tontgáne]   12848
           'to wither away'

The observation that the two schwa morphemes discussed here exceptionally occur in S most often in metrical position two (11 out of 14 cases), seems to find an analogy in so-called "initial inversion": this is the well-known phenomenon in which the iambic strength relation of the first two metrical positions of a line, or sometimes of the first two positions of a line-internal phrase, is reversed (cf. (2)). Initial inversion is quite common in the English iambic pentameter tradition, on average occurring a number of times, for instance, in a 14 line Shakespearean Sonnet. It occurs in the *Lutgart*, too, as shall be shown in the next subsection. The literature has explained this phenomenon by the "Principle of Closure" (Smith 1968, Kiparsky 1975, Hayes 1983, 1989):

(52) Correspondence to a metrical pattern tends to be lax at the beginning of units, strict at the ends. (Hayes 1983: 373)

If this principle can be invoked to explain why a Shakespearean line can start with *[Sermons...*, there seems no reason not to use it to explain the striking relative frequency of schwa syllables in the leftmost S position of the line. Two comments are worth making on this suggestion. First, this case interestingly augments the contention by Hanson and Kiparsky (1996: 298) that "the term INVERSION is really a misnomer, for the licence concerns only the first (weak) position". This *Lutgart* case shows that the Principle of Closure appears to refer to the first position relevant to a constraint, whether W or S. Second, the examples of this section beg the question why, given the choice between *die* and *de* described in subsection 6.1, the latter ([də]) does not sometimes exceptionally occur in metrical position two, too: such cases are completely absent. The answer seems to be that [də] can always be replaced with its sibling *die*, without consequences for the use of the article as such. In other words: FIT can always be fulfilled. Schwa morphemes such as *ge-* and *te*, however, lack a sibling form. They are either used or not, and the Principle of Closure gives FIT the opportunity to boost using them in position two. This is exactly what happens.

6.5. Initial inversion

In absolute line-initial position content words can occasionally be found preceding a relatively non-prominent syllable:

(53) *[Troest van mesquame], clene of groet*   0647
     'Solace from adversity ...'
     [Quaemt in den mont], het moster ut   0695
     'Was thrown up in the mouth ...'
     [Vaste ⌒ in den Godes] prise wart   1548
     'Steady in God's ...'
     [Danc hebbes Got] van hemelrike!   1598
     'Thank have (you) God ...'

[Ghinc hise trosten] ende seide 'Went he them console ...'	1720
[Sprac hi: Got motu] goeden dach 'Said he: God must you ...'	8696

Initial trochaic pairs of syllables can belong to the same word, too, but interestingly inversion is then limited to a specific class of words on the borderline between "function word" and "content word", *i.e.*, adverbs, prepositions, pronouns, and auxiliaries:

(54)
[*Weder* si quaet sijn ochte goet 'Whether they bad are or good'	1003
[*Tuschen* den viant ende hare 'Between the enemy and her'	1633
[*Sonder* kalange moten comen 'Without discord ...'	5249
[*Onder* die vrowen al gemeene 'Among the women ...'	11121
[*Over* dat arme wivekijn 'About that poor little woman'	11355
[*Selken* message, her messagir 'Such a message ...'	12681
[*Waren* si papen ochte clerke 'Were they priests or clerks'	1451(3)
Die bat [*over* die vrowe goet '... about the good woman'	4517
Met slagen groet [*sonder* getal '... without number'	1131
Dat si dar horde [*onder* die silen '... among the souls'	10477
[*Waren* si arm, [*waren* si rike 'Were they poor, were they rich'	7658

All participating words have a specific phonological form: they end in a *schwa-consonant* sequence. Thus, the conjunction *ende* does not (cannot) participate in inversion, nor do similar words such as *ochte* 'or', *beide* 'both', *alse* 'as', *tote* 'to', and so on; they can occur line-initially only by synalepha:

(55) Ende in der goeden lieden mont   0233
      'And in the good people's mouth'
      Alse andre vrowen nutten daer   0691
      'Like other women ate there'
      Tote op den ijoncsten doemesdach   2029
      'Till on the first doomsday'
      Beide oppenbarlic ende stille   3786
      'Both overtly and covertly'
      Ochte anders volgen haren wille   11171
      'Or else according to her wishes'

The fact that closed schwa syllables participate in inversion, and those in open schwa syllables do not, can be taken as independent evidence that the "No Schwa in S" restriction is confined to open syllable schwa, as suggested above.

6.6. Syncope

Synalepha eliminates potential *W-S* schwa syllable sequences. There is some evidence that true Middle Dutch phonology made a contribution towards this, too. Overlong lines occur in which schwa syllable sequences cannot be alleviated by synalepha because the next word is consonant-initial; at the same time, the pertinent word has a variant elsewhere spelt with just a single schwa syllable. Thus, we find pairs of lines such as those below; the first line is overlong, the second is metrically regular.

(56) (a) Syncope pairs

      -    Int *heilege* lant van over zee   0275(3)
           'holy (land)'
           Ende oc dat *heilge* cruce sal   9947
           'holy (cross)'
      -    Die *riddere* mar, die rike man   8545
           'knight (famous)'
           Die *riddre* sijns ambachtes plegen   8788
           'knight'

-	Ghi *andere* vrowen die hir sijt 'other (women)'	1577
	Die daer tevoren *andre* droch 'other (ones)'	0227
-	Hi stont van *wondere* so verdart	8049
	Wat *wondre* dan al hebbic rowe 'miracles'	0591
-	Die *meneger* doeget doet gemessen 'many (people)'	13860
	Van *menger* wonderliker saken 'many (miraculous cases)'	13464

(56) (b) Overlong lines, presumably involving syncope (schwa-less mate unavailable)

Een *edele* nonne, hit Yolent 'noble (nun)'	3774
Ende es te *hemele* wert gevaren '(to) heaven'	0659
Ghi ons met *redenen* hebt verwonnen '(with) reasons'	4487
Want mine *bordene* die ic drage '(my) burden'	5376
Also te *levene* sonder schade '(to) live'	5838(3)

In Modern Standard Dutch a pronunciation such as *andre* for *andere* is quite common, and it seems, because the spelling often represents it, that a(n optional) phonological rule of Syncope had a relatively wide scope in Middle Dutch. Some schwa deletion processes that we can now say have run their full historical course are also attested in the *Lutgart* in the form of spelling-variation; one of them is that of schwa deletion before dental obstruents:

(57) Modern Dutch *maagd* 'virgin'

Lutgart, die *magt* van groten prise	0198
Die Vite van der *maget* vrie	0152
Sent dat die *maget* van hogen prise [overlong]	14425

Modern Dutch *hoofd* 'head'
- Dat *hoft* van hare buke howen — 7244
- Op elker *hovet*, want met cronen — 10467

Modern Dutch present tenses ending in -*C-t*
- Want si mi *brengt* en ongeval — 1428(3)
  'For she me brings...'
- Es ende loes, hi *brenget* gerne — 4115
  '..., he brings gladly'
- Tevoren *brenget*; mar altehant [overlong] 1212(3)
  'in the open brings; ...'
- Oc *heft* dat selve wel getoent — 0526
  'Also has that same ...'
- So *hevet* hi op enen dach — 0831
  'So has he ...'
- Nu *makt* u wech wel drogenere — 5006
  'Now make (you)...'
- Dat si din dommen *maket* vroet — 2950
  '(That she) ... makes'
- Din gi *verleent* din andren silen — 1111
  '(To whom you) give ...'
- *Verleenet* mi so goeden spoet — 0652
  'Gives me ...'

Modern Dutch past tenses ending in -*C-de(n)* [-ə(n)]
- *Volmakde* raste noch verlaet — 9830
  'perfect' (= full-made)
- Die tirst *volmakede* in Latijn — Synalepha 2068
  '(Who first) finished ...'
- So wale *proefde* in dat convent — 9106
  '(So well) recognized ...'
- So wel hem *proeveden* int begin — Syncope 1326
  '(So well him) inspected'
- Ende elke also *bedroefde* hare — 3799
  '... saddened (her)'
- Ende hoe hare oc *bedroevede* das — Syncope 12296

- *Ontfarmde,* doe si quam beweenen 13794
 'moved' (emotionally)
 Want hem *ontfarmede* onser schaden Synalepha 12801

7. Conclusions

Kiparsky (1977: 239-244, 1989: 321) makes a sharp distinction between *metrical and prosodic rules* of metrics:

(58) Resolution and extrametricality both differ in status from the purely PROSODIC (i.e., "paraphonological" as opposed to metrical) processes of elision in vowel sequences. These elision processes also figure in Hopkins. [...] They are sometimes marked in the manuscripts [...], for example, ... *O our oracle!,....off the other* ("Spelt from Sibyl's leaves"). (1989: 321)
 I have been assuming a theory in which a distinction is drawn between metrical rules, which govern the matching between linguistic and metrical representations, and *prosodic rules*, which apply to linguistic representation[s], giving them the form that they must have for the purposes of the metrical rules. (1977: 239)

Thus, *resolution* and *synalepha* both occur in Hopkins's poetry, but they belong to different theoretical components: *metrics* and *prosody*, respectively. It is the former that is crucially involved in "sprung rhythm", motivated, in the parametric theory of Hanson and Kiparsky (1996), by FIT in order to promote the lexicon when S is uncharacteristically constrained so as not to contain weak syllables. Prosody is independent of metrics, and part of a "paralinguistic system that specifies the poetic language as a derivative of the system [...] of ordinary language" (1977: 241).
 Viewed in these terms, this paper has shown that not just the parametric system (*née* metrical rules) can be involved in boosting the lexicon, but also the paralinguistic system. Thirteenth century Middle Dutch is a language with many schwa-final words, partly (but far from exclusively) because of its rich inflectional system; and with many vowel-initial words, mostly function words and prefixed

words. Because of this Willem van Afflighem, the *Lutgart* author, by fully employing the prosodic device of synalepha (and to a lesser extent the Principle of Closure and syncope), was able to produce an intriguing specimen of octosyllabic iambic poetry, of a regularly alternating kind in which *both W and S* are constrained, the latter by *[ə]$_S$, and prosodic means help to satisfy FIT.

Notes

1. This paper is a revised version of one presented in different forms at the *Change in Prosodic Systems Workshop* of the DGfS Jahrestagung at Konstanz University, Germany, 25 February 1999; and at the *Parasession on Stress and Metrics* of the Seventh Phonology Meeting at the University of Manchester, UK, 14 May 1999. I am indebted to the participants at these meetings for comments and criticism, most specifically to Tom Cable, Paula Fikkert, Donna Minkova, and above all to Chris McCully, Martin Duffell and Michael Redford. Remarks by two anonymous referees and several discussions with Erwin Mantingh helped me gain insight into this paper's subject matter.
2. For the literature comprising some of the intermediate stages in these developments, see the references to the latter article; and, for instance, Kiparsky and Youmans (1989), and the references in the contributions to that volume.
3. For elaboration see Weevers (1960) and Zonneveld (1999).
4. A 'diplomatic' edition, differing just marginally from Van Veerdeghem's, was published in 1985 by Maurits Gysseling.
5. The first reference is a reply to a publication which, uniquely so in the *Lutgart* tradition, argued that it, too, is an instance of *heffingenvers*.
6. For further discussion of this point see Redford's contribution to this volume.
7. '(3)' indicates an example taken from the *Lutgart*'s Book III; those from Book II remain unflagged.
8. It would be amazing to find that a poet adds a syllable, however weak, to his language material in order to comply with his isosyllabic norm; as far as can be made out, this is the case here.
9. Michael Redford pointed this out to me.
10. For remarks on the situation in German poetry see Bjorklund (1978: 267ff.).
11. For further information on this system, see Trommelen and Zonneveld (1986).
12. This line is one syllable overlong. The irregularity resides in the preposition *omme*, and is probably due to scribal error. *Om(me)* has both a mono- and a bisyllabic variant, but the idiomatic expression involved occurs 3 times elsewhere as *om wat saken* 'because of what'.
13. The singular *gracie* is attested no fewer than 56 times. The singulars *bedinge*, *koringe* and *nodinge* are not attested, so these words function as *plurale tantum*'s

in the *Lutgart*.
14. This observation was made independently by Donka Minkova and by an anonymous referee.
15. A parenthesized '(⌒)' indicates, not a case of optional synalepha, but an obligatory one immaterial to the discussion.
16. In the *Lutgart* synalepha can span virtually the strongest possible boundaries:
   - [Mar wetti wat die vrow dede ...] *11065 In hemelrike? Eer ver Lutgart* [Ten inde brachte dese wart,]
   'But do you know what those women did ... in heaven? Before lady Lutgart could finish her words, ...'
   - ["Ach, ver Lutgart, wildi mi roeven] *12095 Van minen sinne?" antwerde gaf* [Die broeder ...]
   'Ah, lady Lutgart, will you remove my sin?' answered the friar...
   It must be stressed that synalepha is a purely metrical convention (Halle and Keyser 1971: 141). It is neither an instruction to `slur' word combinations in reciting the poem (although one is of course free to do so, poems can be recited in good or bad ways), nor necessarily a phonological rule of the language stage in question (although some version may be present in the grammar, either in the lexical or the post-lexical component or both).

References

Benson, L.D. (ed.)
    1987   *The Riverside Chaucer*. Oxford: Oxford University Press.
Bjorklund, B.
    1978   *A Study in Comparative Prosody: English and German Jambic Pentameter*. Stuttgart: Akademischer Verlag Hans-Dieter Heinz.
Conner, J.
    1974   *English Prosody from Chaucer to Wyatt*. The Hague: Mouton.
Gollancz, I.
    1940   *Sir Gawain and the Green Knight*. London: Oxford University Press.
Gysseling, M.
    1985   *Corpus van Middelnederlandse Teksten (Tot en met het Jaar 1300). Reeks II: Literaire handschriften, Deel 5: Sente Lutgart*. Leiden: Martinus Nijhoff.
Halle, M., and S.J. Keyser
    1966   Chaucer and the study of prosody. *College English* 28: 187-219. Reprinted in D.C. Freeman (ed.) (1970) *Linguistics and Literary Style*. New York: Holt, Rinehart and Winston: 366-426. (Page references to this latter edition).
    1971   *English Stress: its Form, its Growth, and its Role in Verse*. New York: Harper and Row.

Hanson, K., and P. Kiparsky
1996   A parametric theory of poetic meter. *Language* 72: 336-371.
Hayes, B.
1983   A grid-based theory of English meter. *Linguistic Inquiry* 14: 357-394.
1989   The prosodic hierarchy in meter. In Kiparsky and Youmans (eds.): 201-260.
Horst, J.M. van der, and F.J. Marschall
1989   *Korte Geschiedenis van de Nederlandse Taal.* Amsterdam: Nijgh en Van Ditmar.
Kiparsky, P.
1975   Stress, syntax and meter. *Language* 51: 576-616.
1977   The rhythmic structure of English verse. *Linguistic Inquiry* 8: 189-247.
1989   Sprung rhythm. In: Kiparsky and Youmans (eds.): 305-340.
Kiparsky, P., and G. Youmans (eds.)
         Rhythm and meter. *Phonetics and Phonology* 1, New York: Academic Press.
Loey, A. van
1970   *Schönfeld's Historische Grammatica van het Nederlands.* Zutphen (8th ed.).
Minkova, D.
1991   *The History of Final Vowels in English. The Sound of Muting.* Berlin: Mouton De Gruyter.
Overdiep, G.S., en G.A. van Es
1946   *Vormleer van het Middelnederlandsch der XIIIe Eeuw.* Antwerpen: Standaard Boekhandel.
Robinson, F.N.
1957/1966 *The Works of Geoffrey Chaucer. 2nd edition.* London: Oxford University Press.
Smith, B.H.
1968   *Poetic Closure: A Study of how Poems End.* Chicago, Ill.: University of Chicago Press.
Southworth, J.G.
1962   *The Prosody of Chaucer and his Followers.* Oxford: Basil Blackwell.
Trommelen, M., and W. Zonneveld
1986   Dutch morphology: Evidence for the righthand head rule. *Linguistic Inquiry* 17: 147-170.
Veerdeghem, F. van
1899   *Leven van Sinte Lutgart, tweede en derde boek. Naar een Kopenhaags Handschrift.* Leiden: E.J. Brill.
Verdam, J.
1932   *Middelnederlandsch Handwoordenboek,* revised by C.H. Ebbinge Wubben. The Hague: Martinus Nijhoff.

Weevers, Th.
1960   *Poetry of the Netherlands in its European Context, 1170-1930*. London: The Athlone Press.
Zonneveld, W.
1992/2000 Van Afflighem en Chaucer: Het leven van Sinte Lutgart als jambisch gedicht. *Ruygh-Bewerp XVII,* Dept. of Dutch Language and Literature, Utrecht University. Minimally revised version published by Nodus Publ., Münster.
1993   700 Jaar Nederlandse klemtoon (en weinig veranderd). *Spektator* 22: 198-222.
1999   *Lutgart, Willem and Geoffrey; 13th century Dutch metre in a European Context.* Ms., Research Institute for Language and Speech (O.T.S.), Utrecht University.

From phrase-final to post-initial accent in western Basque

José Ignacio Hualde

1. Introduction

The most widespread accentual pattern in western Basque dialects (those spoken in the provinces of Bizkaia and Gipuzkoa and neighboring areas) is post-initial accent, [+2] (on the second syllable, cf. Txillardegi 1984). Along the Bizkaian coast, however, one finds a pitch-accent system with a lexical unaccented/accented distinction and where the unmarked pattern (in phrases without lexically accented words) is phrase-final accent, [-1]. In small western areas one also finds systems with unmarked penultimate, [-2], and post-post-initial, [+3], accent (see map at the end of the article). There is both internal and external evidence, which suggests that all these systems are historically related and that the most conservative of them is the pitch-accent type with phrase-final accentual prominence. In this paper I will try to demonstrate that the most extreme development [-1] > [+2] has been accomplished following one of three different paths in different areas. In these paths of development, it appears that the accentual and intonational system of Spanish (in which almost all western Basque speakers are bilingual) has been a triggering factor in a direct or indirect manner. To postulate that western Basque has acquired post-initial accentuation under the influence of Spanish may seem paradoxical at first sight, since Spanish words are always stressed on one of the last three syllables of the word, and most commonly on one of the last two. This influence becomes apparent, however, once we consider the typical tone alignment patterns in both languages. In particular, whereas in Spanish abrupt tonal rises are generally associated with stressed syllables, in the most conservative western Basque dialects a non-accentual rise occurs on the second syllable of prosodic units and accentual prominence is, instead, associated with a following fall. Different evolutions have resulted in a greater compatibility between the intonational/accentual systems of the two languages.

In section 2, the northern Bizkaian pitch-accent system is briefly described. After that, in sections 3-6, I consider historical developments leading to accentual systems, which are quite different from what I take to have been the original one.

2. The northern Bizkaian pitch-accent systems

2.1. The Gernika-Getxo type

In the northern part of the Basque-speaking area of the province of Bizkaia (the westernmost Basque province), along the coast and in the immediate hinterland, we find pitch-accent systems with a fundamental lexical distinction between unaccented and accented words, most words belonging to the unaccented class (Hualde 1991, 1993, 1997, 1999). Lexically accented words have an accent on any non-final syllable, although, depending on the variety, there may be restrictions or strong tendencies on the position of lexical accents. As for unaccented words, phrases composed entirely of unaccented words in isolation or in focus position in the sentence receive accentual prominence in the final syllable in most of this area, from the Gernika estuary to Getxo, near Bilbao (Gernika-Getxo type). In the Markina area, to the east of Gernika, however, unaccented phrases receive penultimate prominence (Markina type). Following Jun and Elordieta (1997) we will refer to this accent on the final (or penultimate) syllable of lexically unaccented phrases as 'derived' accent. Both lexical and derived accents are consistently expressed by means of a H*+L contour (in the notation introduced in Pierrehumbert 1980, Pierrehumbert and Beckman 1988, etc.), that is, a tonal peak immediately followed by a valley. The pitch always rises at the beginning of the accentual unit and stays high from the second syllable up to the syllable with lexical or derived accent (unless the accent is on the first syllable, in which case the rise is on this syllable, with a fall on the second).

Figure 1 shows an F0 tracing of the utterance *lagunen amarí gertatu dxatzo* 'it happened to the friend's (sg) mother' pronounced by a speaker of the Bermeo variety (Gernika-Getxo type). The preverbal phrase *lagunen amarí* 'friend-GENsg mother-DATsg' contains two lexically unaccented words and, being in the preverbal focus position, receives a derived accent on the final syllable:

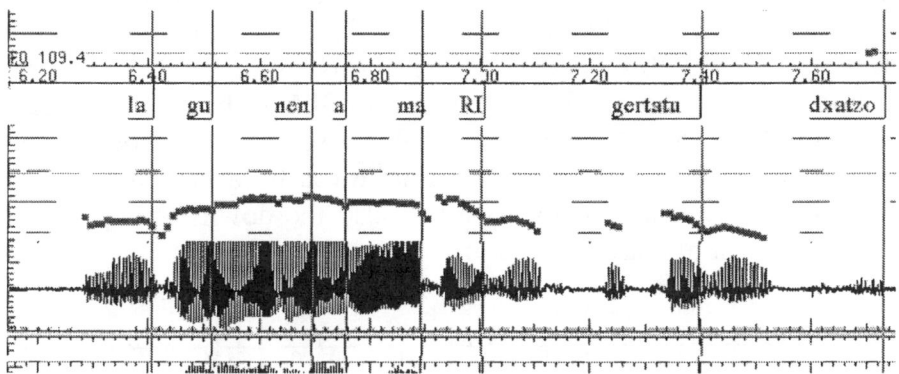

Fig.1   *lagunen   amarí   gertatu dxatzo*
       friend.GENsg mother.DATsg   happen   AUX
       'It happened to the friend's (sg) mother' (Bermeo, Gernika-Getxo type)

As can be seen in figure 1, the pitch level rises on the second syllable of the sentence and remains at a relatively level high pitch up to the last syllable of *amarí*. On this syllable there is a slight rise followed by a fall. As proposed in Jun and Elordieta (1997), Elordieta (1998), this type of tonal contour can receive the following analysis in Pierrehumbert's model (Pierrehumbert 1980, Pierrehumbert and Beckman 1988): %L H- H*+L, where the boundary low tone %L is linked to the first syllable, the phrasal H- is loosely associated with the second syllable and the H*+L pitch-accent occurs on the final syllable of the phrase:

(1)   Tonal analysis of preverbal phrase in fig.1

Subject to dialectal and idiolectal variation, in multi-word phrases non-phrase-initial unaccented words preceded by another unaccented word may also present a (relatively shallow) valley on the initial syllable followed by a rise on the second (a %LH- sequence) (see Elordieta 1998).

The tonal behavior of lexically accented words is shown in figure 2 with includes the F0 contour of a rendition of the sentence *lagúnen amarí gertatu dxatzo* 'it happened to the friends' (pl) mother', by the same speaker. In this sentence, which forms a minimal pair with the one in figure 1, the word *lagúnen* 'friend-GENpl' has lexical accent (like all plural forms). This is reflected in a somewhat steeper rise on the second syllable than in figure 1 followed by a fall on the post-tonic (a H*+L tonal contour). Notice also the downstepping of the derived accent of *amarí*:

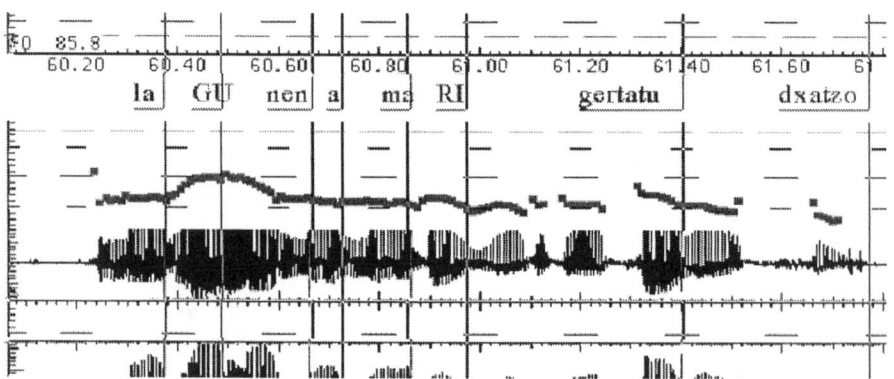

Fig 2. lagúnen   amarí   gertatu dxatzo
       friend.GENpl mother.DATsg happen AUX
       'it happened to the friends' (pl) mother' (Bermeo, Gernika-Getxo type)

This phrase can be analyzed as follows:

(2)   Tonal analysis of preverbal phrase in fig. 2

```
      la gú nen    a ma ri
      |  |  |        |\
      %L H* L        H*L
```

The main properties of this accentual system are thus the following:

a) There is a distinction between lexically accented and unaccented words; most words belonging to the class without lexical accent.
b) Lexically unaccented phrases in focus position or in isolation receive accentual prominence on their final (or, in the Markina area, penultimate) syllable (derived accent).
c) The pitch rises on the second syllable (unless there is a lexical accent on the first syllable) and remains high up to the accented syllable (with lexical or derived accent). The accented syllable is often characterized by a further, smaller, rise. But this is not a necessary feature; the tone may simply remain level from the second to the accented syllable. Following the accentual peak, there is always a fall. In ToBI-style transcription, the pattern is characterizable as %L H- H*L.
d) Accents trigger downstepping of following accents; unaccented words do not induce downstep.

Accented words fall into the following categories:

1. *Preaccenting inflectional suffixes.* Words bearing certain inflectional suffixes have an accent on the syllable preceding the suffix. Preaccenting suffixes include all plural suffixes, as well as the ablative (*-tik* 'from') and the comitative (*-gaz* 'with'). Cf. the following partial inflectional paradigm for the word *adar* 'horn' in Gernika (for more complete paradigms cf. Hualde 1999 as well as Hualde and Bilbao 1992, for the variety of Getxo):[1]

(3)   Gernika: unaccented and preaccenting inflectional suffixes
 SINGULAR PLURAL
 adarra *adárrak*
 'the horn' 'the horns'
 adarrari *adárrari*
 'to the horn, DAT' 'to the horns, DAT'
 adarran *adárran*
 'of the horn' 'of the horns'
 adarrantzat *adárrantzat*
 'for the horn' 'for the horns'

> adarrara
> 'to the horn, ALL'
> adarrátik
> 'from the horn'
> adarrágaz
> 'with the horn'
>
> adárratara
> 'to the horns, ALL'
> adárratatik
> 'from the horns'
> adárrakaz
> 'with the horns'

2. *Preaccenting or accented derivational suffixes.* Many derivational suffixes give rise to accented words. Most of them induce an accent on the preceding syllable (preaccenting derivational suffixes), but in some varieties some polysyllabic suffixes bear the accent on their first syllable. If the word has an accented/preaccenting derivational suffix, any possible accentual effects induced by inflectional suffixes are neutralized.[2] An example of a preaccenting suffix is the ethnonymic *-(t)ar* (for the variety of Getxo, a list of derivational suffixes with indication of their accentual properties is given in Hualde and Bilbao 1992):

(4)   Gernika: preaccenting derivational suffixes (examples in the absolutive case)
      gerníkarra   'the Gernikan'   *gerníkarrak*   'the Gernikans'
      getxótarra   'the Getxoan'   *getxótarrak*   'the Getxoans'

3. *Compounds.* Many compounds have a lexical accent, generally on the syllable preceding the compound boundary. This tends to be a productive phenomenon in the formation of new compounds; e.g.: *begi gorri bat* 'a red eye' but *begí-gorri bat* 'a red-eyed one'.

4. *Accented roots.* Exceptionally, a relatively small number of synchronically monomorphemic roots bear an accent (which is kept in all inflected forms). Words in this group are mostly borrowings (some of them very old, e.g.: *puxíka* 'bladder' < Latin *uesicca*, *dénpora* 'time' < Latin *tempora*, see Hualde 1993). Other words in this group are old compounds or derived words whose structure has become opaque. Only a handful of accented roots have no obvious diachronic explanation. An example is *béste* 'other'.

There is strong evidence suggesting that a pitch-accent system with these characteristics once prevailed throughout the western Basque area and that the other, sometimes very different, systems that we find nowadays in this territory derive historically from the kind of pitch-accent system that we have just briefly described.

Crucial evidence for relatedness is provided by the fact that the same types of words and even the very same lexical items that possess lexical accent in the Gernika-Getxo type tend to present irregular accentuation in other systems as well, even if the manifestation of this irregularity is very different in these other accentual systems. In many systems with regular post-initial, [+2], accent there are some words that irregularly show initial accent. By and large, these items with [+1] accentuation correspond to accented words in the Gernika-Getxo type. We will come back to this in section 5.

Evidence that the Gernika-Getxo type represents the oldest stage is both of an internal and of an external nature. I have presented this evidence elsewhere (Hualde 1993, 1995a). Briefly, the internal or comparative argument is that in the Gernika-Getxo type a greater number of distinctions in the position of the accent is made than in any other dialect and, furthermore, there is a more transparent link between exceptional accentual properties and morphological or etymological structure than in the other accentual types. This conclusion is supported by the fact that the description that the Gipuzkoan writer Larramendi (1729) left us of what at the time were the general accentual patterns in the provinces of Bizkaia and Gipuzkoa corresponds most closely to the patterns still found in the Gernika-Getxo area.

In the remainder of this paper we will be concerned with the development of the other western Basque accentual systems, starting from a stage essentially identical to that still represented by the Gernika-Getxo pitch accent type.

2.2. Markina: From phrase-final to phrase-penultimate and related changes

The accentual system that we have just described in the previous subsection has been altered in parts of the northern Bizkaian area by processes shifting accents one or more syllables to the left or to the right. For instance, in Lekeitio most lexical accents have shifted to the penultimate syllable of the word (see Hualde 1993, 1997, 1999, Hualde, Elordieta and Elordieta 1994, Elordieta 1997). Of particular interest to understand further developments elsewhere are some accentual changes that we find in the Markina area. Since these changes are studied in some detail in another paper (Hualde 2000), here they will be only briefly summarized.

In the Markina area (including Ondarroa, see Hualde 1995b, 1996) the derived accent of unaccented phrases is on the penultimate instead of on the final. There is evidence suggesting that this is because these dialects underwent a process of accent retraction from phrase-final to phrase-penultimate: *gure laguné > gure lagúne* 'our friend' (rather than the varieties of the Gernika-Getxo area having undergone the opposite shift). In its turn, this change triggered a 'compensatory', system-driven retraction of accents in the plural and some other cases in part of this area: *gure lagúnek > gure lágunek* 'our friends'.

(5) Markina: accent retraction

    a. Retraction of phrasal derived accents
    laguné > lagúne   'the friend, ABS'
    lagune dá > laguné da   'it is the friend'
    alarguné > alargúne   'the widow, ABS'

    b. Compensatory retraction of lexical accent in the plural[3]
    lagúnek > lágunek   'the friends, ABS'
    alargúnek > alárgunek   'the widows, ABS'

Notice that, after this shift, the location of the accent in the plural no longer coincides with the morphological boundary, and that in trisyllabic absolutive plural forms the accent now occurs on the initial syllable. The retraction of the accent one syllable to the left took place not only in plural forms but also in other lexically accented words, some of which ended up with initial accent.

In Markina a new generalization arose and all lexical accents were moved to the antepenultimate syllable, causing the accent to occur on different syllables in forms of the same paradigm. In most other dialects that underwent the two changes in (5), however, the paradigmatic generalization that all inflected forms are accented on the same syllable as the absolutive prevailed (see Hualde 2000).

In spite of these changes in the position of accents, the dialects of the Markina area preserve the main features that serve to characterize the northern Bizkaian pitch-accent system as a whole, in opposition to both other Basque accentual systems and other neighboring languages, especially Spanish (Hualde, Elordieta, Gaminde and Smiljanić 2000):

a) A lexical contrast between accented and unaccented words, and
b) A non-accentual phrase-initial rise (%LH-) continued by a high pitch plateau up to the accented syllable.

These are two properties in which the prosody of these Basque dialects differs in a radical manner from that of Spanish, the dominant language of the area. Other Basque dialects have lost one or both of these prosodic features. In the next two sections, we will examine two rather different developments, which have resulted in the elimination of pre-accentual high plateaux, with the consequence that tonal rises now coincide with accented syllables. In both cases, it seems reasonable to assume a direct influence of Spanish prosody in triggering or favoring certain changes, although in two interestingly different manners. In sections 5 and 6, other more complex developments are examined which have also resulted in important modifications to the accentual systems, but where the influence from Spanish, if any, appears to have been more indirect.

3. Bilbao: From phrase-final to post-initial in one fell swoop?

The Gernika-Getxo pitch-accent type extends to the west almost all the way to the city of Bilbao. The Bilbao area is heavily industrialized and overwhelmingly Spanish-speaking. However, as a consequence of the hilly topography of the area, some isolated farmhouses are still found there within a short distance from factories and apartment buildings. In some of these farmhouses, surrounded by an urban Spanish-speaking milieu, the local Basque dialect has somewhat miraculously been preserved. Given its geographical location, we would expect Bilbao Basque to have an accentual system with the properties described above for other northern Bizkaian varieties. However, what we find is very different. Gaminde (1995, 1998a, 1998b) in his study of the indigenous Basque variety of Bilbao notes that in this dialect accent does not have a lexically contrastive value and normally falls on the second syllable of the word.

Reasons of geography lead us to hypothesize that noncontrastive post-initial accent in Bilbao must somehow have developed from the Gernika-Getxo type, which, as has been explained, has a lexical accented/unaccented distinction and unmarked phrase-final accent. Sociolinguistic considerations lead us to suspect the effect of Spanish influence on this change. Now, if we consider the stress patterns of Spanish, it is not immediately clear how Spanish influence may have triggered a change towards post-initial accent in Bilbao Basque. In Spanish the stress falls on one of the three last syllables of the word, the unmarked patterns being penultimate stress, if the word ends in a vowel, and final stress, if the word ends in a consonant.

The clue is found upon consideration of the pitch-contours most commonly associated with stressed syllables in Spanish.

Figure 3 exemplifies a neutral declarative contour in Castilian Spanish. In this figure, which includes the F0 contour of a rendition of the sentence *le diéron el número de vuélo* 'they gave him the number of the flight'[4] (standard orthography supplemented with accent marks on all stressed syllables), there are three tonal peaks corresponding to the three lexically stressed syllables. It can be observed that the tonal peak coincides with the middle of the stressed syllable in the sentence-final word *vuélo* 'flight' but it is displaced to the post-tonic in the words *diéron* 'they gave' and *número* 'number'. The 'displacement' of the tonal peak to the post-tonic syllable in paroxytonic and proparoxytonic words in prenuclear position is a well-known fact of Spanish intonation (see Navarro Tomás 1944, Fant 1984, Garrido et al. 1993, Prieto et al. 1995, Sosa 1999, Hualde forthcoming).

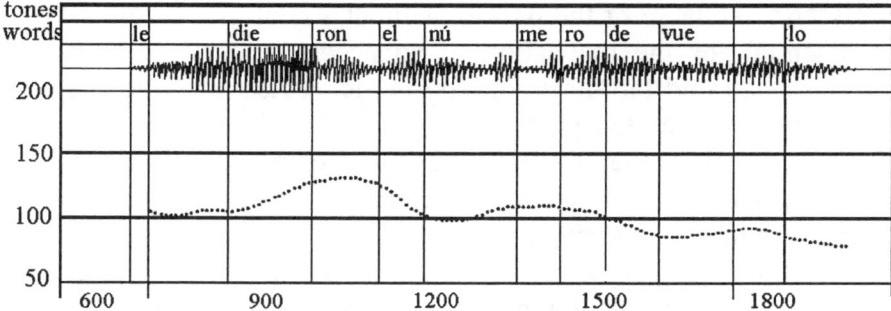

Fig. 3. Spanish *le diéron el número de vuélo* 'They gave him the number of the flight'

Schematically, we have the following configuration, where the boundaries of the stressed syllables are indicated by brackets (on intonational tone alignment, see Cole 2000): a low tone (a tonal valley) at the very beginning of the stressed syllable, followed by a high tone (a tonal peak) which is normally realized on the posttonic in prenuclear position, but on the stressed syllable of words with nuclear accent:

(6) Spanish: tonal analysis of fig. 3

le [dié] ron el [nú] me ro del [vué] lo
   | | | | |
   L*H   L*H   L H* L%

The generalization that arises is that stress in Spanish declarative sentences is usually manifested as a rise in pitch during the stressed syllable. This rise may or may not be followed by a fall. In fact, in paroxytonic and proparoxytonic words the pitch contour will usually continue rising during the post-tonic if the word is not in final position and does not have narrow focus. The tonal contours typically associated with accented syllables in Spanish are thus quite different from those found in the Basque dialects we have examined above. As we saw, in the northern Bizkaian pitch-accent system, the accented syllable is also often accompanied by a rise, but this rise can be very small. In fact, a more pronounced rise is associated with the second syllable of the phrase, without a contrastive value. What is essential for the realization of an accent in northern Bizkaian Basque is a rapid fall during the posttonic. A rise not followed by a fall only indicates the presence of an initial phrase boundary. In Spanish, on the other hand, in neutral declarative sentences tonal rises occur in stressed syllables and there is not necessarily a fall in the post-tonic, as illustrated.

Accentual languages clearly differ in the most distinctive pitch movements, which are typically associated with accented syllables. In languages like Spanish and Greek (Arvaniti, Ladd and Mennen 1998, Botinis 1999) it is a steep rise in pitch across the tonic syllable (in declarative sentences). In other languages like northern Bizkaian Basque and Tokyo Japanese, on the other hand, what most consistently signals the presence of an accent is a fall during the posttonic.

Schematically, we have the following contrast between Spanish and northern Bizkaian Basque regarding the relative importance of rises and falls for the identification of the accented syllable. Notice that in Spanish the pitch remains low up to the first accented syllable, whereas in this Basque dialect the pitch systematically rises on the second syllable:

(7) Role of pitch rises and falls as cues for the position of the accent in Spanish and in Basque

a. Spanish: position of prosodically prominent syllable signaled by rise.

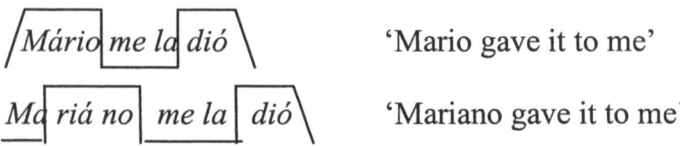

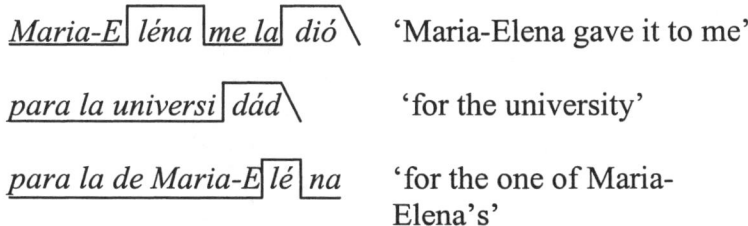

Maria-E| léna |me la| dió \ 'Maria-Elena gave it to me'

para la universi|dád \ 'for the university'

para la de Maria-E|lé|na 'for the one of Maria-Elena's'

b. Northern Bizkaian Basque (Gernika-Getxo type): position of prosodically prominent syllable signaled by fall; rise indicates beginning of phrase.

la |gu ne ná \ 'the one of the friend'

la |gú| ne na 'to the one of the friends'

la |gu né| nak 'the ones of the friends'

In figures 4 and 5 we can see the pitch contour of two renditions of the Spanish sentence *Maria-Eléna me la dió* 'Maria-Elena gave it to me', respectively with broad focus (neutral declarative) and with narrow, contrastive, focus on *Maria-Eléna*. What is apparent is that in both cases there is a pronounced rise through the syllable /le/, which has lexical stress. In neutral intonation (figure 4) the pitch continues rising on the posttonic, whereas under contrastrative focus (figure 5) the peak is reached within the stressed syllable and there is a rapid fall on the posttonic:

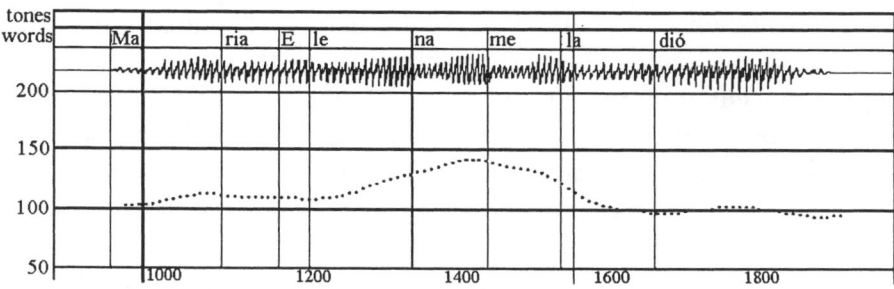

Fig. 4 Spanish *Maria-Eléna me la dió* 'Maria-Elena gave it to me'

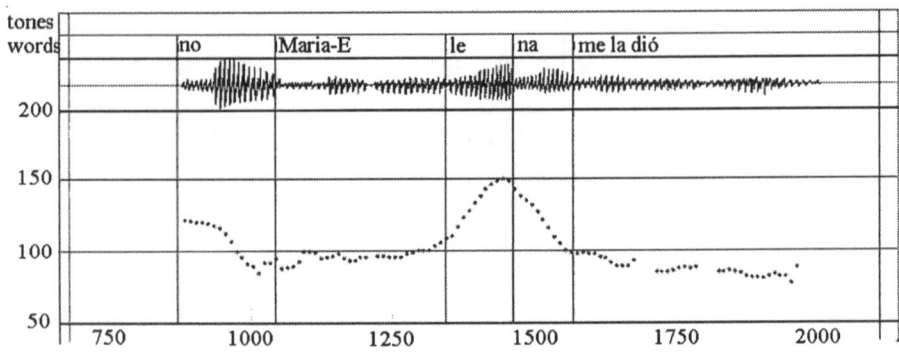

Fig.5 Spanish *No, Maria-Eléna me la dió* 'No, MARIA-ELENA gave it to me'

The functions of tonal rises and falls are thus radically different in the two languages. In Spanish, a pronounced rise in a declarative sentence is associated with a syllable with lexical prominence, whereas the position and steepness of a following fall is used to convey pragmatic information. In northern Bizkaian Basque, on the other hand, the presence of a rise indicates the beginning of a phrase. The syllable with accentual prominence is characterized by an immediately following fall. Given this difference in the function of pitch contours between the two systems, it is apparent that Spanish influence can lead to the reanalysis of the northern Bizkaian pitch-accent system in a situation of intensive bilingualism. It is a fact that Spanish-speakers tend to hear Basque unaccented words as being stressed on the second syllable, where a rise occurs both in unaccented phrases and in accented words (except, naturally, for those accented on the initial syllable), and not to perceive the difference between accented and unaccented words. In connection with this, it should be noted that, in northern Bizkaian Basque, pitch is perhaps the only correlate of accent. Accented syllables do not appear to have increased duration (Hualde, Smiljanić and Cole 1999). For instance, all three words in (7b) will typically be perceived by untrained monolingual Spanish-speakers as stressed on the second. In this case, this leads to the loss of morphological distinctions.

I am proposing that what led to the reanalysis of the accentual system in Bilbao Basque was a transfer of the Spanish perceptual strategy of paying attention to pitch rises and not to falls for the location of accented syllables. When applied to a system of the Gernika-Getxo type this causes the great majority of accentually-based lexical and morphological contrasts to be lost, as has indeed happened in the local Basque variety of Bilbao. The result of reinterpreting the predictable rise on the second syllable as accentual prominence is a system with accent on the second. After this reinterpretation, tonal rises now coincide with accents in declarative sentences, just like in Spanish.

4. Loss of phrasal accents in Antzuola and subsequent developments in neighboring varieties

The influence of the Spanish accentual/intonational system appears to have manifested itself in a quite different manner in other areas of the western Basque provinces. In the area of Antzuola and Bergara, in western Gipuzkoa, the unmarked accentual pattern is [-2] (penultimate), like in Markina. In plural forms, the accent falls on the penultimate of the stem, i.e. two syllables before the plural suffix. Also in verbs, the perfective participle has penultimate accent and in the imperfective the accent falls two syllables before the suffix -*t(z)en*. In addition, there is a group of exceptional stems which are accented on a syllable before the penultimate:

(8)   Antzuola

a. sg. vs. pl.
lagúna   *lágunak*
'the friend'   'the friends'
lagunákin   *lágunekin*
'with the friend'   'with the friends'
lagunandáko   *lágunendako*
'for the friend'   'for the friends'
lagunandakúa   *lágunendakua*
'the one for the friend'   'the one for the friends'
alargúna   *alárgunak*
'the widow'   'the widows'

aberátsa *abératsak*
'wealthy, ABSsg' 'wealthy, ABSpl'

b. perfective vs. imperfective participle
perfective imperfective
apúrtu *ápurtzen* 'to break'
konpóndu *kónpontzen* 'to fix'
aberástu *abérasten* 'to become rich'

c. exceptional words
áizkoria 'the axe', *kótxia* 'the car', *elefantia* 'the elephant'

The distribution of accents in Antzuola is very much as in Markina. However, perceptually these two accentual types are very different. Antzuola Basque sounds much more like Spanish than Markina Basque. Observation of F0 contours reveals one clear reason for this contrast in perception. Schematically, unmarked penultimate accent is realized as follows in the two systems:

(9) Markina vs. Antzuola

Markina type   Antzuola type

la |gu nan tza kú |e   la gu nan da⌐ kú |a   'the one for the friend'

Instead of having a rise in the second syllable, in Antzuola the tone remains low until the accented syllable, where it rises.⁵

It appears that the most straightforward account of the evolution in Antzuola would be to postulate the deletion of the H- tone associated with the second syllable starting from a system basically like the Markina type, as shown in the example:

(10) Antzuola: H- deletion

This change, while preserving all distinctions in the position of accents, has brought the system in line with Spanish by making tonal rises coincide with accented syllables.[6]

This development is very different from what we have claimed for Bilbao. In Bilbao, under the hypothesis that we have defended, the phrasal rise on the second syllable was reinterpreted as indicating the location of the accented syllable, in accordance with the usual Spanish tonal contour-accent correspondence, and the system consequently acquired post-initial accent. In Antzuola, on the other hand, the position of the accent remained stable, but the accented syllable acquired the tonal cues that typically accompany accented syllables in Spanish. It is possible to see the influence from the Spanish accentual/intonational system operating in two rather different ways in these two cases. In one case, lexical prominence is shifted to the syllable where a rise is located; in the other, the rise is shifted to the syllable with lexical prominence. The result in either case is that now rises and prosodic prominence coincide.

Interestingly, after this change, other changes appear to have led also to post-initial accentuation in neighboring varieties. As I argued in Hualde 1998, unmarked penultimate accentuation in a system of the Antzuola type was further reinterpreted as [+3], subject to non-finality (i.e. accent on the third syllable provided it is not the final) in Azkoitia and other towns of the Urola Valley of Gipuzkoa. This reanalysis was aided by the fact that the majority of words are ambiguous between these two interpretations. The differences only emerge in words with 5 or more syllables:

(11) Comparison of [-2] and [+3] non-final systems
      Antzuola [-2]   Azkoitia [+3], non-finality
   a. o ó o   o ó o
      txakúrra   *txakúrre*   'the dog'
      mendíxa   *mendíxe*   'the mountain'

   b. o o ó o   o o ó o
      txakurrári   *txakurréi*   'to the dog'
      alabía   *alabíe*   'the daughter'
      itturríxa   *itturríxe*   'the spring'

c. o o o ó o   o o ó o o
tabernakúa   *tabernákue*   'the one of the tavern'
ieltserúa   *ieltsérue*   'the bricklayer'
emakumía   *emakúmie*   'the woman'

d. o o o o o ó o   o o ó o o o o
emakumiandáko   *emakúmientzako* 'for the woman'

A contributing factor which made the counting-from-the-left reanalysis likely to occur is that in plural forms and in words with accentually marked stems the accent may occur very far from the right edge of the word in the Antzuola system (e.g.: *lágunendako* 'for the friends', *eléfantiakin* 'with the elephant). Finally, a change [+3] > [+2] is currently taking place in the speech of the younger generations in some places like Getaria, to the north of Azkoitia. Both in the change from [+3] to [+2] and in the earlier reanalysis of [-2] as [+3], the possible influence of other neighboring dialects, which had arrived to post-initial accent in other ways should certainly be kept in mind.

Independently of these developments, many of the varieties that have undergone the changes discussed in this section have also lost the lexical contrast between accented and unaccented words.[7]

5. Post-initial systems with exceptional initial accent

In most local dialects spoken in the western provinces of Bizkaia and Gipuzkoa, as well as in the corner of Araba/Alava where the Basque language has been preserved, the predominant accentual system is one with post-initial accent and without a lexical accented/ unaccented distinction. In some of these dialects, the location of the accent on the second syllable has a phonologically contrastive function, since there is a smaller class of words with accent on the first syllable.

Let us consider, for instance, the dialect of Beasain, in the Goierri region of southern Gipuzkoa, which is representative of a large group of local dialects. In this dialect, the accent is generally placed on the second syllable of the word, provided that this is not also the final syllable. This rule, however, has certain exceptions, both morphological and lexical. Starting with the morphological exceptions to post-initial accent, as illustrated in (12a), plural forms have initial accent, except in 'long' words (when the absolutive plural has four or more syllables). Regarding verb forms, imperfective participles also bear initial accent, (12b), again if they have fewer than four syllables:

(12) Beasain : unmarked [+2] vs. marked [+1]
    a. sg. vs. pl.

[+2]	[+1]
lagúne	*lágunek*
'the friend, ABS'	'the friends, ABS'
lagúnei	*lágunei*
'to the friend, DAT'	'to the friends, DAT'
gizóna	*gízonak*
'the man, ABS'	'the men, ABS'
gizónai	*gízonai*
'to the man, DAT'	'to the men, DAT'
zakúrre	*zákurrek*
'the dog, ABS'	'the dogs, ABS'
zakúrrentzat	*zákurrentzat*
'for the dog'	'for the dogs'

BUT:

[+2]	[+2]
alárgune	*alárgunek*
'the widow, ABS'	'the widows, ABS'
abératsa	*abératsak*
'wealthy, ABSsg'	'wealthy, ABSpl'

    b. perfective vs. imperfective

[+2]	[+1]
esán-du	*ésaten-du*
'has said it'	'says it'

etórri-de
'has arrived'
konpóndu-du
'has fixed it'

étortzen-da
'arrives'
kónpontzen-du
'fixes it'

BUT:
[+2]
enténdittu-du
'has understood it'
orgánizau-du
'has organized it'

[+2]
enténditzen-du
'understands it'
orgánizatzen-du
'organizes it'

A strong reason to believe that this system is historically related to the northern Bizkaian pitch-accent system is that the same morphological categories that trigger exceptional [+1] accentuation in Beasain (and other varieties of the same type) are also exceptional in the northern Bizkaian system, where they belong to the lexically accented class. That is, although the surface manifestation of the contrast is very different in the two systems (post-initial vs. initial in Beasain, unaccented vs. accented in northern Bizkaian), there is coincidence in which suffixes condition exceptional accentuation.[8]

A difference between the two accentual systems, however, is that in northern Bizkaian there are no distinctions in behavior conditioned by the number of syllables. In the Gernika-Getxo type, both plural suffixes and the imperfective suffix *-t(z)en* trigger an accent on the preceding syllable, regardless of the number of syllables in the word, as in the following examples (unaccented examples are given with a derived accent on the final syllable, as they would have if pronounced in isolation):

(13) Gernika: unaccented vs. accented
  a. sg. vs. pl.

  la|guné\   la|gú|nek

  'the friend, ABS'   'the friends, ABS'

la gune dá \
'it is the friend'

la gúnek direz \
'they are the friends'

la guneri \
'to the friend, DAT'

la gúneri \
'to the friends, DAT'

gi xoná \
'the man, ABS'

gi xónak \
'the men, ABS'

gi xonarí \
'to the man, DAT'

gi xónari \
'to the men, DAT'

txa kurré \
'the dog, ABS'

txa kúrrek \
'the dogs, ABS'

txa kurrentzát \
'for the dog'

txa kúrrentzat \
'for the dogs'

a larguné \
'the widow, ABS'

a largúnek \
'the widows, ABS'

a beratzá \
'wealthy, ABSsg'

a berátzak \
'wealthy, ABSpl'

b. perfective vs. imperfective

e san-déu \
'has said'

e sáten-deu \
'says'

e| torri-dé \
'has arrived'

e| tór| tzen-da
'arrives'

kon| pondu-déu \
'has fixed'

kon |pón|tzen-deu
'fixes'

or |ganixeu-déu \
'has organized'

or |ganixá| ten-deu
'organizes'

Clearly, this coincidence on which grammatical categories belong to the marked and unmarked accentual classes cannot be explained in any other way but by common origin. We can note that in the Gernika-Getxo system there is a direct relation between the position of the accent and morphological structure. Both plural suffixes and the imperfective suffix trigger an accent on the preceding syllable. It seems reasonable to assume that originally the accent may have marked the internal boundary of a clitic group (Hualde 1993).

In Beasain (and many other dialects), on the other hand, the connection between morphological structure and accentual markedness is considerably less transparent. Under the assumption that this system derives historically from a system like that of Gernika-Getxo, we must explain (a) why marked suffixes, such as the plural suffixes, trigger initial accent and (b) why this does not happen in words of four or more syllables.[9]

I believe that we have a historical explanation for both facts if we assume that, at some historical point, these dialects underwent the shift illustrated above for Markina in (5). Comparing the data in (5) and (12), it is evident that in dialects like Beasain the singular/plural accentual contrast has been preserved only in those cases where the retraction of the lexical accent one syllable to the left had placed it on the initial syllable of the word. This accounts for the fact that in Beasain (and all other [+2] dialects with a singular/plural accentual contrast) this contrast is made with trisyllabic but not with longer words. What appears as a synchronically anomalous fact, the different accentual behavior of "short" and "long" plurals, has a straightforward explanation under the hypothesis I am advancing. What remains to be explained is the loss of the distinction between unaccented words and words with lexical accent on the second or any other non-initial syllable. All these kinds of words have been grouped in the unmarked [+2] accentual class in dialects of the Beasain type. A possibility is that at this point a reinterpretation of surface pitch patterns like the one we have postulated for Bilbao took place:

(14) From Gernika-Getxo to Markina to Beasain
     accent retract.   accent to rise

la guné	>	la gú ne	>	lagúne [+2] 'the friend'
la gúnek	>	lá gunek	>	lágunek [+1] 'the friends'
a larguné	>	a largú ne	>	alárgune [+2] 'the widow'
a largúnek	>	a lár gunek	>	alárgunek [+2] 'the widows'

The evolution may have been somewhat more complicated, though, since we also find varieties, which appear to represent an intermediate stage in this path of development.

6. The acute/grave distinction in Mallabia as an intermediate stage

It appears that an intermediate stage in this evolution is found in the variety of Mallabia, just south of Markina. In his description of his native dialect of Mallabia, Mugarza (1999) distinguishes two types of accent: a rapidly falling accent, which he signals with an acute accent mark, as in *frutérue* 'the fruit bowl', and a slowly falling accent, marked with a grave accent mark, as in *frutèrue* 'the fruit seller' (see figures 8 and 9, where these words appear followed by the copula *da* 'is').

An examination of Mugarza's vocabulary list for Mallabia, which includes over 4000 words, plus the examples of inflected words he gives in other sections of his work, reveals that the distribution of both accents is severely constrained: The acute accent is restricted to one of the two first syllables of the word, and the grave accent to only the second syllable; that is, there are three accentual classes:

(15) Accentual classes in Mallabia

1. Words with initial acute accent; e.g.: *léngosue* 'the cousin', *dómekie* 'the Sunday'
2. Words with postinitial acute accent; e.g.: *dinámittie* 'the dynamite', *korápillue* 'the knot'
3. Words with postinitial grave accent; e.g.: *lagùne* 'the friend', *kontùlarixe* 'the story-teller'. The vast majority of all words fall into this group.

The acute/grave distinction that Mugarza (1999) makes for Mallabia is transparently related to the accented/unaccented distinction of northern Bizkaian. Almost all the words that Mugarza notes with an acute accent correspond to lexically accented words in northern Bizkaian, whereas his grave-accent words correspond to lexically unaccented words.

I have been able to examine data from two Mallabia speakers instrumentally.[10] Whereas Mugarza's 'acute' and 'grave' accent characterization appears to be essentially correct for words in final position, in longer phrases, what is apparent is that words with an acute accent downstep a following accent in the same phrase and words with a grave accent do not. This is shown in figures 6, *lagùnan alàbie da* 'it is the friend's (sg) daughter' and 7, *lagúnen alàbie da* 'it is the friends' (pl) daughter'. We can take this as evidence that grave-accent words are actually lexically unaccented, since they fail to downstep following accents.

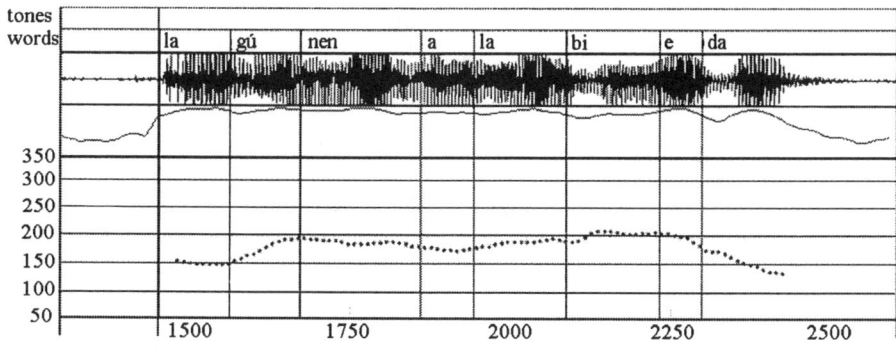

Fig. 6. Mallabia   lagùnan   alàbie   da
                              friend.GENsg   daugther   is
                              'It is the friend's (sg) daughter'

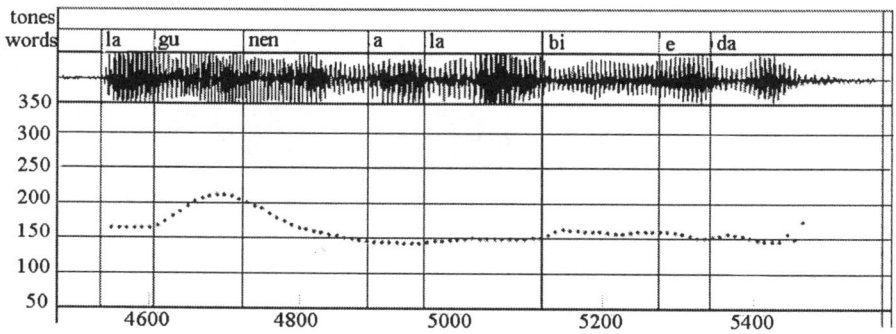

Fig. 7. Mallabia   lagúnen   alàbie   da
                              friend.GENpl   daughter   is
                              'It is the friends' (pl) daughter'

What appears to have happened in Mallabia is that the peak of derived phrase-final accents has been demoted in perception with respect to the phrase-initial H-, which in this dialect tends to occur towards the end of the second syllable or the beginning of the third syllable so that in phrase-final lexically unaccented words the accent is perceived on the second syllable by native speakers. Both H tones may fuse in short phrases.

This development can be schematized as in (16):

(16) Mallabia: diachronic development
H- H* > H* H (=grave accent)
Example:
'it is the fruitseller'

```
fru te ru e dá      >    fru te ru é da     >    fru tè ru e da
 |  |      | \            |  |  |  |              |   |  |  |
%L H-    H* L            %L H- H* L              %L H* H    L%
```

In (16), the first step represents the contour found nowadays in Gernika, the second step corresponds to Markina and the third and final step to Mallabia. An F0 tracing for this example produced by a Mallabia speaker is given in figure 8 and can be compared with the F0 contour for the minimally contrasting *frutérue da* 'it is the fruit-bowl' in figure 9.

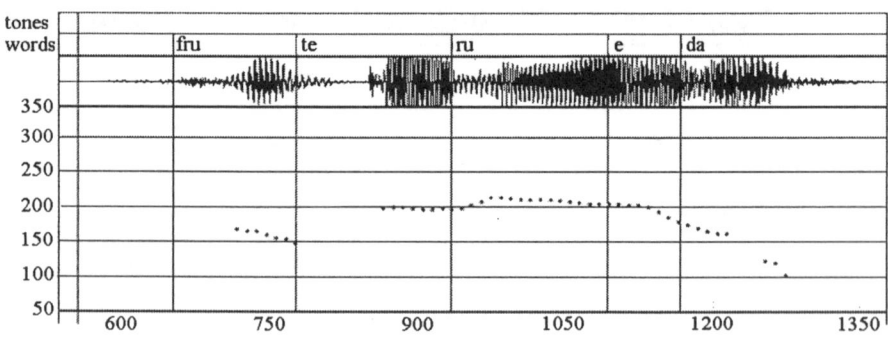

Fig.8 Mallabia *frutèrue   da*
                  fruit-seller is
                  'It is the fruit-seller'

It is easy to see how this system could further develop into a system with a simpler initial/postinitial accent contrast by loss of the distinction between the acute and the grave accent and interpretation of phrasal patterns as word-level properties. In fact, in some neighboring areas we do find systems with this simpler distinction, where most words have postinitial accent but there is a class of exceptional words with initial accent, as we have described for

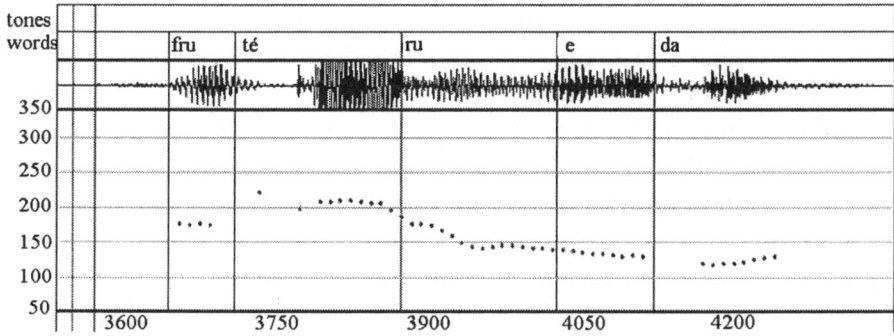

Fig. 9 Mallabia frutérue da
               fruit-bowl is
               'It is the fruit-bowl'

Beasain. Mallabia can be taken to show an intermediate stage in this evolution from unmarked phrase-final to unmarked postinitial accent where the fundamental distinction between lexically accented and unaccented words is still preserved.

7. Conclusion

In this paper we have considered the historical evolutions relating the diverse prosodic systems presently found in the western Basque area. I have made the claim that the most conservative situation is that nowadays represented by the Gernika-Getxo pitch-accent system. This system shows prosodic features, which are very much unlike those of Spanish. In particular the mapping between pitch-events and accentual prominence is rather different. Although some of the changes that we have considered appear to be internally motivated, some other changes have produced a convergence with the prosodic system of Spanish and can be attributed to language contact.

We noted that whereas a non-final abrupt tonal rise from a low point at the beginning of the syllable is typically associated with the stressed syllable in Spanish, in the northern Bizkaian pitch-accent systems a non-accentual, predictable, rise takes place on the second syllable of a prosodic unit.

In a situation of widespread bilingualism with Spanish as the majority language, it is to be expected that the difference between the two prosodic systems will tend to be reduced by convergence towards the Spanish model. The Spanish model requires initial rises to coincide with accented syllables. There are two basic ways in which a system of the northern Bizkaian type can be altered to conform with this requirement: Either the initial rise can be reinterpreted as an accent, or the pitch pattern can be modified so that the rise coincides with the accented syllable (by deletion of the initial H-). As we have seen, both routes appear to have been taken in different areas. In both cases the result is that the rise now coincides with the accented syllable, as in Spanish:

(17) Diachronic realignment of rises and accents

a. Non-accentual H- reinterpreted as accent

$$\underline{la\ |gu\ nan\ tza\ ko\ á\ \searrow}\quad >\quad \underline{la|\ gú|nan\ tza\ ko\ a}$$

(Gernika-Getxo)　　　　　　(Bilbao)

b. Elimination of non-accentual H-

$$\underline{la\ |\ gu\ nan\ tza\ kó|\ a}\quad >\quad \underline{la\ gu\ nan\ tza\ |kó|\ a}$$

(Markina)　　　　　　(Antzuola)

The existence of accentual systems like that used in Mallabia shows that the one-step evolution in (17a) is not the only possible source for [+2] as the unmarked pattern. Rather, in some areas at least, the evolution appears to have had intermediate stages. I believe that the facts reported in this paper and the diachronic hypotheses that have been put forward are of some interest for our understanding of the nature of accent and accentual systems.

Acknowledgements

For comments, I want to thank Gorka Elordieta, Haike Jacobs and Dan Silverman.

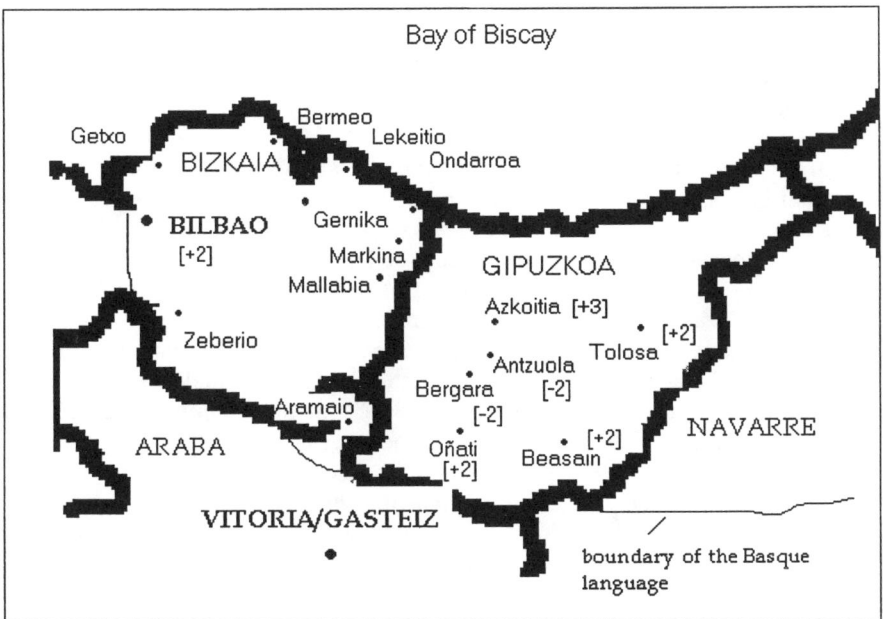

Notes

1. In the absolutive, the plural bears a final -*k*. In other nonlocal cases (ergative, dative, genitive, benefactive), singular and plural are only distinguished by their accentual properties in this dialect. In other central and western dialects (e.g. Antzuola, see section 4) the singular suffix has a vowel -*a*- and the plural a vowel -*e*- in a number of morphological cases, e.g. dative singular, -*ari*, dative plural -*eri*, genitive singular -*an*, genitive plural -*en*. This vowel distinction has been lost in many dialects, like those of the Gernika-Getxo area, that possess a rule raising /a/ to /e/ after a high vowel. In these dialects, the choice between /a/ and /e/ in the suffix is phonologically conditioned by the height of the last vowel of the stem in both singular and plural suffixes (e.g. *adarr-ari* 'to the horn', but *lagun-eri* 'to the friend'). Interestingly, in the dialect of Markina,

which possesses this vowel raising rule, the application of the rule is blocked precisely in those contexts where the distinction between /a/ and /e/ has a morphological function (unlike in Gernika-Getxo where there is no such blocking of the rule).
2. As I have shown elsewhere (Hualde 1993, 1999), the position of the accent in words containing more than one accentually marked morpheme follows from a 'first accent wins' rule.
3. This compensatory retraction did not take place in Ondarroa, where the difference between singular and plural became effectively neutralized in phrase-final position, as explained in Hualde (2000). In Mallabia, we find an intermediate situation. Retraction took place in the plural of stems ending in a vowel; eg.: *eskúek* > *éskuek* 'the hands' vs. sg. *eskùe* 'the hand', but not with stems ending in a consonant; e.g.: *gisónak* 'the men' vs. sg. *gisòna* 'the man', including *i*-final stems, where an epenthetic prepalatal fricative *-x-* is inserted before the suffix; e.g.: *mèndi* 'mountain', *mendìxe* 'the mountain', *mendíxek* 'the mountains' (for the grave accent marks see section 6).
4. I take the text for this example from Sosa 1999, where renditions of this utterance in a number of Spanish dialects are considered.
5. The same development has taken place in Arratia and Zeberio, in southern Bizkaia (for the accentual patterns of these varieties see Hualde 1999 and for experimental evidence demonstrating the lack of phrase-initial rise in Southern Bizkaian see Hualde, Elordieta, Gaminde and Smiljanić 2000). A difference between the two systems is pointed out in fn. 7.
6. The exact location of the valley preceding the accentual peak in Antzuola remains to be determined. If it turns out that, as in Spanish, the valley is precisely aligned at the beginning of the accented syllable, a more adequate ToBI notation would require a L at this location.
7. In the experiment reported in Hualde, Elordieta, Gaminde and Smiljanić (2000), the speakers from Bergara, near Antzuola, did not show any evidence for a contrast between accented and unaccented words, whereas all speakers from the Southern Bizkaian area did. Both dialects, Bergara and Southern Bizkaian, lack the phrase-initial rise that is typical of the Northern Bizkaian dialect.
8. Nevertheless some accented forms in Gernika-Getxo have unmarked cognates in Beasain and other Gipuzkoan varieties. This is the case, for instance, with the ablative singular. That is, all accentually exceptional morphological categories in dialects of the Beasain type are also exceptional in Gernika-Getxo, but the reverse implication does not always hold.
9. As for exceptional stems, here too we find a great deal of agreement throughout the whole area regarding which specific items have marked accentuation. Thus, words like *óllar* 'rooster', *léku* 'place', *béste* 'other', *léengusu* 'cousin', etc. which have marked initial accent in Beasain (both in singular and plural, e.g. *óllarra* 'the rooster', *óllarrak* 'the roosters') are also lexically accented in Gernika-Getxo.
10. For which I want to thank Pello Mugarza.

References

Arvaniti, Amalia, D. Robert Ladd and Ineke Mennen
    1998   Stability of tonal alignment: The case of Greek prenuclear accents. *Journal of Phonetics* 26: 3-25.

Botinis, Antonis
    1998   Intonation in Greek. In: Daniel Hirst and Albert Di Cristo, eds., *Intonation in Greek: A survey of twenty languages*, 288-310. Cambridge: Cambridge Univ. Press.

Cole, Jennifer
    2000   Integrating the phonetics and phonology of tone alignment. In: Michael B. Broe and Janet B. Pierrehumbert, eds., *Papers in Laboratoy Phonology V: Acquisition and the lexicon*, 168-179. Cambrigde: Cambridge Univ. Press.

Elordieta, Gorka
    1997   Accent, tone and intonation in Lekeitio Basque. In: Fernando Martínez-Gil and Alfonso Morales-Front, eds., *Issues in the phonology and morphology of the major Iberian languages*, 1-78. Washington, DC: Georgetown Univ. Press.
    1998   Intonation in a pitch accent variety of Basque. *ASJU, International Journal of Basque Linguistics and Filology* 32: 511-569. [revised version of Elordieta 1997].

Fant, Lars
    1984   *Estructura informativa en español: Estudio sintáctico y entonativo*. Acta Universitatis Upsaliensis 34. Stockholm: Almqvist & Wiksell.

Gaminde, Iñaki
    1995   *Bizkaieraren azentu-moldeez*. Bilbao: Labayru Ikastegia.
    1998a   *Euskaldunen azentuak*. Bilbao: Labayru Ikastegia.
    1998b   Bilbo eta euskara 700 urte geroago. In: Rodríguez Bornaetxea, Fito and Imanol Esnaola Arbiza, eds., *Euskara mintzatuaren erronkak*, 103-115. Leioa: Univ. of the Basque Country.

Garrido, Juan M., Joaquim Llisterri, Carme de la Mota and Antonio Ríos
    1993   Prosodic differences in reading style: Isolated vs. contextualized sentences. *Proceedings of Eurospeech*.

Hualde, José I.
    1991   *Basque phonology*. London: Routledge.
    1993   On the historical origin of Basque accentuation. *Diachronica* 10: 13-50.
    1995a   Reconstructing the ancient Basque accentual system: Hypotheses and evidence. In: José I. Hualde, Joseba Lakarra and R.L. Trask, eds. *Towards a history of the Basque language*, 171-188. Amsterdam: Benjamins.
    1995b   Análisis del sistema acentual de Ondarroa. *Anuario del Seminario de Filología Vasca "Julio de Urquijo"* 27: 241-263.

1996 Accentuation and empty vowels in Ondarroa Basque. *Lingua* 99: 197-206.
1997 *Euskararen azentuerak*. Donostia and Bilbao: Gipuzkoako Foru Aldundia and Euskal Herriko Unibertsitatea [Univ. of the Basque Country].
1998 A gap filled: postpostinitial accent in Azkoitia Basque. *Linguistics* 36: 99-117.
1999 Basque accentuation. In: Harry van der Hulst, ed., *Word prosodic systems in the languages of Europe*, 947-993. Berlin: Mouton de Gruyter,
2000 On system-driven sound change: Accent shift in Markina Basque. *Lingua* 110: 99-129.
forthc. Intonation in Spanish and the other Ibero-Romance languages: Overview and status quaestionis. In: Caroline Wiltshire and Joaquim Camps, eds., *Romance phonology and variation: Selected papers from the 30th Linguistic Symposium on Romance Languages*.

Hualde, José I. and Xabier Bilbao
1992 *A phonological analysis of the Basque dialect of Getxo*. Donostia-San Sebastián: Diputación de Gipuzkoa (Supplements of *Anuario de Filología Vasca "Julio de Urquijo"* 29)

Hualde, José I., Gorka Elordieta and Arantzazu Elordieta
1994 *The Basque dialect of Lekeitio*. Bilbao and Donostia-San Sebastián: Universidad del País Vasco and Diputación de Gipuzkoa (Supplements *of Anuario de Filología Vasca "Julio de Urquijo"* 34).

Hualde, José I., Gorka Elordieta, Iñaki Gaminde and Rajka Smiljanić
2000 From pitch accent to stress accent in Western Basque. Presented at LabPhon 7, Nijmegen, June 2000.

Hualde, José I., Rajka Smiljanić and Jennifer Cole
1999 The accented/unaccented distinction in western Basque. Presented at Berkeley Linguistic Society 26.

Jun, Sun-Ah and Gorka Elordieta
1997 Intonational structure of Lekeitio Basque. In: Antonis Botinis, Georgios Kouroupetroglou and George Carayiannis, eds., *Intonation: Theory, models and applications. Proceedings of an ESCA Workshop*, 193-196. Athens: European Speech Communication Association.

Larramendi, Manuel de
1729 *El impossible vencido: Arte de la lengua bascongada*. Salamanca: Antonio J. Villagordo Alcaraz. [Repr., Donostia: Hordago, 1979].

Mugarza, Pello
1999 Mallabiko hiztegia. Ms., Euskal Herriko Unibertsitatea [Univ. of the Basque Country].

Navarro Tomás, Tomás
1944 *Manual de entonación española*. New York: Hispanic Institute of the United States.

Pierrehumbert, Janet
    1980   *The phonology and phonetics of English intonation.* Ph.D. dissertation, MIT.
Pierrehumbert, Janet and Mary Beckman
    1988   *Japanese tone structure.* Cambridge, Mass.: MIT Press.
Prieto, Pilar, Jan van Santen and Julia Hirschberg
    1995   Tonal alignment patterns in Spanish. *Journal of Phonetics* 23: 429-451.
Sosa, Juan M.
    1999   *La entonación del español.* Madrid: Cátedra.
Txillardegi [Alvarez Enparantza, J.L.]
    1984   *Euskal azentuaz.* Donostia: Elkar.

Swiss German vowel length through time

Astrid Kraehenmann

1. Introduction

Lengthening and shortening phenomena in Germanic have attracted a lot of attention in the past as well as in current research. In particular, recent literature on the historical development of vowel length in West Germanic has concentrated on Open Syllable Lengthening and Trisyllabic Shortening in the standard dialects of English, German, and Dutch (Bermúdez-Otero 1998; Dresher 2000; Lahiri and Dresher 1999; Lahiri and Fikkert 1999; Minkova 1982, 1985; Minkova and Stockwell 1998). While the issue of Open Syllable Lengthening is controversial and subject to ongoing debate for English, the effects of this process are obvious and straightforward for Standard Dutch and Standard German.[1] According to most handbooks on Middle Dutch, Open Syllable Lengthening was completed at the end of the Old Dutch stage, which is much earlier than in German for which it is assumed to have been active in the thirteenth and fourteenth century (e.g. Van Bree 1977; Fikkert 2000; Van Loey 1969; Prokosch 1939; Van den Toorn et al. 1997; Wright 1907). The process involved lengthening of main-stressed vowels when they occurred in open syllables. This change had different consequences for the individual language systems since it interacted with other language-specific processes, as will be shown in detail in this paper: both reanalysis of underlying stems and concomitant analogical levelling due to phonological lengthening went different ways in the different languages.

Compared to the standard dialects of German and Dutch, the effects Open Syllable Lengthening in some non-standard dialects has been disputed. Particularly the High Alemannic dialects have been claimed not to have undergone the process at all (e.g. Bermúdez-Otero 1998; Hotzenköcherle 1986).[2]

Here we will trace the historical development of two Swiss German dialects with different synchronic vowel length patterns and compare it to the developments in Standard German and Dutch. The dialects presented are Grison, spoken in the canton of Graubünden in the south-east of Switzerland, and Thurgovian, spoken in the canton of Thurgau in the north-east of Switzerland (see x-marks on map in (1)). Thurgovian is especially interesting since its synchronic data display paradigmatic alternations in the opposite direction to the two standard systems *and* Grison. For example, the Dutch pair *dag–da[:]gen* 'day/days', which is transparently alternating, compares to Thurgovian *ta[:]g–tage* with the reverse pattern.

The dialectal data are particularly useful to show that the Swiss German dialects are not a homogeneous group as is often more or less implicitly suggested, but rather that the individual dialects are systems in their own right and, therefore, react differently to changes, even if the change in question originally was the same, as we claim was the case for Open Syllable Lengthening. The differences between the dialects as well as between the dialects and the standard languages are explained in terms of both (a) the interaction of Open Syllable Lengthening with syllable-closing processes such as the Second Consonant Shift or gemination and (b) the different role of paradigmatic levelling due to different application domains of Open Syllable Lengthening.

Before detailing the historical developments in Standard Dutch, Standard German, Grison, and Thurgovian in turn, some geographical and historical background in relation to Standard German is given for the Alemannic branch, which the Swiss German dialects belong to.

2. Situating Alemannic

(1) Alemannic-speaking area

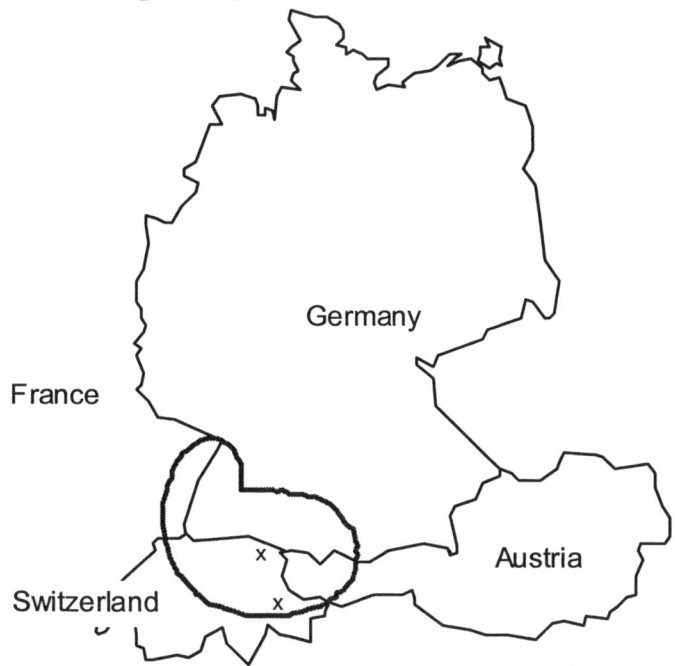

Alemannic dialects are in general spoken in the south-west of the German-speaking area. This area comprises now the German-speaking part in Switzerland, the Vorarlberg region and portions of the Tyrolese Lech valley in Austria, the area in Bavaria west of the river Lech, the main part of Baden-Württemberg in Germany, and the Alsace in France (Besch et al. (1983: 829-836); Jutz (1931: 1)). In (1) the Alemannic-speaking area is roughly circled on the map. Romance languages border on the Alemannic area in the west (French) and the south (Italian and Raeto-Romance). The Germanic dialects of Franconian, Bavarian, and Austrian adjoin to the north, north-east, and east respectively.

Alemannic people migrated into this area between the fifth and seventh century. It is widely acknowledged that around the same time the *Second Consonant Shift* or *Old High German Consonant*

Shift originated in Alemannic, setting off the Old High German period (Sonderegger 1963: 33 and references therein, among many others). It was not until the late Middle High German period, the thirteenth and fourteenth century, that the Alemannic spoken in what is now Switzerland had started developing distinct innovations in all aspects of the language system, which eventually set Swiss German Alemannic apart from its northern and eastern neighbours (Müller 1963: 72-74 and references therein). Like Bavarian, Alemannic belongs to the Upper German dialect group of the High German branch. Almost all Swiss German dialects are categorized as High Alemannic; only the dialect spoken in the canton of Wallis (southwest corner of Switzerland) is Highest Alemannic (e.g. Voegelin and Voegelin 1977, Wright 1907).

It is important to keep in mind with respect to the Swiss German dialects discussed in this paper that (a) they are, like Standard German, descendants of Old High German and therefore have undergone the Second Consonant Shift, and (b) Open Syllable Lengthening was a regular active process at the time as the Swiss German dialects began to go their own way.

3. Development in Dutch

In order to have a good reference point for the comparison of the three German language systems we briefly review the historical vowel length patterns of Dutch, since they are most elucidating. Of all the West Germanic languages, Dutch is the most transparent with respect to developments in vowel length. Old Dutch presumably had contrastive vowel length in open syllables. This contrast was virtually lost in the middle stage of the language, largely due to the process of regular Open Syllable Lengthening. In this section as well as in section 4 we draw substantially from earlier work done on the process of Open Syllable Lengthening by Lahiri and Dresher (1999).

3.1 Lengthening in open syllables

With respect to Open Syllable Lengthening (OSL), the focus now and in the remainder of the paper is on singular–plural pairs. Of particular interest to us are words of early Old Dutch in which the stressed initial syllable is open, as shown in (2a), and words in which the stressed initial syllable becomes open through the addition of singular and/or plural endings (2b-c).

(2)	endings	V length	singular	plural	gloss
Old Dutch					
a)	Ø – Ø	V – V	wapen	wapen	
b)	Ø – V	V – V	dag	daga	
c)	V – V	V – V	tala	tala	
Middle Dutch with OSL					
a)	Ø – Ø	V: – V:	wa:pen	wa:pen	
b)	Ø – V	V – V:	dach	da:ghe	
c)	V – V	V: – V:	ta:le	ta:le	
Modern Dutch					
a)	Ø – -s	V: – V:	wa:pen	wa:pens	'weapon'
b)	Ø – -en	V – V:	dag	da:gen	'day'
c)	Ø – -en	V: – V:	ta:l	ta:len	'language'

Considering that vowel lengthening in the middle stages of the West Germanic languages was conditional on the openness of a stressed syllable, the long vowels of the Middle Dutch forms in (2a) and (2c), as compared to the short vowels in early Old Dutch, are as expected. Also expected and predicted in (2b) are the short vowel in the closed syllable of the singular *dach* and the long vowel in the plural *da:ghe*. The trigger of vowel lengthening in Middle Dutch is synchronically transparent and specially noticeable in example (2b).

In Modern Dutch the alternating singular–plural pairs that remain are termed "exceptional" or "special" and almost all of them came from Germanic roots that belonged to the short *a*-stem noun class. This was the largest class, which had a CVC-CVCV singular-plural pattern. In the modern stage of the language, Open Syllable Lengthening is no longer a productive mechanism. In the course of time, words of type (2a) and (2c) have been reanalyzed as having underlying long vowels, e.g. /wapen/ > /waːpen/ and /tal+e/ > /taːle/.[3]

3.2 WGmc changes leading to closed syllables

At a time before West Germanic split up into its major language groups, the process of *West Germanic Gemination* closed open syllables in certain classes of words by geminating consonants: i.e. sequences of Germanic [CV.Cj] became [CVC$_1$.C$_1$(j)].[4] The fact that during the middle stage all the words affected by West Germanic Gemination retained short vowels in all descendent languages is strong additional evidence that the process of Open Syllable Lengthening indeed lengthened vowels because they were in open syllables. As an illustration the Dutch examples in (3) are given in comparison to Gothic, which was not affected by West Germanic Gemination.

(3) Short vowels before West Germanic geminates in Dutch

	V length	singular	plural	gloss
Gothic				
a)	V	*badi*	*badja*	
b)	V	*fani*	*fanja*	'silt'
Middle Dutch				
a)	V – V	*bedde*	*bedden*	
b)	V – V	*venne*	*vennen*	
Modern Dutch				
a)	V – V	*bed*	*bedden*	'bed'
b)	V – V	*ven*	*vennen*	'pool'

The vowels were short in Middle Dutch where the geminates had closed the stressed syllables and prevented Open Syllable Lengthening. In Modern Dutch the vowels are still short even though the following consonants are not geminates any longer. Geminates degeminated some time after Open Syllable Lengthening was productive in Dutch. Although the resulting consonants are not phonologically long, they are still ambisyllabic, i.e. syllable-closing. The present-day spelling of the plural forms in (3) simply reflects an older stage of the language.

4. Development in German

The situation in German was not quite as straightforward as in Dutch. Like Old Dutch, Old High German had contrastive vowel length. Late Middle High German[5] underwent an Open Syllable Lengthening process which was basically the same as in Middle Dutch, but it had different effects because there were other phonological changes that interacted with it.

4.1 Lengthening in open syllables

The visible effects of Open Syllable Lengthening (OSL) in Middle High German were the following: originally disyllabic stems with short open syllables as in (4a), regularly became long and carried this length on to Modern German. Also the vowels in (4c) were long from Middle High German onwards. Thus the words of type (4a) and (4c) behaved the same as the Dutch (2a) and (2c) examples, respectively: plural *and* singular have long vowels. While this length was derived by Open Syllable Lengthening in the middle stage of the language, it is present in the underlying form in Modern German.

(4)	endings	V length	singular	plural	gloss
Old High German					
a)	Ø – Ø	V – V	bibar	bibar(e)	
b)	Ø – V	V – V	tag	taga	
c)	V – V	V – V	meri	mere	
Middle High German with OSL					
a)	Ø – Ø	V: – V:	bi:ber	bi:ber(e)	
b)	Ø – V	V – V:	tac	ta:ge	
c)	V – V	V: – V:	me:re	me:re	
Modern German					
a)	Ø – Ø	V: – V:	bi:ber	bi:ber	'beaver'
b)	Ø – -e	V: – V:	ta:g	ta:ge	'day'
c)	Ø – -e	V: – V:	me:r	me:re	'sea'

The words of type (4b) in Modern German, however, differ from the Modern Dutch (2b) cases. Where no other earlier processes prevented Open Syllable Lengthening, i.e. where gemination and consonant doubling – two processes which will be discussed below – did not apply, there we find long vowels in both the singular and plural forms in the modern language. In particular, forms with a short–long alternation in Dutch singular–plural pairs turn out either all short, due to open syllables having been closed, or all long, due to the restructuring of underlying forms based on the plural form which was lengthened by regular Open Syllable Lengthening. Thus the synchronic data of Modern German obscure the effects of Open Syllable Lengthening much more than in Modern Dutch.

4.2 Interaction with syllable-closing processes

As a West Germanic language, like Dutch, German displays the reflexes of West Germanic Gemination: short vowels in open syllables which were closed by geminated consonants at the older stage were never subject to Open Syllable Lengthening in the middle stage. The examples given in (5) illustrate this point. The non-geminated Gothic forms are listed for comparison.

(5) Short vowels before West Germanic geminates in German

	V length	singular	plural	gloss
Gothic				
a)	V	*badi*	*badi*	
b)	V	*halja*	*haljōs*	
Middle High German				
a)	V – V	*bett(e)*	*bette*	
b)	V – V	*helle*	*helle*	
Modern German				
a)	V – V	*Bett*	*Betten*	'bed'
b)	V – V	*Hölle*	*Höllen*	'hell'

As for Modern Dutch, the standard spelling of Modern German mirrors the actual historical development, but the sounds represented by the double graphemes are no longer geminates. The double graphemes nowadays indicate that the preceding vowels are short.

In addition to West Germanic Gemination a number of other consonant doubling processes occurred before Open Syllable Lengthening was active in German.

One of these processes was the Second Consonant Shift, also called the Old High German Consonant Shift since it only affected High German. The Second Consonant Shift changed Germanic voiceless stops into geminate fricatives in intervocalic position. As can be seen in the examples in (6) below, which are mostly verbs, this change occurred after short as well as after long vowels.

(6) The Second Consonant Shift:[6]

	Germanic				Old High German		
	p	t	k	>	ff	ȝȝ	hh
V̌_	opan	ëtan	makōn	>	offan	ëȝȝan	mahhōn
	'open'	'to eat'	'to make'				
V̄_	slāpan	lātan	tēkan	>	slāffan	lāȝȝan	zeihhan
	'to sleep'	'to let'	'sign'				

Other consonant doubling specific to German involved, for example, Old High German /d/ and /m/ becoming late Middle High German /tt/ and /mm/, respectively, as the examples in (7) show.

(7) a. OHG /d/   > MHG /t/   > late MHG /tt/:
     budar   > *buter*   > *butter* 'butter'
   b. OHG /m/ before *-er* or *-el*   > late MHG /mm/:
     himil   > *himel*   > *himmel* 'sky'

A consequence of the various doubling processes mentioned in (5-7) was that the few remaining single medial consonants were all *voiced* in German. According to Lahiri and Dresher (1999: 688), this may be an explanation for why German restructured its roots in favour of the long vowels, i.e. (4b) Old High German /tag/ > Modern German /taːg/: the phonetic length generally associated with voiced consonant adjacency (see also Reis 1974) may have been reinterpreted as phonological length since there were phonologically long vowels in some plural forms.

In conjunction with the developments of the various early syllable-closing processes, this paradigmatic levelling obscures the fact that Open Syllable Lengthening has, at one point, applied systematically also in German.

5. Swiss German

In order to compare the effects of Open Syllable Lengthening in the two Swiss German dialects of Grison and Thurgovian with the two standard languages German and Dutch, we now look at the relevant patterns in the contemporary dialects. It will be shown that the length patterns of Grison are much like the ones we see in Standard German, whereas Thurgovian displays a pattern entirely different from all the other systems.

It is important to note at this point that both Swiss German dialects have at an early stage undergone West Germanic Gemination (WGmcG), the Second Consonant Shift (OHG CS), and other consonant doubling processes. These changes removed a number of contexts in which Open Syllable Lengthening would have applied at the middle stage of the dialect development. In this respect they are exactly like Standard German, that is they are on the one hand different from their West Germanic relative Dutch which did not undergo the "German" changes, and on the other hand different from their East Germanic relative Gothic which did not undergo any of these changes. The examples in (8) illustrate this point.

(8) Changes in West Germanic systems compared to Gothic

	Gothic	Dutch	German	Grison	Thurgovian
WGmcG	*badi*	*bedden*	*Bett*	*Bett*	*Bett*
OHG CS	**hitjō*	*hitte*	*Hitze*	*Hitz*	*Hitz*
	watō	*wa:ter*	*Wasser*	*Wasser*	*Wasser*
d > tt		*we:(de)r*	*Wetter*	*Wetter*	*Wetter*
m > mm		*ha:mer*	*Hammer*	*Hammer*	*Hammer*

Thus, like Gothic, Dutch shows short vowels in the first two examples, *bedden* 'bed (pl.)'[7] and *hitte* 'heat', where West Germanic Gemination applied, but not in the other three where the initial syllables remained open. German, Grison, and Thurgovian have short vowels also in *wasser* 'water', *wetter* 'weather', and *hammer* 'hammer' where various consonant doublings caused the closing of the initial syllables. While the double graphemes in Dutch and German no longer represent geminates, they still do so in the synchronic system of Modern Grison and Thurgovian.[8]

Before discussing Grison and Thurgovian in more detail in the next two sections, it is necessary first to look at the nominal declension system of Swiss German since it is quite different now from what it was in the old and middle stages. A consequence of this change in the declension system was that words, which originally belonged to the same declension class, regrouped into different ones and now have diverging singular–plural patterns.

Following Schobinger (1984: 43) and Baur (1939: 34), Swiss German has four main ways to build plural forms. These are listed with examples[9] under points (A) to (D) in (9):

(9) The four main declension classes of Swiss German

A) *Plural = Singular (no endings: [Ø– Ø])*:
- most masculine and a few neuter nouns with non-umlauting stem vowel
    Wind – Wind 'wind'   *Chind – Chind*   'child'
- masculine nouns ending in *-el* and *-er*
    Schlüssel – Schlüssel 'key'   *Cheller – Cheller* 'cellar'
- masculine and neuter nouns ending in *-i*, *-li*, *-eli*
    Kafi – Kafi   'coffee'   *Bieli – Bieli*   'axe'
- feminine nouns ending in *-e*, *-le*, *-ere* (tend to switch to C)
    Huube – Huube 'hood'   *Windle – Windle* 'diaper'

B) *Plural = Singular plus Umlaut (no endings: [Ø– Ø/U])*:
- most masculine nouns with umlautable stem vowel
    Saal – Sääl   'hall'   *Huet – Hüet* 'hat'

- very few feminine nouns
    Nacht – Nächt 'night'   *Chue – Chüe* 'cow'

C) *Plural = Singular plus -(n)e ([Ø– -(n)e]):*
- masculine nouns (mostly terms for persons and animals)
    Maa – Mane   'man'   (also: *Maa – Männer*)
- feminine nouns ending in *-ig, -igung, -et, -hait, -t, -ai, -schaft*, as almost all other feminine nouns
    Wonig – Wonige 'apartment'   *Taat – Taate* 'deed'

- feminine nouns ending in *-i, -in, -e*
    Mitti – Mittene 'middle'   *Türe – Türene* 'door'

D) *Plural = Singular plus -er plus Umlaut ([Ø– -er/U]):*
- most neuter nouns
    Blatt – Blätter 'leaf'   *Muul – Müüler* 'mouth'

The details in (9) can be summarized as follows: it appears that the gender of a noun may determine how the plural is formed. Umlaut and plural endings play a crucial role. While the plural of most masculine nouns tends to have no ending and may be both umlauted or not, feminine and neuter noun plurals tend to have the endings *-(n)e* and *-er*, respectively, and additional Umlaut is only characteristic of neuter nouns. These facts are schematically listed in the table in (10) below.

(10) Tendencies in Swiss German plural formation

	ending	Umlaut	declension class
masculine	no	no	A
		yes	B
feminine	-(n)e	no	C
neuter	-er	yes	D

5.1 Grison

Let us now direct our attention to the dialect of Grison.[10] Considering the close relatedness of Grison with German (cf. (8)), one can assume that, like Standard German, it ought to have all long vowels where Dutch has a length alternation (cf. (2b)). Exceptions to this would be those cases where the Second Consonant Shift caused consonant doubling, in which case the vowels would have to be all short.

The table in (11) shows the Grison equivalents of some of the Dutch alternating singular–plural pairs. All of these are former Germanic *a*-stems, i.e. all used to belong to the same declension class before Old High German times.

(11)

	endings	V length	singular	plural	class	gloss
Modern Dutch						
a)	∅ – -en	V – V:	pad	pa:den		
b)	∅ – -en	V – V:	hof	ho:ven		
c)	∅ – -en	V – V:	dag	da:gen		
d)	∅ – -en	V – V:	glas	gla:zen		
e)	∅ – -en	V – V:	dal	da:len		
f)	∅ – -en	V – V:	schip	sche:pen		
g)	∅ – -eren	V – V:	blad	bla:deren		
h)	∅ – -en	V – V	bed	bedden		
Grison						
a)	∅ – ∅	V: – V:	pfa:d	pfa:d	A	'path'
b)	∅ – ∅/U	V: – V:	ho:f	hö:f	B	'court yard'
c)	∅ – -(n)e	V: – V:	ta:g	ta:ge	C	'day'
d)	∅ – -er/U	V: – V:	gla:s	glä:ser	D	'glass'
e)	∅ – -er/U	V: – V:	ta:l	tä:ler	D	'valley'
f)	∅ – ∅	V – V	schiff	schiff	A	'ship'
g)	∅ – -er/U	V – V	blatt	blätter	D	'leaf'
h)	∅ – -er	V – V	bett	better	D	'bed'

What we find is indeed as similar to Standard German as expected: the disyllabic plurals in (11c-d) and (11e) have all long stressed vowels, as do the monosyllabic singular and plural forms (11a-b). The short vowels in (11f-g) are due to the Old High German doubling processes which prevented Open Syllable Lengthening, while the ones in (11h) are due to West Germanic Gemination preempting lengthening, hence the short vowels also in Dutch.

The similarity of Grison to the Standard German system is also maintained if we look at disyllabic stems such as the ones in (12) shown with the Old High German forms as the reference point: vowels in main-stressed open syllables are long, regardless of whether the Old High German stem had a short or a long vowel. This in fact is true for any word, not just for the examples given in (11) and (12).[11]

(12)

	endings	V length	singular	plural	class	gloss
Old High German						
a)	∅ – ∅	V – V	honag	honag	a	
b)	∅ – ∅	V – V	namo	namo-n	n	
c)	∅ – ∅	V – V	bira	birū-n	n	
d)	∅ – ∅	V – V	scado	scado-n	n	
e)	∅ – -a	V: – V:	tiufal	tiufala	a	
Grison, Standard German						
a)	∅ – ∅	V: – V:	ho:nig	ho:nig	A	'honey'
b)	∅ – ∅/U	V: – V:	na:me	nä:me	B	'name'
c)	∅ – ∅	V: – V:	bi:re	bi:re	C	'pear'
d)	∅ – ∅/U	V: – V:	scha:de	schä:de	B	'damage'
e)	∅ – ∅	V: – V:	tü:fel	tü:fel	A	'devil'

A short note on the Old High German declension system must be added at this point. The comments made here are crucial for understanding the development in the Thurgovian system discussed in section 5.2 below.

Germanic noun inflections arose from the conjunction of the word stem with a stem-final element – which marked declension class membership and is called the *theme* or *stem extension* – and the case endings: STEM + EXTENSION + INFLECTIONAL SUFFIX. Nouns were grouped into declension classes according to the extension they showed. In Old High German there were two major declension classes left: the *vocalic* or *strong* declension, which contained nouns whose stems originally ended in a vowel (e.g. *a-*, *ō*, *i-*, *u-*); and the *consonantal* declension, which contained nouns whose stems originally ended in a consonant (e.g. *n-* or *weak*, *r-*, *nt-*). The traditional labels for the declension classes were kept in Old High German although a number of changes made extensions difficult to recover from the surface forms. In many of the inflected forms the old theme vowels were no longer recognizable: what remained discernable as an "ending" mostly was the result of the fusion of the theme vowel with the respective case and/or number ending. Due to various reduction processes from the time of Proto-Germanic onwards, many inflectional endings merged and/or disappeared altogether, as for example for the *ō*-nouns and *a*-nouns. The consonantal declensions, however, differed in that respect because the theme consonants generally remained. For example, in the *n*-nouns, as seen in (12), the theme *n* was present in all case forms except the nominative singular where it was deleted (cf. section 5.2.1). Henceforth, themes – if present – will be attached to the stem by a hyphen as in (12) in order to stress the fact that they are different from inflectional endings.

The vowel length patterns in (12) match each other in the two language systems Grison and Standard German. Thus we can assume that the process of Open Syllable Lengthening applied in the same manner. This means that, as a consequence of Open Syllable Lengthening, restructuring of the underlying forms occurred in favour of the long variant in Grison as well.

Notice also how the words in (11) have rearranged into different declension classes (cf. (9)). These former *a*-nouns were all masculine or neuter, as they still are in the present Grison system. However, the three masculine nouns (11a-c) now belong to three different declension classes, namely classes (A-C) respectively (see column 'class' in (11)). The neuter nouns in (11d-e) and (11g) regrouped in class (D), whereas (11f) now is found in class (A). Special attention has to be drawn to the masculine noun *ta:g* in (11c) which is in a declension class predominantly used by feminine nouns: beside *ta:ge* there exists an alternative, equally frequent plural form, namely *tä:g* (class (B)), which is a prototypical masculine plural.[12]

5.2 Thurgovian

The facts about gender and the reorganization of declension classes hold for Thurgovian as they do for Grison. It is in the vowel length pattern where we see a difference, not only from Grison and Standard German but also from Dutch. The table in (13) shows the Thurgovian forms of the same list of words as in (11), again in comparison to the Dutch alternating pairs.

Except for examples (13c-d), the Thurgovian data are the same as in Grison: both singular and plural have either long vowels (13a-b) or short vowels (13f-h). While the plural of (13c) *tage* also has the variant *tä:g*, the plural of (13d) is always *gläser* with a short vowel.

(13)

	endings	V length	singular	plural	class	gloss
Modern Dutch						
a)	Ø – -en	V – V:	pad	pa:den		
b)	Ø – -en	V – V:	hof	ho:ven		
c)	Ø – -en	V – V:	dag	da:gen		
d)	Ø – -en	V – V:	glas	gla:zen		
e)	Ø – -en	V – V:	dal	da:len		
f)	Ø – -en	V – V:	schip	sche:pen		
g)	Ø – -eren	V – V:	blad	bla:deren		
h)	Ø – -en	V – V	bed	bedden		
Thurgovian						
a)	Ø – Ø	V: – V:	pfa:d	pfa:d	A	'path'
b)	Ø – Ø/U	V: – V:	ho:f	hö:f	B	'court yard'
c)	Ø – -(n)e	V: – V	ta:g	tage	C	'day'
d)	Ø – -er/U	V: – V	gla:s	gläser	D	'glass'
e)	Ø – -er/U	V: – V:	ta:l	tä:ler	D	'valley'
f)	Ø – Ø	V – V	schiff	schiff	A	'ship'
g)	Ø – -er/U	V – V	blatt	blätter	D	'leaf'
h)	Ø – -er/U	V – V	bett	better	D	'bed'

There are many more such regular long–short alternating pairs in Thurgovian. Some additional examples with this pattern are given in (14). All of these had short stem vowels and belonged to the *a*-stem nouns in Old High German times.[13]

(14) Former *a*-stem nouns with length alternation in Thurgovian

	endings	V length	singular	plural	class	gloss
Old High German						
a)	∅ – -ir/U	V – V	(h)rad	(h)redir	a	
b)	∅ – ∅	V – V	bad	bad	a	
c)	∅ – ∅	V – V	grab	grab	a	
	∅ – -ir/U	V – V		grebir		
d)	∅ – ∅	V – V	gilid	gilid	a	
Thurgovian						
a)	∅ – -er/U	V: – V	ra:d	räder	D	'wheel'
b)	∅ – -er/U	V: – V	ba:d	bäder	D	'bath'
c)	∅ – -er/U	V: – V	gra:b	gräber	D	'grave'
d)	∅ – -er	V: – V	gli:d	glider	D	'limb'

(15) Former *a*-stem nouns in Dutch, Standard German, and Grison

	Endings	V length	singular	plural	class	gloss
Modern Dutch						
a)	∅ – -eren	V – V:	rad	ra:deren		
b)	∅ – -en	V – V:	bad	ba:den		
c)	∅ – -en	V – V:	graf	gra:ven		
d)	∅ – -er	V – V:	lid	le:der		
Grison, Standard German						
a)	∅ – -er/U	V: – V:	ra:d	rä:der	D	'wheel'
b)	∅ – -er/U	V: – V:	ba:d	bä:der	D	'bath'
c)	∅ – -er/U	V: – V:	gra:b	grä:ber	D	'grave'
d)	∅ – -er	V: – V:	gli:d	gli:der	D	'limb'

In all the Thurgovian plural forms in (14) the stem vowel is short as in Old High German, while in all the singular forms it is long, which is exactly the opposite of the Dutch pattern of these words, given for comparison in (15), which are exceptional plurals as the ones in (2b) and (11). With respect to Standard German and Grison, whose forms of the same words as in (14) are also given in (15), only the plural vowels are different: in Standard German and Grison they are all long while they are all short in Thurgovian.

In contrast to Standard German and Grison, the examples in (14) as well as (13c-d) so far suggest that their *underlying* vowel quantity has not changed from what it used to be in Old High German. If it is really true that some type of words systematically have retained the old vowel length, what is the common denominator which makes this group different from the others which *did* change? Let us next consider some additional data.

(16)

	endings	V length	singular	plural	class	gloss
Old High German						
	disyllabic stems					
a)	∅ – ∅	V – V	honag	honag	a	
b)	∅ – ∅	V – V	namo	namo-n	n	
	∅ – ∅	V – V	bira	birū-n	n	
	∅ – ∅	V – V	scado	scado-n	n	
c)	∅ – -a	V: – V:	tiufal	tiufala	a	
	monosyllabic stems					
d)	∅ – ∅	V: – V:	wīb	wīb	a	
e)	∅ – ∅	V: – V:	mūl-a	mūl-ā	ō	
f)	∅ – -i	V – V	sun-u	suni	u	
Thurgovian						
	disyllabic stems					
a)	∅ – ∅	V – V	honig	honig	A	'honey'
b)	∅ – ∅/U	V – V	name	näme	B	'name'
	∅ – ∅	V – V	bire	bire	A	'pear'
	∅ – ∅/U	V – V	schade	schäde	B	'damage'
c)	∅ – ∅	V: – V:	tü:fel	tü:fel	A	'devil'
	monosyllabic stems					
d)	∅ – -er	V: – V:	wi:b	wi:ber	D	'wife'
e)	∅ – -er/U	V: – V:	mu:l	mü:ler	D	'mouth'
f)	∅ – ∅/U	V: – V:	so:(n)	sö:(n)	B	'son'

If we consider disyllabic and monosyllabic stems from different old declension classes as in (16), the picture becomes more complicated, but it reveals two facts: a) if there was a change in vowel length, it systematically went from short to long, never from long to short; and b) endings play a crucial role. In other words, it is important what the status of an ending was in Old High German (i.e. stem extension or suffix), whether there was an ending at all, and – if there was one – whether it still is present in Thurgovian.

Disregarding the last two examples in (16) for the moment, the following can be said: in stems which were disyllabic in Old High German and remained disyllabic, the Old High German length is retained in Thurgovian: short remains short in (16a-b), long remains long in (16c). Example (16d) illustrates that Old High German long vowels of monosyllabic stems remained long in Thurgovian regardless of whether the forms are mono- or disyllabic now. Thus the disyllabic plural form *wi:ber* also has a long vowel, as opposed to the plural forms of (13c) *tage* and (13d) *gläser* which originate from former *short* vowels.

What makes (16e-f) different from the other cases is the way the singular (and plural) was formed in Old High German: here we had a stem plus an extension or theme vowel: /mūl-a + Ø/; /sun-u + Ø/, /sun-u + i/. The effect of these extensions was that they created an open stem syllable by causing syllabification of the stem-final consonant in the onset of a following syllable. The reflex of this in Thurgovian is that formerly short vowels are now long in forms such as (16f) *so:n–sö:n*. In contrast, (16e) *mu:l–mü:ler* was long to begin with. Diachronically then the data in (14) and (16) tell us that the underlying vowel quantity only changed for the (16f) subset of Old High German short vowels.

However, if we take into consideration again our initial data in (13), we notice that there are two other instances where short Old High German vowels have long reflexes in Thurgovian: in monosyllables which are closed by a single consonant and in the case of (13e) *ta:l–tä:ler* 'valley'.

The vowels in monosyllables ending in a single consonant are traditionally explained by a process termed *Leichtschlussdehnung* (also called *hochalemannische Dehnung* 'High Alemannic Lengthening' by Bohnenberger (1953: 155), see also endnote (2)), which basically is a synchronic lengthening process that makes monosyllables heavier. This treatment, however, has at least one serious drawback, namely that it cannot explain why (13e) type of words patterns systematically different from (13c-d).

In search for an explanation to the *ta:l–tä:ler* case, let us consider the additional examples in (17) which show the same vowel length pattern. (13e) is repeated as (17g).

(17)

	endings	V length	singular	plural	class	gloss
Old High German (all monosyllabic *stems*)						
a)	Ø – Ø	V – V	ban-a	ban-ā	ō	
b)	Ø – Ø	V – V	zal-a	zal-ā	ō	
c)	Ø – Ø	V – V	wal-a	wal-ā	ō	
d)	Ø – Ø	V – V	scar-a	scar-ā	ō	
e)	Ø – Ø	V – V	spor	spor	a	
f)	Ø – Ø	V – V	spil	spil	a	
g)	Ø – -ir/U	V – V	tal	telir	a	
Thurgovian						
a)	Ø – -e	V: – V:	ba:n	ba:ne	C	'course'
b)	Ø – -e	V: – V:	za:l	za:le	C	'number'
c)	Ø – -e	V: – V:	wa:l	wa:le	C	'choice'
d)	Ø – -e	V: – V:	scha:r	scha:re	C	'troop'
e)	Ø – -e	V: – V:	spu:r	spu:re	C	'track(s)'
f)	Ø – -er	V: – V:	spi:l	spi:ler	D	'game'
g)	Ø – -er/U	V: – V:	ta:l	tä:ler	D	'valley'

Note that all the stems of the examples are monosyllabic and build their plural with a vowel-initial suffix. In the Old High German plural forms of (17a-d) the final *-ā* is a combination of the stem extension and the plural suffix. What these examples all have in common is that the stems end in a sonorant consonant.[14] Additionally, the formerly short vowels of monosyllabic stems now are long throughout the para-digm. The most obvious explanation for the lengthening in (17) is that the stem-final sonorant consonant of these words must have played a role in determining the length of the preceding vowel. But what was this role?

Let us consider the possibilities to explain the diachronic changes in Thurgovian:

Hypothesis 1: There was no Open Syllable Lengthening at an older stage in Thurgovian. Under this hypothesis, all those cases need another explanation where we actually do find short Old High

German vowels having a long correspondence in Thurgovian. The traditional *Leichtschlussdehnung* could account for the lengthening in monosyllables. Lengthening in disyllables, however, is more complex: why do we have long vowels in the plural forms in (17) when they are short in forms such as in (14)? It cannot be morphologically conditioned since the examples intersect with respect to declension class as well as gender. In addition, the set of words, which was affected, is far too systematic for lengthening to possibly have been accidental.

Hypothesis 2: Open Syllable Lengthening occurred only before sonorant consonants. This proposal could account for the forms in (17). Yet, it would falsely predict long vowels in words such as (16a) **ho:nig*, (16b) **na:me–*nä:me*, and **bi:re*.

Hypothesis 3: Regular Open Syllable Lengthening occurred with subsequent reanalysis. This proposal looks the most promising but requires a number of additional assumptions. It must be possible to explain why Thurgovian does not look like Grison, i.e., why it has retained short vowels in most open syllables such as in (13d) *gläser* and only applied lengthening in a minority of cases such as in (13e) *tä:ler*. It is clear that the lengthening cannot have applied as in Grison and Standard German. As will be shown in detail below, by restricting lengthening to affect only derived environments, exactly the right type of words are targeted. A reinterpretation of Open Syllable Lengthening to lengthening before sonorant consonants in those cases where an alternation existed in the paradigm made it possible to split off the *ta:l* type from the *gla:s* type. The former type then restructured the underlying form with a long vowel.

The development as we propose it in the third hypothesis above can best be demonstrated by going through the stages from Old High German to Thurgovian with the relevant examples step by step.

5.2.1 The Old High German stage

The former *a*-stems *tal*, *glas*, and *pfad* as well as the *u*-stem *sunu* and the weak stem *namo* will serve as illustration in (18-21). In the tables we give the assumed underlying forms with the corresponding attested surface forms and explain in the text how these surface forms are obtained.

(18) Old High German

	singular		plural		gloss
a)	/tal+∅/	[tal]	/tal+ir/	[tɛlir]	'valley'
b)	/sun-u+∅/	[sunu]	/sun-u+i/	[suni]	'son'
c)	/namo-n+∅/	[namo]	/namo-n+∅/	[namon]	'name'
d)	/glas+∅/	[glas]	/glas+ir/	[glɛsir]	'glass'
e)	/pfad+∅/	[pfad]	/pfad+a/ /pfad+∅/	[pfada] [pfad]	'path'

In (18) the neuter noun *tal* had the plural form *telir* (beside the regular *tal*) from late Old High German on. The final *-ir* marked the plural of the *-iz/-az*-nouns and caused Umlaut on the stem vowel. This way of building the plural was extended to quite a few more former neuter *a*-stem nouns (cf. also endnote (13)).

The masculine *u*-stem noun *sunu* had vocalic endings in both the singular and the plural: in the singular it was the stem extension *-u*, in the plural it was the suffix *-i* which ended up next to the stem. In the latter case the stem extension *-u* prevented Umlaut before it was deleted.

For the masculine weak or *n*-stem *namo* we assume an underlying form with stem-final *n* for several reasons. First, the Old High German weak declension is the only class in which *n* occurred in virtually all case markings, except the nominative singular. Second, some of the weak nouns have reinstated the final *n*, as for example in *balken* 'beam (sg.)'. This levelling of the Middle High German *-n* of the oblique cases into the nominative happened only with *n*-stems. Finally, with exactly this type of noun Thurgovian and other Swiss German dialects exhibit regular "linking n" in phrasal contexts if the adjacent word starts in a vowel (e.g. *ä blueme-n-aaluegä* 'to look at a flower').[15] In addition, the plurals of the feminine nouns of this class all end in *-ne*. The conclusion, therefore, seems very reasonable to assume that the *n* is underlying and is deleted only in the nominative singular. The crucial point here is that the plural *namon* then differs from all the others in (18) in being non-derived.

The word *glas* is equivalent to *tal*, the only, very important difference being that the stem ends in an obstruent as opposed to a sonorant consonant. The plural form with Umlaut and *-ir* existed from early on beside the regular *glas*.

Like a number of other masculine *a*-stems, the word *pfad* alternatively was also neuter in Old High German. Consequently two plural forms existed: the masculine *pfada* and the neuter *pfad*. We keep both listed here because Thurgovian has kept the two possibilities to this day.

5.2.2 The Middle German stage

As illustrated in (19), two important developments happened in the middle stage: there were no longer any stem extensions – hence the morphological form was STEM + SUFFIX – and regular Open Syllable Lengthening started.

(19) Middle German

	singular		plural		gloss
a)	/tal+∅/	[tal]	/tal+ər/	[tɛ:lər]	'valley'
b)	/sun+∅/	[sun]	/sun+ə/	[sy:nə]	'son'
c)	/namən+∅/	[namə]	/namen+∅/	[namən]	'name'
d)	/glas+∅/	[glas]	/glas+ər/	[glɛ:sər]	'glass'
e)	/pfad+∅/	[pfad]	/pfad+ə/ /pfad+∅/	[pfa:də] [pfad]	'path'

The application of Open Syllable Lengthening, however, must have been different in High German and in the precursor of Thurgovian, which we call Middle German here, otherwise we would also expect long vowels in the singular and plural of (19c) *name*. If we assume that Open Syllable Lengthening initially was a lexical rule which only applied to derived environments, the forms given in (19) fall into place: lengthening occurs in the disyllabic plural forms of *tal*, *sun*, *glas*, and *pfad*, but not in *name*. As for the other changes, *tal* and *glas* build their plural by the suffix *-er* plus Umlaut, *sun* by the suffix *-e* plus Umlaut (like former *i*-stems), and *pfad* has one variant plural with the suffix *-e* but without Umlaut. For the weak noun *name* nothing has changed: a morphological rule removes the stem-final *n* in the singular.

Since the present-day forms of *tal* and the others given in (17) clearly have long stem vowels throughout their paradigms, which suggests that their underlying forms were restructured, the Middle German singular forms must have undergone a further change. Possibly, at a late stage, the process of Open Syllable Lengthening was reanalyzed as lengthening before a sonorant consonant in those cases where a length alternation existed, i.e. in the *tal* and *sun* cases in Middle German. This is reminiscent of the reinterpretation in Standard German where lengthening came to occur before voiced consonants. In fact, the reinterpretation in late Middle German could have been just that, namely lengthening before voiced consonants, because by this time Alemannic had switched from a voice distinction to a quantity distinction within the obstruents, and the only voiced consonants left were the sonorants (Kraehenmann 2001).[16] The difference between *tal* and *glas* then is that the stem-final consonant in the latter is not voiced or not sonorant and therefore the lengthening did not apply. Lengthening did not affect *name* because it still only occurred in derived environments.

Thus at a late stage the Middle German forms must have been as given in (20) below. The lengthening in the singular form of *tal* and *sun* was in effect a stem levelling. It furnished the basis for the restructuring of /tal/ to /ta:l/ and /sun/ to /su:n/ at the modern stage. With the exception of the monosyllabic forms *glas* and *pfad*, the vowel quantity of the surface forms in (20) is the same as in Modern Thurgovian. Up until now monosyllables such as *glas* and *pfad* obviously were perfectly acceptable prosodic words.

(20) Late Middle German

	singular		plural		gloss
a)	/tal+∅/	[ta:l]	/tal+ər/	[tɛ:lər]	'valley'
b)	/sun+∅/	[su:n]	/sun+ə/	[sy:nə]	'son'
c)	/namən+∅/	[namə]	/namən+∅/	[namən]	'name'
d)	/glas+∅/	[glas]	/glas+ər/	[glɛsər]	'glass'
e)	/pfad+∅/	[pfad]	/pfad+ə/ /pfad+∅/	[pfadə] [pfad]	'path'

5.2.3 The modern stage

At this stage, Open Syllable Lengthening is no longer an active process. Recall from (13), (14), and (17) that monosyllables closed by a single consonant have long vowels in Modern Thurgovian with no exception, regardless of the vowel quantity in Old High German. In the present system, there obviously is a condition for minimal words to be at least bimoraic.

(21) Thurgovian

	singular		plural		gloss
a)	/ta:l+∅/	[ta:l]	/ta:l+ər/	[tɛ:lər]	'valley'
b)	/so:n+∅/	[so:n]	/so:n+U/	[sø:n]	'son'
c)	/namən+∅/	[namə]	/namən+∅/	[nɛmə]	'name'
d)	/glas+∅/	[gla:s]	/glas+ər/	[glɛsər]	'glass'
e)	/pfad+∅/	[pfa:d]	/pfad+ə/ /pfad+∅/	[pfadə] [pfa:d]	'path'

While a form like /namən/ is bimoraic without any additions, forms such as /glas/ and /pfad/ in (21) need prosodic enhancement, which suggests that the final consonants do not count for prosodic word status, i.e. are extrametrical. Considering that Open Syllable Lengthening was the source of monosyllabic lengthening for the *ta:l* and *su:n* type of cases in Middle German, it is conceivable that it served as model for the general lengthening in monosyllables as well, particularly if one takes into account the nature of the original Open Syllable Lengthening process. In essence, it was a prosodic lengthening: it lengthened a vowel in a stressed open syllable, i.e. a vowel in a particular prosodic position. The effect was that the main stressed syllable received a second mora and became heavy or bimoraic.

Thus the early Thurgovian system already had the means to cause prosodic lengthening, it only had to change its area of application. Having reinterpreted Open Syllable Lengthening to apply to subminimal prosodic words then has as its logical consequence that word forms which meet the minimal word condition receive no lengthening any longer, which is exactly what we find in Thurgovian today: in (21) the stem vowels of the plural *gläser* and the plural variant *pfade* are short while they were long in Middle German (cf. (20)). Therefore we can say that vowel lengthening became functionally different, no longer occurring in open syllables, but serving as a mechanism to fix subminimal prosodic structure.

The fact that the plural forms of (13e) *tä:ler* and the examples given in (17) are long is testimony to Open Syllable Lengthening in Middle German, which was reanalyzed in late Middle German as lengthening before sonorants, as proposed in (20). Otherwise it is not clear why *tä:ler* is still long. There is no other source of lengthening possible since we also have stems ending in sonorant consonants which have *not* undergone restructuring (e.g. *name*). The vowels in the plurals of forms like (13c) *tage* and (13d) *gläser* are short because the stem-final consonants are not sonorant and did not trigger reinterpretation of Open Syllable Lengthening and subsequent stem levelling in Middle German. Considering the development in these two types, the prediction is that we never find restructuring of Old High German short to Thurgovian long vowels before obstruents; or wording it positively: where restructuring of vowel length occurs the vowel is always followed by a sonorant consonant. To our knowledge, this prediction is borne out by the present-day data.

Under this account then, the contemporary long vowels of monosyllabic words ending in a single consonant have three different sources: some are underlyingly long and have been long throughout their development (e.g. *wi:b* 'wife'); some are underlyingly long but were short in Old High German, lengthened in the plural (OSL) in the middle stage, and later levelled the stems (e.g. *so:n* 'son', *ta:l* 'valley'); some are underlyingly short, get synchronically lengthened due to a minimal word requirement, and are the only ones displaying a long–short singular–plural alternation (e.g. *ta:g* 'day', *gla:s* 'glass').

6. Conclusion

The question remains why the two High Alemannic dialects of Grison and Thurgovian are so different and why Grison and Standard German are so much the same with respect to their vowel length developments. Open Syllable Lengthening cannot have been a phenomenon that originated in one area and then just simply spread, since Thurgovian geographically sits between Grison and the area where Standard German is spoken. Moreover, Grison is considered "*Ostschweizerdeutsch*" 'East Swiss German' (Hotzenköcherle (1986: 74) first and foremost, closely related to the St.Gall dialect of the Rhine valley, which in turn connects via the main St.Gall dialect to Thurgovian. It is commonly acknowledged that the High Alemannic dialects are very conservative and become more conservative the higher up the Alps one goes (Besch et al. 1983: 832). But if Grison actually does reflect an older linguistic stage than Thurgovian, why did Thurgovian keep much more of the underlying vowel quantities and not Grison? While the closeness of the Thurgau to the town of St.Gall, at a time the prescriptive center of the Alemannic speech community, may certainly have had an influence on the level of language preservation, this simply cannot be the whole story.

The fact that the Grison vowel length development resembles much more the Standard German system than that of its Alemannic relative is striking, but it could be explained by how Open Syllable Lengthening applied originally: in Middle High German and in the precursor of Grison it applied to all open main-stressed syllables, probably as a post-lexical rule, while in Middle German, the stage before Modern Thurgovian, only derived open syllables were targeted by a lexical rule of lengthening. Thus the domain of application of Open Syllable Lengthening played a crucial role. Why Open Syllable Lengthening should have had a different status in Thurgovian as opposed to in Grison and Standard German is difficult to answer at this point, but it is a question worth pursuing in future research.

Acknowledgements

This work was supported in part by the *Sonderforschungsbereich* 471 funded by the *Deutsche Forschungsgemeinschaft*. Parts of this paper have been presented in the talk 'Open Syllable Lengthening in High German dialects' at the fourteenth ICHL, August 1999, in Vancouver, Canada. Thanks go especially to Aditi Lahiri for extensive discussions on the topic, to Elan B. Dresher, Paula Fikkert, Jennifer Fitzpatrick, Mirco Ghini, Frans Plank, Michael Redford, and Henning Reetz for valuable comments and suggestions for improvement on earlier drafts, to the commenting audience members at the fourteenth ICHL, and to an anonymous reviewer. All errors are my own.

Notes

1. By Standard German we mean the northern pronunciation of the *Hochsprache*.
2. Of the two most frequently quoted standard references on this subject, only Hotzenköcherle (1986: 319) explicitly says that Open Syllable Lengthening did not apply ("Ausbleiben der nhd. Dehnung") in the Swiss German dialects. Keller (1961: 32-33, 43) mentions that Middle High German short vowels have mostly remained short in open syllables but have become long in monosyllables closed by a lenis consonant. He does not, however, relate these developments to the regular Middle High German lengthening in any way.
3. Gussenhoven (1998) presents an account in which he claims that vowel length is predictable in Modern Dutch. Nevertheless, he has to distinguish vowels by a feature like [tense]/[lax].
4. According to the standard view (e.g. Braune 1989), /j, w, r, l, n, (m)/ caused gemination of the preceding consonant, but the strongest trigger by far was /j/.
5. By Middle and Old High German we mean the East Franconian dialects, in particular the Rhine-Franconian dialect taken as the standard in most German grammars.

6. Old High German spelling correspondences: <ë> = [ɛ]; <ȝȝ> = [ss]; <hh> = [xx]; bar diacritic = long vowel.
7. The plural form was chosen here because the singular spelling *bed* 'bed' does not reflect the fact that gemination indeed had occurred. Recall that the double graphemes do no longer refer to long consonants in the modern system.
8. For a discussion on the historical development of the geminate–singleton opposition see Kraehenmann (2001) and Kraehenmann and Lahiri (1999).
9. Spellings with double vowel graphemes indicate long vowels.
10. All Grison data come from the town of Chur which is considered the center of the High Alemannic speech community in the canton of Grison (Hotzenköcherle 1986: 73).
11. See also Meinherz (1920: 25), according to whom vocalic length stands for old length as in *hūs* 'house' and for old lengthened shortness as in *rēge* 'rain'.
12. The class (C) plural is more likely to denote the abstract notion of time, whereas the class (B) plural is often used to refer to the measurable and experienced unit of time. In most cases, however, they can be used interchangeably.
13. The fact that these forms in (14) as well as (13d) and (13g) now have an *-er* ending and Umlaut has its roots in Old High German. According to Wright (1907: 171, 190) and Braune (1989: 185-186) in Old High German a few neuter *a*-stem nouns switched to the *-iz/-az*-declension in the plural, resulting in forms such as *blat–bletir* beside the regular *blat–blat*. This switching of declension class continued through Middle High German into modern times so that nowadays about one hundred nouns build the plural in *-er* plus Umlaut (< *-ir*).
14. One clear difference from *ta:l–tä:ler* is the lack of Umlaut in the plurals of (17a-e). This, however, is due to the fact that all these nouns are feminine which typically have no Umlaut (cf. (9C) and (10)). *Ta:l* and (17f) *spiil* are neuter nouns, have the characteristic *-er* ending, and Umlaut where possible.
15. "Linking n" does not occur before a consonant-initial word.
16. Note that for this reason no *Auslautverhärtung* as in Standard German occurred in Middle German, therefore the form *pfad* and not *pfat* is given. As is evident from this example, in order not to complicate things unnecessarily, I have used the symbols for voiced and voiceless sounds to stand for short and long sounds respectively in Alemannic. Since it is the vowels which we are interested in, this shorthand seemed reasonable.

References

Baur, Arthur
1939   *Praktische Sprachlehre des Schweizerdeutschen.* Zürich: Rigi-Verlag.
Bermúdez-Otero, Ricardo
1998   Prosodic optimization: the Middle English length adjustment. *English Language and Linguistics* 2. 169-197.
Besch, Werner, Ulrich Knoop, Wolfgang Putschke und Herbert E. Wiegand (eds.)
1983   *Dialektologie: Ein Handbuch zur deutschen und allgemeinen Dialektforschung.* Band 2. Berlin: Walter de Gruyter.
Bohnenberger, Karl
1953   *Die alemannische Mundart: Umgrenzung, Innengliederung und Kennzeichnung.* Tübingen: J.C.B. Mohr (Paul Siebeck).
Braune, Wilhelm
1989   *Althochdeutsche Grammatik.* (Sammlung kurzer Grammatiken germanischer Dialekte.) 14. Auflage. Bearbeitet von Hans Eggers. Tübingen: Niemeyer. Erste Auflage 1886.
Bree, Cor van
1977   *Leerboek voor de historische grammatica van het Nederlands* [textbook for the historical grammar of Dutch]. (Klank- en vormleer met een beknopte grammatica van het Gotisch [phonology and morphology with a concise grammar of Gothic].) Groningen: Wolters Noordhoff.
Dresher, Bezalel Elan
2000   Analogical levelling of vowel length in West Germanic. In: Aditi Lahiri (ed.), *Analogy, levelling, markedness: principles of change in phonology and morphology.* 47-70. Berlin/New York: Mouton de Gruyter.
Fikkert, Paula
2000   Prosodic variation in the 'Lutgart'. In: Aditi Lahiri (ed.), *Analogy, levelling, markedness: principles of change in phonology and morphology.* 301-332. Berlin/New York: Mouton de Gruyter.
Gussenhoven, Carlos
1998   Vowel duration, syllable quantity and stress in Dutch. Ms., Centre for Language Studies, Catholic University of Nijmegen.
Hotzenköcherle, Rudolf
1986   Aspekte und Probleme der Vokalquantität im Schweizerdeutschen. In: Robert Schläpfer und Rudolf Trüb (eds.), *Dialektstrukturen im Wandel: Gesammelte Aufsätze zur Dialektologie der deutschen Schweiz und der Walsergebiete Oberitaliens.* 319-333. Aarau: Sauerländer.

Jutz, Leo
1931   *Die alemannischen Mundarten: Abriss der Lautverhältnisse.* Halle: Niemeyer.
Keller, Rudolf Ernst
1961   *The German dialects: phonology and morphology.* Manchester: University Press.
Kraehenmann, Astrid
1999   Open Syllable Lengthening in High German dialects. Talk presented at the 14th International Conference on Historical Linguistics, August 1999, Vancouver B.C., Canada.
Kraehenmann, Astrid
2001   Quantity and prosodic asymmetrics in Alemannic: synchronic and diachronic perspectives. Doctoral dissertation, university of Konstanz, Germany.
Kraehenmann, Astrid and Aditi Lahiri
1999   Phonological quantity contrast in Swiss German stops: history and acoustics. Ms., University of Konstanz.
Lahiri, Aditi and Bezalel Elan Dresher
1999   Open Syllable Lengthening in West Germanic. *Language* 75: 678-719.
Lahiri, Aditi and Paula Fikkert
1999   Trisyllabic Shortening in English: past and present. *English Language and Linguistics* 3/2: 229-267.
Loey, A. van
1969   *Middelnederlandse Spraakkunst* [Middle Dutch grammar]. I. Vormleer [Morphology]. Groningen: Wolters Noordhoff.
Meinherz, Paul
1920   *Die Mundart der Bündner Herrschaft.* (Beiträge zur Schweizerdeutschen Grammatik.) Band XIII. Frauenfeld: Huber und Co.
Minkova, Donka
1982   The Environment for Open Syllable Lengthening in Middle English. *Folia Linguistica Historica* III: 29-58.
1985   Of rhyme and reason: some foot-governed quantity changes in English. IN: Roger Eaton, Olga Fischer, Willem Koopman and Frederike van der Leek (eds.), *Current Issues in Linguistic Theory.* 163-178. Amsterdam: John Benjamins.
Minkova, Donka and Robert P. Stockwell
1998   The origins of long-short allomorphy in English. In: Jacek Fisiak and Marcin Krygier (eds.), *Advances in English historical linguistics 1996.* 211-239. Berlin/New York: Mouton de Gruyter.
Müller, Ernst Erhard
1963   Zur Stellung des Schweizerdeutschen im Alemannischen. In: Paul Zinsli, Oskar Bandle, Peter Dalcher, Kurt Meyer, Rudolf Trüb und

Hans Wanner (eds.), *Sprachleben der Schweiz: Sprachwissenschaft, Namenforschung, Volkskunde.* 57-74. Bern: Francke.

Prokosch, Eduard
  1939   *A Comparative Germanic Grammar.* Philadelphia, Pennsylvania: Linguistic Society of America, University of Pennsylvania.

Reis, Marga
  1974   *Lauttheorie und Lautgeschichte.* München: Fink.

Schobinger, Viktor
  1984   *Zürichdeutsche Kurzgrammatik.* Zürich: pendo-verlag.

Sonderegger, Stefan
  1963   Die althochdeutsche Schweiz: Zur Sprach- und Siedlungsgeschichte der deutschen Schweiz bis 1100. In: Paul Zinsli, Oskar Bandle, Peter Dalcher, Kurt Meyer, Rudolf Trüb und Hans Wanner (eds.), *Sprachleben der Schweiz: Sprachwissenschaft, Namenforschung, Volkskunde.* 23-55. Bern: Francke.

Toorn, Maarten C. van den, Wilhelmus J.J. Pijnenburg, Jan A. van Leuvensteijn, Joop M. van der Horst (eds.)
  1997   *Geschiedenis van de Nederlandse Taal* [History of the Dutch language]. Amsterdam: Amsterdam University Press.

Voegelin, Charles Frederick and Florence Marie Voegelin
  1977   *Classification and Index of the World's Languages.* Amsterdam: Elsevier Scientific publishing Company.

Wright, Joseph
  1907   *Historical German Grammar.* Vol. 1: Phonology, Word-Formation and Accidence. Oxford: University Press.

The prosodic structure of prefixed words in the history of West Germanic*

Paula Fikkert

1. Introduction

Prefixes have long been recognized as disturbing factors in analyses of the prosodic structures of words in the history of West Germanic languages. Disregarding prefixed words, main stress in the older stages of the West Germanic languages was uncontroversially assigned to the first syllable of the word or root. However, prefixed words behave notoriously difficult: although all handbooks give as a rule of thumb that prefixed nouns have stress on the prefix, and prefixed verbs stress on the root, the exceptions to this rule are numerous, as we will see in section 2. Given this complex situation regarding stress in prefixed words in the older stages of the languages, it is of interest to investigate how prefixed loan words entered the different languages in the middle period, where the situation in English will be compared to that of the sister language Dutch. In section 3, we will sketch how unprefixed Romance loans, derived and underived, entered the English and Dutch language.

In section 4, we will discuss the borrowing of word pairs of the type *abstráct*$_V$ - *ábstract*$_N$, which in English differ in stress patterns and morphosyntactic class. These word pairs have evoked substantial research in both phonology and morphology (cf. Jespersen 1909, Kingdon 1958, Chomsky & Halle 1968, Halle & Keyser 1971, Aronoff 1976, Kiparsky 1982, Minkova 1997). The concern of this paper is not to show how different theories account for these facts (cf. Redford, *this volume,* McCully, *this volume*). Rather, it aims to clarify how word pairs like *abstráct*$_V$ - *ábstract*$_N$ first arose. After the Norman Conquest many Romance words entered the English language. Some examples are given in (1). The dates given in (1), and elsewhere for English words, denote the first occurrence of a word according to the OED.

(1) Romance disyllabic loans into English

Nouns		Verbs	
a. íncline	(1600)	inclíne	(1300)
ímpress	(1590)	impréss	(1374)
tránsport	(1456)	transpórt	(1374)
cónflict	(1440)	conflíct	(1432)
cómbine	(1610)	combíne	(1440)
éxport	(1690)	expórt	(1485)
cóntrast	(1597)	contrást	(1490)
ímport	(1588)	impórt	(1508)
áccent	(1581)	accént	(1530)
b. présent	(1225)	presént	(1290)
púrport	(1278)	purpórt	(1300)
cónduct	(1290)	condúct	(1400)
ábsent	(1382)	absént	(1400)
cóntract	(1386)	contráct	(1548)
ábstract	(1387)	abstráct	(1542)
prótest	(1400)	protést	(1440)
próject	(1400)	projéct	(1477)

Since the word pairs in (1) are all loan words, the question is when and how did these words enter the language.

A straightforward analysis for the facts in (1) would be that they are borrowed and incorporated analogous to the Old English noun-verb pairs, as suggested by Sweet (1891) and Jespersen (1909), and this analysis will also be defended in this paper in section 4. This view, however, is explicitly denied in the influential work of Halle & Keyser (1971) and more recently, and more subtle, in Minkova (1997). In section 5 we will see that, rather than account for the patterns in (1) by analogy, both argue that the Old English stress system changed under influence of loan words, although they account for the change in different ways.

In section 6, we will compare the way in which Romance loans entered into English with the situation in Middle Dutch. Here too, I will argue that foreign words were incorporated into the native prosodic system, in both English and Dutch; neither did they enter the language initially with their foreign stress pattern, nor did these words immediately lead to a change into the prosodic system of the language. However, small differences in the prosodic systems of English and Dutch at the time of borrowing lead to different prosodic structures for borrowed nouns and verbs. Unlike in English, as shown in (1), Romance nouns were usually borrowed with final stress in Dutch, because the language allowed final stressed syllables. However, Romance verbs were borrowed with a stressed verbal derivational ending. Some examples are given in (2).

(2) Romance loans into Dutch

Nouns		Verbs		
advíes	(1265-1270)[1]	adviséren	(1467-1490)	'advise'
presént	(1240)	presentéren	(1240)	'present'
arrést	(1308-1346)	arrestéren	(1276-1300)	'arrest'
appél	(1336-1339)	appeléren	(1281)	'appeal'
adrés	(1574)	adresséren	(1512)	'address'
dispúut	(1566)	disputéren	(1240)	'dispute'
excúus	(1546)	excuséren	(1353)	'excuse'
protést	(1582)	protestéren	(1400)	'protest'
transpórt	(1506)	transportéren	(1503)	'transport'
accént	(1240)	accentuéren	not given	'accent'
contráct	(1391)	contractéren	not given	'contract'
projéct	(1613)	projectéren	(1650)	'project'
profíjt	(1265)	profitéren	(1451)	'profit'
prodúct	(1508)[2]	producéren	(1697)	'produce'

Besides differences in the prosodic systems of English and Dutch, there are also important morphological and syntactic differences between the two in the middle stages of the languages. Although both Dutch and English had two types of prefixed verbs in the older period – separable prefixed verbs with stress on the prefix, and inseparable prefixed verbs with stress on the verb root – Middle English – unlike Middle Dutch – no longer had separable prefixed verbs: ME *upstart* corresponds to ModE *to start up* (cf. Marchand 1969, Strang

1970, Hiltunen 1983). Separable prefixed verbs have largely been replaced by simple verbs followed by a post-particle[3] or by a Romance loans. The explanation for the decline of separable prefixed verbs is usually accounted for by the change of word order from SOV to SVO.[4] Thus, this is in principle unrelated to the decline of inseparable prefixed verbs. Not only were separable prefixed verbs lost, there also was a decline in inseparable prefixed verbs in English. The common understanding of the decline of inseparable prefixed verbs is that the unstressed prefixed eroded,[5] just like unstressed endings, whereby the unstressable prefixes like *ge-*, were the first ones to disappear.[6]

However, there are at least two problems with this account. First, while native verbs with inseparable unstressed prefixes were on the decline in English, there was the rise of loan words with inseparable and unstressed prefixes, particularly the prefixed verbs in (1), which remains to be explained (cf. Strang 1970: 191, Samuels 1972: 164, Lutz 1997).[7] Second, a language like Dutch, which has also lost many morphological endings in the course of its history, has nevertheless retained its unstressed verbal prefixes. Prefixes' lack of stress, therefore, cannot be a sufficient motivation for losing prefixes altogether.

Finally, Dutch did not borrow the Romance loans analogous to the native prefixed nouns and verbs, for several reasons. First, the prosodic system was preferring final stress on (super)heavy syllables, which caused Romance nouns to have final stress. Second, the distinction between nouns and verbs on the basis of stress was far less clear in Dutch than in English, due to the coexistence of stressed and unstressed prefixed verbs. Dutch nevertheless maintained a distinction between verbs and nouns from Romance by borrowing the Romance stressed infinitival suffix. Neither verbs nor nouns behave as being prefixed in Dutch. Unlike in English, the Romance prefixes never became productive in Dutch.

To summarize, the paper is organized as follows. In section 2 the special role of prefixes in the older stages of the West Germanic prosodic system is briefly discussed. Section 3 presents previous accounts of how Romance loans entered the English language. Section 4 gives arguments for the analogy analysis for Romance word pairs such as those in (1). Section 5 presents previous accounts for the different stress patterns in Romance nouns and verbs. In section 6 it will be shown that the subtle differences in the prosodic systems of Middle English and Middle Dutch can account for the differences in the way loans were borrowed in the two languages. Moreover, also differences in morphology and syntax between the two languages play a role in explaining the differences. Finally, section 7 summarizes the main conclusions.

2. Prefixes in the word prosodic systems of older West Germanic

2.1. Stress on prefixed words in the history of English and Dutch

Although prefixes have received considerable attention in phonology, morphosyntax and semantics (cf. Hiltunen 1983, Brinton 1988, Kastovsky 1996, Lutz 1997), their role in prosody has been underresearched. The prosodic systems of the West Germanic languages — of which I shall only refer to English and Dutch — have changed dramatically over time (cf. Lahiri et al. 1999). Whereas the modern languages all are claimed to have main stress assigned from end of words (cf. Kager 1989, Hayes 1995, Zonneveld et al. 1999), in the older stages of these languages stress was basically *root*-initial (cf. Kluge 1891, Streitberg et al. 1936, Van Loey 1970, Krahe & Meid 1969, Van Bree 1977, 1987, Suphi 1988, McCully & Hogg 1990) or *word*-initial (cf. Kuhn 1863, Scherer 1878, Franck 1910, Hammerich 1921, Wright & Wright 1925, 1928, Halle & Keyser 1971). Thus, some researchers regard unstressed prefixes to be an anomaly to the otherwise straightforward analysis of word-initial main stress, while others view stressed prefixes as anomalous to the otherwise regular analysis of root or stem initial stress. From this description it is clear that prefixes obscure the regular pattern of initial stress.

The controversy in the literature about whether Old English stress is phonological or morphological is also largely due to 'misbehaving' prefixes. Suphi (1988), for instance, claims that stress is morphologically determined: prefixes to nouns are attached at level 1, and undergo the stress rules (leading to word-initial stress), while prefixes to verbs are attached at level 2, i.e. after stress assignment.

McCully & Hogg (1990), on the contrary, argue that prefixes to verbs are extrametrical and are invisible for stress assignment. Minkova (1997) and Minkova & Stockwell (1994) have also argued that stress is morphological in Old English. Under this view, prefixes in nouns are considered part of the root. Halle & Keyser (1971) assume that stress in Old English was root-initial, but that prefixed nouns underwent a Stress Retraction Rule. We will discuss this analysis in more detail in section 5.1.

Although main stress was on the root in most prefixed verbs and on the prefix in most prefixed nouns (3a), Old English also had verbs with stress on prefixes. First, in the oldest period of the language, compound verbs had stress on the first element if the verbs was separable (Wright & Wright, 1925: §14), as in (3b). Already in Old English these separable verbs were declining and they no longer exist in Middle and Modern English. Second, some verbs were derived from nouns, and kept initial stress, as in the case of *ándswàrian* 'to answer' from the noun *ándswàru* 'answer', as in (3c). Third, some prefixes like *ge-* were considered unstressable. These never bore stress, independent of whether they were prefixed to nouns or verbs, as shown in (3d). Most of these prefixes no longer exist in Modern English. Fourth, already in the oldest period of the language many nouns were formed from verbs containing an inseparable particle. Accordingly, these had main stress on the second element (Wright & Wright 1925: §12), as shown in (3e). These forms, too, are declining in Old and Middle English. The patterns in (3) were found in the older stages of all West Germanic languages, and all of them are still attested in Modern Dutch, as shown in (4).

(3) Prefixed words in OE

	Nouns		*Verbs*	
a.	ándgiet	'intelligence'	ongíetan	'to understand'
	ándsaca	'adversary'	onsácan	'to deny'
	bīgang	'practice'	begángan	'to practice'
	wíersàca	'adversary'	wiþsácan	'to oppose'
b.	'æfterfòlgere	'follower'	'æfterfòlgian	'to pursue'
	fóresprèca	'advocate'	'æftersprècan	'to claim'

			ófadrīfan	'drive away'
			fóregangan	'to precede'
			bístandan	'to support'
c.	ándswaru	'answer'	ándswarian	'to answer'
	ándwyrde	'answer'	ándwyrdan	'to answer'
	fúltum	'support'	fúltumian	'to support
d.	gemóte	'meeting	gebǣran	'to behave'
	geféoht	'fight'	abéran	'to bear'
e.	forbód	'prohibition'	forbĕodan	'to forbid'
	forlór	'destruction'	forlĕosan	'to lose'
	begáng	'practice'	begángan	'to practice'

(4) Prefixed words in Modern Dutch

	Nouns		*Verbs*	
a.	wéerstand	'resistance'	weerstáan	'to resist'
b.	bíjstand	'support'	bíjstaan	'to support'
c.	ántwoord	'answer'	ántwoorden	'to answer'
d.	gelóof	'believe'	gelóven	'to believe
e.	verlíes	'loss'	verlíezen	'to lose'

The role that prefixes play in determining the prosodic structure of words is far from obvious.

2.2. Word stress in the history of English and Dutch

There is also little consensus on the prosodic structure of unprefixed words of Old and Middle English. That main stress was largely initial in Old English is hardly controversial, but there are large disagreements on the location of secondary stress, and on the exact foot structure of Old English. While most scholars claim that Old English was not a quantity-sensitive language (cf. Halle & Keyser 1971, Minkova & Stockwell 1994, Minkova 1997), others have argued that stress in Old English was quantity-sensitive (Dresher & Lahiri 1991, Lahiri & Dresher 1999, Lahiri et al. 1999, and Lahiri & Fikkert 1999). Under the latter view, Dresher & Lahiri (1991) have proposed the Germanic foot, which is characterized as a foot whose head must contain two moras. Weight was entirely straightforward: syllables with long vowels and closed syllables are bimoraic. If the first syllable of the word is a light monomoraic syllable, it forms the head of the foot with the following syllable, whether light or heavy. This results in a resolved moraic trochee, as shown in (5):

(5) The Germanic Foot (Dresher & Lahiri 1991)
Foot type: resolved expanded moraic trochee ([μ μ (μ)] μ)
Direction of parsing: left to right
Main stress: Left
Sample parsings

```
   (x    .)      (x    .)      (x     .)
   ([μμ] μ)      ([μ μ] μ)     ([μ μμ] μ)
    H L           L L L          L H L
   wor da        we ru da       cy nin ga
```

Feet were built iteratively from left to right, and main stress was assigned to the first foot. The arguments for the Germanic foot come from main and secondary stress, High Vowel Deletion in Old English and Sievers' Law in Gothic. Other important features of Old English stress is that unstressed syllables never had long vowels, i.e. were usually light, and final syllables never bore stress. Dresher & Lahiri argue that final feet underwent Final Defooting, which defooted feet without a dependent syllable (non-branching feet), which ultimately led to consonant extrametricality, as argued by Lahiri et al. (1999) and Lahiri & Fikkert (1999). No provision is made for the treatment of prefixed words as these words were left out of the analysis.

3. The prosodic structure of trisyllabic loans into Middle English

Lahiri & Fikkert (1999) provide additional evidence for the Germanic foot in Old and Middle English from loan word phonology. They discuss the phenomenon of Trisyllabic Shortening, which applied to native words in Old English, as shown in (6a), as well as in Romance loan words into Middle English, as shown in (6b). The singular (6a) and the 'underived' forms (6b) have a long vowel, whereas their corresponding forms to the right, respectively the plural and 'derived' forms, have a short vowel.

(6) TSS
  a. Late Old English

Singular	Plural	
cīcen	cĭcenu	'chicken'
hēafod	hĕafodu	'head'
ǣnig	ǣnige	'any'
clōver	clăvere	'clover'
hǣring	hǣringas	'herring'

  b. Romance loans into Middle English (from Lahiri & Fikkert 1999)

sāne	(1628)	sănity	(1432)
vāin	(1300)	vănity	(1230)
chāste	(1225)	chăstete	(1305)
brīef	(1325)	brĕvity	(1509)
clēar	(1297)	clărity	(1340)

Lahiri & Fikkert argue that the motivation behind the alternation in vowel length is the optimization of the prosodic structure of these words. The preference for (a) maximal feet and (b) a complete syllable parse led to vowel lengthening is disyllabic words. This is referred to as Open Syllable Lengthening (cf. Lahiri & Dresher 1999), as shown in (7a), and as vowel shortening in trisyllabic words (7b). A short vowel in the disyllabic forms in (7a), would be less preferred, as the foot only consists of a head, rather than a head plus a dependent, i.e. weak branch of the foot. The preference for heavy stressed syllables is a long noted tendency, known as Prokosch' Law (Prokosch 1939). However, words with short stressed vowels are nevertheless allowed, as shown in (6) and (7b), in which an initial heavy syllable would result in a prosodic structure in which the final syllable is left stranded. By shortening the initial vowel, this situation is improved resulting in an acceptable Germanic foot.

(7) Open Syllable Lengthening and Trisyllabic Shortening

a. (x   .)   (x   .)
    ([μμ] μ)   ([μ μ])
     H   L   >>   L L
    cī ce\<n\>   cī ce\<n\>
    sā ne   sā ne

b. (x   .)   (x   .)
    ([μ μ] μ)   ([μ μ]) μ
     L L L   >>   H L   L
    cĭ ce nu   cĭ ce nu
    să ni ty   să ni ty

A number of interesting facts need to be mentioned. First, English did not borrow stress nor vowel length from the donor language. Latin words like *perso:na* 'person', which have a long stressed vowel in the penultimate syllable are borrowed with initial stress and a short penultimate vowel in Middle English *persone* (cf. Luick 1907: 33–38, Danielsson 1948: 37, Minkova 1997, Lahiri & Dresher 1999, Lahiri & Fikkert 1999). Second, Middle English no longer has inflectionally related nouns that differ in the length of their initial vowels. Pairs like those in (6a) no longer exist in Middle English and length distinctions in inflectionally related words have been leveled out (cf. Lahiri & Dresher 1999). However, derivationally related pairs, as those in (6b) have survived into Modern English. In an analysis of contemporary English, Prince (1990) has argued that due to prosodic optimization trisyllabic words undergo trochaic shortening resulting in a moraic trochee, under extrametricality.

Given that Romance loans like *sane – sanity* adopted the native Middle English prosodic system upon entering the English language, there would be no reason to assume that at the same time other Romance loans that entered the language would not be incorporated into the native prosodic system. Let us now look at 'prefixed' Romance loans into Middle English.

4. Prefixed loans in Middle English

Prefixed loans, such as *abstráct*$_V$ - *ábstract*$_N$, first occurred in Middle English. If the prosodic system at the time of borrowing was as described above, both nouns and verbs would have entered the language with initial stress. Therefore, we have to account for the fact that Romance verbs seem to have entered the language mostly with final stress. On the assumption that the prosodic system still had not changed, the only possible account can be that these words were considered prefixed. There were several reason for the speakers of Middle English to do so.

First, by the Middle English period, prefixed verbs with stressed particles (separable prefixed verbs), like those in (3b) had mostly disappeared. The only verbs with stressed prefixes were the verbs derived from nouns, as in (3c). Therefore, almost all native prefixed verbs that still existed in the language were inseparable and had stressless prefixes. Second, all native verbs were either strong or weak. The strong verbs were monosyllabic and had ablaut grades; the weak verbs were mostly denominative verbs with the *–jan* ending, such as *árian* 'to honor', *baþian* 'to bathe', *célan* 'to cool', etc., which had initial stress. Therefore, disyllabic verbal roots did not exist in the language. The only native disyllabic verbal forms were the prefixed verbs. The natural interpretation of foreign disyllabic verbs was therefore to consider them prefixed.

As we will see in the next section, one of the reasons for Halle & Keyser (1971) to assume that these loans words – both nouns and verbs – all had final stress in early Modern English (by means of the Romance Stress Rule) is based on Levins 1570 pronouncing dictionary. Levins marks stress on a number of words, and mentions just a handful of pairs where the noun has initial and the verb final stress. The complete list found in Levins in given in (8) below:

(8) Complete list of noun-verb pairs which differ in stress in Levins

óutlawe	924	outláwe[8]	10..
míschiefe	1300	mischéefe	1330
quárel	1225	quarél	1390
rébel	1400	rebéll	1340

326 *Paula Fikkert*

dývine	<1303	divíne	13..
députe	1405	depúte	1382
récorde⁹	1300	recórde	1225

This can be taken to mean that these homophonous pairs, which only alternate in stress, were not common at that time, an interpretation given in Halle & Keyser (1971). It could also be the case, however, particularly because many words in Levins are not marked for stress, that stress was mostly marked in Levins if it was not predictable. It is therefore of interest to investigate which word pairs are marked for stress in Levins to establish the predictable stress patterns.

The complete list of Romance verbs that receive initial main stress in Levins, just like the corresponding nouns, is given in (9).

(9)   Initial-stressed Romance noun-verb pairs according to Levins (1570)

Noun   *Verb*

a. *Nouns attested earlier than verbs according to the OED*

hónoure	1200	hónoure	1290
réason	1225	réason	13..
méritit	1225	mérit	1484
méasure	1225	méasure	1300
lánguage	1290	lánguage	1636
cóloure	1290	cóloure	1300
púrpose	1290	púrpose	1382
pásture	1300	pásture	1390
pórture	1305	pórture	1394
stómake	<1340	stómake	1523
láyvel	1340	leývel	1440
pléasure	1368	pléasure	1559
férie	1377	féry	1496
múrmur	1381	múrmur	1386
éffect	1385	éffecte	1494
mórgage	1390	mórgage	1530
géllie	1393	géllie	1601
prómise	1400	prómise	1420
gésture	1410	gésture	1542

túmulte	1412	túmulte	1570
gárbage	1430	gárbage	1542

b. *Nouns attested before verbs, where the verbs originally had final stress according to the OED*

énvie	1280	énvie	1386
óutrage	1297	óutrage	1303
cáptive	1400	cáptive	1430
cónquest	1300	cónquest	1375

c. *Verbs attested earlier than Nouns according to the OED*

cómpasse	1300	cómpasse	1297
cóver	1300	cóver	1297
rével	<1350	révell	1325
práctice	1494	práctice[10]	1460
áccent	1538	áccent	1530

The verbs in (9a) have entered the language after their corresponding nouns, according to the OED. In (9c) the verbs are borrowed earlier than the nouns, and the verbs in (9b), which have initial stress according to Levins, seem to have had final stress earlier, according to the OED. Overwhelmingly, the verbs occurred later than the nouns, and one could argue that they could have been derived from the corresponding nouns,[11] parallel to the native English verbs derived from nouns, as for example the verb *ándswàrian* 'to answer' from the noun *ándswàru* 'answer' in (3c).

In (10) all occurrences in Levins are presented in which both verbs and nouns are marked with final stress. Recall that the only nouns which did not bear stress on the prefix in Old English were the ones with unstressable prefixes, such as *ge-* in (3d), and those derived from inseparable verbs without changing stress, like those in (3e), as has been reported to be the case for *debate*. Although these prefixes which never bore stress were declining in Middle English, they have survived into Modern English, as in *belief – believe*. Here, it seems that in many cases the noun could have been derived from the verb, although this leaves the cases in (10b) unexplained. Possibly, the prefixes in (10b) were beginning to belong to the category of unstressable prefixes (cf. Lutz 1997 and footnote 6).

(10) Final-stressed Romance noun-verb pairs according to Levins (1570)

Noun　　　　　　　　　Verb

a. *Verbs reported to exist before nouns (OED)*

excúse	1374	excúse	1225
exchange	1374	exchánge	1300
accómpt	1300	accómpt	1303
rewárde	<1338	rewárd	<1315
refúse	1330	refúse	<1330
discharge	1460	dischárge	<1330
mysúse	1398	mysúse	1374
disúse	1552	disúse	1375
distract	1624	distráct	1380
abúse	1538	abúse	1413
retrácte	1553	retráct	1432
extrácte	1549	extráct	1489

b. *Nouns reported to exist before verbs (OED)*

reléefe	1225	reléefe	1374
debáte	1300	debáte	1340
suspéct	1300	suspéct	1483
decrée	1303	decrée	1399
contráct	1315	contráct	1530
regárde	1340	regárde	1430
afféct	1374	afféct	1483
respéct	<1391	respéct	1542
prospéct	1430	prospécte	1555
awárde	1300	awárde	1393

To summarize, Levins gives a number of word pairs in which both members have initial stress (9). Here it seems that the verbs are derived from the corresponding nouns, as overwhelmingly the nouns were borrowed before the corresponding verbs. For the word pairs with final stress on both members (10), the situation is less clear. However, although the words with stressless prefixes were declining, they still occur in the modern language, as in *abúse* (N, V). Apparently, the pattern was still strong enough in Middle English to allow new word pairs of this type, and the prefixes were presumably considered weak. Finally, Levins presents a small number of pairs with stress on the prefix in nouns, and on the verbal root in verbs, as in (8). Pairs with a stressed prefix for verbs and an unstressed one for nouns do not occur. Moreover, many prefixed words are not marked for stress. Given these facts, it seems not quite right to conclude that all disyllabic Romance nouns and verbs bore final stress. The situation was more complex than that. Although not all pairs were borrowed uniformly into the language, they nevertheless followed a pattern familiar from Old English.

Therefore, it is argued that Romance verbs entered the language as prefixed, because the language did not have disyllabic verbal stems. The only exceptions are verbs that are derived from nouns, which have stress on the prefix, as the verbs with a stressed separable prefix had ceased to exist in Middle English. Romance nouns, on the other hand, would under all analyses of Middle English stress receive stress on the prefix, unless the prefix was unstressable, and unless the noun was derived from the verb: in those cases the word would carry stress on the second part. Before turning to Dutch, let us first discuss previous accounts of stress assignment in Romance prefixed words.

5. Previous accounts of prosodic structure in Romance loans

5.1. Halle & Keyser (1971): The RSR and Stress Retraction

In their monumental work on English stress, Halle & Keyser (1971) sketch the development of the English stress system from Old English to Modern English. They assume the following stress pattern for Old English: stress is on the first syllable of the root, due to the Initial Stress Rule. Prefixed nouns[12] subsequently undergo a stress retraction rule, which moves stress to the initial syllable. Due to massive borrowing from Romance, both from Latin and Anglo Norman, the Middle English stress system underwent several changes. First, next to the Old English stress rules, the Romance Stress Rule (RSR) was introduced into the language, given in (11). Second, the vocabulary was divided into two sets of words each with its own stress pattern: the unmarked native words underwent the Old English stress rules, the non-native set the RSR.

(11) Romance Stress Rule (RSR) (Halle & Keyser 1971: 101)

$$V \rightarrow [1\text{stress}] / [X\text{---}C_0 ((\begin{bmatrix} -\text{tense} \\ V \end{bmatrix} C^1_0) \begin{bmatrix} -\text{tense} \\ V \end{bmatrix} C_0)]$$

They acknowledge the fact that there are stress doublets in Middle English – particularly in the language of Chaucer (cf. Redford *this volume*). In their view this is due to the coexistence of two different stress rules: i.e. native words could be stressed by RSR, and vice versa non-native words by the Old English stress rules. However, and more importantly for us, they furthermore claim that the Romance stress doublets with different morphosyntactic categories, like those in (1) did not yet exist in Middle English. If initially-stressed Romance nouns (or verbs) occurred, they must have received stress by the Old English stress rules.

Moreover, even the early modern English dictionary of Levins (1570) do not have word pairs like *permít$_V$ – pérmit$_N$*; these disyllabic word pairs usually have final stress in Levins according to Halle & Keyser.[13,14] Thus, as stress is no longer variable at the time of Levins, Halle & Keyser argue that in Early Modern English all words receive stress by a uniform system. They claim that in Early Modern English the Old English Initial Stress Rule is given up and replaced by the RSR. Thus, both 'Romance' nouns and verbs receive final stress by the RSR. However, to account for the fact that words with final lax vowels, such as *impórt, convérse, protést,* receive final stress, they have to assume a prefix boundary (=), which is not otherwise motivated. The Stress Retraction Rule is also changed to prevent its application to Romance disyllabic prefixed nouns, while still allowing stress retraction in the native disyllabic prefixed nouns. Thus, prefixed Romance nouns, [con=tráct]$_N$ have a different structure from prefixed native words, the later undergoing the stress retraction rule, as in [ánt#giet]$_N$.

Halle & Keyser claim that reliable evidence for stress retraction in Romance nouns only exists from 1634 on (based on Cooper's *English Teacher*). For early Modern English they suggest that both nouns and verbs (both native and non-native) are stressed by the RSR, but the nouns undergo the revised Old English Stress Retraction rule, which is now changed to apply to both [cón=tràct]$_N$ and [ánt#gìet]$_N$. Two further remarks need to be made. First, Halle & Keyser assume that nouns, like *pérmit* are derived from the corresponding verbs, and that these nouns therefore have the structure [[per=mit]$_V$]$_N$. However, from the dates given, we can infer that sometimes the verb occurred earlier than the noun. Moreover, the earlier initially stressed non-native nouns were assumed to have been separate lexical items, and were not derived from verbs (cf. footnote 14). Second, the stress retraction rule now becomes less restricted and may apply to all categories of words, except to non-nouns with a native prefix: that is, verbs like *undergo* and *overtake* remain finally stressed. Why the stress retraction rule for non-native words only applies in Modern English and not in Middle English remains "somewhat surprisingly" (Halle & Keyser 1971: 112). It seems that the new early Modern English system is more analogous to the Old English pattern than the Middle English system was. Moreover, the stress retraction rule becomes even more general at the time of Walker's *Pronouncing Dictionary* (1791), where the stress retraction rule also applies to verbs, accounting for initially stressed verbs like *vacate* (1643), *dictate* (1592), although this does not seem to affect prefixed native and non-native verbs. They argue that there are two different stress retraction rules, with the choice between those two being lexically determined. However, it seems that native prefixed verbs never undergo stress retraction to the prefix.

There are a number of puzzling factors in this analysis. First, it seems that during the early Middle English period the lexicon was divided into two sets, which collapsed during early Modern English, but was reintroduced in Modern English. Second, under their analysis the Early Modern English stress system seems to bear more resemblance to the Old English stress system, than to the Middle English stress system. This is particularly due to the prevention of stress retraction in Romance prefixed disyllabic nouns in Middle English, pairs like those in (1) only being introduced in Modern English.

Third, Romance prefixed nouns are assumed to be derived from the corresponding verbs, which is not obvious if we consider the times of their earliest occurrences according to the OED. Furthermore, as we saw above, trisyllabic (unprefixed) loans entered the language adopting the native prosodic system. Given this fact, it would be remarkable if other, i.e. disyllabic loans, took on their own foreign prosodic system.

The evidence for both the variation of stress in Middle English words and the non-variation of stress in words like the ones in (1), is questioned by Minkova (1997), among other people. She shows that variation was limited, and that the evidence points to 'an early and rapid adaptation of many of the Romance loans to the still dominant OE prosodic structure'.

5.2. Minkova 1997: Different Grammar for different lexical strata

Unlike Halle & Keyser, Minkova argues that the stress system did not change dramatically from Old English to Middle English. What changed was that foreign words from Latin and Anglo-Norman entered the language, and as long as they were part of the peripheral lexical stratum, they obeyed the foreign stress rules. However, as soon as they become part of the core vocabulary of the language, they follow the native stress rules. Thus, variation in stress in loan words is due to the fact that they are in different lexical strata. This is, however, not her account of the different stress patterns in pairs like *abstráct*$_V$ - *ábstract*$_N$, for which she assumes the Latinate stress system.

Minkova (1997) proposes an analysis of Old and Middle English stress in an Optimality Theoretical framework. In her view, the ranking of constraints determines the prosodic pattern of words in Old English, where ROOT STRESS – the first syllable of every lexical root carries stress – and INITIAL PROMINENCE – the left edge of a morphological category root is matched to the prosodic category of stress – are unviolated. According to Minkova the native words all receive stress through the Old English stress system. Prefixed words have a special status: if the prefix is specified as part of the root, the prefixed word behaves as if it is monomorphemic and will receive initial root stress; otherwise it is invisible for the constraint ROOT STRESS. In the example in (11), the prefix *ge-* is not specified as being part of the root, unlike most nominal prefixes, which are considered part of the lexical root, as shown in (12) for *ánd₊ᵣₒₒₜswaru*. However, verbal prefixes are not part of the root, as shown in (13) for *forwíernan* 'to refuse'.

(11) OE Constraint ranking

(ge).fór *'died, sg'*	Root stress	Initial Prominence	Nonfin	WSP	Right Stress
ge.fōr			*!		
gé.fōr	*!	?¹⁵		*	*

(12) OE Constraint ranking

ánd₊ᵣswaru 'answer'	Root stress	Initial Prominence	Nonfin	WSP	Right Stress
ándswaru					*!*
andswáru		*!		*	*
andswarú	*!	**	*	*	

(13) OE Constraint ranking

(for)wíernan 'to refuse'	Root stress	Initial Prominence	Nonfin	WSP	Right Stress
fórwiernan	*!				**
forwíernan					*!
forwiernán	*!	**	*		

Crucially, Minkova's analysis can only account for the stressed prefix in nouns such as *ándswaru* 'answer' by assuming that 'prefixes can be root-like with respect to stress'. Otherwise the preferred form should have stress on the root, given the unviolated constraints INITIAL PROMINENCE and ROOT STRESS. Moreover, unstressed verbal prefixes must be invisible for the INITIAL PROMINENCE constraint. This information is part of the lexical representation. Under those assumptions, stress is uniformly assigned by the Old English constraint ranking, and differences between prefixed verbs and nouns are expressed in the lexical representations of nouns and verbs: prefixed nouns phonologically behave as underived, but prefixed verbs are morphologically composed of prefix plus root.

According to Minkova, Middle English stress differs from the Old English stress system only in the following aspect: Next to the Old English stress rules, there is another lexical stratum that conforms to the Latinate stress system. This system is composed of the same constraints, but they differ in ranking. In the Latin stress system NONFINALITY dominates INITIAL PROMINCE, and the WEIGHT-TO-STRESS PRINCIPLE (WSP) plays a role, and makes the system quantity sensitive. The crucial part of the Latinate constraint ranking is 'NONFINALITY > WSP > INITIAL PROMINENCE'.

In Minkova's analysis both the Old English and Latinate rankings produce the same results for *disyllabic* loans, because the high-ranked constraints NONFINALITY and INITIAL PROMINENCE are never in conflict in such words. She argues that, therefore, these words are borrowed with the native stress system, as shown in (14), adapted from Lahiri & Fikkert (1999):

(14) Disyllabic Romance loans in English, German and Dutch

English	First recorded in English	Dutch	First recorded in Dutch
channel	1300	kanáal	1376
pánel	1300	panéel	1280
sátin	1366	satíjn	1599
tálent	893	talént	1400
métal	1340	metáal	1240
móral	1380	moráal	1528

córal	1305	koráal	1287
prófit	1325	profíjt	1265
sénate	1205	senáat	1858
pálace	1290	paléis	1240
jéalous	1250	jalóers	1300
básin	1220	basín	1824
fámous	1400	faméus	1488
móment	1240	momént	1485
páper	1374	papíer	1361
pátent	1387	patént	1588
prócess	1330	procés	1295
ráisin	1382	rozíjn	1288
vácant	1290	vacánt	1569
clóset	1370	closét	1847

Some Romance disyllabic words nevertheless have final stress in English. These words follow neither the native stress rules, nor the Latinate, but are in yet another stratum of the lexicon where they obey the Anglo-Norman stress rules, in which RIGHTWARD MAIN STRESS is high-ranked, and dominates both NONFINALITY and INITIAL PROMINENCE. These words are clearly perceived as foreign, according to Minkova. Once they become part of the core vocabulary stress shifts and becomes initial.

In non-prefixed inflected *trisyllabic* words there are only minor difference in the Old English and Latinate stress systems: High-ranked INITIAL PROMINENCE and high-ranked NONFINALITY both dismiss the final syllable as a candidate for stress. However, according to the Old English stress system, INITIAL PROMINCE determines that stress is initial; the Latinate system leaves the decision between initial or medial stress to the WSP. If both syllables are of equal weight, the next constraint (INITIAL PROMINCE) decides (LLX, HHX),[16] and these forms would receive initial prominence, although Minkova states that HHX-words have stress on the second syllable. If the second syllable is heavier than the first, stress will be on the penultimate syllable (LHX), because of WSP. Thus, only for LHX (and in Minkova's view also HHX) words the Latin stress rules give different results than the Old English stress rule. There is, therefore, large overlap between the Latin and Old English stress systems, which made these loans so easy to incorporate.

Thus, Minkova (1997: 162) argues that 'The only change [from OE to ME stress] in the prosodic patterning was the newly developed differential treatment for disyllables and trisyllables. The former obeyed the Old English constraint ranking, the latter conformed either to the Old English pattern (*continent, dividend, invalid, lavender, orchestra, vanity*), or the late Latin pattern which respects NONFINALITY (*imagine, omitted, possesses, tormented, united*)". This newly differentiated treatment for disyllables and trisyllables, which are lexically marked and allow INITIAL PROMINENCE violations, is the crux in her account of the difference in stress in Romance nouns and verbs. Minkova assumes that nouns lost inflectional endings earlier than verbs, resulting in trisyllabic forms for verbs (*contact*+verbal inflection) versus disyllabic forms for nouns (*contact*). Both the Old English and the Latin constraint force initial stress on the nouns, but the Latinate stress system may result in penultimate stress for inflected verbs. The difference between nouns and verbs is therefore unrelated to their morphological structure; it is purely based on phonological grounds. To account for the stress differences in word pairs like *abstráct*$_V$ - *ábstract*$_N$ the idea of convergence to the Old English system is therefore unnecessary and wrong according to Minkova.

The account given by Minkova raises a number of questions though. As we have seen in section 3, LHX nouns mostly had initial stress (as Minkova herself notes too), and Latinate HHX words were borrowed into the language with a short first syllable, resulting in a resolved moraic trochee: ([LH]X). The need for the Latinate stress system is thus far from evident. Moreover, stress was already weight sensitive, given the possibility of a resolved moraic trochee.

Furthermore, Minkova argues that disyllabic and trisyllabic nouns are adopted according to the Old English stress pattern, whereas both disyllabic and trisyllabic verbs fall under the Latin stress system. However, why this is so, remains unclear. In particular, as nouns and verbs with native prefixes in OE (where inflectional endings were present for both nouns and verbs) have different lexical representations: stressed prefixes have root-like status, unstressed prefixes are invisible for the constraint rankings, it remains unclear why borrowed words would not follow a similar lexicalization process. That non-native word pairs exist with the same 'morphosyntactically conditioned' alternation is under this account purely accidental. Another fact to be explained is that when Middle English verbs lost their endings this did not effect stress. However, the prediction is that words would now be produced in the language with the 'nominal' stress pattern.[17] Finally, in section 3 we have seen that vowel length alternations are maintained in derivationally related pairs, but that in inflectionally related pairs the vowel length alternation is leveled out. Here too, one would expect that the alternation, in this case of stress, would cease to exist after the loss of inflectional endings, as stress is purely assigned on the basis of phonological structure. This is, however, not the case.

Although Minkova is undoubtedly right about the fact that verbal inflections were maintained longer than nominal inflections, this is unlikely to be the source of the stress alternation in Romance verb-noun pairs, particularly given the strong native pattern of stress alternation in prefixed nouns and verbs. Moreover, the fact that other loans, particularly the trisyllabic ones discussed in section 3, have adopted the native stress pattern, it seems but natural to adopt the analogy analysis for prefixed loans, too.

6. Loans in Middle Dutch

As mentioned in the introduction, Dutch borrowed word pairs like English *abstráct*$_V$ - *ábstract*$_N$ in quite a different fashion. First, nouns are borrowed with final stress. Second, the verb is borrowed with a stressed suffix. Recall from section 2 that at the time of borrowing, Middle Dutch had the Germanic foot, just like Old English. However, there were significant differences between Dutch and English in the middle period (cf. Fikkert 2000), which will be discussed in section 6.1.

6.1 Comparing Middle English and Middle Dutch prosodic systems

There is much uncertainty as to the exact stress system of Middle Dutch, as very little research has been carried out on the subject. All handbooks on Middle Dutch (cf. Franck 1910, Van Loey 1970, van Bree 1977, 1987) describe the Middle Dutch stress system as being similar to the older West Germanic system described in section 2: stress is word- or root-initial, unless the word is prefixed. However, most handbooks also note that the many French words and suffixes generally kept their original accent. This then weakened the feeling for accenting the first syllable and increased the chance for stress shifts in native words and word groups (cf. Van Loey 1970).

The question then is, whether or not Romance loans entered the language with Romance stress, unlike the situation in English. In Fikkert (2000) I argue against this analysis, on the basis of the study of stress alternations in the Middle Dutch text 'Sente Lutgart' (cf. Zonneveld, *this volume*). There are several types of words that showed variation to some degree and their structures are given in (15). The only disyllabic words with variable stress are the words with two heavy syllables, and thus two feet. Normally these are expected to have stress on the initial foot, but instead they sometimes have final stress.[18] Words of the type LL, HL and LH invariably have initial stress, as these words form a single foot.

(15) *Variation in prosodic forms*
    form   expected structure   attested structure
    a.   HH   (H̲)(H)   (H̲)(H) and (H)(H̲)
    b.   HHL   (H̲)(HL)   (H)(H̲L) and sometimes (H̲)(HL)
    c.   HLL   (H̲L)L   (H)(L̲L) and sometimes (H̲L)L

Of interest is that in the HH type words, most variation is found with the native monomorphemic and prefixed nouns. Suffixed nouns almost always have initial stress; Romance loans on the other hand invariably have final stress. Furthermore, almost all HH words with final stress have a heavy first syllable and a superheavy final syllable. It therefore seems that the heaviest foot receives main stress.

Trisyllabic words can be of several types. LLL and LHL words form one Germanic foot, and do not have variable stress (16a). As predicted, the structures in (16b) all have initial stress and no variation.[19] There are only two patterns that have variable stress, which are given in (16c). Interestingly, these are exactly the structures that were prone to Trisyllabic Shortening in English.

(16) Middle Dutch dominant stress patterns

a.	LLL	(LLL)	mŏneke 'monk'
	LHL	(LHL)	cŏninge 'king'
b.	HHH	(H)(H)(H)	wónderlíc 'strange'
	HLH	(HL)(H)	brūdegóem 'groom'
	LHH	(LH)(H)	běsechheit 'activity'
	LLH	(LL)(H)	stédekíjn 'town, dim'
c.	HHL	(H)(HL)	abdésse 'abbess', ambáchte 'trade'
	HLL	(H)(LL)	līchăme 'body', blīschăpe 'joy'

The forms in (16c) have in common with those in (16b) in that one foot is more complex then the other. However, they differ also significantly: the forms in (16b) have alternating stress, whereas the forms in (16c) contain a stress clash, which is usually resolved in favor of the most complex foot (cf. Dresher & van der Hulst 1995, 1998).

The difference with Middle English, which favored Trisyllabic Shortening in these cases, is that whereas Middle English had no final stressed syllables, these did occur in Middle Dutch. Long vowels in closed syllables did probably did exist in the older stages of Dutch and German, as in OHG *hanōm* (dat. pl. 'cock') and *zungūn* ('tongue' nom./acc. pl.), and, Dutch also had many derivational (native) suffixes consisting of a superheavy syllable that bore at least secondary stress and are still superheavy to this day (cf. Dutch *–loos*, *-heid*, etc.). Note that the corresponding native suffixes were reduced syllables in English (*-less*, *-ness*). As final stress was possible in Dutch (but not in English), Romance loans could also enter the Dutch language with final stress, particularly as many of them were having superheavy final syllables. It seems, therefore, that in general superheavy syllables are exempted from the older West Germanic Final Defooting rule in Dutch. As mentioned in section 2, Final Defooting applied to all non-branching feet in English. In Dutch, the superheavy syllables seem to behave as if they were equivalent to a branching foot. On the other hand, heavy syllables in Dutch mostly had monosyllabic feet ending in –VC, which were subject to destressing. This special status of monosyllabic -VC feet in Dutch has been preserved into Modern Dutch and is accounted for in many different ways: some claim that final syllables, except the superheavy ones, are made extrametrical (cf. Trommelen & Zonneveld 1989). Others claim that a monosyllabic -VC foot is made extrametrical (cf. Lahiri & Koreman 1988, Kager 1989).

To summarize, whereas Middle English has no final heavy or superheavy syllables, and no final stressed syllables, Middle Dutch seem to have all of these. However, superheavy final syllables bore stress. Moreover, if the final foot was the most complex foot in the word, it would attract main stress, as is the case with many disyllabic Romance loans, as shown in (2) and (14). The prosodic pattern of the language at the time of borrowing is therefore responsible for the final stressed nouns like *contráct* 'contract'. However, this does not account for the fact that the corresponding verbs borrowed the stressed infinitival suffix from French.

6.1 Comparing Middle English and Middle Dutch prefixed verbs

With respect to prefixed words, the Middle Dutch stress system was consistent with the older West Germanic system described in section 2: Stress is word- or root-initial, unless the word is prefixed. Just like Old English and Modern Dutch, all prefixed patterns described in (3) and (4) are attested in Middle Dutch. Thus, whereas prefixed nouns usually bore stress, unless preceded by an unstressable prefix, prefixed verbs could have both stressed and unstressed prefixes. Stress was therefore not a very unreliable factor for distinguishing nouns and verbs. It seems that the language chose another way to distinguish foreign nouns and verbs: by borrowing the infinitival suffix from French, which was always a branching foot, and therefore stress-bearing.

Importantly, this was not the case for English: In Middle English separable prefixed words no longer existed, and therefore verbs with initial stressed prefixes no longer occurred in large numbers, whereas most prefixed nouns had stress on the prefix. Stress pattern and morphosyntactic class were therefore fairly reliably related.

A second distinction between prefixed verbs in English and Dutch is that prefixed verbs with unstressed prefixes were declining in English. As noted in the introduction, the common understanding of the decline of inseparable prefixed verbs is that the unstressed prefixed eroded, just like unstressed endings. Here the unstressable prefixes like *ge-*, were the first ones to disappear. However, as in English, Dutch unstressed endings also eroded, yet this was not the case with unstressed prefixes. Rather, in Middle Dutch sometimes prefixes have been added to words which did not have prefixes in the older stages of the language, as in the case of the past participle prefix *ge-*: the Middle Dutch forms *worden, bracht,* etc. are now realized as *geworden* and *gebracht* 'became, brought, past ptc.'. Stresslessness of the prefix itself can therefore not be a sufficient motivation for losing prefixes altogether.

Although the development of prosodic structures in the history of Dutch certainly needs to be studied in more detail, it seems clear that it differed from the Middle English stress system. The difference does not seem to be related to foot structure, because both have been argued to still have the Germanic foot in the middle stages. Rather, the differences are particularly due to differences in the preservation of vowel length in Dutch, versus the loss of length distinctions in English unstressed and final syllables. Due to these differences, Romance loans were borrowed differently in the two languages. Moreover, whereas English maintained a fairly reliable stressed-based distinction between nouns and verbs, this was not true in Dutch, because separable verbs with stress on the prefix were both frequent and productive in Dutch.

7. Summary and conclusions

In the older stages of the West Germanic languages there were two broad types of prefixed verbs: (a) verbs with stressed and separable (native) prefixes, and (b) verbs with unstressed and non-separable (native) prefixes. Whereas both types still exist in Dutch, Modern English no longer has verbs of category (a) and words of type (b) are declining. In the literature on prefixed verbs in English several reasons have been given for this decline of prefixed verbs (cf. Hiltunen 1983, Lutz 1997). The most common account for the decline of separable verbs in English is that this is due to the change in word order from SOV to SVO. The decline of inseparable prefixed verbs in English has been argued to be due to general erosion of unstressed syllables, often combined with semantic bleaching (cf. Lutz 1997). It has also been argued by some that it is due to the influence of French, which led to the borrowing of non-native words, both prefixed and unprefixed, which replaced the native words (cf. Marchand 1969). Moreover, the French influence on Dutch has also been considerable, but did not lead to the decline of prefixation. Rather, native prefixation is still very productive.

Instead, we have argued here that Romance loans into English were incorporated into the prosodic pattern of the language at the time of borrowing. As all disyllabic native verbs were prefixed, this was also the way disyllabic Romance verbs were analyzed. Prefixed disyllabic nouns usually have initial stress, and Romance nouns are borrowed similarly. The Middle Dutch prosodic system allowed final superheavy syllables with main stress, and this is how many Romance loans were borrowed.

Moreover, whereas prefixed nouns and verbs are fairly reliably distinguished by different stress patterns in English, this is not the case in Dutch which kept both initially stressed separable prefixed verbs and inseparable verbs with stress on the verbal root. As there was no predominant stress pattern for prefixed verbs, Romance verbs were borrowed with a finally verbal suffix, which often bore stress under the normal stress system at that time. Although many details of the analysis need further investigation, it has become clear that the prosodic systems of English and Dutch led to different ways in which Romance loans were incorporated. However, by and large, in both cases Romance loans were adapted into the native prosodic system of the language at the time of borrowing.

Notes

* I would like to express my appreciation to Haike Jacobs, Astrid Kraehenmann, Aditi Lahiri, Frans Plank and Tania Zamuner for helpful comments on earlier versions of this paper. This research was funded by the Royal Dutch Academy of Science.
1. The date mentioned in (2) and elsewhere for Dutch words, denotes the first occurrence of a word according to van der Sijs (2001).
2. The meaning of the early attested word was not related to the verb: 'result of multiplying quantities'. The meaning 'product' only occurred in 1752.
3. It is not the case that the preverb changed into a postverbal particle: often a different particle than the preverbal one was used, as in OE *atgo*, *atflee* corresponding to ModE go to, to flee from, respectively.
4. If there is a direct relation between the decline of prefixed verbs in English and word order changes, it follows that if the word order did not change, as in Dutch and German, no decline of prefixed verbs is expected. Dutch and German have indeed retained both separable stressed, and inseparable, unstressed prefixed verbs.
5. The general view is that stressed prefixes have an independent semantic meaning unlike the unstressed ones; unstressed prefixed are claimed to have undergone semantic bleaching, and often have little meaning, or an idiosyncratic meaning: *únderstandan* 'to stand under' vs. *understándan* 'understand'.
6. Lutz (1997) argues that native prefixes were losing ground in Old and Middle English because of general phonological reduction rules. Prefixes with reduced vowels were particularly vulnerable to these reduction rules, which are based on phonological strength. This could lead to the loss of entire lexical units (thus, also prefixes), and to the replacement by a semantically suitable alternative. In the history of English two alternatives were available: verb-particle constructions and Romance loans.
7. Strang (1970) argues that the increase of Romance prefixed loans was triggered by the decline of native prefixed words, which caused a chain shift.
8. Outlaw and mischieve are now stressed on the initial syllable.
9. The OED remarks that originally stress was final, which remained as late as 19th century.
10. According to the OED, the verb 'practice' previously had final stress.
11. For some verbs the OED explicitly mentions that they are derived from the nouns.
12. Halle & Keyser (1971: p 94) notice that some prefixes never bear stress, and thus nouns with such prefixes never undergo the stress retraction rule. However, they leave open the question of specifically how to deal with prefixes like ge- and assume only that they are somehow marked as exceptions to the stress assignment rules.
13. Comparing (9) and (10) this is not so obvious.

14. To account for the exceptional pairs given in (8), Halle & Keyser assume that the nouns were separate lexical entries, not derived directly from the verbs, and presumably did not have a prefix = boundary.
15. Minkova gives no violation here, and although it is not relevant as to optimal candidate is determined by the higher ranked constraint, ge- does not seem to be a root in itself.
16. Underlining refers to stress.
17. Moreover, verbs that enter the language after the loss of inflectional endings for verbs, should all have initial stress. This seems to be true.
18. Line final feet are not considered, because this position in general permits more variation.
19. As stress is alternating in these words it is impossible to distinguish between main and secondary stress on the basis of meter. These forms are therefore uninformative as to the location of main stress.

References

Aronoff, Mark
    1976   *Word formation in generative grammar.* Cambridge, MA: MIT Press.

Bree, Cor van
    1977   *Leerboek voor de historische grammatica van het Nederlands. Klanken vormleer met een beknopte grammatica van het Gotisch.* Groningen: Wolters-Noordhoff.
    1987   *Historische grammatica van het Nederlands.* Dordrecht: Foris.

Brinton, Laurel J.
    1988   *The development of English aspectual systems. Aspectualizers and post-verbal particles.* Cambridge: Cambridge University Press.

Campbell, A.
    1959   *Old English Grammar.* Oxford: Clarendon Press.

Chomsky, Noam & Morris Halle
    1968   *The sound pattern of English.* New York: Harper & Row.

Danielsson, B.
    1948   *Studies on the accentuation of polysyllabic Latin, Greek, and Romance loan-words in English.* Stockholm: Almqvist & Wiksells Boktryckeri.

Dresher, B. E. & Harry van der Hulst
    1995   'Head-dependent asymmetries in phonology'. In H. van der Hulst & J. van de Weijer (eds.), *Leiden in last: HIL phonology papers I.* The Hague: Holland Academic Graphics. 401-431.
    1998   'Head-Dependent asymmetries in phonology: complexity and visibility'. *Phonology* 15: 317-352.

Dresher, B. Elan & Aditi Lahiri
  1991   The Germanic foot: metrical coherence in Old English. *Linguistic Inquiry* 22. 251–286.
Fikkert, Paula
  2000   'Prosodic variation in Lutgart'. In A. Lahiri (ed.), *Analogy, levelling, markedness. Principles of change in phonology and morphology*. Berlin: Mouton. 301-332.
Franck, J.
  1910   *Mittelniederländische Grammatik*. Mit Lesestücken und Glossar. Leipzig: Chr. Hem. Tauchnitz.
Halle, Morris & Samuel J. Keyser.
  1971   *English Stress. Its form, its growth, and its role in verse*. New York: Harper & Row.
Hammerich, Louis L.
  1921   *Zur Deutschen akzentuation*. Copenhagen: Bianco Lunos Bogtrykkeri.
Hayes, Bruce
  1995   *Metrical stress theory: Principles and case studies*. Chicago: Chicago University Press.
Hiltunen, Risto
  1983   *The decline of the prefixes and the beginnings of the English phrasal verb*. Turku: Turun Yliopisto.
Jespersen, Otto
  1909   *A Modern English grammar on historical principles, Part 1: Sounds and spelling*. Heidelberg.
Kager, Rene
  1989   *A metrical theory of stress and destressing in English and Dutch*. Dordrecht: Foris.
Kastovsky, Dieter
  1996   'Verbal derivation in English: A historical survey. Or much ado about nothing'. In: Derek Britton (ed.), *English historical linguistics 1994*. Amsterdam/Philadelphia: John Benjamins.
Kingdon, R.
  1958   *The groundwork of English stress*. London.
Kiparsky, Paul
  1982   *Explanation in phonology*. Dordrecht: Foris.
Kluge, F.
  1891   Vorgeschichte der altgermanischen Dialekte. In H. Paul (ed.), *Grundriss der Germanischen Philologie*. Band I. Strassburg: Karl J. Trübner. 300–406.
Krahe, H. & W. Meid.
  1969   *Germanische Sprachwissenschaft*. Berlin: Walter de Gruyter.
Kuhn, A.
  1863   Review of C. W. M. Grein: Ablaut, reduplication und sekundäre Wurzeln der starken Verba dôn und iddja. *Zeitschrift für vergleichende Sprachforschung* 12. 142–145.

Lahiri, Aditi & B. Elan Dresher
1983-4 Diachronic and synchronic implications of declension shifts. *The Linguistic Review* 3. 141-163.
1999 'Open syllable lengthening in West Germanic'. *Language* 75: 678-719.

Lahiri, Aditi & Paula Fikkert
1999 'Trisyllabic shortening: past and present'. *English Language and Linguistics*. 229-267.

Lahiri, Aditi & Jacques Koreman
1988 'Syllable weight and quantity in Dutch'. H. Borer (ed.), *Papers from the West Coast Conference of Formal Linguistics 7*. 217-228.

Lahiri, Aditi, Tomas Riad & Haike Jacobs
1999 'Diachronic prosody'. In Hulst, H. G. van der (ed.), *Word prosodic systems in the languages of Europe*. Berlin: Mouton de Gruyter. 335-421.

Levins, P.
1969 *Manipulus Vocabulorum (1570)*. Menston, England: Scolar Press.

Loey, A. van
1970 Schönfeld's *Historische grammatica van het Nederlands*. Zutphen: Thieme.

Lutz, A.
1997 Sound Change, Word Formation and the Lexicon: The History of English Prefix Verbs. *English Studies* 3. 258-290.

Luick, K.
1907 'Beiträge zur englischen grammatik V. Zur quantitierung der romanischen lehnwörter und den quantitätsgesetzen überhaupt'. *Anglia* 30: 1-55.

Lutz, Angelika
1997 'Sound change, word formation and the lexicon: The history of the English prefix verbs', *English Studies* 3: 258-290.

Marchand, Hans
1969 *The Categories and Types of Present-Day English Word-Formation. A Synchronic-Diachronic Approach*. München: C. H. Beck'sche Verlagsbuchhandlung.

McCully, Chris & Richard Hogg
1990 'An account of Old English stress'. *Journal of Linguistics* 26: 315-339.

Minkova, Donka & Robert Stockwell.
1994 Syllable weight, prosody, and meter. *Diachronica* 11 (1). 35-64.

Minkova, Donka
1997 'Constraint ranking in Middle English stress-shifting'. *English Language and Linguistics* 1: 135-175.

Oxford English Dictionary
1933 Edited by J. A. H. Murray et al. Oxford: Clarendon Press.

Prince, Alan
  1990   'Quantitative consequences of rhythmic organization'. In Ziolkowski, M., M. Noske & K. Deaton (eds.) *Parasession on the syllable in phonetics and phonology*. Chicago: CLS. 355–398.
Prince, Alan & Paul Smolensky
  1993   Optimality theory: Constraint interaction in generative grammar. Ms. Rutgers University.
Prokosch, E.
  1939   *A comparative Germanic grammar*. Linguistic society of America, University of Pennsylvania, Philadelphia.
Samuels, M. L.
  1972   *Linguistic evolution. With special reference to English*. Cambridge: Cambridge University Press.
Scherer, W.
  1878   *Zur Geschichte der deutschen Sprache*. Berlin: Weidmannsche Buchhandlung.
Sijs, Nicoline van der
  2001   *Chronologisch woordenboek. De ouderdom en herkomst van onze woorden en betekenissen*. Amsterdam/Antwerpen: Uitgeverij L.J. Veen.
Strang, Barbara
  1970   *A history of English*. London: Methuen.
Strauss, S.
  1982   *Lexicalist phonology of English and German*. Dordrecht: Foris.
Streitberg, Wilhelm, V. Michels & Max H. Jellenick.
  1936   *Geschichte der indogermanischen Sprachwissenschaft*. Teil II. Die Erforschung der indogermanischen Sprachen: Germanisch. Berlin: Walter de Gruyter.
Suphi, M.
  1988   'Old English stress assignment'. *Lingua* 75: 171-202.
Sweet, H.
  1891   *A history of English sounds*. Oxford.
Trommelen, Mieke & Wim Zonneveld
  1989   *Klemtoon en metrische fonologie*. Muiderberg: Coutinho.Wright, J. & E. M. Wright. (1925). *Old English Grammar*. Second Edition. Oxford: Oxford University Press.
Walker, J.
  1791   *A critical pronouncing dictionary and expositor of the English language*. London.
Wright, J. & E. M. Wright.
  1925   *Old English Grammar*. Second Edition. Oxford: Oxford University Press.
  1928   *An elementary Middle English Grammar*. Second Edition. London: Humprhey Milford Oxford University Press.

Wurzel, W. U.
    1984   *Flexionsmorphologie und Natürlichkeit*. Berlin: Akademie-Verlag.

Zonneveld, Wim
    1992/2000   Van Afflighem en Chaucer: Het leven van Sinte Lutgart als jambisch gedicht. *Ruygh-Bewerp* XVII. Vakgroep Nederlands, Universiteit Utrecht. Herzien uitgegeven, Münster: Nodus Publikationen (2000).
    1993   '700 jaar Nederlandse klemtoon (en weinig veranderd)'. *Spektator* 22: 198-222.

Zonneveld, Wim, Mieke Trommelen, Michael Jessen, Curtis Rice, Gösta Bruce & Kristjan Árnason
    1999   'Wordstress in West-Germanic and North-Germanic languages'. In Harry van der Hulst (ed.), *Word Prosodic Systems in the languages of Europe*. Berlin: Mouton. 477-603.

Left-hand word-stress in the history of English

Chris McCully

1. Theoretical and historical backgrounds

1.1. Approaches to the problem

This paper addresses a phonological problem concerning the history of stress in English, and in doing so addresses issues concerning the descriptive adequacy of competing explanations for, and descriptions of, the history of English stress. For instance, in handling the stress patterning of present-day English (PDE) bisyllabic acronyms such as ACAS (Arbitration and Conciliation Advisory Service), or the primary+secondary patterning of "marked" or somewhat exceptionally derived nouns such as *proton*, or another problematic class of polysyllabic nouns bearing secondary stress on their final syllables (*mackintosh, Hottentot, ampersand*), standard versions of stress theory (Hayes 1982; Hayes 1995; Halle and Idsardi 1995), though differing in detail, would describe the retention of secondary stress in final syllables via lexical marking, or, more brutally, via the frank ascription of "exceptional" status. That is, such items misbehave, or are arguably marked, in terms of "normative" present-day English stress principles, which begin to assign prominence within a three-syllable window working from right-to-left across words, ignoring extrametrical material. (At least, this is the case in rule-based, piece-by-piece derivations; as we will see, the position in Optimality-theoretic (OT) accounts, where whole words are harmonically evaluated, is somewhat different.) Notably, in the examples given above, had final syllables been labelled as extrametrical prior to the right>left application of stress assignment then they would surface as merely weak.

Yet the observation that such items carry primary stress on (Root-) initial syllables may capture a completely normative "fact" about English stress, and about the historical persistence of Root-initial prominence – what the title of this papers refers to, informally, as "left-hand stress". The further observation that such items display secondary stress on their final syllables may be interpreted to mean that such items behave rather like compound nouns, and thus may behave in a relatively stable and expected fashion within the evolution of the English stress system, rather than patterning as exceptions.

Directly related to the presence or otherwise of secondary stress within words is the problem of where, and how, primary stress is distributed in English. Within the modern and present-day synchronies, primary stress has seemed to be rightmost, i.e. it is rightmost constituents (non-extrametrical feet within words) to which word-level prominence migrates. Historically, however (see 1.2. below), word-stress was in Old English (OE), as in other Germanic languages, unambiguously leftmost, i.e. Root-initial. Interestingly, within the Present Day English pattern, "rightmost primary word stress" is subject to a number of exceptions: there are word-final feet which are nevertheless non-primary stressed (the examples above are cases in point). Whether such items show the historical persistence of leftmost primary stress is arguable, and will be discussed below.

(1) summarizes some of the problems to be addressed in what follows:

(1)   Some problems of Present Day English primary stress

	Item	Observation	Problem
a.	balloon affair guitar cigar...	rightmost primary	exception to extrametricality
b.	ACAS NATO SOGAT AWOL...	leftmost primary	exception to (rhyme/syllable) extrametricality; secondary stress on final syllables

Item	Observation	Problem
c. stress-shift black-board hand-stand water-garden...	leftmost primary	under an approach using extrametricality, final feet (here coextensive with morphological Words) must be extrametrical; secondary stress on final syllables (Prosodic Words)
d. caravan catamaran garage...	stress rightmost/leftmost	how to account for variation
e. gorilla vanilla	stress on medial L(ight)	"eye-stressing"? spelling pronunciation? true exception?

In earlier incarnations of non-linear theory, the problems sketched in (1) could simply be stated as little more than a piece of derivational mechanics (how to construct and constrain the relevant rules). In one current version of the theory, that of OT, derivational mechanics give way to constraint-based modelling where the history and distribution of English stress is captured in constraint re-ranking (Minkova 1997; Gasiorowski 1998; see also Kager 1999). An object of the present paper is to ask which account of the problem might be most compelling. Is modelling the history of a stress system in terms of overlap between sub-parts of parameterized rules less, or more adequate than modelling the same system in terms of the shifting relations between a set of constraints?

In pre-OT models of non-linear stress theory in English (most recently Halle and Vergnaud 1987 [1990]; Hayes 1995; Halle and Idsardi 1995; Halle 1998) "word-level" stress rules work in Present Day English on the output of foot-formation processes. They do so while respecting parameters, and/or any extrametrical material. That is, a word-level rule will assign/project the main stress of a lexeme. A rule like this is familiar from the literature in different guises and under several names:

(2a) Liberman and Prince (1977; adapted)

LCPR. [L(exical) C(ategory) P(rominence) R(ule), abbreviated]

For any pair of sister nodes $[N_1, N_2]_L$ where L is a lexical category and N is a foot or dominates a foot, then **N_2 is strong** iff one of the following conditions is met:

- A. N_2 branches (*hiatus, expensive determine...*)
- B. N_2 is [+F] (*cigar, antique, bizarre...*)
- C. L is non-nominal and N_1 doesn't branch (*thirteen...*)
- D. L is a verb and N_2 directly dominates the stem (*permit, advance...*)

Otherwise, N_2 is weak

(2b) Hayes (1982)

WTCR. [W(ord) T(ree) C(onstruction) R(ule)]

For any pair of feet within a word **the second is strong(er)**

(2c) Prince (1983), Selkirk (1984), Hayes (1995)

End Rule, **Right** (after Hayes 1995: 60-61)

- a. Create a new metrical constituent at the top of the existing structure
- b. Observing the Continuous Column Constraint, place the grid mark forming the head of this constituent in the (leftmost/rightmost) available position (**Present Day English = rightmost**)

(2d) HV (adapted)

After line 0 parameter settings/heads have been projected

- Line 1 parameter settings are [+HT, -BND, right]
- Construct constituent boundaries on line 1
- Locate the head of the line 1 constituent on line 2
- Conflate lines 1 and 2

Partial derivation (material in < > is extrametrical):

```
                                    *
 *   *   *         (.   .   .   *)
(* *)(* *)(*) .     *   *   *   (*)
 o no ma to pei <a>  o no ma to pei <a>
```

(2e) Halle and Idsardi (1995; a parameters and projections approach, here abbreviated as SBG - Simplified Bracketed Grid)

Parameters for projection of main word stress:

Line 1: Edge RRR ("Insert a right bracket to the right of the head of the rightmost Foot")
Head R ("Project main word-stress on the rightmost stressable element")

Partial derivation

```
                        *
     *)            *)
* (* *)<.>    * (* *)<.>
a me ri ca    a me ri ca
```

What each account has in common - as the bold emphasis (supplied) written into each rule indicates - is that main word stress is invariably projected on the rightmost available foot, or (as in Selkirk 1984) the rightmost basic beat, or (as in SBG) the rightmost available edge constituent of a word.

The productivity of the notion "right edge" in Present Day English word-stress assignment is also captured in OT-theoretic work, as in (2f):

(2f) Align-Head (Pater 1995: 17; cf. Kager 1999: 167)

Align (PrWd, R, Head (PrWd), R) - ALIGN-HEAD
("Align the *right edge* of the Prosodic Word with the *right edge* of the head of the Prosodic Word")

One might reasonably ask what "headedness" means in this context: does this constraint refer to the general tendency in Present Day English to prefer the strongest feet in a Prosodic Word to lie as close as possible to the right edge of that word? Or by transitivity does the constraint refer not to rightmost feet but to the head of the rightmost foot? If the former, then one may also have grounds to assume a further constraint, All-F(ee)t-X (where X ranges Left/Right, Kager 1999: 163), by which "Every foot stands at the left/right edge of the prosodic Word". In present versions of OT, therefore, two constraints,

Alignment and All-Ft-X, are mutually responsible for ensuring that (i) a foot is optimally aligned with the right edge of the (Prosodic) word, and (ii) that peaks are rightmost/leftmost (in Present Day English, the assumption would be "rightmost"). At the same time one might justifiably question the need for two constraints (where derivational theories place main stress with a single rule); and further, one may query the justification for thinking of the projection of main word stress as a top-down, evaluative procedure. Historically, one can and should ask where such a procedure originated, given that the constraints operative in earlier synchronies (Old English, for example) would appear to align strongest word-stress with (the left edge of) Root-initial syllables.

By way of summary of 1.1: rule-based accounts assume that at some period in the history of English, parameters were re-set so that stress assignment begins to iterate right>left, rather than left>right. OT, meanwhile, would appear to assume not that parameters, as such, were re-set but that Alignment and Footing constraints were re-ranked. Teasing out the implications of these respective positions may prove insightful in terms of evaluating the processes of historical phonological change.

1.2. Diachrony (I): evidence from Middle English, and the "Catastrophe Model"

In terms of the history of English, accounts of stress change have tended to focus on the replacement of "Germanic, left-strong" rules with "Romance stress" patterns that privilege rightmost constituents. The first statement of such replacement within generative phonology may be found in Chomsky and Halle (1968; SPE), modified in Halle and Keyser (1971), and developed in much of the subsequent literature, however these rule-based analyses were subsequently developed into parameterized accounts (Lass 1992; McCully 1997), or derivational accounts focussed on the presumed longevity of the "Germanic foot" (Dresher and Lahiri 1991; Lahiri et al. 1999, cf. McCully, forthcoming). The various analyses have in common that "left-handed" Germanic stress, with strongest word-initial prominence, is held to be replaced, or subsumed, early in the ME period, by a "right-handed" Romance pattern. The subsequent existence of stress doublets - *hónour(e)* vs. *honóur(e)*, *Vénus* vs. *Venús* - is often cited to support the general case of change, usually accompanied by the rider that such doublets were sometimes, though by no means always, accommodated, sooner or later, to native stress patterns. (For a suggestive account of such replacement, see Minkova 1997; see also Redford, this volume). Further, in derivational accounts of English stress, Romance principles could be shown to be compatible with native vocabulary, since sub-parts of Romance rules, or elements of the relevant parameterization, would apply by default to native items. This is clearly (and trivially) the case with lexical monosyllables; it is also the case with bi-syllables with light finals, and polysyllables with light medials. On this view, the phonological crisis provided by the spectacle of incoming Romance rule(s) is played down, precisely *because* much of the native Old English vocabulary proves susceptible to re-analysis. It is difficult to resist the temptation to imagine Old English hanging around in linguistic history, looking hopefully through the stained glass of a three-syllable window, and waiting to speak with a French accent.

Crucial data on stress changes in Middle English is often held to be provided by the metrical and phonological structures presumed to be manifest in the work of Chaucer, and it is worthwhile looking at how this evidence is typically handled. What consequences, for the evolution of the English stress system, are entailed by the "evidence" provided through the metrical work of this poet?

Chaucer, speaking and writing in a language contact situation not far removed from – and at least weakly analogous to – that of today cannot, of course, be assumed to have had a form of linguistic competence radically different from that of any other native (and literate) speaker. And under the terms of the Uniformitarian Hypothesis, the language contact situation pertaining in many parts of England during the fourteenth century cannot be assumed, without heavy qualification, to have given rise to unprecedented innovation in (the phonology of) English. Yet "linguistic innovation may turn out to mean nothing new".

Generalizing about Chaucer's language is enabled by the fact that, compared (for example) to other English poets of the period, a great deal is known about his life, reading, and continental sojourns. It is known that Chaucer's education, as a court page, must have included instruction in French and Latin. His sojourns abroad included service in France, and diplomatic visits to France, Italy, and Spain (where one infers from the offer of safe conduct issued to Chaucer by Charles the Bad that the poet was on pilgrimage to Santiago de Compostela). It is assuredly the case that Chaucer's knowledge of both French and Italian not only made possible the great early translations, including the *Book of the Duchess* (1369-70; see Robinson 1957: xxix), but also allowed Chaucer single-handedly to invent the metre that has become canonical in the English tradition, the iambic pentameter (Duffell 1996; 2000). The single decisive factor that allowed Chaucer to achieve this was his ruling out of the triple-time hemistich- and line-closures he found in his Italian models, and the imposition of strict rhythmic alternation on the final two feet (or four metrical positions, W S W S) of the decasyllabic line ("Chaucer had to restrict in his verse the two minor rhythms of Boccaccio's (the first in triple time, the second in *fragmento adónico*)....[] Chaucer also borrowed the Italians' favourite rhythm…because a duple-time rhythm (one of *moraic trochees*) happens to underlie both the Italian and the English languages….." Duffell 2000: 284, 283-284).

Whatever Chaucer's individual linguistic and literary competence, rather more important is the linguistic environment of England – specifically, of London – out of which Chaucer and many of his readers were born, and into which Chaucer's verse penetrated. It is a handbook commonplace, surely, that the linguistic milieu of London, of educated, literate, bourgeois and court London, was heavily influenced by Parisian French:

> It is important to recognise that after the Norman Conquest, the French language imported into England soon developed its own individual variety, that of Anglo-Norman, and that monarchs like Edward III and Richard II, like their predecessors, were French-speaking, presiding over largely francophone courts. Two issues are points of linguistic debate: first, whether French was the mother tongue of those residing in court circles, or always or mostly an acquired second language; and second, whether French was ever a living language even in the lower echelons of society, and if so, to what extent, and according to which geographical distribution. Even when in Chaucer's age English started to regain its strength and French started to recede, French remained a language of culture, of record, of ideas in science, medicine, history, agriculture, the law, administration, and theology. It is estimated that

in these lexical areas and others, some ten thousand French words were adopted in English in the Middle Ages, of which approximately three quarters have survived to our day.... (Zonneveld 1999: 120).

Strang (1970: 250-51) adds that "borrowing requires more than contact between two speech-communities. It requires bi-lingualism, at least in some measure. And Anglo-French bilingualism, on any significant scale, was slow to develop. Once it did, the sluice-gates opened, and there poured into English the greatest flood of loans from a single source by which the language has ever been inundated...."

In terms of the stress phonology of English, it is exposure to French, the development of bilingualism, and the inundation brought about by successive phases of borrowing, that are widely assumed to have triggered not only end-stress on native items (while retaining, as expected, primary stress on final syllables of the borrowed "Romance" loans), but also to have developed quantity-sensitive patterns of Latinate stress retraction on native and non-native polysyllables alike. On this view, English is subject to the incursions of at least two "new" stress rules (one to handle French items, one to handle many Latin polysyllables). Along the way, it is claimed (Halle and Keyser 1971: 102), many native Germanic words, with weight-blind, root-initial stress, were stressed in accordance with one of the "Romance" rules, while many French and Latin borrowings were, or came to be, stressed in accordance with the existing "Germanic" rule (= Root-initial-strongest). Although the foregoing is an oversimplification for the sake of theoretical economy, this is the assumption that underlies even relatively recent work such as Lass 1992 ("It looks as though English underwent a change of "handedness" [from left>right prominence assignment, with initial stress, to right>left assignment, with primary stress on the final foot of the word: McC]) and McCully 1997. Let us here call this view of innovation in the English stress system the "Catastrophe Model" (because English stress is held to lurch from crisis to crisis, each crisis being co-extensive with an incoming rule, or co-operative set of rules). The Catastrophe Model depends on re-structuring beginning, perhaps, in Anglo-Norman, and more certainly, in Parisian French.   In (3) I spell out some consequences of the "Blame English stress on the French" analysis:

(3) Some formal consequences of Blaming It On The French

- massive French borrowing (c.1100-1450) brings with it a(t least one) new stress "rule"
- such a rule applies to non-native and native items alike, though not predictably in native items
- meanwhile, existing "Germanic" rules apply (though not everywhere, and not always) to some borrowed "Romance" items
- speakers develop a subdivided lexicon (Halle and Keyser 1971: 99), where "a special subdivision" deals "with stress placement in words that were being introduced from French and other, primarily Romance, languages" (Halle and Keyser, ibid.)
- meanwhile, Chaucer (and other poets) were able to write a highly cultured verse where both native and non-native bisyllables (for example) could be stressed W S or S W, and
- this new, highly cultured verse provides evidence for the interpenetration of the "Germanic" and "Romance" rules in an arguably sub-divided lexicon.

Picked apart, however, such a (non) theory is revealed to be impeachable on at least the grounds of bad logic. Some theoretical and other drawbacks of (3) are detailed in (4) below:

(4) Drawbacks of the *Let's Blame It On The French* Hypothesis

- it is implausible in terms of the Uniformitarian Hypothesis
- it misrepresents the extent and degree of "French influence"
- it misrepresents linguistic change, and does so at the expense of continuity
- it brings with it the danger of circular argumentation, since the evidence for reconstruction is almost wholly based on verse (and often, worse, on the assumed form of words in line-final, rhymed position)
- it misrepresents the nature of the English lexicon.

In terms of "French influence" it's not the case that words of French origin were felt to be equally prestigious, and thus available to be shunted into that subdivision of the English lexicon to which such foreign, prestige words belonged. Burnley (1983) properly asks whether a purely etymological, synchronic distinction can be made between words of French and English origin, and suggests that such a distinction might be "a misrepresentation of the way in which Chaucer's compatriots would perceive their language. At the least, we must distinguish between established French borrowings, which have become incorporated into the common core of the language, and those which are new and are still felt as foreign. Statistical statements to the effect that Chaucer's vocabulary contains 51.8 per cent of Romance loan words are of little use in assessing Chaucerian style, and indeed simply ignore the crucial factor of the contemporary perception of the status of the words" (1983: 135). Burnley's further observations form such an interesting counter-suggestion to the idea of a rigidly stratified lexicon that they are worth quoting separately:

> in assessing Chaucer's vocabulary, degree of familiarity and frequency of use are more important than etymological origins.... The co-existence of two languages in the everyday life of Chaucer's circle would inevitably lead to a certain "fuzziness" in the demarcation between their two language skills. English was regarded as shifting and various, and the extent of its resources was uncertain; French was often written, at least in technical fields, with a phrasing and syntax owing much to English, whereas English had long ago adopted many of the phrasal idioms of French. In the minds of men with bilingual competence, the boundaries of the languages would be particularly ill-defined....(Burnley 1983: 135-136)

Burnley interestingly highlights the fact that many of the earlier Anglo-Norman loans were not felt to be particularly "foreign" (*castel, prisoun, daunce, werre* 'war'). Further, early calques such as 'to do justice' (*faire justice*) and 'to have (or grant) mercy' (A-N *grant mercy, gramercy*) testify to the fact that certain syntactic constructions were familiar in English contexts. And moreover, it is clear that many French borrowings, both early (Anglo-Norman) and later (Parisian French), were entirely amenable to native English stress principles. This is most clearly the case with Anglo-Norman, and with later borrowing of monosyllables (trivially) and bisyllables (see below, figures (5-7)). It is also the case, less clearly but still ascertainably, in some trisyllables as well (i.e. those that did not have heavy medial syllables).

Burnley's work suggests that English stress is as messy – in Burnley's words, there's a "certain "fuzziness"" – for our contemporaries as it was for Chaucer's. There's frequency of use; there's prestige. There is, in short, sociolinguistic variation. (See below for empirical data for Present Day English.) There is also the sense that the lexicon is organized not into layers, but in terms of a core vocabulary, accessible to (and partly constituted by) a familiar set of rules or constraints, together with peripheral items, items that perhaps are felt to be "non-native" because their phonological form is constituted precisely by a set of non-native, and/or low-ranked constraints. One doubts whether a neatly subdivided lexicon existed in the mind of Chaucer, Gower, Thomas Usk, or the woman who sold eel pies on Billingsgate Market. Following Minkova (1997) it is possible to conceive of the English lexicon of the period in terms of the model developed by Ito and Mester (1995). The Middle English lexicon "can be stratified into a core consisting of native and already assimilated words for which all relevant constraints obtain, and increasingly peripheral lexical strata mapped like concentric circles around the core, for which the core constraints are progressively weakened. The boundaries between all strata allow fluctuation"(Minkova 1997: 153).

Is it possible to find empirical data for "fuzziness" in stress patterns? Can "Chaucerian stress", and the language-contact situation that precedes and includes it, be studied today? Given that diachronic change may be studied by analysing analogous synchronic problems, the answer is a qualified affirmative.

Consider the following fragment of data. It scores Subject 05's response to a "Stress Questionnaire" distributed as part of a pilot study of English stress underway (and still in progress) in Manchester. Native and non-native speaker-subjects were provided with a list of bi- and polysyllabic items, most of them loans from French, and asked to read back the items in three different styles, (a) a single-word, list style, (b) a phrase-list style (which allows analysis of rhythmically driven stress-shift within the target items), and (c) a reading passage style (which allows analysis of the same items

Left-hand word-stress in the history of English 361

pronounced rather more informally, and at a normative tempo). At the same time, the Subjects' age, sex, current occupation, holiday destinations, L1 (and L2 and L3, if any), and other relevant information, were recorded. (For the Stress Questionnaire in full, see Appendix.) One object of the pilot study was to obtain firm data on what possible linguistic interferences, vis à vis English stress patterning, might obtain from L2 learning and/or exposure. It is also proving possible to study sociolinguistic variation in English stress patterning. (5) gives the scores for Subject 05, a 17-year old white male from Glasgow.

(5) Results from Stress Questionnaire for respondent 05

Informant	Single word 05	Phrase 05	Reading 05
L1	BrE (Glasgow)	BrE (Glasgow)	BrE (Glasgow)
L2	F (minimal)	F (minimal)	F (minimal)
Age	15-20 (17)	15-20	15-20
Sex	M	M	M
chateau	/ \	/ \ and \ /	/ \
garage	/ x	/ x	/ x
pate	/ \	/ \	/ \
defense	\ /	\ /	\ /
offense	\ /	x /	x /
flambe	Didn't recognise word		
technique	\ /	\ /	\ /
debris	/ \	/ \	/ \
coupon	/ \	/ \	/ \
cliché	/ \	/ \	/ \
Bordeaux	\ /	/ \ and \ /	\ /
homage	/ x	/ x	/ x
salon	/ \	/ \	/ \
diverse	\ /	n/r	\ /
bureau	/ \	/ \	/ \
café	/ \	/ \	/ \
souffle	/ \	/ \	/ \
ballet	/ \	/ \	/ \
nouveau	x /	\ /	\ /

mobile	/ \	/ \	/ \
End-stressed	**6**	**6** (4 + 2 Reversal)	**6**
Initial-stressed	**14**	**14**	**14**
monument	/ x x	/ x x	/ x x
versatile	/ x \	/ x \	/ x x
fiance	x / \	x / \	x / \
premier	/ x \	/ x \	/ x \
harassment	x / x	x / x	x / x
Beaujolais	\ x /	\ x / and / x \	/ x \
End-stressed	**1**	**1**	**0**
Initial-stressed	**3**	**3 + 1 Reversal**	**4**
Other	**2**	**2**	**2**
controversy	/ x \ x	/ x \ x	/ x \ x
quantitative	/ x \	/ x x \ or / x (x)	/ x (x)
advertise-ment	/ x \ x	/ x \ x	/ x \ x
Initial-stressed	**3**	**3**	**3**

For this speaker, in the single-word list 14/20 items are initial-stressed, and it seems largely to be the most overtly "French" items that are pronounced with end-stress (*technique, nouveau, Bordeaux*). Elsewhere, this speaker appears to have a Root-initial stress default.

It's worthwhile comparing Subject 05's results with that of Subject 03, a 28-year old speaker of General American with native-like Spanish as her L2:

(6) Result of Stress Questionnaire for Subject 03

Summary of results

Bisyllables, Single word list
    Initial-stressed   7
    End-stressed 13

Trisyllables
    Initial-stressed   2

End-stressed 0
Other   4

Polysyllables
Initial stressed   3 (pattern / x \ x throughout)

Unlike Subject 05, this speaker appears at first glance to have a form of default rightward stress, although this is modified by an unreliable (a "fuzzy") tendency towards left-alignment. A more penetrating look at the data, however, suggests that while this speaker has end-stress in some overtly "French" items, elsewhere the un-predictabilities are great enough to make one suspect that end-stress is a variant driven by sociolinguistic considerations, possibly associations with prestige. (These upredictabilities include initial vowel reduction: *garáge* BUT *pàté*; exceptions to \ / patterning in bisyllables: *salón* BUT *hómage* and *bállèt, sóufflè*; unpredictability of Reversal, rhythmic alternation (phrase list): *flàmbé > flámbè (flambe steak)*, BUT cf. single-word *bállèt* vs. Northern *bàllét*, the last possibly with phrase-final, intonational lengthening.) In other words, for this speaker, left-hand word stress could still be the default.

Perhaps the most surprising result, to date, of this pilot study comes in the form of data provided by a native speaker of French:

Informant	Single word 02	Phrase 02	Reading 02
L1	F	F	F
L2	BrE	BrE	BrE
Age	20+	20+	20+
Sex	F	F	F
chateau	/ \	/ \ and \ /	/ \
garage	x /	/ \	x /
pate	x /	\ / and / \	/ \
defense	\ /	\ /	/ \
offense	/ \	\ /	/ \
flambe	/ \	/ \ and \ /	/ \
technique	\ /	\ /	\ /
debris	/ \	/ \	/ \
coupon	/ \	/ \	/ \
cliché	/ \	/ \	/ \

Bordeaux	/\	/\ and / x	/\
homage	/\	/\	/\
salon	\/	/\	/\
diverse	/\	n/r	\/
bureau	/\	/\ and \/	/\
café	/\	x / and /\	/\ and \/
souffle	/\	/\	/\
ballet	/\	/\	/\
nouveau	/\	\/	/\
mobile	/\	/\	/\
End-stressed	5	5 up to 8	4
Initial-stressed	15	15 up to 14	16

monument	/ x x	/ x x	/ x x
versatile	/ x \	\/ x (!)	x / x (!)
fiance	/ x \	\/\	/ x \
premier	/\	\/ and / x \	/ x \
harassment	\/ x	x / x and \/ x	x / x
Beaujolais	\\/	/ x \	/ x \
End-stressed	1	1	0
Initial-stressed	4	2	4
Other	1	3	2

controversy	/ x \ x	\/ x x	\/ x x
quantitative	\/ x x	\/ x x	\/ x x
advertisement	/ x \ x	/ x \ x and x /\ x	x /\ x
Initial-stressed	2	2	0

In the single-word list, this speaker had of all respondents the highest proportion of initial-stressed items, suggesting that in a language-contact situation, speakers consciously or unconsciously learning an L2 readily adopt (and even over-generalize) the L1's default primary word-stress pattern. In this case, it is a left-hand pattern.

To underscore this point concerning the patterned "fuzziness" of stress in the linguistic competence of Chaucer's contemporaries, we might briefly compare Chaucer's own employment of bisyllabic loan-words in verse with respondent 05's perception of such items. In (7), the stress patterns of 10 French loan-words in the opening of the *Canterbury Tales* are analysed. ("Assumptions" are those often made in the literature; "Comment" has something, if only a little, to say about each preceding assumption.)

(7) A comparison of Chaucer's linguistic competence, and that of respondent 05

    Token: *licour*
    Example: *And bathed every veyne in swich licour*
    Assumption: *licour* appears in W S position in the verse. It's a French loan. therefore it's linguistically W S.
    Comment: Yes, probably. Rhymes with full-stressed mono-syllable *flour* BUT evidence from rhyme is problematic, since rhyme position can match full unstress with stress: rhyme isn't a reliable diagnos-tic for primary stress.

    Token: *vertu*
    Example: *Of which vertu engendred is the flour* (GProl. 5)
    Assumption: *vertu* appears in W S position in the verse. It's a French loan. Therefore its underlying stress pattern is W S
    Comment: the word can quite easily be both linguistically and metrically S W. There's no need to *assume* it's W S. If metrically S W, one might expect elision of <u#~#e>, and this doesn't appear to occur, so it's *probable* that the pattern is W S.

    Token: *palmeres*
    Example: *And palmeres for to seken straunge strondes* (Gprol. 13)
    Assumption: It's a French loan, stands in S W position of verse. Appears to be initial-stressed.
    Comment: Right. The tilting power of metre, or prior linguistic S W.

    Token: *season*
    Example: *Bifil that in that seson on a day* (GProl. 19)
    Assumption: French loan, stands in S W position of verse. Appears to be initial-stressed.
    Comment: Right.

    Token: *devout*
    Example: *To Caunterbury with ful devout corage* (GProl. 22)
    Assumption: French loan, linguistically W S. Verse W S
    Comment: Linguistically W S (and metrically, a trochee in that position would be unusual – at least, in Chaucer's verse - to the point of being impossible).

Token: *corage*
Example: *To Caunterbury with ful devout corage* (GProl. 22)
Assumption: French loan, linguistically and metrically W S
Comment: Right

Token: *pilgrim*
Example: *In felaweshipe, and pilgrimes were they alle* (GProl. 26)
Assumption: French loan (< Provencal *pelegrin*), stands in S W position of verse, therefore linguistically S W
Comment: Assumption's right, but derived for wrong reason. Word simply patterns with other early borrowings, bisyllables compatible with native stress principles (= initial stress). It was *already* S W before being used that way in verse.

Token: *honour*
Example: *Trouthe and honour, fredom and curteisie* (GProl. 46)
Assumption: French loan, appears in W S position of verse, therefore linguistically W S. Used W S elsewhere.
Comment: Wrong assumption. And why make it? Line could begin with two trochees, S W S W (line-beginnings have more metrical freedom). Further, your metrical reading of S W W S, though possible, is unlikely given the parallelism of [S (and)] [S W] [S W] – *truth, honour, freedom* all put into parallelistic alignment.

Token: *degree*
Example: *No Cristen man so ofte of his degree* (GProl. 55)
Assumption: French loan, W S in line-final position. Linguistically W S. Maintains stress pattern into Present Day English. Vowel Shift. Linguistically W S.
Comment: Right.

Token: *army*
Example: *At many a noble armee hadde he be* (GProl. 60)
Assumption: French loan. S W in verse. Linguistically S W.
Comment: Right. Spelling indicated /i:/ or (conservatively) /e:/. Secondary-stressed syllables (if this is one) could freely be used in metrical W positions.

Results for 10 tokens

Incontrovertibly end-stressed: 4
Incontrovertibly initial-stressed: 4
Probably initial-stressed: 2

Recall respondent 05's scores. For twenty bisyllabic French loans, sixteen were initial-stressed, four end-stressed (single-word style). That is, 80% of the items were initial-stressed. For Chaucer, on the plausible assumption that *linguistically* many of the bisyllabic loans of (7) are S W, 60% of the sample turns up as initial-stressed. Of the remainder, all occur in metrical positions (line- or hemistich-final) that obligatorily demand W S. Certainly, it is a miniscule sample, and one arrived at randomly (in (7), merely by taking the first ten bisyllabic French loan words to occur in the text), but the percentages indicate that Chaucer's linguistic competence, with respect to the perception of English and French stress patterns, may not have been radically different from that of today's seventeen-year-old Glaswegian. (For a similar, indeed more telling, set of percentages see Minkova 1997: 149-51.) It would be unsafe to assume that respondent 05, with his vanishingly small knowledge of French, has a subdivided, indexed lexicon, with "native" and "Romance" rules earmarked for application within those sub-divisions. Under the terms of the Uniformitarian Hypothesis, it would be equally unwise to assume such specified rule-application, and such a configured lexicon, for Chaucer or for his contemporaries. English stress in the late fourteenth century, and the history that underpins it, is a fuzzier, messier, more complex and more in-teresting matter than rules, lists, and the particularities of linguistic indexation. Therefore the Catastrophe Model, which at least implies, and in its strongest versions demands, drama – incoming rule, parametric switch, and change of "handedness" – seems im-peachable. It appears to drive the history of English stress by assuming the prior existence of indexed rules, and thus may stand charged with putting the theoretical cart before the analytical horse. But data cannot be compelled by theory, and the data, studied above in brief, suggest that speakers, in the late fourteenth century as now, may have an uneasy sense that some item is "foreign" (and may be so pronounced, for reasons of prestige, earnestness, or sheer bafflement), while fuzzily judging the degree of native non-likeness against well-established native default patterns.

Derivationalists may here object that during the period of Catastrophe, while native and non-native rules and parameters are jostling for space within the English lexicon, there will be an unavoidable period of confusion, and that (therefore) rules may over-apply, or may be over-generalized. One might counter by saying that Subject 05 does not appear to be a rule-governed entity, and still manages to end-stress some of the target words. Subject 02 generalizes the left-hand pattern not because she is learning a (new) rule, with its accompanying, ordered subrules (e.g. of extrametricality), but because she has picked up on an underlying default, and adopts this as a piece of appropriate phonology in her specific language-contact situation. The emerging picture seems to be a matter of sociolinguistic variation and default, rather than of rule-driven catastrophe. It remains to be seen whether, and to what extent, derivational or OT accounts are better suited to accounting for this variation, and the linguistic history through which it persists.

1.3 Diachrony (II): extrametricality and the history of English

The most comprehensive and elaborate derivationalist account of the history of English stress to date is that found in Lahiri et al. (1999). The paper attempts to show how the history of English stress – and the history of stress in cognate languages, such as Dutch and German – is intimately bound up with the interaction between the persistence of the structure informally called the "Germanic foot" (an augmented moraic trochee), and the restructuring consequent on the development of (different forms of) right-edge extrameticality in the respective languages. Some crucial assumptions of this account are detailed in (8):

(8)   Lahiri et al. 1999. Extrametricality and the Germanic foot

- the foot that carries primary and secondary stress in Common Germanic (and in Old English, Old High German, Middle Dutch) was the Germanic foot (called in the 1999 paper the resolved moraic trochee, see also Lahiri et al. 1999: 404 fn.1)
- iteration takes place: "[In Common Germanic] the direction of parsing...was left-to-right, with main stress assigned at the left edge, while in the modern languages the parsing is from right to left, with the rightmost foot being the most prominent" (1999: 345)
- as a result of iteration – and the over-generation it entails – various devices are assumed to have operated in the respective Germanic stress phonologies, most significantly

- final destressing (non-branching final feet are deleted in Old English, thus æþeling, 'prince', with final destressing, but æþelinges (g.sg., / x \ x), and
- extrametricality (of final consonants, see Lahiri et al. 1999: 348ff.), driving inter alia Trisyllabic Shortening in Old English (OE *hēringes > heringes, cf. PDE herring) so that acceptable Germanic feet are generated (the LHL syllable structure of heringe(s) maps nicely into a SWW Germanic foot).

It is not my intention here to revisit all details of Lahiri et al.'s arguments, since many of these are the subject of a separate paper (McCully, forthcoming). It is perhaps sufficient to note here that the Germanic foot would be an addition, and a somewhat ungainly one, to the universal foot inventory proposed by Hayes (1995); that the assumption of final consonant extrametricality, while well motivated, still leaves a residue of derivations to be handled under the theoretically-suspect terms of Final Destressing; and that Final Destressing, as a repair strategy, is as unwelcome in the grammar as Initial Destressing is (or was) in Present Day English. As we shall see, however, the notion that certain edge-constituents (word-final consonants, syllabic Rhymes, perhaps even final feet) may not count in calculations of stress is essentially correct, and is cross-linguistically attested (see Kager 1999, especially chapter 4). Yet one has the impression of a clever derivationalist model designed in order to account, somewhat conspiratorially, for a central assumption: that stress in English switched direction, and main stress switched word-edge (see second point above). But this is merely an assumption. It may be that default main word stress in many if not all varieties of English has remained leftmost (see again the materials in (5-7) above), though subject to a whole host of more or less explainable exceptions. If so, then English stress may flow in at least some of its old channels, and the historical task would be not so much to account, however ingeniously, for the shock of the new (the Catastrophe Model), but the persistence of the old.

If we are truly in the environment of historical persistence, it is equally clear that the "rules" that arguably operate in the tenth century are no longer productive in the twenty-first. The "Germanic Stress Rule" is assumed to work from left-to-right, ignoring unscannable (extrametrical) material such as verbal prefixes, and it is transparently obvious that such a rule would scarcely work for much of Present Day English – though it would work for some of the Present Day English lexicon, some of the time. (It would work, trivially, for lexical monosyllables, for bisyllables of the form L(ight)+L(ight) or H(eavy)+Light, and for trisyllables of the form H/L+L+L. It would not elegantly work for L+H bisyllables, for prefixed verbs, and for large classes of polysyllabic adjectives.) At even a cursory glance, then, one could not readily assume that some unmodified rule-block provided an enduring framework for English stress. Nor would it be easy to construct a level-ordered account of the history of English stress, since even if one were to assume two levels of derivation for Old English (and thus account among other things for the structuring of secondary stress), it would be unclear how, and when, those erstwhile levels of derivation conflated...or where, if at all, cyclicity kicked into the derivational pattern. (For some suggestions along these lines, see Hutton 1998, and the development of Hutton's work into a level-ordered form of OT in McCully 1999.) And what, in any case, would be the point of refining the Catastrophe Model, if what little evidence there is points towards the radical persistence of the old?

2. Developing a theory of evolution: the persistence of the old

2.1. Evidence for left-hand stress from Present Day English

How might the persistence of the old be studied? Once again we might turn to word-form and (crucially) to word-creation in Present Day English, and look at two interesting classes of items. One is a small class of relatively rare, and largely technical, words, whose final syllables exceptionally bear secondary stress. The second is the much larger, and fast-growing, class of acronyms. Some data are schematised in (9):

(9) Studying initial stress in Present Day English: learned loans, and acronyms
   a. prótòn, nárthèx, hélìx...and in derivational words e.g. gýmnàst.
   b. bisyllabic acronyms, all initial+secondary stressed, / \:
      ACAS, AWOL, HOTOL, NATFHE, NATO, SOGAT, UMIST...

This is a partial set of data, and of course there are several trisyllabic acronyms where main stress is medial (*UNESCO, UNITA*). Vennemann (personal communication, 1995 *International Conference on Historical Linguistics*) proposes that there is nothing in fact exceptional about these trisyllabic items, and that they are to be handled completely straightforwardly under normative Romance principles. Yet in fact normative Romance principles would, allowing for extraprosodicity of final syllables, oblige final syllables to surface as unstressed in the bisyllabic word-class, and thus Romance principles do not seem to apply *tout court*. (In theories which avoid the necessity for marking constituents as extraprosodic, e.g. Halle and Idsardi 1995 (see especially the account of Latin stress, 425ff., and cf. the edge-marking analysis of Halle 1998), the same effect is achieved through a specified form of Edge Marking and Head Projection. Notably, in every non-linear account to date, items such as bisyllabic acronyms carrying / \ stress would have to be handled as exceptions to normative principles.)

For the class of acronyms, which are clearly cases of word-creation where every segment (grapheme) "counts", it is probably undesirable to posit extraprosodicity at all, see here McCully and Holmes (1988). That is, one cannot leave the final syllables invisible and/or unparsed.

The problem is two-fold: to account for the presence of secondary stress on final syllables, and primary stress on initials. Rule-based accounts work at some cost: the final syllables have to bear lexically assigned feet (or have lexically-projected Heads); then extrametricality applies, with the effect of making the final (lexical) foot – not just the final Rhyme – invisible; then a foot is assigned to the word-initial syllable. At this point, right-hand word-level stress applies, but cannot see the extrametrical final foot. Word-level stress is dumped on the initial syllable. Thereafter, the skipped foot is incorporated into a higher-level left-hand structure of the form

```
(*     .
(*...<*>)    <*>: "extrametrical" final foot
 A   B
```

Paradoxically, a right-hand default here obtains a left-hand result (primary stress on A) but only because the final syllable (B) has been brutally assigned a lexical foot prior to the derivation, and is subsequently extrametrical.

Given the apparent "naturalness" of initial stress on such items, one might ask whether there is a simpler account. One possibility lies in OT, where instead of Prosodic Words (PrWds) being prosodified piecemeal and step-wise, whole PrWds are harmonically evaluated by a language-specific ranking of universal constraints. Just four relevant constraints, here used largely as cover terms (these constraints turn out to be more complicated entities later on), are Root, Initial Prominence, Non Finality, and Parse Syllable.

The constraint Root (Minkova 1997) demands that lexical words are assigned prosodic structure somewhere in their Roots. In this sense the constraint is drawn from earliest work in OT (Prince and Smolensky 1993), and is elaborated in Kager (1999: 152 and *passim*.) as GrWd=PrWd ("A grammatical word must be a prosodic word"). Initial Prominence demands that "Initial syllables of Roots are stressed". That this constraint turns out to be a cover term stems from work by Kager (1999), who shows clearly that word-initial stress is matter for both Align-Head-X (Align-Leftmost: "The head foot is leftmost in PrWd", cf. Kager 1999: 167) *and* word-alignment constraints (e.g. Align-Word-Left: "Every PrWd begins with a foot", cf. Kager 1999: 169). Non Finality, which may turn out to be OT's problematic star of the piece in reconstructing the history of the English stress system, demands that "No foot is final in the PrWd". And Parse Syllable demands that "syllables are parsed into well-formed feet" (Kager 1999: 162; Pater 1995: 4).

Notice that in common with all constraint rankings, constraints are in potential conflict. This, for instance, a constraint such as Align-Head-Right would be in direct competition with Non Finality. Yet violations are in principle allowed, and where constraints conflict, matters are settled in favour of the output that incurs fewest penalties.

What might a fragmentary constraint ranking look like? For English, as for many other languages, Root is apparently inviolable, and if structure is assigned within a Root, then the parsed syllable or syllables must be part of a well-formed foot. (That the well-formed foot on English is a moraic trochee is independently attested, see Pater 1995, Kager 1999 and, for typology, Hayes 1995. The relevant constraint runs as Foot Binarity, abbr. Ft-Bin, which demands that "feet must be binary under moraic or syllabic analysis", see Kager 1999: 156.) Non Finality, which forces stress off final syllables, appears to be violated by our bisyllabic acronyms, each of which have a surface final foot, yet it may be that such violation is allowed if the disobedient items fulfil the terms of some higher-ranked constraint, possibly what is here called Initial Prominence. And Parse Syllable appears to be fulfilled in each of our example outputs – yet we know independently that it will be widely violated elsewhere (e.g. the initial syllables of *a(gen)da*, the "stranded" syllable *–ma-* of *(Tata)ma(gouchi)*, see Pater 1995: 14), in favour of Ft-Bin. Therefore it is unlikely to be as high-ranked in the constraint set as Root, or Initial Prominence, but may take its place above Non Finality.

These informal remarks suggest the constraint ranking Root>>Initial Prominence>>Parse Syllable>>Non Finality. Spelled out:

It is more important for   *than it is for*
Lexical words to be prosodified   words to have initial prominence
Words to have initial prominence syllables to be parsed into feet
Syllables to be parsed into feet final feet not to be footed

How do proposed competing outputs fare?

(10) Working (and wrong) ranking

ACAS /eɪ.kas/	Root	Initial Prom	Parse Syll	Non Finality
(éɪ)(kàs)				*
(á)kas			*!	
(èɪ)(kás)				*

Given this tableau, there is no way of deciding between the top and bottom competitors (the middle competitor is out because of its violation of Parse Syll). The problem seems to be in the formulation of Initial Prominence, which in its present guise only requires that initial syllables be stressed, rather than primary stressed. Recall, however, that this was used as a cover term, and includes Align-Leftmost, which requires that the head foot of the PrWd is leftmost in the prosodic word. A revised tableau capturing this, and specifying Initial Prominence as L(eftmost), brings a satisfactory result:

(11) Revised (and better) tableau for ACAS

ACAS	Root	Head-Leftmost	Parse Syll	Non Finality
☞ (á)(càs) (éı)(kàs)				*
(á)cas			*!	
(à)(cás) (èı)(kás)		*!	*	*

For the winning candidate, even though there is a violation of Non Finality, syllables are exhaustively parsed and strongest prominence is left-aligned. The same ranking appears to account straightforwardly for learned items such as *ilex, narthex, helix, proton*, and for *gymnast* etc., with the wrinkle that footedness of the final syllable is not guaranteed by a presumed graphemic: phonemic correspondence (recall that acronyms are specific instances of word-*creation*). Notice also that if there were a high-ranked Head-Rightmost constraint (the kind of constraint borrowed from "rightmost-prominent" derivational accounts, and operative for Present Day English in e.g. Pater 1995), then all of these items would output as end-stressed.

The ranking Root>>Head-Leftmost and, by transitivity, Head-Leftmost>> Non Finality is particularly interesting if one enquires into its possible historical persistence.

Minkova (1997) argues that constraint re-ranking holds the key to the evolution of the English stress system, and in doing so, eschews earlier arguments about the productivity of a supposed left > right parametric switch in the English stress system of Midlle English: "[t]he...results [of Minova's analysis: McC]...repeal the need to posit stress-shifting as part of the dynamics of the phonological system of ME" (1997: 162).

Minkova's main arguments, which are focussed largely if not exclusively on primary stress, may be summarised as in (12):

(12) Minkova on constraint re-ranking

i. primary stress in Old English was weight-blind, and morphologically assigned on the initial syllable of lexical roots (1997: 137)
ii. root stress overrides the preference for initial stress (1997: 138-39)
iii. large portions of incoming Latinate (late Latin, Anglo-Norman) vocabulary were stressable by native constraints (1997: 140-44)
iv. problem cases - trisyllabic loans with a heavy medial syllable - are handled by postulating constraint re-ranking (Initial Prominence>>Weight-to-stress (WSP) becomes WSP>> Initial Prominence; 1997: 144), but...
v. Non-Finality - a principle entirely compatible with the native stress principles - still dominates (i.e. is highly ranked within) native and non-native stress patterning (1997: 145)
vi. the evidence from stress doublets (*pardóun* vs. *párdoun*) has been over-interpreted; the evidence - from sound-change, spelling, lack of syncopation - compels the view that such words were, or quickly became, initial-stressed, a pattern adopted from the Initial Prominence constraint of Old English, and supported by the (re)ranking of Non-finality (1997: 148)

In (13a-c) illustrative tableaux, drawn directly from Minkova 1997, are given:[1]

(13a) Old English optimal stress (Root Stress>>Initial Prominence>>Non Finality>>WSP, Rightward Main Stress)

na.me.na	Root	Initial Prominence (Head-Leftmost)	Non Finality	WSP	RMS
☞ .ná.me.na				*	**
.na.mé.na	*!	*		*	*
.na.me.ná	*!	**	*	*	

Here, primary stress outputs in a completely weight-blind fashion (Weight-to-Stress is low ranked to the point of dormancy, as is – another cover term – Rightward Main Stress).

(13b) late Latin stress (provisional version: Root Stress>>Initial-P>>Non Finality>>WSP, RMS)

.lu.pus	Root	Initial Prominence	Non Finality	WSP	RMS
☞ .lú.pus				*	*
.lu.pús		*!	*	[.pus]	

(13c) late Latin trisyllables (where WSP>>Initial Prominence)

.vo.lū.men	Root	Non-Finality	WSP	Initial-Prominence	RMS
☞ .vo.lú.men				*	*
.vó.lu.men			*!		**
.vo.lu.mén	OK	*!	OK	**	OK

In these aggressively top-down analyses, two important and, in terms of the history of the English stress system, significant points emerge: first, the relatively high ranking of Non-Finality, and the relative dormancy of Weight-to-Stress, whose role here is limited to handling trisyllabic forms with heavy medial syllables (13c). Elsewhere, WSP is inactive, and Rightward Main Stress is needed - or will become needed - only in order to "license the iambic rhythm of [Anglo-Norman] loans" (Minkova 1997: 139; in fully specified OT terms, RMS is a cover term for Align-Head-Rightmost and All-Feet-Right, see Kager 1999: 163). In terms of the development of the system, the two significant points are these: traditional analyses would (perhaps) favour increased ranking of RMS, with WSP, in conjunction with Right-Alignment, acting as decisive in accounting for at least "right hand" stress assignment in later forms of English. A further factor, in this posited (and fictional) account, would possibly be the eventual, and final (Renaissance?) disprivileging of Initial Prominence, in conjunction with the upward re-ranking of WSP and the continued high rank of Non Finality, in order to help accommodate the apparent fact that an erstwhile morphological system became at least partly phonological. But Minkova argues that such a hypothetical account must be problematic: it fails to distinguish between the various competing systems that were converging on English through the earlier and later medieval period. It fails to account for the persistence of Non Finality in the system - something for which there is independent evidence. And crucially, the evidence from verse on which such an account might be based - like the evidence often cited to support the notion of parametric switch - would perhaps lead to an over-determination of the extent to which supposed Romance principles ousted native ones, cf. the data in (5-7) above, which support Minkova's analysis. Minkova concludes that "the adoption and accommodation of Romance nouns to the native stress system was much less cataclysmic than has generally been assumed" (1997: 152).

If this is on the way to being the correct analysis, then Minkova's contention that in the stress system inherited from ME, "the dominant core ranking" (Minkova 1997: 155) had survived from Old English, and was by no means subsumed by the Latinate constraint set, becomes particularly interesting as an illustration of just that historical persistence whose form was sketched above. Notably, in both sets of constraints Non Finality dominates WSP, and it is only Initial Prominence, undominated in Old English except for Root Stress, that re-ranks, ceding to Non Finality and the rise of WSP. Minkova goes so far as to pose the question as to "when and how and *if* WSP became indispensable for main stress placement in English" (1997: 163; Minkova's emphasis). That "if" remains tantalising.

2.2. Reinterpreting Weight-to-Stress as constraint interaction in Present Day English

Items often used to support the idea that heavy syllables attract stress in Present Day English include words such as *agenda, defender, aroma, hiatus, angina, synopsis* (examples taken from Pater 1995: 1). It is therefore assumed, as was seen in the preceding section, that Weight-to-Stress (WSP) plays an important role in Present Day

English (although not in Old English, where Head-Leftmost is blind to whether the leftmost head is light or heavy). Yet as Kager (1999: 171ff.) points out, quantity-sensitivity is not a linguistic property which is switched either on or off. There may be degrees of quantity-sensitivity, and within OT, these may be handled by interaction of a constraint set that includes not only WSP, but also other constraints bearing on the size of feet (FtBin, for example – the requirement that foot must be binary under moraic or syllabic analysis), the shape of feet (i.e. whether feet are optimally iambic or trochaic), the form of feet (whether optimal feet are perfectly bimoraic, LL, trochees, or perfect, LH, iambs, for example), and even the form of foot-closure. This last possible constraint is suggested by Kager 1999: 174: his Rh-Contour, "A foot must end in a strong-weak contour at the moraic level", captures a requirement that the "micro" prominence of morae within feet is optimally falling, thus helping to explain the cross-linguistic preference for, and asymmetry between, perfect trochees (LL = [* .]) and uneven iambs (LH = [.] [* .]).

Re-analysing the history of English stress largely in terms of the re-ranking of WSP (largely dormant in Old English, but playing its full role in words such as *aroma* by, presumably, the early Modern period) may, then, be something of an oversimplification. To clarify this, consider the analysis Pater gives for the *aroma* class of words. His constraint Align-Head is indexed for rightmost-ness, cf. (2f) above:

(14) Tableau for *aroma* (Pater 1995: 17)

Input: aroma	Non Finality	Align-Head (R)
☞ a(ró)ma		*
(áro)ma		**!
(àro)(má)	*!	

It may also be the case, as we have seen, that Align-Head (Right) may not in fact be the "correct" constraint for Present Day English, given the evidence there is for the persistence of the left-handed pattern. If one were to substitute AlignHead (Left) without further ado, however, *(áro)ma* wins out over its rivals. Yet this would be to ignore the existence of other constraints that militate towards outputs containing perfect, rather than sub-optimal and unbalanced, trochees. Some relevant candidates for constraint-hood are FtBin, Troch, Rh-Type T(rochee). Allow these into the ranking, and it is their concert, rather than the brute need for "WSP", or a critical interaction between Non Finality and Align-Head (R), that determines the optimal form:

(15) Tableau for *aroma*, augmented

Input: aroma	Ft Bin	Non Finality	Troch	Rh-Type T	Align-Head (L)
☞ a(ró)ma					*
(áro)ma				*!	
(àro)(má)	*!	*	*	*	*

That is, it is the need, in modern and present-day Englishes, for perfect trochees that appears to determine the optimal output pattern, rather than the crude fact that a medial H syllable has somehow acquired stress.

To develop this historically, one might plausibly construct an argument whereby the need for perfect trochees was less important in Old English than the need to have binary feet (moraic OR syllabic trochees), i.e. where Ft Bin>>Rh-Type T. Couple this putative fragment of ranking with high-ranked Non Finality, and Head-Leftmost, and the grammar would predict that (i) Roots will be prosodified, (ii) that stress will not fall on final syllables, but preferentially on Root-initial syllables, and that (iii) feet will be trochaic, but include *both* LL (the moraic trochee) and LH (the syllabic trochee). It is possible that Troch includes many of the "Germanic feet" of pre-OT accounts. Taken together, one is looking at a minimally quantity-sensitive system, that of Old English primary stress:

(16) Tableau for OE *cyning*

Input: cyning	Root	Non Finality	Ft Bin	Troch	Head-Leftmost	Rh-Type T
☞ (cý.ning)						*
cy(níng)		*!			*	
cy.ning	*!					
(cý)(nìng)		*!	*	*		*

In terms of the history of English stress, it seems that the historical stamina of Non Finality, coupled with the arguable persistence of Head-Leftmost, and the re-ranking of Rh Type T (and possibly, WSP), provides a stable framework in which native items largely retain their left-hand stress, *and* where incoming loans will *either* retain their right-hand stress patterns iff they are LH and Rh-Type T>>Head-Leftmost, *or* where such items will "nativize" in dialects where Head-Leftmost>>Rh Type T. This re-structuring is not a case of an incoming rule, or rule-block; it is a set of quiet readjustments to a constraint ranking – or a subset of such a ranking – so that final syllables will continue to be optimally dispreferred from bearing stress. Yet there is a further complication in the pattern, and that is the existence of secondary stress within PrWds.

2.3. A note on Old English secondary stress

The evidence for secondary - or tertiary - stress in the Old English system, and their possible relationship to syllable weight, is particularly difficult since it is typically based on verse structure, and, very largely, on work that goes back at least to Sievers (1885). However, Fulk (1992: 178) shows that the spelling evidence for tertiary stress - in affixes such as *-feald* and *-dom*, say - is reliable, coupled with alternation between stressed and unstressed forms of suffixes (which, on Fulk's view, ultimately that of Luick, provides "evidence for the preservation of tertiary stress in inflected forms, with loss in uninflected ones" (1992: 178)). Since there is some spelling evidence for tertiary stress, it would not be surprising to find the same kind of evidence operating for secondary stress. And this is in fact is what is found. Crucially, Fulk's view is that "syllable length plays a greater role [in determining the relationship between stress and metrical ictus: McC] than previously imagined" (1992: 223). In particular, the syllabic length of affixes is critical for the operation of Kaluza's Law (presence or suspension of resolution), and Fulk goes so far as to suggest that "the role of stress has been overestimated" (1992:224).

In the context of this paper, and abbreviating the analysis, it appears that WSP may well be operative in non-root-initial syllables in Old English. WSP may be not quite as dormant, in terms of secondary and tertiary stress, as Minkova 1997 - focussed though that is on primary stress - implies. If there is a more active WSP operating within the Old English system, would not this be one contributory factor, aligned with the re-ranking of WSP under the influence of late Latin, and/or the re-ranking of Rh Type T, to a later reinterpretation of the constraint ranking so that WSP came to have a more significant role for the determination of primary stress than might have otherwise been the case? Alternatively, the position might be that an independently-motivated constraint required for handling secondary and tertiary stress in Old English comes to be reinterpreted as WSP. One such independently-attested constraint might in fact be Ft-Bin, the requirement that feet are binary at some level of analysis. (McCully [MS., 1999] argues that constraint rankings for Old English, for Old Norse and, to a lesser extent, for Old Saxon, fell synchronically into two blocks, one to handle primary stress, one to handle secondary stress. If correct, this analysis mightily complicates Pater's 1995 claim that stress assignment within OT can be integrated into a single level.)

Some derivational syllables that are candidates in Old English for bearing secondary - or perhaps tertiary - stress are the items seen in (17):

(17) Some well-known candidates for secondary/tertiary stress in Old English

-full, -ness, -dom, -feald, -od(e)....

One perennial puzzle is why, again on presumed metrical evidence, these items often appear to have no stress when they are not followed by a weaker syllable, but do stand in ictic position of the verse when they are so followed. Further, when these derivational syllables are preceded by a light syllable, they are unstressed, but preceded by a heavy, they are analysable as stressed. The minimal contrast is between e.g. *tímbròde* 'he built' and *bífode* 'it trembled'. These items are analysed in (18), where Parse Syll (cf. (10) and (11) above) is reintroduced. In conjunction with Ft-Bin, Parse Syll helps to account for the apparent primary-secondary distinction. Note that low-ranked WSP is largely dormant, but does help to determine why *–brode* (LL, a violation of Faithfulness in any case, see Kager 1999: 102) is dispreferred:

(18) Tableau for OE *timbrode*, 'he built' (Class II Weak verb)

tim.brō.de	Head-Leftmost	Ft-Bin	Parse-Syll	WSP
☞ (tím)(brōde)				
(tím)(brō)de			*!	
(tím)(brŏde)				*!

In this case, if *-od(e)* is analysed as containing an historically long penultimate vowel (Campbell 1959; Hogg 1992: 47-52), thus satisfying WSP, it is Parse Syll that picks the optimal candidate. Compare the analysis with that for *bifōde*:

(19) Tableau for OE *bifōde*

bi.fō.de	Head-Leftmost	Ft-Bin	Parse-Syll	WSP
(bí)(fōde)		*!		* (bi-)
☞ (bífō)de			*	*
(bífo)(de)		*!	*	*
(bifode)		*!	*	*

As the example of *bifōde* shows, it seems to be the interaction of constraints - in this partial tableau, headed by Head-Leftmost - that determines the stressing. The puzzle is how Ft-Bin fits into the picture: in *timbrōde*, the heaviness of the initial syllable, together with the presumed heaviness of medial *-ōd-*, ensures that exhaustivity and binarity choose the optimal candidate; while in *bifōde*, depriving the initial syllable of its well-formed syllabic trochee (in order to satisfy Ft-Bin and WSP elsewhere) violates the ranking. On this analysis, considerations of weight, notably within the alignment of left edges with moraic and syllabic trochees, cannot be entirely de-coupled from the determination of primary stress. WSP, in short, is not altogether dormant in the determination of Old English secondary stress, although it plays at best a minimal role in the determination of primary stress.

This analysis can help to handle the *æpel/æpeling* cases, where word-final *-ing* appears to surface as unstressed, but bears secondary stress when followed by an inflection (*æpelinges*). Presumably, and if taken to refer to any kind of primary or secondary stressed syllable, Non-Finality also has a role to play here:

(20) Tableau for OE *æpeling*

.æ.þe.ling	Non-finality	Ft-Bin	Parse-Syll
(æþel)(ing)	*!		
☞ (æþel)ing			*
(æþeling)		*!	

(21) Tableau for OE *æpelinges*

.æ.þe.lin.ges	Non-finality	Ft-Bin	Parse-Syll
☞ (æþel)(inges)			
(æþel)(ing)es			*!
(æþeling)es		*!	

If the ranking Non Finality, Ft Bin>>Parse Syll disfavours final stress on derivational affixes, Root Stress, which is crucially ranked above Non-finality, ensures that compounds retain stress somewhere in the second elements of their roots, while leftmost prominence is still preferred at superordinate Word level, see (22):

(22) Tableau for OE *magodriht*, 'band of young retainers'

[[mago][driht]]	Root Stress	Non-finality	FTBIN	Head-Leftmost
[[(mágo)][(drìht)]]		*		
[[(mágo)][driht]]	*!			
[[[(màgo)][(dríht)]]]		*		*!

3. Conclusions

The analysis suggests that considerations of syllable weight – whether these are arrived at by the determining influence of WSP, or more subtly, by the interaction of Parse Syll, Ft Bin, and/or Rh Type T - cannot be entirely decoupled from Old English stress assignment, particularly since structures such as the erstwhile "Germanic foot" appear to be at least partially licensed by the interaction of foot binarity, exhaustive parsing, and weight-to-stress. The "Germanic foot", in its LL, HL, and LH guises, in fact falls quite naturally out of the present OT-based model: these last are structures available as more-or-less optimal outputs given the ranking Ft-Bin>>Rh Type T. Explicit in this analysis is also the idea that WSP, in conjunction with Non-Finality and Ft-Bin, plays an interactive role in secondary stress placement, whereas it plays only a marginal role (at best) in assigning primary stress, being crucially outranked by Root Stress, Head-Leftmost, and indeed a whole battery of necessarily prior constraints.

The excursus into Old English stress patterning was driven by the suspicion that long-standing assumption concerning the "right-hand" nature of Present Day English primary stress might prove to be mistaken. This paper has argued that setting up analyses of the history of English stress partly in order to justify parametric re-setting, or a change in edge-marking, or conspiracies between rule-orderings, may equally be mistaken. It might even turn out to be that an enduring constraint block (including the phonological equivalents of marathon runners, Non Finality and Head-Leftmost) optimizes left-hand primary word-stress – as was the case in Old English and as may be the case in many Present Day English dialects.

Table (23), a collation of results to date from the Manchester pilot study (cf. (5-7) above, and see Appendix), underscores the idea that analysts ought to remain open-minded to the idea of leftmost primary stress for English – not applying across the board, certainly, but in sufficient cases to be interesting, and worth studying as a possible reflex of linguistic history.

(23)

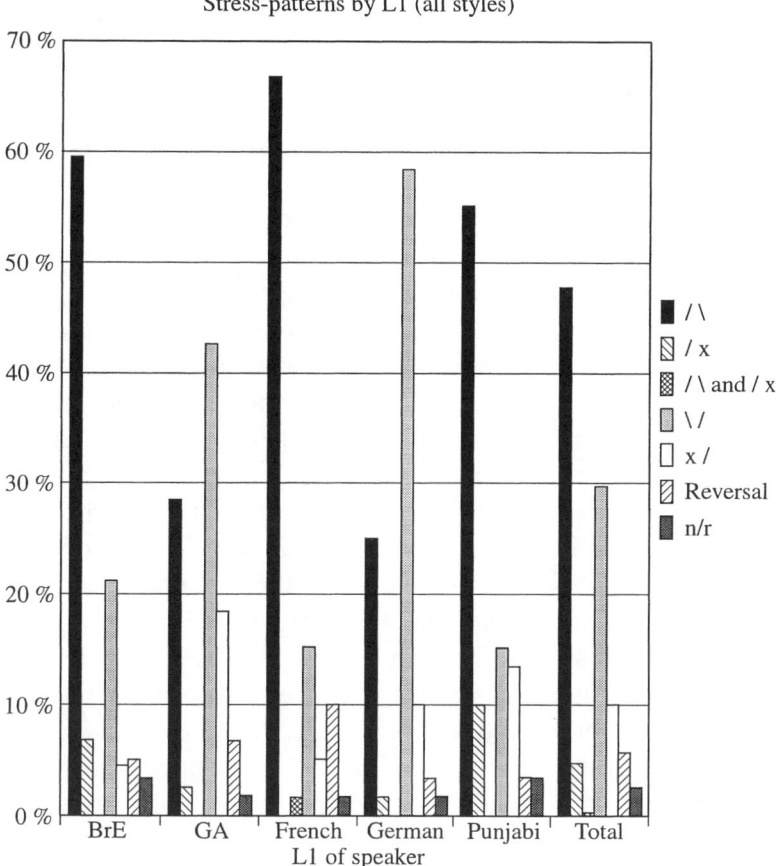

There are interesting anomalies in the data: the speaker of German, for example, whose bisyllabic default seems to be weak+strong, puzzled us – until we realized that in present-day German, primary stress is attracted to superheavy (VVC or VCC) final syllables (G. *Studént*) *and* that this respondent had fluent L2 French (and spent long holidays in France). Yet for all the anomalies, it seems that for native British English (BrE) speakers, and speakers/learners of L2 BrE, "left-hand strong" would seem to be an operative word-stress principle. Nor, in terms of the analysis presented above, does quantity-sensitivity account *on its own* for rightwards stress placement in words such as *aroma, agenda*. WSP works with other (and more highly ranked) constraints to ensure that the foot that is here favoured with main word-stress falls on the only syllable capable of maintaining itself as a perfect trochee. Nevertheless, even here there is speaker-specific variation – compare e.g. *enígma* with "left-hand" *énigma*, where left-hand stress is ranked over the creation of an unlovely trochee.

In terms of the problem items listed in (1), the analysis being developed here accounts, with a greater or lesser degree of elegance (if not economy), for all except the true exceptions, *gorilla* and *vanilla* (*vánilla). For these, rather than positing an SPE-style "explanation" positing underlying geminate <l>, I would claim that these are genuine eye-spellings, and (therefore) genuine exceptions to what would appear to be a normative left-hand pattern. That is not to pretend that there are not significant problems remaining in a study of this kind. To date, despite a large and growing literature, OT has seemed relatively incoherent as an explanatory theory of the history and form of English word-stress, and there are still, one suspects, deep weaknesses in the model – not least, in the formulation of Non-Finality, which may require (and see Kager 1999: 166, and 166 fn.8) an indexed reformulation so that it applies to morae, syllabic rhymes, feet, and possibly, PrWds as well, in this way recapitulating the effects of extrametricality. Nor has OT – or any other account of word-stress theory - begun to theorize the sociolinguistic variation that may have existed, and may still exist, in the patterning of English stress. Yet if the present paper has begun to point to some of those challenges, suggested that even more careful interpretation of data is even more necessary than usual in the reconstruction of word-prosodic histories, and pointed out that diachronic persistence is as interesting, theoretically speaking, as linguistic catastrophe, then it will have achieved some of its original purposes.

Appendix

Testing for a mess of stress (Thomas and McCully, in progress)

A. Single word list

Bisyllabic:
*chateau   garage   pate   defense   offence   flambee   technique   debris
coupon   cliche   Bordeaux   homage   salon   recourse   bureau   cafe
souffle   ballet   nouveau   mobile*

Trisyllabic:
monument   versatile   fiance   premier   harassment   Beaujolais

Polysyllabic:
controversy   quantitative   advertisement

B. Phrase list

1 a) Beaujolais Nouveau
    b) nouveau cuisine
    c) a fine Beaujolais

2 a) offence and defense

3 a) the shuttered chateau
    b) the grand chateau

4 a) Federal Bureau
    b) Bureau de Change

5 a) French cafe
    b) riverside cafe

6 a) money-off coupon
    b) free coupon

7 a) steak flambe
    b) flambe steak

8 a) double garage
    b) unlocked garage

9 a) hairdresser's salon
    b) a new salon

10 a) favourite cliche
    b) bad cliche

11 a) my friend's fiancee
    b) fiancee from Santa Fe

12 a) falling debris
    b) some old debris

13 a) the duck pate
    b) tasty pate

14 a) film premier
    b) the premier doctor

15 a) the Bordeaux region
    b) the wine of the Bordeaux

16 a) homage to the dead
    b) they went to the homage

17 a) cafe souffle
    b) the souffle on the menu

18 a) the Northern Ballet
    b) the sad ballet

19   mobile home

20 a) a billboard advertisement
    b) new car advertisement

21 a) a good technique
    b) a useful technique

22 a) versatile cameraman

b) versatile performer

23   war monument

24 a) unwanted harassment
   b) sexual harassment

25 a) quantitative measurement
   b) quantitative mathematics

26 a) the news was filled with controversy
   b) a raging controversy

C. Reading passage

"Life at the chateau would have been extremely diverse. The image, quite a cliche, of courtiers drinking fine wines such as a vintage Bordeaux or a Beaujolais Nouveau, is actually not far from the truth. Often the evening would have included a trip to the ballet with friends, or an extravagant dinner of many courses. In modern times, these castles stand as a monument, paying homage to a time in history when armies would have been made mobile to begin their offence towards their enemies, ready to ensure the defense of the kingdom.
 "Today of course, more is needed to attract visitors to such treasures than simple historical value alone and they must be seen as more than just the debris of an earlier age. Now tourist boards must use advertisements in order to promote a versatile image for the future.
 "One successful technique which has been used to attract a greater number of visitors to the area has been the addition of a good cafe nearby. It would seem that punters never fail to be satisfied by a good souffle, a flambee steak or the speciality duck liver pate.
 "However, the project has been criticised by some and has caused controversy amongst traditionalists. In particular, there was one well publicised incident where the fiance of a local resident was the victim of harassment from a group of tourists. Many say that an increase in the number of visitors to the area will bring yet more problems and that quantitative research must be carried out to help assess the pros and cons of such schemes."

(July 10, 2000. Initial data collected July-early September 2000.)

Specimen Informant Questionnaire

Informant Number:	03
Age:	28
Gender:	F
Occupation:	Student/English teacher

Nationality:	American
Country of Birth:	USA
Country of Residence:	Temporarily UK; normally US
Exact Place of Residence:	Florida, Fort Myers
First Language:	English
Second Language:	Spanish
Other Languages:	n/a
Length of Residence in UK:	1 yr + 10 months. 2 x visits
Length of Residence in USA:	25 years
Length of Residence in other countries:	Columbia, 2 years
Educational Background:	Florida State U. BA. Specialism in Creative Writing
	TEFL MA at Manchester (UK)
Occupational Background:	ELT teaching and service
Knowledge of French:	Studied in high school and at U., but not proficient.

Note

1. Michael Redford (personal communication) points out that WSP>>RMS should be reversed. In fact nothing crucial hinges on the synchronic ordering here, as the hatched line separating the two constraints indicates. Historically, Redford is almost certainly correct, and his observation that the constraint-set Root>>Initial-Prominence>>Nonfinality is 'historically persistent' is borne out by the present paper.

References

Archangeli, D. and D. Terence Langendoen (eds.)
    1997   *Optimality Theory: an Overview*. Oxford: Blackwell.
Bermudez-Otero, Ricardo.
    1996   Stress and quantity in Old and early Middle English: evidence for an optimality-theoretic model of language change. Rutgers University, New Brunswick: Rutgers Optimality Archive = ROA 136-0996
Bermudez-Otéro, Ricardo et al. (eds.)
    2000   *Generative Theory and Corpus Studies*. Berlin/New York: Mouton De Gruyter

ten Brink, Bernhardt
  1881 *Chaucers Sprache und Verskunst*. Leipzig: T.O. Weigel.
Burnley, David
  1983 *Chaucer's Language*. London: Macmillan.
Burzio, Luigi
  1994 *Principles of English Stress*. Cambridge: Cambridge University Press
Campbell, Alistair
  1959 *Old English Grammar*. Oxford: Clarendon Press
Chomsky, Noam and Morris Halle
  1968 *The Sound Pattern of English*. New York: Harper and Row
Dresher, Elan B.
  1999 A cue-based approach to prosodic change. Paper presented to the *Change in Prosodic Systems* Workshop, DGfS, University of Konstanz.
Dresher, Elan B. and Aditi Lahiri
  1991 The Germanic foot: metrical coherence in Old English. *Linguistic Inquiry* 22: 251-86.
Duffell, Martin
  2000 "The craft so long to lerne": Chaucer's invention of the iambic pentameter. *The Chaucer Review* 34:269-288
Fulk, Robert D.
  1992 *A History of Old English Meter*. Philadelphia: University of Pennsylvania Press
Gasiorowski, Piotr
  1998 *Optimal Stress for English*. Poznan: Motivex
Halle, Morris
  1998 The stress of English words, 1968-1998. *Linguistic Inquiry* 29: 539-568.
Halle, Morris and J.-R. Vergnaud
  1990 [revised edition of Halle and Vergnaud 1987] *An Essay on Stress*. Cambridge, Mass.: MIT Press
Halle, Morris and W. Idsardi
  1995 General properties of stress and metrical structure. In: John Goldsmith (ed.), *The Handbook of Phonological Theory*, 403-444. Oxford: Blackwell
Halle, Morris and S. Jay Keyser
  1971 *English Stress: its Form, its Growth, and its Role in Verse*. New York: Harper and Row
Hayes, Bruce
  1982 Extrametricality and English stress. *Linguistic Inquiry* 13: 227-76
  1995 *Metrical Stress Theory: Principles and Case Studies*. Chicago: Chicago University Press.
Hogg, Richard
  1992 *A Grammar of Old English*. Oxford: Blackwell

van der Hulst, Harry (ed).
  1999   *Word Prosodic Systems in the Languages of Europe.* Berlin: Mouton de Gruyter
Hutton, John
  1998   Stress in Old English, *giet ongean. Linguistics* 36: 847-885
Ito, Junko and R.A. Mester
  1995   Japanese phonology. In Goldsmith J. (ed.) *A handbook of phonological theory.* Cambridge, MA.: Blackwell, 817-839.
Kager, Rene
  1999   *Optimality Theory.* Cambridge: Cambridge University Press
Labov, William
  1993   *Principles of Linguistic Change.* Oxford: Blackwell
Lahiri, Aditi, Tomas Riad and Haike Jacobs
  1999   Diachronic prosody. In ed. Harry van der Hulst, *Word Prosodic Systems in the Languages of Europe.* Berlin and New York: Mouton de Gruyter, 335-421.
Lass, Roger
  1992   Phonology and morphology. In: Norman Blake (ed.); R.M. Hogg (gen,ed.) *The Cambridge History of the English language*, Vol. II, 1066-1476. Cambridge: Cambridge University Press, 23-155.
Luick, Karl
  1896   *Untersuchunger zur Englischen Lautgeschichte.* Strasburg: Karl Truebner
McCarthy, John and Alan Prince
  1993   Generalized alignment. In eds. Geert Booij and Jaap van Marle, *Yearbook of morphology 1993.* Amsterdam: Kluver, 79-153
McCully, ChristoPher B.
  1997   Stress, survival and change: Old to Middle English. In: Jacek Fisiak (ed.), *Studies in Middle English Linguistics*, 283-300. Berlin: Mouton de Gruyter.
  Forthcoming What's afoot with word-final C#? Metrical coherence and the history of English. To appear in *Proceedings of the XII ICEHL* (Santiago de Compostela).
  (MS, in prep.) Secondary stress in Old English and other Germanic languages. Department of English and American Studies, University of Manchester. [Paper originally presented to the International Conference on Historical Linguistics, Vancouver, 1999].
McCully, Christopher B. and Martin Holmes
  1988   Some notes on the structure of acronyms. *Lingua* 74: 27-43.
Minkova, Donka
  1997   Constraint ranking in Middle English stress shifting. *English Language and Linguistics* 1/1: 135-75.

Pater, Joe
  1995   On the nonuniformity of weight-to-stress and stress preservation in English. MS, Rutgers University, New Brunswick: Rutgers Optimality Archive = ROA 107-0000
Prince, Alan and Paul Smolensky
  1993   *Optimality Theory: Constraint Interaction in Generative Grammar.* MS, Rutgers University, New Brunswick (= RUCCS 2; ROA)
Redford, Michael
  Forthcoming Middle English stress doubles: new evidence from Chaucer's meter. Forthcoming in eds. Paula Fikkert and Haike Jacobs, *Developments in prosodic systems.* Berlin: Mouton de Gruyter. This volume.
Robinson, F.N.
  1957   *The Complete Works of Geoffrey Chaucer.* second edition. London: Oxford University Press
Sievers, Eduard
  1885   Zur Rhythmik des germanischen Alliterationsverses. *Beiträge zur Geschichte der deutschen Sprache und Literatur* 10: 209-314, 451-545
Thomas, Helen and C.B. McCully
  In progress Theorizing a mess of stress. MSS., Dept. of English and American Studies, University of Manchester
Zonneveld, Wim
  1999   *Lutgart, Willem and Geoffrey: 13th century Dutch Metre in a European Context.* Research Institute of Language and Speech, Utrecht University.

Why preantepenultimate stress in Latin requires an OT-account

Haike Jacobs

1. Introduction

The well-known Classical Latin stress rule (stress is on the penultimate syllable if heavy and otherwise on the antepenultimate syllable) has been well studied in metrical theory (Hayes (1995), Halle (1997), Prince and Smolensky (1993), Mester (1994), among others). There is one important fact, however, that, although well-known in the traditional literature (cf. Lindsay (1963) among others), has never received any attention in recent metrical theory. In Early Classical Latin (by the time of Plautus and Terence; third/second century BC) there was a systematic exception to the Classical (first century BC) stress rule. In words of exactly four syllables with the first three syllables light, main stress was on the initial syllable. Some examples are *fácilius* 'easy', *fáciliter*, 'easily', *básilicus* 'royal', *múlierem* 'woman', *bálineum* 'bath' and *ínopiam* 'poverty'.

In this paper, we will stress the implications and theoretical importance for metrical theory of the facts mentioned above, and, we will show that the proposed analysis of Early Classical Latin provides a principled account of the typological intricacies of previous foot-extrametricality. Moreover, it will be argued that the facts of Early Classical Latin cannot be adequately described in a rule-based framework, but, instead, require an OT-account.

2. The Constraint NONFINALITY and Main Stress in Latin

Prince and Smolensky (1993) have provided an OT-analysis of Classical Latin. Here we will concentrate on the constituent structure they derive and not go into the details of their analysis with respect to the various shortening processes (cf. Jacobs (2000a and 2000b). The constraints they assume are given in (1) and (2), of which those in (1) are supposed to be undominated. Main stress is indicated by underscoring.

(1) Constraints for the Form of Feet

Lx ≈ Pr: A member of MCAT corresponds to a PrWD, a lexical item must be prosodically analyzed.
FTBIN: Feet are binary at some level of analysis (m,σ)
RHTYPE (T): The rhythm type is trochaic, that is feet are trochees.
RHHRM: Rhythmic harmony or *(HL): an uneven trochee is forbidden.

(2) Constraints for Position/Parsing

NONFINALITY (F̲, σ̲) » EDGEMOST (σ̲ ,R)

No head of PrWd is final in PrWd (both foot and head syllable) dominates the constraint that forces the stressed syllable to be located at the right word edge.
Motivation for the ranking: (L̲L)L is better than L(L̲L)

EDGEMOST (σ̲, R) » PARSE-σ

Parse syllables into feet is dominated by stressed syllable location.
Motivation for the ranking: L(L̲L)L is better than (L̲L)(LL)

In order to clarify the various constraints we give in (3) a tableau for an input HLL, HLH and LLL.

(3) Main Stress in Classical Latin

(a) /HLL/	NonFin	Edgemost	Parse-σ
(1) ☞ (H̱)(LL)		σ σ	
(2) (H̱L)L		σ σ	*!
(3) (H)(ḺL)	*!	σ	
(b) /HLH/	NonFin	Edgemost	Parse-σ
(1) (H)L(H̱)	*!		*
(2) (H̱)LH		σ σ	* *!
(3) (H̱)L(H)		σ σ	*!
(4) ☞ (H̱)(LH)		σ σ	
(c) /LLL/	NonFin	Edgemost	Parse-σ
(1) L(ḺL)	*!	σ	*
(2) ☞ (ḺL)L		σ σ	*

An input HLL (3a) is optimally parsed as (H̱)(LL). The output candidate (H̱L)L (a2) not only violates the undominated constraint *(HL), but also Parse-σ. The output candidate (H)(ḺL) (a3) violates NonFinality, given that the foot with main stress is in final position. It is clear from the above examples that main stress will not always be on the final foot. Sometimes main stress is on the final foot as in L(ḺL)L, (ḺL)L, (H̱)L or (ḺL) cases, but other times on the prefinal foot: as in (H̱)(LL) and ((H̱)(LH) cases. In this respect, the analysis of Latin main stress is clearly different from an approach along the lines of Hayes' (1995) End Rule Final/Initial. The constraints responsible for main stress Align Head-Foot, R, PrWd, R (H/R) and (Align Head-Foot, L, PrWd, L (H/L) (the OT translation of the End Rule cf. Kager (1999)), which demand that the head-foot be final or initial, must be dominated by NonFinality.

Let us next consider an alternative analysis of Classical Latin. The constraints assumed are given in (4). We will leave the constraints in (1) unaltered, except crucially for the constraint banning the uneven trochee: *(HL) (cf. Prince and Smolensky, 1993). Prince and Smolensky assume that this constraint is universally undominated. We will assume that this constraint can, in fact, be dominated by other constraint, and that, in Latin, it is dominated by PARSE-σ. Also, instead of the constraint EDGEMOST, we will use ALIGN-constraints to account for the location of main stress.

(4)   *Undominated constraints:*

Lx ≈ Pr, FTBIN, RHTYPE (T)

Modified constraints:

NONFINALITY: A foot may not be final
ALIGN (PRWD,R, FT,R)   (W/R)
ALIGN (HEAD-FOOT, R, PRWD, R) (H/R)

Ranked constraints:

NONFIN » W/R » H/R » PARSE-σ » QS » *(HL)

The constraints in (4) (and with NONFINALITY *doubly* simplified) will always yield main stress on the final foot. A foot will never be final except if forced by the higher ranked constraint: FTBIN. This accounts for monosyllabic words. This also means that HH will be optimally parsed as (H̲)H and not as (H̲)(H), given that the parsing of the final syllable results in a violation of the higher-ranked modified NONFINALITY constraint. A bisyllabic input LH will still be (LH̲) and not (L̲)H which violates FTBIN. Although both L(H̲) and (LH̲) violate NONFINALITY, (LH̲) will be evaluated better. Although it does violate QS it avoids a violation of PARSE-σ ranked above QS, the constraint responsible for quantity-sensitivity, which demands that heavy syllables are stressed.

Preantepenultimate stress in Latin 399

Words ending in HLL will optimally be parsed as (HL)L, because (H)(LL) (the optimal candidate of (3)) violates NONFINALITY and because (H)LL entails one more violation of PARSE-σ ranked above *(HL). Words ending in HLH will be optimal if (HL)H. The joint effect of these modifications (NONFINALITY simplified (neither reference to main foot nor to stressed syllable) and *(HL) dominated by PARSE-σ) results in main stress being uniformly on the last foot. In (5) this is illustrated for the crucial HLL and HLH cases.

(5) Main Stress in Classical Latin

(a) /HLL/	NONFIN	W/R	H/R	PARSE-σ	QS	*(HL)
(H̲)(LL)	*!		σ σ			
(H̲)LL		σ σ!	σ σ	**		
☞ (H̲L) L		σ	σ	*		*
(H)(L̲L)	*!					
(b) /HLH/	NON-FIN	W/R	H/R	PARSE-σ	QS	*(HL)
(H̲)L(H)	*!		σ σ	*		
(H̲)LH		σ σ!	σ σ	**	*	
(H̲)(LH)	*!		σ σ		*	
☞ (H̲L)H		σ	σ	*	*	*

It goes without saying that the proposed analysis has considerable consequences for the analysis of both shortening and syncope in Latin. We refer for a more detailed account to Jacobs (2000a and 2000b). In the next section we will concentrate on the constraint NONFINALITY and show why the proposed modification is necessary on typological grounds. It will be demonstrated that the constraint NONFINALITY as proposed by Prince and Smolensky leads to the prediction of quaternary stress, and, that therefore, a modification of the constraint is independently required.

3. NONFINALITY (F̱, σ̱) and quaternary stress systems

It is a well-known fact that quaternary systems do not occur (cf. Hayes (1995) and van der Hulst (1999). What may occur in a language, though, is a quaternary pattern. That is, as in Early Classical Latin mentioned above, sometimes stress can fall on the pre-antepenultimate, the fourth, syllable from the end, but not systematically in all words.

In Prince and Smolensky's analysis of Latin in (1)-(3) above we saw that a ranking NONFINALITY (F̱,σ̱) » EDGEMOST » PARSE-σ resulted in preferring L(ḺL)L to (ḺL)(LL) and in preferring (H̱)(LL) to (H)(ḺL).

In (6) we have presented the same constraints, but in a different order. We have ranked PARSE-σ above NONFINALITY (F̱, σ̱), which has the consequence of deriving a stress system where main stress is systematically on the fourth syllable from the right-edge. This is illustrated for words containing four, five and six light syllables. For ease of exposition, we have abstracted away from quantity-sensitivity.

(6) A Systematic Quaternary Stress System

a. /σ σ σ σ/	PARSE-σ	NONFIN (F̱, σ̱)	W/R	H/R
☞ (σ̱ σ)(σ σ)				σ σ
σ (σ̱ σ) σ	*! *		σ	σ
(σ̱ σ) σ σ	*! *		σ σ	σ σ
(σ σ)(σ̱ σ)		*!		

b. /σ σ σ σ σ/	PARSE-σ	NONFIN(F̱, σ̱)	W/R	H/R
☞ σ (σ̱ σ)(σ σ)	*			σσ
(σ̱ σ) σ (σ σ)	*			σσσ!
σ (σ σ)(σ̱ σ)	*	*!		
(σ σ)(σ̱ σ) σ	*		σ!	σ

c. /σ σ σ σ σ σ/	Parse-σ	NonFin(F, σ)	W/R	H/R
☞ (σ σ)(σ̱ σ)(σ σ)				σ σ
(σ σ)(σ σ)(σ̱ σ)		*!		
σ (σ σ)(σ̱ σ) σ	*! *		σ	σ

It is obvious from (6) that the constraint NonFinality (F, σ) makes the unwanted prediction of the possible existence of quaternary stress systems.

Before proceeding our discussion, we have illustrated in tableau (7) that the modified constraint NonFinality, as in (4), which we used for Latin, does not lead to the same prediction, but correctly excludes systematic quaternarity.

(7) Systematic Quaternary Stress Excluded

a. /σ σ σ σ/	Parse-σ	NonFin (F)	W/R	H/R
(σ̱ σ)(σ σ)		*		σ!σ
σ (σ̱ σ) σ	*! *		σ	σ
(σ̱ σ) σ σ	*! *		σ σ	σ σ
☞ (σσ) (σ̱ σ)		*		

b. /σ σ σ σ σ/	Parse-σ	NonFin (F)	W/R	H/R
σ (σ̱ σ)(σ σ)	*	*!		σ σ
☞ (σ σ)(σ̱ σ) σ	*		σ	σ
(σ̱ σ) σ (σ σ)	*	*!		σσσ
σ (σ σ)(σ̱ σ)	*	*!		

c. /σ σ σ σ σ σ/	Parse-σ	NonFin (F)	W/R	H/R
(σ σ)(<u>σ</u> σ)(σ σ)		*		σ!σ
☞ (σ σ)(σ σ)(<u>σ</u> σ)		*		
σ (σ σ)(<u>σ</u> σ) σ	*! *			σ

In this section, we have argued that a modification of the constraint NONFINALITY is needed in order to exclude the existence of quaternary stress systems. However, we still have to account for existing quaternary patterns in a language, such as Early Classical Latin. In the next section, we will first discuss how in rule-based theory, more specifically extrametricality theory, the concept of foot-extrametricality permits to account for quaternary patterns in a language.

4. Foot and syllable extrametricality

Hayes (1995) has proposed to use Foot-extrametricality for a number of languages. The use of Foot-extrametricality can be divided into two types: one, to which we will refer as Free Foot-Extrametricality and the other, to which we will refer as Clash Foot-Extrametricality. Clash Foot-Extrametricality is a restricted use of extrametricality. First, the word is parsed into feet and then the last foot is made extrametrical, but only if in clash with a preceding foot. Turkish non-final stress in loanwords and toponyms (cf. Hayes, 1995:262, based on Sezer (1983)) is analyzed in two possible ways, one of which invokes Clash Foot-Extrametricality.

First, (i) moraic trochees are constructed from right-to-left, then, (ii) the final foot is made extrametrical if in clash with a preceding foot. Finally, (iii) the application of the End Rule Final produces main stress on the final foot. Sample derivations are given in (8).

Preantepenultimate stress in Latin 403

(8) Turkish Foot Extrametricality in Clash

    a.   lo   kán   ta   'restaurant'
         L   H   L

  (i)   (x)
  (ii)   not applicable
  (iii)   (x)
      (x   )

    b.   an   ták   ya   Place Name
         H   H   L

  (i)   (x) (x)
  (ii)   not applicable
  (iii) (x) (x)
      (x   )

    c.   ka   ná   pe   'couch'
         L   L   L

  (i)   (x   .)
  (ii)   not applicable
  (iii)   (x   .)
      (x   )

    d.   án   ka   ra   Place Name
         H   L   L

  (i)   (x) (x .)
  (ii)   (x) <(x .)>
  (iii) (x) <(x .)>
      (x   )

Although the final foot in (8b) is in clash with the preceding foot, the final foot is not peripheral and, hence, not subject to extrametricality.

    Only in (8d) the final foot is both in clash with the preceding foot and peripheral, and, hence, subject to foot-extrametricality. In the other cases in (8), there is no clash and, hence, no foot-extrametricality (cf. Hayes (1995) and Gussenhoven and Jacobs (1998) for more discussion).

In cases of Free Foot-Extrametricality the final foot is made extrametrical irrespective of clash considerations. A typical example is Palestinian Arabic, where preantepenultimate stress occurs in words ending in four light syllables. Hayes (1995: 126/127) assumes, final consonant extrametricality, left-to-right moraic trochees, final foot extrametricality and End Rule Final. Some examples are given in (9).

(9) Palestinian Arabic Foot Extrametricality

    a.   ká   ta   bu   'they wrote'
        L   L   L

        (x   .)
        (x   )

    b.   sá   ja   ra   tu<n>   'a tree'
        L   L   L   L

        (x   .) <(x   .)>
        (x   )

    c.   sa   ja   rá   tu   hu   'his tree (nom.)'
        L   L   L   L   L

        (x   .)   (x   .)
        (x   )

The final foot in (9a) and (9c) is not peripheral and cannot be made extrametrical due to the Peripherality Condition. In (9b) the last syllable is treated as light, due to the prior application of a rule of consonant-extrametricality (cf. Hayes, 1995: 129). After making the final foot extrametrical, as in (9b), End Rule Final will promote the first foot to main stress status.

Hayes (1995) reports no cases of syllabic trochees with Free Foot-Extrametricality, which would result in systematic quaternarity. Now, quite strikingly, cases of left-ward footing (feet are assigned from right-to-left) plus Free Foot-Extrametricality are rare, if existant at all. There is one example given in Hayes (1995), Hindi, to which we will return below. All the examples of Free Foot-Extrametricality occur in rightward (feet are assigned from left-to-right) iambic or moraic trochee stress systems. The languages which are given in Hayes (1995) are: Palestinian Arabic, Munsee, Unami, Cayuga, Radio Cairene Arabic, Cyrenaican Bedouin Arabic, Negev Bedouin Arabic and Eastern Ojibwa (cf. Hayes (1995) for a more detailed account).

This directional asymmetry in Free Foot-Extrametricality is unexplained in a derivational theory, but makes perfect sense in OT, but only if NONFINALITY is indeed modified as we have proposed above for Latin. That is, the modification of NONFINALITY, as proposed here, according to which any foot in final position is disallowed, has the effect that parsing of syllables into feet will stop exactly two light syllables from the word end if footing is rightward. In leftward parsing NONFINALITY can be minimally satisfied by skipping just one syllable. Minimal violation is enforced by PARSE-σ. Hence, preantepenultimate stress is expected if the four last syllables of a word are light in rightward systems, but not in left-ward systems.

Let us now consider Hindi stress. In Hindi, we do find cases of preantepenultimate stress due to Free Foot-Extrametricality. Moraic trochees are constructed going from right to left. The final foot is made extrametrical and main stress is accounted for by the End Rule Right. Hayes (1995:165) notes that his analysis predicts the preantepenultimate maximum to occur only in cases with two disyllabic feet, which, by the definition of the moraic trochee, implies that the four last syllables are light. An example is *ánumati* 'approval' illustrated in (10).

(10) Hindi Pre-antepenultimate Stress

```
    (x            )
    (x    .)   <(x   .)>

     á    nu    ma    ti
```
Such a quaternary pattern can arise by the ranking given in (11).

(11) A Quaternary Pattern

/σ σ σ/	Non-Fin	W/L	W/R	H/R	Parse-σ
☞ (σ́ σ) σ			σ	σ	*
σ (σ́ σ)	*!	σ			*
/σ σ σ σ/	Non-Fin	W/L	W/R	H/R	Parse-σ
σ (σ́ σ) σ		σ!	σ	σ	* *
(σ́ σ)(σ σ)	*!			σ σ	
☞ (σ́ σ) σ σ			σ σ	σ σ	* *
/σ σ σ σ σ/	Non-Fin	W/L	W/R	H/R	Parse-σ
☞ (σ σ)(σ́ σ) σ			σ	σ	*
σ (σ́ σ)(σ σ)	*!	σ		σ σ	*
(σ σ) σ (σ́ σ)	*!				*
/σ σ σ σ σ σ/	Non-Fin	W/L	W/R	H/R	Parse-σ
☞ (σ σ) σ (σ́ σ) σ			σ	σ	* *
σ (σ σ)(σ́ σ) σ		σ!	σ	σ	* *
(σ σ)(σ́ σ)(σ σ)	*!			σ σ	

In (11) we have, for clarity's sake, abstracted away from quantity-sensitivity. The pattern that emerges from (11) is antepenultimate stress in longer words, but pre-antepenultimate stress being restricted to words of exactly four light syllables.

There are two important differences, however, between the analysis in (10) and (11). First, Hayes' analysis predicts that in a pentasyllabic word with the four last syllables light, main stress will also be on the fourth syllable from the word edge. Again, moraic trochees are constructed from right-to-left and the final foot is made extrametrical. This is illustrated in (12).

(12) Pre-antepenultimate Stress in Longer Words as Well

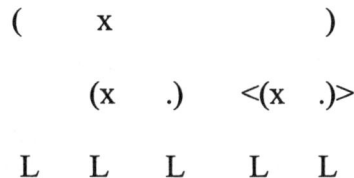

The analysis in (11), on the other hand, produces preantepenultimate stress only in tetrasyllabic words, but not in pentasyllabic ones. I have found no examples for Hindi in order to evaluate either analysis. In Early Classical Latin, however, which seems to work exactly like Hindi, only tetrasyllabic words show preantepenultimate stress, but not pentasyllabic ones.

Second, the analysis in (11) produces, in cases of words of four syllables, only one stress: on the first syllable and no secondary stress on the prefinal syllable. Hayes' analysis (cf. 10) predicts a secondary stress on the prefinal syllable in these words. Gupta (1987) notes explicitly that *ánumàti* is ill-formed in Hindi. Let us next turn to Early Classical Latin.

5. Early Classical Latin

In Early Classical Latin (Plautus 244-184 BC) preantepenultimate stress occurred only in quadrisyllabic words with the first three syllables light, but where the final syllable may be either light or heavy. Some examples are *fácilius* 'easy', *fáciliter*, 'easily', *básilicus* 'royal', *múlierem* 'woman' and *bálineum* 'bath'. Pentasyllabic words obey the antepenultimate maximum, such as, *maleficium* 'crime' or *domicílium* 'house' (cf Allen (1973, Fraenkel (1928), Thierfelder (1928) and Lindsay (1963) among others).

There are two good arguments supporting the traditional scholars' view of initial stress in these cases.

First, in the comedies of Plautus and Terence there was a strong tendency to harmonize verse ictus (the strong position in the verse foot) and word accent, and as Lindsay (1963: 158) puts it: "the metrical treatment of [these words] in the plays of Plautus and Terence, indicate that the pronunciation of such words in their time laid the accent on the first, and not on the second syllable. [...] the incidence of the metrical ictus in all other types of words points to the prevalence of the Paenultima Law for all words, except for these quadrisyllables with the first three syllables short."

Second, in some of these quadrisyllabic words it is exactly the syllable which under the Classical stress rule would have had the main stress, that is syncopated, such as, for instance, *bálineum* > *bálneum*.

Finally, it is important to mention that there seems to be no morphological reason whatsoever supporting initial stress in precisely these cases. This is clear when one compares *lábor fácilior* 'more easy work; nom.sg.' and *labórem faciliórem* 'more easy work; acc. sg.' or *básilicus* 'royal; nom.sg.' *basilicórum* 'royal; gen.pl.'.

For Early Classical Latin, there is no direct way in which foot-extrametricality and a moraic trochee can reach the preantepenultimate syllable in quadrisyllabic words with a final heavy syllable, given that the final heavy syllable will form a foot on its own (viz. L(LL)<(H)>). If, prior to foot-extrametricality, the last consonant is made extrametrical, which has the effect of making the final syllable light, one could in principle stress the initial syllable in these cases (viz. (LL)<(LL)><-C>). Notice that in these cases the final consonant must be supposed to be part of the syllable, in order to escape unallowed 'chained' or 'embedded' extrametricality, which is excluded by Hayes (1995:107) on principled grounds.

Moreover, given the fact that the use of both final consonant- and final foot-extrametricality has to be restricted to words of four syllables with the initial three syllables light, because in all other words the classical three-syllable window is respected, makes the analysis, if acceptable at all, completely ad-hoc.

A ranking such as the one in (11) above straightforwardly derives Plautinian Latin as shown in (13).

(13) Preantepenultimate Stress in Early Classical Latin

L L L H ba-li-ne-um	NonFin	W/L	W/R	Parse-σ
(L̲ L) L (H)	*!			*
L (L̲ L) H		σ!	σ	* *
(L̲ L) (L H)	*!			
☞ (L̲ L) L H			σ σ	* *

In (14), we show for a pentasyllabic word, such as, for instance, *maleficium* 'crime' or *domicilium* 'house', that in all other cases the three-syllable window is respected.

(14) Pentasyllabic Words Have Antepenultimate Stress

L L L L H ma-le-fi-ci-um	NonFin	W/L	W/R	Parse-σ
(L̲ L) (L L) (H)	*!			
L (L̲ L) L H		σ!	σ σ	* * *
L (L̲ L) (L H)	*!	σ		*
☞ (L L) (L̲ L) H			σ	*

Now, Early Classical Latin differs with respect to the rankings of the constraints in only one aspect from Preclassical Latin.

In Preclassical Latin stress always was on the initial syllable (cf. Lindsay (1963) among others), a situation which can be accounted for by the ranking in (15). The constraint which demands that the Prosodic Word starts with a foot, W/L, dominates the constraint that demands that the Prosodic Word ends with a foot, W/R. Furthermore, in order to obtain initial instead of final stress, H/L must dominate H/R.

(15) Preclassical Latin Initial Stress

/σ σ σ σ/	NonF	W/L	W/R	H/L	H/R	Parse-σ
σ (σ σ) σ		σ!	σ	σ	σ	**
(σ σ) σ (σ)	*!				σσ	*
(σ σ) (σ σ)	*!				σσ	
☞ (σ σ) σ σ			σ σ		σσ	**
/σ σ σ σ σ/	NonF	W/L	W/R	H/L	H/R	Parse-σ
☞ (σ σ)(σ σ) σ			σ		σσσ	*
σ (σ σ) (σ σ)	*!	σ		σ	σσ	*
σ σ (σ σ) σ		σ!σ		σσ	σ	***
(σ σ) σ σ σ			σσ!σ		σσσ	***

High-ranking W/L and H/L will always produce initial stress. Quantity-insensitivity (cf. *fénestra*) is achieved, although not indicated in (15), by ranking the QS-constraint below the Alignment-constraints.

The evolution from Preclassical to Plautinian or Early Classical Latin can now be described more precisely as a reranking of the constraints H/L and H/R as in (16).

(16) Preantepenultimate Stress in Quadrisyllabic Words Only

/LLLH/ o-pi-tu-mus	NonF	W/L	W/R	H/R	H/L	Parse-σ
(L L) L (H)	*!			σ σ		*
L (L L) H		σ!	σ	σ	σ	**
(L L) (L H)	*!			σ σ		
☞ (L L) L H			σ σ	σ σ		**

Tableau (17) shows, in a more precise way than (14), the effect of this ranking for penta- and hexasyllabic words.

(17) Early Classical Stress: Antepenultimate Stress in Longer Words

a. /L L L L σ/ o-pi-fi-ci-na	NonF	W/L	W/R	H/R	H/L	Parse-σ
(L̠ L)(L L) σ			σ	σσ!σ		
☞ (L L)(L̠ L) σ			σ	σ	σσ	*
L (L̠ L)(L σ)	*!	σ		σσ	σ	*
(L L) L (L̠ σ)	*!				σσσ	*
b. /L L L L L σ/ re-stu-pe-fa-ci-o	NonF	W/L	W/R	H/R	H/L	Parse-σ
☞ (L L) L (L̠ L) σ			σ	σ	σσ σ	**
L (L L)(L̠ L)σ		σ!	σ	σ	σσ σ	**
(L L)(L̠ L)(L L)	*!			σ σ	σ σ	

The change from Early Classical to Classical Latin can then simply be described as the reranking of the AL-PrWD constraints, which has the efffect that preantepenultimate stress is no longer possible, as shown in (18).

(18) No Preantepenultimate Stress In Classical Latin

L L L H	NonFin	W/R	W/L	H/R	H/L	Parse-σ
(L̠ L) L (H)	*!			σ σ		*
(L̠ L) (L H)	*!			σ σ		
☞ L (L̠ L) H		σ	σ	σ	σ	**
(L̠ L) L H		σ σ!		σ σ		**

6. Why derivational analyses fail and why OT is required

In section 4, it was argued that the directional asymmetry in Free Foot-Extrametricality (that is, the observation that it occurs only in systems with rightward footing, but never in systems with leftward footing) is left unexplained in a derivational theory, but receives a principled explanation in OT, but only if the constraint NONFINALITY is modified as we have proposed above for Latin main stress. The constraint NONFINALITY has the effect that parsing of syllables in feet will stop exactly two light syllables from the word end if footing is rightward (that is, from left-to-right) and in leftward parsing (from right-to-left) NONFINALITY is minimally satisfied by skipping just one syllable, forced by PARSE-σ. Hence, preantepenultimate stress is expected if the four last syllables of a word are light in right-ward systems, but not in left-ward systems.

In section 5, it was shown how the quaternary pattern of Early Classical Latin can be accounted for in OT. However, in derivational terms, footing in Latin is leftward and not rightward. Preantepenultimate stress is due to the ranking of PRWD-LEFT (W/L) above PRWD-RIGHT (W/R) and the ranking of H(EAD-FOOT)/L (H/L) above H(EAD-FOOT)/R (H/R), as shown in (16) and (17).

Nick Clements (personal communication) pointed out an alternative derivational analysis for both Hindi and Preclassical Latin, which makes the same predictions with respect to preantepenultimate stress being limited to tetrasyllabic words, and which essentially mimicks the OT-account of section 5. The analysis is: (i) first construct one moraic trochee at the left word edge (mimicking high-ranked ALIGN-PRWD-LEFT (W/L)), then, (ii) after final syllable extrametricality, (iii) construct moraic trochees from right-to-left, followed by (iv) End Rule Right. This is illustrated for Latin in (19).

(19) A Rule-based Alternative I

    a.   ba   si   li   cus
         L   L   L   H

i	(x	.)		
ii				<σ>
iii	n.a			
iv	(x			)

    b.   ma   le   fi   ci   um
         L   L   L   L   H

i	(x	.)			
ii					<σ>
iii			(x	.)	
iv	(		x		)

It is important to observe that this analysis does not need the concept of Foot-Extrametricality to describe Early Classical Latin or Hindi. This, then, implies that, as far as we know, all cases of Free Foot-Extrametricality occur in right-ward stress systems. What is left unexplained in the derivational account is why syllable-extrametricality occurs in left-ward stress systems, but foot-extrametricality only in right-ward stress systems. It is not easy to see how, within a derivational account, one could generalize over these two types of extrametricality. The modification of the constraint NONFINALITY proposed here, on the other hand, does precisely this. It not only generalizes over syllable-extrametricality and foot-extrametricality, but, moreover, formally captures and straightforwardly explains the directional asymmetry of previous foot-extrametricality.

There is a second rule-based alternative that we have to consider. Mirco Ghini (personal communication) proposed the following straightforward analysis for Early Classical Latin. First, (20-i) the final syllable is made extrametrical, then (20-ii) moraic trochees are constructed, not from right-to-left, but from left-to-right. Finally, (20-iii) End Rule Final produces main stress on the final foot.

(20) A Rule-based Alternative II

```
    a.   ba   si   li   cus
         L    L    L    H

i                        <σ>
ii       (x   .)
iii      (x                )


    b.   ma   le   fi   ci   um
         L    L    L    L    H

i                             <σ>
ii       (x   .)  (x   .)
iii      (         x            )
```

There are two word types where there is a crucial difference between this rule-based analysis and the OT-account in section 5, or, for that matter, the Rule-based Alternative I, in (19), which mimicks the OT-account. Both in words of 6 syllables with the first 5 syllables light and in words of 5 syllables with the first syllable heavy, followed by three light syllables, preantepenultimate stress is predicted, whereas the OT-account and Alternative I in (19) both predict antepenultimate stress. Words of the first prosodic shape (6 syllables, first 5 light) are not easy to find. One might think of cases such as *restupefacio* 'to make silent again' or *recalefacio* 'to heath again'. Words of the second prosodic shape (5 syllables, first heavy followed by three lights and a final syllable) are quite common. Some examples are *aedificium* 'building', *perceleriter* 'very fast' or *arefacio* 'to dry'. In (21), the different predictions for these words are illustrated.

(21) Different Predictions for L L L L L σ and H L L L σ words

Rule-based Alternative I (19):

	L	L	L	L	L	
	re	stu	pe	fa	ci	o
i	(x	.)				
ii						<σ>
iii				(x	.)	
iv	(			x		)

Rule-based Alternative II (20):

	L	L	L	L	L	
	re	stu	pe	fa	ci	o
i						
						<σ>
ii	(x	.)	(x	.)		
iv	(		x			)

Rule-based Alternative I (19):

	H	L	L	L	
	a	re	fa	ci	o
i	(x)				
ii					<σ>
iii			(x	.)	
iv	(		x		)

Rule-based Alternative II (20):

	H	L	L	L	
	a	re	fa	ci	o
i					<σ>
ii	(x)	(x	.)		
iv	(	x			)

There is one crucial piece of evidence that helps us deciding between the two analyses: Lindsay (1963: 184) gives *arfacio* for *arefacio* as a possible case of syncope, which clearly points to the fact that the second syllable has to be unstressed. Although Allen (1973) remarks that in the Plautinian period in words of the type *adsimiliter* 'according' (first heavy, followed by three lights), the ictus, too, was preferentially on the fourth syllable from the end, Lindsay, who has edited the complete works of Plautus, is quite explicit with his "except for quadrisyllables with the first three short". In conclusion, of the two possible rule-based alternatives (19) and (20), only the one in (19) seems to be observationally adequate. The most important flaw of both analyses, as indicated above, is their impossibility to generalize over extrametricality effects.

7. Summary

In this paper we have modified Prince and Smolensky's NONFINALITY constraint. We have argued that the proposed simplification of NONFINALITY was needed independently of Latin in order to exclude quaternary systems. We have shown that the account provided in this paper of quaternary stress patterns (as in Early Classical Latin and Hindi) is superior to a derivational account. On the hand, it proved capable of generalizing over syllable-extrametricality and foot-extrametricality, relating the two to different directions of parsing, and, on the other hand, it straightforwardly accounts for the directional asymmetry of previous foot-extrametricality. Moreover, we have demonstrated that the facts of Early Classical Latin cannot be adequately described in a rule-based model, but require and OT-account.

Acknowledgements

This paper is a revised and elaborated version of Jacobs (1999). I have profited from the comments of a number of people, of whom I would like to thank especially Nick Clements, Twan Geerts, José Hualde, and Mirco Ghini.

References

Allen, W. S.
    1973   *Accent and Rhythm*. Cambridge, Cambridge University Press.

Corssen, W.
    1870   *Uber Aussprache, Vokalismus und Betonung der lateinischen Sprache*. Leipzig, Tubner.

Fraenkel, E.
    1928   *Iktus und Akzent im lateinischen Sprechvers*. Berlin, Weidmannsche Buchhandlung.

Gupta, A.
    "Hindi word stress and the Obligatory-Branching parameter" *CLS* 23; 134-148.

Gussenhoven, C. and H. Jacobs.
    1998   *Understanding Phonology*. London, Arnold.

Halle, M.
    1997   "On Stress and Accent in Indo-European," *Language* 73, 275-313.

Hayes, B.
    1995   *Metrical stress theory: Principles and case studies*. Chicago, Chicago University Press.

Hulst, van der H.
    1999   "Word Accent" H. van der Hulst (eds.) *Word Prosodic Systems in the Languages of Europe,* 3-115. Berlin, Mouton.

Jacobs, H.
    1999   "Constraining Constraints: NonFinality and the Typology of Foot-Extrametricality" *Linguistics in the Netherlands 1999*, 111-120. Amsterdam/ Philedphia, John Benjamins.
    2000a   "The Revenge of the Uneven Trochee: Latin Main Stress, Metrical Constituency, Stress-related Phenomena and OT." A. Lahiri (eds.) *Analogy. Levelling, Markedness: Principles of Change in Phonology and Morphology*, 333-352. Berlin, Mouton.
    2000b   The Emergence of Quantity-Sensitivity in Latin: Secondary Stress and Brevis Brevians. ms.

Kager, R.
    1999   *Optimality Theory: A Textbook*. Cambridge, Canbridge University Press.

Lindsay, W.   *The Latin language*. New York/London, Hafner. 2nd edition. [1894]
    1963

Mester, R. A.
    1994   "The Quantitative Trochee in Latin," *Natural Language and Linguistic Theory* 12, 1-61.

Prince, A. and P. Smolensky
    1993   *Optimality Theory: constraint interaction in generative grammar*. Technical Report 2, Rutgers University.

Sezer, E.
    1983. "On Non-Final Stress in Turkish" *Journal of Turkish Studies*, 5, 61-69.
Thierfelder, A.
    1928 "Iktierungen des Typus *facilius*" in E. Fraenkel.

From prosody to place:
The development of prosodic contrasts into place of articulation contrast in the history of Miogliola

Mirco Ghini†

1. Introduction[1]

This paper examines the historical development of the metrical system in the Ligurian (Gallo-Italian) Romance dialect spoken in Miogliola, Northwest Italy. The loss of Latin phonemic length for both vowels and consonants resulted in a new system, in which new segmental contrasts developed. Moreover, lexical stress made its appearance, syllable extrametricality turned into rhyme extrametricality, and mora insertion, either via Vowel Lengthening or Ambisyllabicity, substituted the Latin revocation of extrametricality in repairing degenerate feet.

The focus of this paper is on the development of prosodic contrasts into segmental ones. In this respect, interesting asymmetries between obstruents and sonorants are observed. Old prosodic contrasts were maintained as segmental ones among the obstruents through the occurrence of lenition first, which created a new series of voiced fricatives previously unknown to the system, and degemination thereafter, whose effect was to replace the slots left empty by the lenited singletons. Sonorants, however, did not undergo lenition; nonetheless, they too managed to rescue old prosodic contrasts as new segmental ones. But the "rescuing" was limited to coronal sonorants, a possibility predicted by any phonological theory where the feature [Coronal], as universal default feature, is normally left unspecified in underlying representations, but can, in marked cases, be present underlyingly to contrast with phonemes unspecified for place. In that case, one of the pair in the prosodic contrast can be marked as coronal, whereas the other can be left unspecified. This is exactly what happened in Miogliola, where old geminate coronals pattern now as underlyingly specified coronals, whereas old coronal singletons pattern as underlyingly unspecified segments.

The paper is organized as follows. After a brief description of the Miogliola dialect and the basic assumptions in section 1, the prosodic systems of Latin and the Migliola dialect are discussed in section 2. In section 3 the evolution of the Latin system into the Miogliola Ligurian (MgLig) system is presented. The question of how prosodic contrasts developed into segmental ones is discussed in section 4 and the role of underspecification in accounting for those changes in section 5. The conclusions are summarized in section 6.

1.1. Miogliola

The dialect spoken in Miogliola belongs to Ligurian. Ligurian is one of the Gallo-Italian dialects spoken in Northern Italy, together with Lombard, Veneto, Piedmontese, and Emilian-Romagnol (Pellegrini 1977). Unlike Standard Italian – which is based on the central dialect of Florence and the Central and Southern Italian dialects – Northern Italian dialects pattern with the rest of West Romance in having undergone the historical processes of Obstruent Lenition and Degemination. The village of Miogliola lies in Northwest Italy, more precisely on the left bank of a small river flowing along the border between the two provinces of Savona and Alessandria, the former belonging to the region of Liguria, the latter to the region of Piedmont, north of Liguria. Although Miogliola lies on the Piedmontese side of the river, its dialect belongs to Ligurian, at least following traditional classification criteria. Following Forner (1988:453), the main isogloss defining Ligurian Romance is the palatalization of Vulgar Latin labials before [l], unknown to Piedmontese. This isogloss does not always follow the borders of the present day Ligurian administrative region, deviating sometimes to include Southern Piedmontese areas (such as Gavi and Ovada), or excluding parts of the Ligurian territory (such as its south-eastern end Beverino and

Lerici). Miogliola is included within the territory defined by this isogloss. With respect to palatalization, in Miogliola the output for Vulgar Latin *blanku* 'white' is [dʒaŋk], whereas in Cartosio, the next village a few kilometers north of Miogliola, one can hear [bjaŋk].

1.2. Background assumptions

In spite of the phonetic and functionalist turn which phonology has undergone in recent years (Steriade 1997; Hayes 1999), I argue for a highly abstract model of phonology, in which underspecification plays an important role. Unlike recent views according to which phonology is not multistratal (Prince and Smolensky 1993, Steriade 1995 and OT literature in general), the phonological component of the language is assumed to be organized in levels (Kiparsky (ms.)), with Lexical Minimization governing the shape of underlying representations and full specification characterizing the acoustic signal perceived by the language listener (Lahiri 1999; Reetz 1998, 1999). Unmarked features as well as redundant and predictable featural information have no place in mental representations (cf. Lahiri 1999, Lahiri and Reetz 2002). It will be shown that underspecification plays an important role in the phonology of Miogliola and interacts in intricate ways with prosodic structure.

I assume a hierarchical syllable structure, where the syllable node dominates the onset and rhyme, and the rhyme node dominates the nucleus and coda (cf. Blevins 1995, Broselow 1995 and references therein. From this classical syllable model moraic structure is derived, so as to allow length and weight to be represented on independent tiers (Lahiri and Koremann 1988) to capture the behavior of those languages where phonemically long vowels (Dutch) and long consonants (Malayalam) contribute as much weight to the syllable as their short counterparts. Furthermore, I assume the basic bounded foot inventory in (1), drawn from Hayes (1995).

(1) *Foot inventory*
Syllabic trochee ('σσ)
Moraic trochee ('σ_{μμ}) or ('σ_μσ_μ)
Iamb (σ_μ'σ_{μ(μ)}) or ('σ_{μμ})

The quantity evenness and unevenness characterizing respectively trochaic and iambic rhythm in (1) can be reversed to create more marked uneven trochees (Dresher and Lahiri 1991; Jacobs 1997) and even iambs. In the unmarked case, feet are constructed starting from a designated edge. In the marked case, however, foot structure can be assigned by either ignoring one prosodic unit at one edge (extrametricality: Hayes 1995:56-58), or adding one prosodic unit without phonetic content at one edge (catalexis: Kiparsky 1991; Kager 1993). Both extrametricality and catalexis will be shown to be of importance to the prosodic systems under discussion.

A final assumption concerns the relationship between word stress and foot structure. I assume that every language has a way of computing stress. There are languages where main stress is always predictable, whereas in others a subset of the vocabulary is marked, i.e. exceptional, for having stress in a different place from the expected one. Thus, the existence of pairs like Italian *ancóra* 'again' and *áncora* 'anchor' does not mean that stress is unpredictable for both members of the pair, but rather indicate that one and only one of the two words is lexically marked for a deviant stress pattern. The regular stress pattern is derived via foot structure assignment. In the case of the deviant stress pattern, foot structure is built around lexical stress in a metrically coherent way by constructing around the preexisting lexical stress the same foot structure which stands in a causal relationship to regular stress.

2. The Latin and Miogliola Ligurian metrical systems

In this section I first give an overview of the metrical systems of Latin, in section 2.1, as this is the ancestor of Miogliola stress and subsequently I describe Miogliola Ligurian (MgLig) stress in section

2.2. Section 2.3 is devoted to the historical processes which bridge the two metrical systems.

2.1. The Latin metrical system

The Latin stress patterns are shown in (2): Latin monosyllables are invariably heavy and are stressed on the only available syllable (2a), whereas disyllables (2b-e) are predictably stressed on the penult. In words of more than two syllables, heavy penults are stressed (2f-h), otherwise antepenults (2i). Due to the later loss of phonemic vowel length and consonant length in Miogliola, penults whose heaviness was due solely to the presence of either a long vowel (2c, g) or of a long consonant (2d, h) have been distinguished from cases where the heaviness of the penult is due to the presence of a heterosyllabic cluster, with or without a long vowel (2b, f).

(2)   *Latin stress patterns*
      ($<>$ = extrametrical units;] = right edge of a foot)
      Monosyllabic words
        a.   'CV: / 'CVC(C)
      Disyllabic words
        b.   'CV(:)C]<σ>
        c.   'CV]<σ>
        d.   'CVC$_j$]C$_j$(C)<R>
        e.   'C(C)V]<σ>
      Polysyllabic words
        f.   ...'CV(:)C]<σ>
        g.   ... 'CV:]<σ>
        h.   ...'CVC$_j$]C$_j$(C)<R>
        i.   ... 'σ C(C)V] <σ>

The patterns illustrated in (2) are captured by the parameter settings in (3) (cf. Hayes 1995, Mester 1994, Jacobs 1997).

(3) *Latin setting of metrical parameters and repair strategy*
    a.   *Foot type*: Moraic trochee
    b.   *Direction of parsing*: Right to left
    c.   *End rule*: Right
    d.   *Extrametricality*: Final syllables
    e.   *Lexical stress*: NO
    f.   *Repair strategy*: Degenerate feet are repaired by revoking extrametricality

In (2), all stress types but (2a) and (2c) are straightforwardly accounted for by the parameter values in (3a-d). In (2a) and (2c) extrametricality is revoked as otherwise no well-formed moraic trochee can be constructed. Under extrametricality no stressable syllable would remain in (2a), while in (2c) stress could fall on the remaining light penult, which is therefore the head of a degenerate foot. Notice, however, that in both type of words stress is predictable and therefore by no means lexical.

2.2. The Miogliola Ligurian metrical system

MgLig has the following metrical parameters (Ghini 2001):

(4) *Miogliola Metrical Parameters*
    a.   *Foot type*: Moraic trochee
    b.   *Direction of parsing*: Right to left
    c.   *End rule*: Right
    d.   *Extrametricality*: Final light rhymes
    e.   *Catalexis*: All surface final consonants but [ŋ] are followed by a catalectic mora

f. *Lexical stress*: YES. Penultimate pre-stress light syllables in words with more than two syllables

g. *Repair strategy*: Degenerate feet undergo mora insertion, either via vowel lengthening or ambisyllabicity

The MgLig metrical system has maintained the Latin foot, direction of parsing, and End Rule. However, it has restricted extrametricality to final light rhymes and has acquired lexical stress and mora catalexis. Finally, degenerate feet are now no longer repaired by revoking extrametricality, but rather by inserting a mora. Mora insertion applies in two different modes, Vowel Lengthening (VL) and Ambisyllabicity (AMB), depending on the consonant that follows. The split between 'lengthening', i.e. triggering VL, and 'non-lengthening', i.e. triggering AMB, consonants is shown in the MgLig consonantal inventory below.

(5)   *MgLig consonantal inventory*
            Non-Lengthening   Lengthening

	Non-Lengthening	Lengthening	
obstruents	p, t, ts, tʃ, k		voiceless
	b, d, dz, dʒ	g	voiced
fricatives	f, s, ʃ		voiceless
		v, z, ʒ	voiced
nasals	m, n, ɲ, N		
liquids	l	ɾ, r	

(6) illustrates VL before lengthening consonants. The lengthening applies in penultimate position (6a), but not in antepenultimate position (6b). Due to extrametricality, it is only in the former case, that the stressed syllable can be the head of a degenerate foot. In (6b) the

penultimate and antepenultimate syllable form a moraic trochee and do not need a repair strategy.

(6) *MgLig Vowel Lengthening before lengthening consonants*
    a. *In stressed open penults*   b. *In stressed open antepenults*

lú:[v]i	'wolves'	ní[v]uɾa	'cloud'
ɔ́:[z]a	'donkey'	á[g]avɛ	'agave'
vúː [ʒ]ɪ	'voices'	mý[ʒ]ika	'music'
amí:[ʒ]a	'friend.fem'	fí[ʒ]ika	'physics'
fi:[g]i	'fig trees"	ká[ɾ]iga	'load'
kɔ́:[r]i	'wagons'	mó[g]anʊ	'mahogany'
kɔ́:[ɾ]i	'dear.pl'	u mé[ɾ]ita	'he deserves'

Parallel to (6) is (7), where non-lengthening consonants are ambisyllabic (but short) after stressed penults, but not after stressed antepenults. ᶜC stands for a short ambisyllabic consonant.

(7) *MgLig Ambisyllabicity before non-lengthening consonants*
    a. *After stressed open penults*   b. *After stressed open antepenults*

sý[ᵖp]a	'soup'	u ká[p]ita	'it happens'
gø[ᵇb]a	'hump'	nó[b]ilɛ	'noble'
go[ᶠf]a	'stupid.fem'	u ʒbrý[f]uɾa	'he crumbles'
rú[ᵗt]a	'broken.fem'	bé[t]ula	'taverne'
ʃpý[ᵉè]a	'stunk'		
buɾí[ᵈd]a	'stewed fish'	má[d]ida	'soaked'
it mú[ᵈᶻdz]i	'you grumble'		
rú[ˢs]a	'red.fem'		
kú[ᶜc]a	'dog's basket'		

kú[ᵈ³dʒ]a	'pair'	á[dʒ]ilɛ	'skillful'
bi[ʃʃ]a	'snake'	bí [ʃ]uɾa	'piggy bank'
bǽ[ᵏk]i	'beaks'	má[k]ina	'car'
dʒǽ[ᵐm]a	'gem'	u ɛzá[m]ina	'he examines'
tú[ⁿni]	'tuna fish.pl'	á[n]ima	'soul'
pý[ⁿɲ]i	'blows'	u ɲá[ɲ]uɾa	'he whines'
bú[ˡl]a	'delivery note'	é[l]ika	'propeller'

Notice that, unlike VL in (6), AMB is not directly detectable: the non-lengthening consonants following a stressed penult and antepenult are absolutely identical. That indeed they are ambisyllabic in the former, but not in the latter, is shown on independent grounds in Ghini (2001). AMB and VL are therefore complementary in repairing a monomoraic degenerate foot by making it bimoraic. Notice also that AMB makes the onset of the final syllable into the coda of the preceding stressed penult. The rhyme, then, and not the syllable, is the extrametrical constituent in MgLig.

With respect to Latin, MgLig has acquired Catalexis. Words ending in a consonant in MgLig have a final catalectic mora. This makes final consonants into onsets rather than codas.

(8) *Catalectic words*

kup$^\mu$	'roofing tile'	pedz$^\mu$	'worse'	vuːʒ$^\mu$	'voice'
ljévit$^\mu$	'yeast'	dudʒ$^\mu$	'double'	ɑɾɑːm$^\mu$	'copper'
bæk$^\mu$	'beak'	ʃtuf$^\mu$	'bored'	pɑːn$^\mu$	'cloth'
dɑːd$^\mu$	'die'	fis$^\mu$	'fixed'	ɑɾɑːɲ$^\mu$	'spider'
tyb$^\mu$	'tube'	liʃ$^\mu$	'smooth'		
káɾig$^\mu$	'fig'	luːv$^\mu$	'wolf'	kɔɾː$^\mu$	'dear'
puts$^\mu$	'well'	riːz$^\mu$	'rice'	fæːr$^\mu$	'iron'

The only exception to (8) is constituted by the words ending in [ŋ], which are not catalectic and syllabify the final nasal as a coda, making the syllable heavy.

(9) *Non-catalectic words*
    baʃtóŋ   'stick'
    krɛtéŋ   'dumb'
    bakáŋ   'uproar'
    dzadzǿŋ   'fasting'

[ŋ]-final words are also the only words ending in a consonant which are predictably stressed on the final syllable, consistently with the catalexis hypothesis outlined above. The data in (7), on the other hand, show that only light syllables are extrametrical at the right edge. Heavy final rhymes, instead, attract stress (9). Evidence for catalexis will be discussed in section 4.1. I will first provide a brief outline of the evolution of the Latin system into the MgLig one.

3. The evolution of the Latin system into the MgLig system

In the evolution of the Latin system into the MgLig system I distinguish three main steps. First, phonemic vowel length was lost, which led to Open Syllable Lengthening (OSL) in Italian, to overcome the introduction of degenerate feet (3.1). Subsequently, in MgLig further lenition and degemination processes occurred that affected the obstruents, which turned OSL into VL (3.2). Finally, the sonorants replaced prosodic contrasts with new segmental contrasts (3.3).

3.1. The loss of phonemic vowel length

Both vowel and consonant length were phonemic in Latin. Therefore, beyond heterosyllabic clusters following the penultimate vowel, either underlying vowel length or underlying consonant length could make a penult heavy and attract stress on it (2c, d, g, h). After the loss of phonemic vowel length in Vulgar Latin, those words which bore stress on the penult because they had an underlyingly long vowel in that position (2g), but not (2c), lost their motivation for penultimate stress. Penultimate stress in these words became therefore unpredictable and had to be lexically marked. Notice that one obvious way of avoiding penultimate lexical stress would have been the elimination of extrametricality from the metrical system, so as to include the last vocalic mora into foot construction. Although this would no longer have required lexical stress marking for words of type (2g), it would have entailed the lexicalization of antepenultimate stress and therefore would still involve lexical stress. Thus, one would expect that such a scenario could only take place if the amount of items bearing lexical stress would be significantly different under the two options.

MgLig, like Italian, appears to have preserved extrametricality and, as a consequence, has introduced penultimate lexical stress. As shown in (6), VL in stressed open syllables is limited to penultimate position; in antepenultimate position VL never applies. This asymmetry between stressed penults and antepenults finds a parallel in Italian, which had a process of Open Syllable Lengthening (OSL), a prosodic lengthening which stressed vowels in open syllables. However, OSL in antepenultimate position is unknown in Italian (D' Imperio and Rosanthall 1999)[2]. Such weight asymmetry receives a straightforward explanation if extrametricality is resorted to. VL in MgLig and OSL in Italian are necessary in penultimate position in order to meet the bimoraic weight requirement imposed by the moraic trochee, which has been inherited from Latin. By contrast, in antepenultimate position it is always the case that a moraic trochee can be constructed, given that a second mora for the weak branch of the foot is always available to the right of its head. At the same time, the assignment of a moraic trochee from right to left, given extrametricality, derives stress on the antepenultimate syllable iff the penult is light. If the penult is stressed in a polysyllabic word, stress MUST be analyzed as lexical both in MgLig and Italian, at least in the derivational mode adopted here.

MgLig VL and Italian OSL are parallel in being restricted to penultimate position. However, while Italian OSL is prosodically conditioned, the vowel lengthening process in MgLig is segmentally conditioned, due to the later phonological processes of degemination and lenition, as will be shown below. These processes were unknown to Italian. VL represents therefore a further development of OSL, which took place in Romance after the loss of phonemic vowel length. Notice that once phonemic vowel length was lost, OSL applied to all stressed light penults. OSL provided the extra mora for the construction of the moraic trochee not only in those cases where stress had become unpredictable and therefore lexical (2g), but also in those disyllables whose penults had already been (2e) or had now become (2c) the head of a degenerate foot. After the loss of phonemic vowel length, then, derived length became the repair strategy for degenerate feet, a strategy not resorted to in Latin, which had phonemic vowel length and therefore preferred revoking extrametricality.

3.2. Degemination and obstruent lenition in MgLig

Later phonological processes which affected the metrical system of MgLig and of the other Gallo-Italian dialects are Obstruent Lenition (OBST-LEN), affecting short onset obstruents in word-internal position, and degemination (DEGEM) of (phonemically) long consonants, both obstruents and sonorants.

The historical process of OBST-LEN applied after the Latin system developed palatals. A detailed account of palatalization in MgLig is beyond the scope of this paper. The interested reader is referred to Lausberg (1969), Rohlfs (1966) and Forner (1988) for an exhaustive picture of the different and successive palatalization processes in Romance and Ligurian. OBST-LEN lenited obstruents, including the newly developed palatals, to voiced fricatives. Velars voiced but did not spirantize. Dental stops lenited to zero. Notice that among the onsets which were lenited by OBST-LEN were also those following the stressed penult lengthened by OSL. Hence, the historically lenited consonants gave rise to the lengthening obstruents in (5, 6). This can easily be SEEN if one compares MgLig with Italian, where OBST-LEN did not take place:

(10) *Obstruent Lenition in MgLig compared to Italian*

MgLig	Italian	gloss
lúː[v]ᵘ	lúː[p]o	'wolf'
fyː[z]ᵘ	fúː[s]o	'spindle'
vúː[ʒ]ᵘ	vóː[tʃ]e	'voice'
adɔ́ː[ʒ]i	adáː[dʒ]o	'slowly'
fiː[g]ᵘ	fíː[k]o	'fig tree"

The historical process of DEGEM shortened all long consonants in the MgLig system. Thus, after phonemic vowel length, phonemic consonant length was lost as well. By the time DEGEM applied, OSL had ceased to be operative, and the stressed vowels preceding the degeminated consonants failed to lengthen. This in turn gave rise to the nonlengthening consonants in (5, 7). i.e. to the consonants which under penultimate stress underwent AMB. The combined effect of OBST-LEN and DEGEM is shown in (11).

(11) *The consonant system to which OBST-LEN and DEGEM applied*
  a. *Consonants to which DEGEM applied*

pp	tt	tsts	tʃtʃ	kk
bb	dd	dzdz	dʒdʒ	(gg)
ff	ss		ʃʃ	

  b. *Consonants after DEGEM*

p	t	ts	tʃ	k
b	d	dz	dʒ	--
f	s		ʃ	

  c. *Consonants to which OBST-LEN applied*

p	t		tʃ	k
b	d		dʒ	g
f	s			

d. *Consonants after* OBST-LEN

v   z   3   ɣ

Notice that, since there were no long voiced fricatives to degeminate to begin with, there were no degeminated voiced fricatives in the resulting system. Moreover, MgLig does not exhibit any word where a [g] has resulted from degemination of */gg/, which must have been quite rare. As a consequence, in MgLig /g/ patterns with the voiced fricatives in consistently going back to old singletons (11d) and triggering VL (from OSL) of preceding stressed penultimate vowels. By contrast, VL is not allowed before the historically degeminated obstruents (11b), which make up the rest of the obstruent inventory.

To sum up, the combined effect of OBST-LEN and DEGEM was to turn old prosodic contrasts into new segmental ones. For instance, regarding the labial place of articulation the old contrasts pp/p, bb/b, ff/f were now represented by the newly developed contrasts p/v, b/v, f/v. Moreover, the system now exhibited a prosodic split. The obstruents in (11d) now became lengthening, as shown in (6), or non-lengthening (11b), as shown in (7), simply because the historical geminates preserved the syllabic structure through ambisyllabicity. Thus, the non-lengthening obstruents are syllabified in both the coda of the stressed syllable and the onset of the final syllable, like their contrastively long predecessors. However, within the MgLig synchronic system the ambisyllabicity of the intervocalic short consonants (7 and 11b) follows stress assignment, rather than preceding it. The same is true for VL in (6) before the lengthening consonants in (11d). Thus, the historical processes which led to the loss of phonemic vowel and consonant length both inversed the relation between stress and weight. In Latin, long vowels and geminates were underlyingly long and therefore, if the penultimate syllable contained a long vowel or a geminate, stress would always fall on the penultimate syllable. After the loss of phonemic vowel length stress was no longer based on the heaviness of the penultimate syllable. Rather, lexical stress invoked either VL or ambisyllabicity. Thus, vowel length or ambisyllabicity became a consequence of stress and both processes complement each other in repairing degenerate feet.

DEGEM was also responsible for limiting the domain of extrametricality. This is because in the system which arose after degem, the only prosodic slot the non-lengthening consonants were provided with had to be available to foot construction as well, so as to build the coda of the stressed, obligatorily heavy, penult.

It was the combined effect of OBST-LEN and DEGEM which was responsible for the development of the prosodic split between lengthening and non-lengthening consonants and for turning old prosodic contrasts into new segmental ones. As sonorant consonants did not undergo lenition, the prediction is that they were not involved in similar processes. However, this prediction is wrong: the sonorants did split up in lengthening and non-lengthening, and did turn old prosodic contrasts into new segmental ones, at least in some cases. No phonemic vowel length arose because of sonorant DEGEM. The details follow in the next section.

3.3. Changes in the sonorants

The prosodic and segmental properties of some of the sonorants fall out from the combined effect of DEGEM and historical processes other than lenition. In the remaining cases, an 'analogical' extention of the prosodic split must be assumed. Some of the sonorants developed new segmental contrasts replacing older prosodic ones, as will be discussed in detail in section 4. However, I will first outline the relevant facts about the prosodic and segmental development of MgLig sonorants.

Perhaps not surprisingly, the nasal /ɲ/ is a non-lengthening consonant. The fact that in modern Italian the intervocalic palatal nasal is always long (12), supports the view that MgLig /ɲ/ must be the exclusive output of degem.

The rhotacization of */l/ to /r/ has left older */ll/ as the only source for synchronic /l/, which therefore acts as a non-lengthening consonant. The evolution of */r-rr/ is similar to that of the obstruents: it represents a case of a prosodic contrast which turned into a segmental manner-like one: /ɾ-r/. The phoneme /ɾ/ itself, going back to either rhotacized */l/ or to /r/, but crucially not to */rr/, behaves predictably as a lengthening consonant. By contrast, /r/, being the result of the degemination of */rr/, should be expected to behave as a non-lengthening consonant in the synchronic system. Contrary to any prediction, this is not the case and /r/ belongs to the subset of consonants which lengthens a preceding stressed penult. Even more surprising is the extension of the lengthening properties of both rhotics to coda position, where they appear in complementary distribution: [r] before coronals, [ɾ] elsewhere.

Another prosodic contrast which was rescued as a segmental one is represented by */n-nn/. Old */nn/ developed into /n/, a non-lengthening consonant. By contrast, */n/ developed into an unexpectedly non-lengthening, place-alternating nasal, realized as [n] in prevocalic, as [ŋ] in preconsonantal position. I have indicated this phoneme as /N/ in (12). Observe that the prosodic neutralization of */n-nn/ went in the opposite direction with respect to */r-rr/: the latter pair became lengthening /ɾ-r/, whereas the former pair resulted in non-lengthening /N-n/. It is also worth mentioning that the old prosodic contrast */n-nn/ did turn into a segmental one, like for the obstruents and the rhotics, but unlike them, the resulting segmental contrast was one of place of articulation, rather than one of manner of articulation.

Finally, Miogliola /m/ never lengthens a preceding stressed penult in the synchronic system, thus behaving as if */mm/ were its only predecessor, despite the fat that it represents both earlier /m/ and /mm/. The picture is summarized in (12).

(12) *Sonorants before and after* DEGEM
    Lengthening consonants are in bold

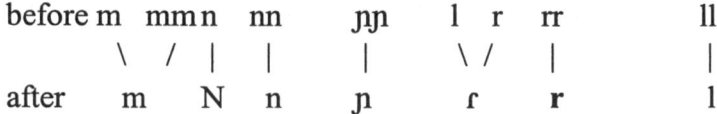

As is clear from (12), both lengthening and non-lengthening sonorants can go back to both singletons and geminates. This contrasts with the obstruents in (11), where lengthening consonants have a singleton as ancestor, while non-lengthening consonants originate from a geminate. In this paper I do not address the reasons behind the fact that certain sonorants developed unexpected prosodic properties. Instead, I am here concerned with the way in which some sonorants developed segmental contrasts out of prosodic ones. We have already seen that among obstruents the loss of prosodic contrasts was made up somehow by the conjunct effect of OBST-LEN and DEGEM, which turned prosodic contrasts into segmental ones. This is also the case for sonorants: */n-nn/ and */r-rr/ turned into /N-n/ and /ɾ-r/. Why, though, did not all of the sonorants turn old prosodic contrasts into segmental ones? Investigating the real nature of such segmental contrasts in the resulting synchronic system may help answer this question. This is the aim of section 4.

4. Changing old prosodic contrasts into segmental ones

We have seen that in the course of the history old Latin prosodic contrasts have turned into segmental ones in MgLig. Obstruents underwent both OBST-LEN and DEGEM. OBST-LEN changed manner and voicing features in singletons, whereas DEGEM filled the slots left empty by the shifted singletons. As a result, contrasts became underlyingly qualitative, no longer quantitative. Unlike obstruents, sonorants did not lenite. However, DEGEM did not neutralize all the prosodic contrasts existing in the sonorant system either. As pointed out above, after DEGEM, */r-rr/ turned into /ɾ-r/, whereas */n-nn/ turned into /N-n/. DEGEM must have been accompanied by another process to account for the existing system.

Notice that labeling the process which turned */r/ into /ɾ/ and */n/ into /N/ as lenition does not really help answer this question. Abstracting away from the fact that obstruent and sonorant lenition would have to be featurally characterized in a different way, no answer would be provided to the question of why lenition applied to just /r/ and /n/. To explore this issue section 4.1 investigates in detail the nature of the synchronic /ɾ-r / and / N-n / segmental contrasts in MgLig.

4.1. Catalexis

The segmental nature of the /ɾ-r and / N-n / segmental contrasts in MgLig can be accounted for by making use of the notion catalexis which interacts in interesting ways with underspecification, as will be shown below. Catalexis singles out a subset of consonants within the system which cannot be captured as a natural class. I argue that what the members of this subset have in common is that they are all underlyingly unspecified for PLACE. This set of consonants is /t, d, N, l, ɾ/. By contrast, the other consonants, and crucially the other coronals, within the system are analyzed as underlyingly specified for PLACE. Under this hypothesis the newly developed /ɾ-r/ and /N-n/ contrasts are in fact contrasts between underspecified and specified place of articulation. The historically old geminates underwent [Coronal]-insertion, whereas old singletons were left unspecified for place of articulation. The following data support this hypothesis.

One argument for catalexis comes from the distribution of vowels in stressed position before a single surface coronal nasal [n]. In (13) this distribution is given for the eight-vowel system of MgLig in both open and closed syllables. The vowel [ø] is systematically absent in closed syllables.

(13) *Miogliola vowels*
open syllable   *closed syllable*

open syllable		closed syllable	
dɾ[í]tʃa	'straight.f.'	p[í]ʃ.ta	'track'
s[ý]pa	'soup'	fɾ[y]ʃ.ta	'worn out.f.'
r[ú]sa	'red.f'	kɾ[ú]ʃ.ta	'crust'
ɪt v[é]nɪ	'you come'	b[é]ʃ.tja	'beast'
k[ǿ]tʃa	'sunburn'		
kar[ó]ta	'carrot'	p[ó]ʃ.ta	'mail'
bɾ[ǽ]ta	'cap'	t[ǽ]ʃ.ta	'head'
v[ɑ́ː]³ka	'cow'	p[ɑ́]ʃ.ta	'pasta'

The stressed vowel system above is not found before [N]. Instead, in this position a reduced vowel inventory occurs consisting of four vowels: [ɛ, œ, a, ɔ]. If [ŋ] is in word-final position, the mid vowels are raised and the reduced vowel system has the realization [e, ø, a, o]. This is illustrated in (14).

(14)　*Vowels before [ŋ]*

in preconsonantal position		in word-final position	
it f[ɛ́]ŋdzɪ	'you pretend'	kam[e]ŋ	'walk'
it r[œ́]ŋpɪ	'you break'	dʒadʒ[ǿ]ŋ	'fast'
ti ʃp[á]ŋdzɪ	'you spill'	s[a]ŋ	'healthy'
f[ɔ́]ŋdzɪ	'mushrooms'	s[o]ŋ	'sound'

The distribution of the reduced vowel system in preconsonantal position in (14) is not limited to the position immediately preceding [ŋ], but can also occur before [n], as in (15).

(15)　*The reduced vowel system before [n]*[4]

f[ɛ́:]na	'fine.f'
l[œ́:]na	'moon'
l[á:]na	'wool'
b[ɔ́:]na	'good.f'

However, before [n] also the vowel system in (13) is found, as shown in (16):

(16)　*The default stressed vowel system before [n]*

p[í]na	'fin'	t[ú]nɪ	'dumb.pl'
[ý]nɪ	'Huns'	n[ó]nʊ	'grandpa'
ɪt v[é]nɪ	'you come'	k[ɑ́:]na	'reed'
aŋt[ǽ]na	'antenna'		

The distributional facts point to the existence of two types of the intervocalic surface [n], one patterning with [ŋ] and preceded by the reduced vowel system, and one being preceded by the unreduced vowel system. The nasal preceded by the reduced vowel system is the nasal which I have been referring to as /N/, realized as coronal in intervocalic position and as velar in coda position. This is the only nasal in the system which is allowed as a syllabic coda. The nasal preceded by the unreduced vowel system is /n/ and does not exhibit any alternation in its place of articulation. Like the other nasals in the system, /n/ is ruled out as a syllabic coda. This analysis, which exclusively relies on synchronic patterns, finds support in the historical perspective, where intervocalic [n] < /N/ goes back to */n/ and intervocalic [n] < /n/ to */nn/.

Consider now the set of data in (17):

(17) *Word-final nasal contrasts*

a.	b.	c.
saŋ 'healthy'	váːn 'insipid'	váːn$^\mu$
kaméŋ 'walk'	a kaméːn 'I walk'	a kaméːn$^\mu$
dzadzǿŋ 'fast'	a dzadzœ́ːn 'I fast'	a dzadzœ́ːn$^\mu$
soŋ 'sound'	a sɔːn 'I ring'	a sɔːn$^\mu$

In (17), both the words in (a) and (b) end in a nasal. From the patterning of the vowels preceding the nasal, we know that we are not dealing with the /N-n/ contrast here. In both cases we have to posit the same underlying nasal, namely /N/, realized as coda in (a), as onset in (b). In the latter case a catalectic mora is assumed, so as to warrant the nasal's onset status, as shown in (c). Further support for the catalexis hypothesis comes from the fact that word-final [n] can be preceded by the reduced vowel system, as in (17), as well as by the unreduced vowel system, mirroring the vowel distribution before the two intervocalic [n]'s in (15) and (16). The parallelism can easily be captured if [n] from /n/ in final position is also catalectic, as shown in (18), where 'V$_{+R}$' and 'V$_{-R}$' stand for 'reduced' and 'unreduced' vowel inventory, respectively.

(18) *The vowel distribution before final [n]*

$$/N^\mu\#/ \rightarrow ['V_{+R}n^\mu\#] \qquad /n^\mu\#/ \rightarrow ['V_{-R}n^\mu\#]$$

The catalectic 'formula' in (18) allows generalization to the environment where /n/ and /N/ contrast, i.e. in onset position. If words ending in [n] from /n/ were not catalectic, the final nasal would be in coda position, leaving it a mystery why the very same segment cannot occur in word-internal codas as well.

To sum up, /N/ can be found in final position dressed up as both coda and onset, due to the absence or presence of a catalectic mora, respectively. This nasal is not the only consonant in the inventory which exhibits such a behavior: /t, d, l, ɾ/ do as well, as will be shown shortly. In contrast, the other consonants in the inventory share the behavior of /n/, that is, they fail to exhibit any kind of alternation. In Ghini (2001) I support the view that all of them appear in final position in catalectic forms, consistently with the analysis of final /n/ proposed in this section. The reader is referred to Ghini (2001) for a lengthy discussion on the theoretical aspects that lead to this conclusion. On comparative grounds, it is interesting to observe that in the Ligurian dialects which did not undergo apocope all the words analyzed as catalectic in MgLig exhibit a final vowel. However, even if the same words were to be treated as non-catalectic, the fact remains that a small subset of consonants is singled out by their 'double' behavior in final position: /N/, and, to be examined in the following paragraphs, /t, d, l, ɾ/. Why this is, is the interesting question addressed here.

4.2. Ghost consonants

Consider now the ghost consonants in (19). In (c), the final consonants /t, d, l, ɾ/ surface due to the presence of a derivational suffix. If an inflectional suffix (a) or no suffix at all (b) is added, these consonants are dropped. These consonants are obviously part of the underlying form (19d), and drop unless they become non-final by the end of the derivational morphological component.

(19) *Ghost consonants /t, d, l, ɾ/*

a.	b.	c.	d.
mɛɾkɔ́ːɪ 'markets'	mɛɾkɔ́ 'market'	mɛɾka[t]éŋ 'market.dim'	/mɛɾkat/
péːɪ 'feet'	pe 'foot'	pɛ[d]ɔ́ 'kick' /ped/	
kapéːɪ 'hats'	kapé 'hat'	kap[l]áts 'hat.pej'	/kapel/
katsýːɪ 'ladles'	katsý 'ladle'	katsʏ[ɾ]éŋ 'ladle.dim'	/katsyɾ/

The data in (20) show that the very same consonants do not require the presence of a derivational suffix to their right to surface. The contrast between (19a-c) and (20a) can be readily accounted for if we assume the consonants in (20a) to be followed by a catalectic mora in the underlying representation (20b), which means that they are actually onset consonants. In contrast, in the underlying forms in (19d), the final consonants have no catalectic mora and, therefore are true coda consonants.[5]

(20) */t, d, l, ɾ/ in word-final position*

a.			b.
rut	'broken'	→	rut$^\mu$
dɑːd	'cube'	→	dɑːd$^\mu$
kol	'neck'	→	kol$^\mu$
dyːɾ	'hard'	→	dyːɾ$^\mu$

To summarize, MgLig exhibits five consonants which can occur in stem-final position in non-catalectic forms: /t, d, N, l, ɾ/. Unlike the ghost consonants, /N/ surfaces irrespective of its derivational history. The asymmetry in the surface behavior of the ghost consonants on the one side and /N/ on the other side is not relevant here. The interested reader is referred to Ghini (2001), where I offer an account based on Rice (1996). The main issue here is to find the common denominator which allows all of them to occur in a position where the rest of the consonant inventory is excluded, that is in stem-final, non-catalectic position. The following section focuses on the question why this is so and whether the answer to this question can shed any light onto the historical development of */n-nn/ and */r-rr/ into /N-n/ and /ɾ-r/, respectively.

5. Underspecification in MgLig

Before we address the question how to capture the relevant structures in MgLig, I first present the basic assumptions regarding segmental phonology.

5.1. Underspecification theory

I assume that the structure around which featural information is organized is provided by Universal Grammar and is represented as the feature tree in (21):

(21) *Feature geometry*

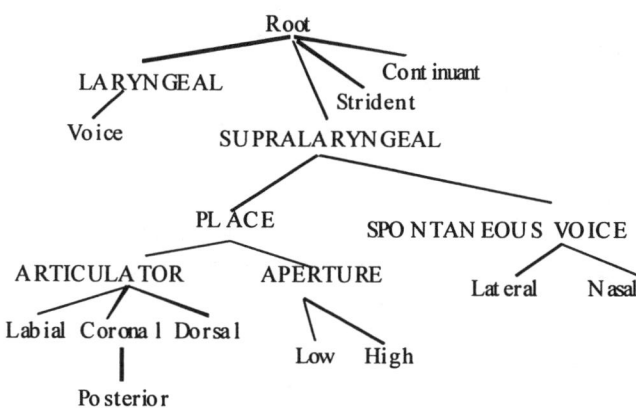

The tree above provides the landing site for all linguistically relevant featural information, underlying and derived. For PLACE being organized in two further organizing nodes, ARTICULATOR and APERTURE, see Lahiri and Evers (1991). For SPONTANEOUS VOICE see Avery and Rice (1989) and Rice and Avery (1991, 1993). Features are assumed to be monovalent (Rice 1996) and shared by vowels and consonants (Clements 1989, 1991), although the constraints which features are subject to may be different for vowels and consonants (Ghini 2001). Featural specification in underlying representations is assumed to be minimal. All redundant information relating to feature cooccurrence restrictions is absent. (see Contrastive Underspecification: Steriade 1987, 1995). Thus, since sonorants are always voiced, they will never contain the specification [Voice] in their underlying representations. Moreover, the unmarked/marked status of the members of contrastive pairs is directly mirrored in UR, where they are represented as contrasts of the type Ø/marked: only the marked element of any pair bears the distinctive specification, the unmarked element always being unspecified (see Radical Underspecfication: Kiparsky 1982, 1985, 1993; Steriade 1995). For the sake of clarity, in a two-height system [Low] will suffice to express the contrast between the lower and the higher unit. Even if the higher unit is phonetically high, the claim is that it will not be phonologically [High], given that [High] does not fulfill any distinctive function in such a scenario. By contrast, in a three-height system both [Low] and [High] will be necessary to make the three units distinct. As the basic principle governing the specification of information in the underlying featural tree is the contrastive force of such information, with features being specified only to the extent that phonemes must be differentiated, I find 'distinctive underspecification' a proper name for this view of underspecification.

There is another way in which the notion of contrast is encoded in underlying representations. This is captured by the Dominating Node Principle in (22), which I assume to complement the shape of underlying representations. This principle is a generalization of the Organizing Node Principle in Ghini (2001). Both have the Node Activation Condition in Avery and Rice (1989) as forerunner.

(22) *Dominating Node Principle (DNP)*
If a feature F has contrastive force within a given class, then the node dominating F, be it a content or an organizing node, is present in the underlying representation of both members of the contrastive Ø/F (unmarked/marked) pair.

To illustrate this principle, consider the case of a language where [Voice] is distinctive. This will trigger the presence of the feature [Voice] under the voiced obstruents, whereas the unmarked members, the voiceless obstruents, will lack specification for voicing. In both obstruent series, however, the node of which [Voice] is a dependent, the organizing node LARYNGEAL, will be specified in the underlying representation. By contrast, in a language where obstruents do not contrast in voice, neither [Voice] nor LARYNGEAL will ever be specified in UR. The same holds true for sonorants, whether in a system where the obstruents do or do not contrast in voicing. Given that within the class of sonorants [Voice] never has contrastive force, the LARYNGEAL node will be left out of the underlying representation altogether. The representation of contrastive voicing in a /t, d, n/ system is illustrated in (23).

(23) *The representation of contrastive [Voice]*

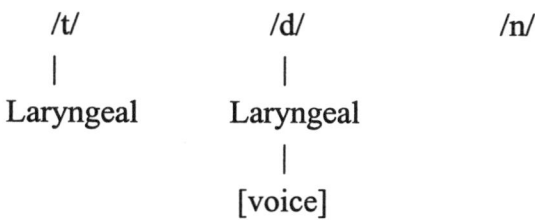

Notice that the presence of the bare LARYNGEAL node in (23) is not directly contrastive. Once /d/ is specified for [Voice], the pair /t, d/ is already distinct and the presence of LARYNGEAL can even be seen as redundant. As a principle of grammar, the DNP encodes grammatically relevant categories in the underlying featural tree, making it explicit that in a system like (23) LARYNGEAL distinctions are contrastive for obstruents. Notice, also, that the effects of the NDP depend on what classes are already available, i.e. what features have already been assigned. To say that LARYNGEAL distinctions are contrastive for obstruents but not for sonorants crucially implies that the feature distinguishing obstruents and sonorants is already available, arguably acquired. For discussion on the matter of feature ordering assignment, the reader is referred to Ghini (2001) and Dresher, Piggot and Rice (1994).

Different predictions are made as to class membership and target behavior of the underspecified segments, depending on the presence or absence of bare nodes. On the assumption that coronal is the default place of articulation coronality is normally not marked in the UR of coronals. In that case, [Coronal] is inserted by a default rule at a later stage, to be present in the surface representation (see Lahiri (1991) for ABSENCE of [Coronal] in UR and PRESENCE of the same feature in SR). The feature involved in the representation of contrasting 'front' and 'back' coronals is [Posterior], a dependent of [Coronal]. Thus, in a /p, t, k/ system the feature [Coronal] is absent from the underlying representation of /t/, even though the Dominating Node Principle triggers the presence of a bare PLACE node in its UR, as illustrated in (24). The structure of PLACE is simplified, ARTICULATOR and APERTURE not being shown.

(24) *The representation of coronals in a /p, t, k/ system*

By contrast, in a /p, t, c, k/ system the contrastive value of [Posterior] triggers the presence of [Coronal] in the representation of both /t/ and /c/. This is illustrated in (25).

(25) *The representation of coronals in a /p, t, c, k/ system*

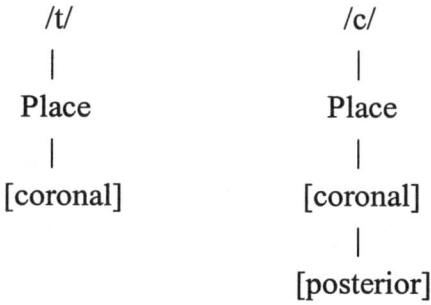

Evidence for the presence of [Coronal] in the UR of /t/ in a system like (25), and hence for the DNP, has to do with cross-linguistic patterns of assimilation and dissimilation, as well as other phonological processes like default feature insertion and transparency.

Under the assumption that rules are only feature filling, and not feature changing, and that assimilation is due to spreading, typically, the /t/ in a /p, t, k/ system assimilates in place of articulation to following labials and dorsals. However, this is not the case so in a /p, t, c, k/ system, where /t/ assimilates to /c/, but not to the labials and the dorsals. If the /t/ in the /p, t, k/ system has a bare PLACE node, this makes it prone to assimilation to the other places of articulation. By contrast, if the /t/ in a /p, t, c, k/ system has the specification [Coronal], but lacks specification underneath it, this makes it prone to assimilation to the specified coronals only, but not to the non-coronal places of articulation. For extensive discussion about this point the reader is referred to Avery and Rice (1989).

A well-known phenomenon across languages is the constraint that consonants share the same place of articulation within the root. Typically back and front coronals do not appear to be able to escape such constraints, showing that they rather share the same place of articulation, than belong to different ones. If both front and back coronals are specified for [Coronal], these facts can easily be captured.

Consider now a last point concerning the feature [Coronal]. Coronals are unmarked consonants and often unspecified for place of articulation. Yet, the presence of [Coronal] in URs is not banned completely. As we have seen, reasons of contrast can require its presence in URs as well, as captured by the DNP. As a consequence both coronals and placeless segments are in principle available as two separate categories of underlying consonants. The question that immediately follows is: can these two classes contrast? The DNP triggers the presence of [Coronal] in (25). Since its presence is triggered, by definition it cannot be contrastive, unlike the presence of [Posterior] in the same system. The question then is can [Coronal] be used contrastively in such cases? Can the Ø/marked representational type be instantiated as Ø/[Coronal]? In the system outlined above, there is nothing preventing this. Actually, Underspecification predicts such a possibility, although it is quite marked. Imagine inserting a new place contrast in (24) by making use of [Coronal]: the resulting system would be /p, T, t, k /, as in (26), where /t/ is now specified as coronal, /T/, by contrast, placeless.

(26) *Underlying Ø/[Coronal] contrast*

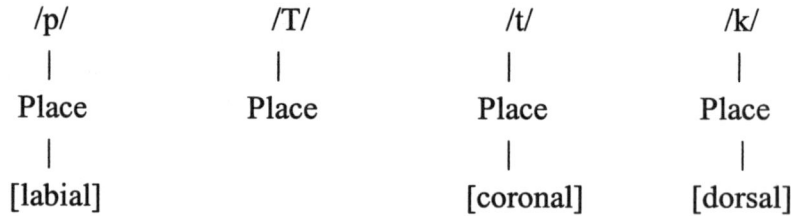

If /T/ undergoes the default insertion of the feature [Coronal], as normally assumed in underspecification literature, the contrast is neutralized and, all things being equal, not recoverable. So, given that underlyingly placeless segments are USUALLY realized as coronals, underlying contrasts of the Ø/[Coronal]-type are expected to be UNUSUAL. However, in a view of phonology where phonetic details of particular sounds do not find an immediate and automatic place in the grammar, but are rather evaluated with respect to the system in question and to the patterns exhibited by the particular sounds, one might conceive of other possible scenarios for the realization of the Ø/[Coronal] phonological contrast. Actually, a possible scenario could be one in which a phonological PLACE contrast is realized in

From prosody to place 447

the phonetics in a different articulatory dimension from place of articulation which can be both segmental and prosodic. MgLig appears to have such a system.

5.2. Underspecification in Miogliola Ligurian

The five consonants singled out by catalexis can only form a single class if we assume that they are all placeless. Any full specification approach would have no chance to capture the same subset of consonants as a class sharing a particular phonological property. This will immediately become clear if one considers the coronal-velar alternating nasal /N/. A full specification approach should mark this nasal as underlyingly [Dorsal], since there is a non-alternating coronal nasal in the system which must be specified as [Coronal]. Once the alternating nasal is underlyingly specified for [Dorsal], it becomes a complete mystery why the nasal marked [Dorsal] patterns with /t, d/ in being able to occur in stem-final non-catalectic position, and, on the other hand, why the nasal marked [Coronal] patterns with /k, g/ (among others) in being ruled out in the same position. By contrast, under the assumption that segments can be unspecified for a given class of features, /t, d, N, l, ɾ/ can all share the lack of PLACE specification in their underlying representation. Notice that the lack of PLACE specification in just these consonants is not an *ad hoc* trick; if the assumptions in the preceding section are accepted, it falls out in a principled way from the set of relationships within the whole system, i.e. it is inventory-driven.

Consider first the set of sibilants in the MgLig system. Since they contrast within the coronal space of articulation, the DNP triggers the presence of the feature [Coronal] in the underlying representations of both anterior and posterior sibilants, as shown in (27).

(27) *The Representation of* PLACE *of the Strident Coronals*

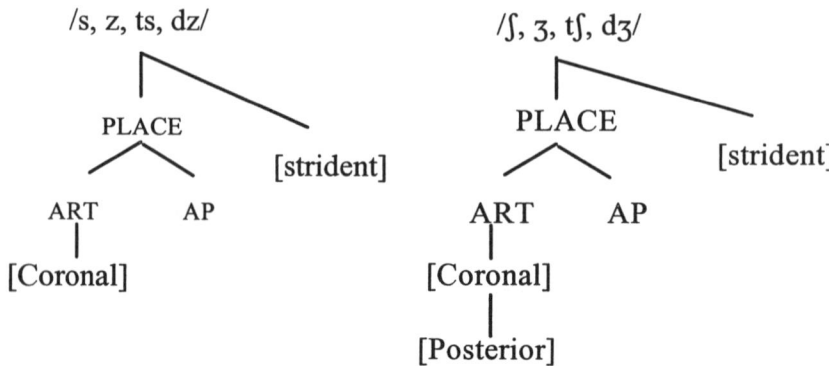

The plain coronals have no posterior counterparts. Therefore, the DNP is not activated, neither is the feature [Coronal] underlyingly present. Notice, however, that the DNP is active at the immediately higher level in the hierarchy: since PLACE specifications are distinctive within the class of obstruents, the DNP triggers the presence of a bare PLACE-node in the representation of the plain coronals.

Let us now turn to the sonorants. If the possibility of an underlying Ø/[Coronal] contrast, i.e. of the possibility of contrasting underlyingly placeless and underlyingly coronal segments is accepted, behavior and class membership (?) of the sonorants in MgLig can be readily accounted for. The phonological patterning of the two rhotics suggests that the shorter, alternating tap/approximant /ɾ/ has an underlying bare PLACE-node, whereas the trill /r/ has an underlying PLACE-node specified for [Coronal]. Again, since PLACE-specifications have distinctive force among the liquids, the DNP triggers the presence of the PLACE-node in the underlying representation of both /l, ɾ/. Consequently, the underlying PLACE-nodes of the liquids have the structures in (28).

(28) PLACE *structure of the liquids*

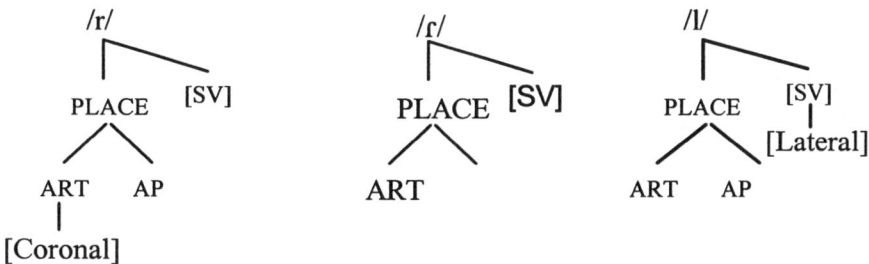

An even more complex pattern of contrast is exhibited by the nasals. Here the combination of the DNP and the [Coronal]/Ø contrast type leads to the quite marked three-way contrast illustrated in (29).

(29) *Underlying* PLACE *structure of the nasals surfacing as coronal*

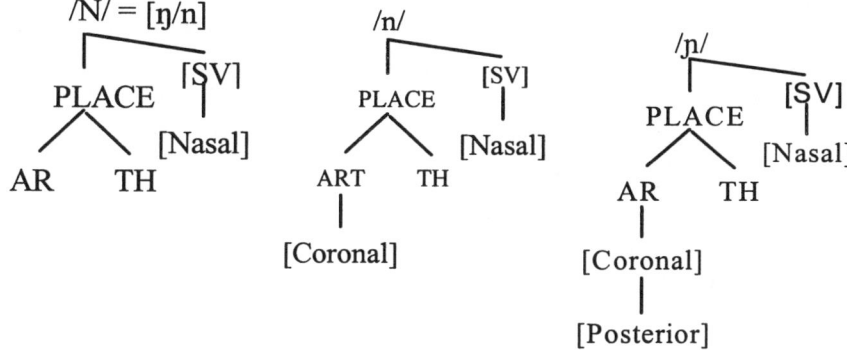

6. Conclusions

I have argued that the synchronic behavior of the phonological system in MgLig can be accounted for under the Distinctive Underspecification Theory outlined above. It has been shown that the contrasts /N-n/ and /ɾ-r/ are of the type Ø/[Coronal]. Both /N/ and /ɾ/ pattern with a subset of coronals which can only form a class under the assumption that they are underlyingly placeless. By contrast, /n/ and /r/ pattern with the rest of the consonantal inventory, with which they share the specification of the PLACE node. This Ø/[Coronal] contrast has not always been part of the language.

Historically, the Ø/Coronal contrast exhibited by the /N-n/ and /ɾ-r/ pairs arose from a length contrast which, as a result of DEGEM, was lost. Within a scenario where old prosodic contrasts among obstruents turned into segmental contrasts via OBST-LEN and DEGEM, the sonorants, which did not undergo lenition, rescued the contrast by a marked system, a possibility open to Underspecification Theory: the historical geminates were now marked for [Coronal], leaving the historical singletons unspecified. Quite obviously, this could only happen to coronal sonorants, which is readily accounted for by Underspecifcation Theory. Short and long [LABIAL] nasals had no chance of rescuing their prosodic opposition as a segmental one – and neutralized. Short and long laterals neutralized too, in spite of their coronality, but this is because */l/ rhotacized. Thus, the fact that /l/ from older */ll/ behaves as unspecified for PLACE in the synchronic system is not a surprise, given that for independent reasons a single lateral was left in the system.

The markedness of a system contrasting underlyingly placeless and coronal segments is obviously related to the implementation of the contrast: placeless segments must be realized somewhere; if they are realized in the coronal space of articulation, as assumed here, then the contrast is lost. Therefore, other ways must be resorted to in order to realize the underlying contrast. MgLig does this in different ways for the two pairs concerned: the underlyingly placeless nasal exhibits a coronal-velar alternation in its surface realization, whereas the underlyingly coronal does not. In those cases where the placeless nasal is realized as coronal, the system still tells us which surface coronal is which through the patterning of the preceding vowels. As for the rhotics, the underlyingly coronal one is longer, the underlyingly placeless one is shorter. Moreover, the former is a trill, the latter alternates between a tap and an approximant.

The generalization here seems to be that the underlying Ø/[Coronal] phonological contrast is realized through a set of phonetic properties which, as the SYSTEM tells us, have no primary phonological function, but rather serve the purpose of recovering primary phonological functions, i.e. contrastiveness. Consider the length difference between the two rhotics. Length cannot be the phonological contrast here; it would be manifested in just this particular pair. Consider now the manner difference of the two rhotics. Is the trill marked [Continuant]? Or should /ɾ/ be marked as such? The phonetics does not provide the answer. Trills have been claimed to be both, and MgLig /ɾ/ is both too, because it is realized as either a tap or as an approximant. All the phonetics has to say about the two rhotics is that they are PHONETICALLY different. One might assume an underlying manner contrast for the two rhotics in an attempt of mirroring the phonetic fact that they are phonetically different in manner and not in place. Although this brings the phonetics closer to the phonology, as is the spirit of much present research, it would completely obliterate the SYSTEMATIC facts. By contrast, if a view of phonology as a mental grammar of sounds is accepted, where the whole system and not the phonetic details of sounds unveil the value of single linguistic units, everything falls into place (and PLACE): the pairs /N-n/ and /ɾ-r/ have an underlying Ø/[Coronal] contrast. The phonetics has to live with that and adapt.

Notes

1. Mirco Ghini passed away in January 2001. Before he died, he had incorporated most of the comments by the reviewers, but was unable to complete it to his satisfaction. Based on his comments, Paula Fikkert, Astrid Kraehenmann and Aditi Lahiri added the finishing touches to the document.
2. In spite of the weight asymmetry between stressed penults and antepenults, D' Imperio and Rosanthall assume antepenultimate stress to be lexical. This, however, does not follow from their analysis, but rather motivates it. They just assume, as in most traditional literature, that antepenultimate stress is lexical whereas penultimate stress never is, and rank the constraints so as to justify their assumption. They might as well have assumed the opposite and reranked the constraints accordingly.
3. In stressed position, the vowel /ɑ/ shows up as [ɔː] before lengthening consonants, as [ɑː] in the environment in which the other vowels are short and followed by an ambisyllabic consonant, as [ɑ] before heterosyllabic clusters.
4. /N/ is a non-lengthening consonant, as shown by the fact that, unlike the rhotics, it does not lengthen a preceding stressed vowel when it occurs in the coda.

The length of the vowel before onset /N/ is accounted for in Ghini (2001) and does not have any bearing here.
5. The final stress in the (19b) forms is due to a derived catalectic mora (via Final Consonant Deletion plus footing). For details see Ghini (2001: 133).

References

Avery, Peter and Keren Rice
    1989   Segment structure and coronal underspecification. *Phonology* 6/2: 179–200.

Blevins, Juliette
    1995   The syllable in phonological theory. In John A. Goldsmith (ed.), *The handbook of phonological theory*. 206–244. Cambridge, MA: Blackwell.

Broselow, Ellen
    1995   Skeletal positions and moras. In John A. Goldsmith (ed.), *The handbook of phonological theory*. 175–205. Cambridge, MA: Blackwell.

Clements, George N.
    1989   A unified set of features for consonants and vowels. Ms., Cornell University.
    1991   Place of articulations in consonants and vowels. *Working Papers of the Cornell Phonetics Laboratory* 5: 77–123.

D' Imperio, Mariapaola and Sam Rosanthall
    1999   Phonetics and phonology of main stress in Italian. *Phonology* 16/1: 1–28.

Dresher, B. Elan and Aditi Lahiri
    1991   The Germanic foot: Metrical coherence in Old English. *Linguistic Inquiry* 22: 251–289.

Dresher, B. Elan, Glynn Piggott and Keren Rice
    1994   Contrast in phonology: Overview. *Toronto Working Papers in Linguistics* 13: iii-xvii.

Forner, Werner
    1988   Italienisch: Areallinguistik I: Ligurien. In Günther Holtus, Michael Metzeltin and Christian Smitt (eds.), *Lexikon der Romanistischen Linguistik*. Volume 4. 453–469. Tübingen: Max Niemeyer Verlag.

Ghini, Mirco
    2001   *Asymmetries in the phonology of Miogliola.* Berlin/New York: Mouton de Gruyter.
Hayes, Bruce
    1995   *Metrical stress theory.* Chicago: University of Chicago Press.
    1999   Phonetically-driven phonology: The role of optimality theory and inductive grounding. In Michael Darnell et al. (eds.), *Functionalism and formalism in linguistics.* 243–285. Amsterdam: John Benjamins.
Jacobs, Haike
    1997   Latin enclitic stress revisited. *Linguistic Inquiry* : 28/4: 648-661.
Kager, Rene
    1993   Consequences of catalexis. In Harry van der Hulst and Jeroen van der Weijer (eds.), *Leiden in Last: First HIL conference in phonology.* 269–298. The Hague: Holland Academic Graphics.
Kiparsky, Paul
    1982   From cyclic phonology to lexical phonology.' In Harry van der Hulst and Norval Smith (eds.), *Structure of phonological representations.* Volume 1. Dordrecht: Foris. 131–175.
    1985   Some consequences of lexical phonology. *Phonology Yearbook* 2: 85-137.
    1991   Catalexis. Ms., Stanford University and Wissenschafts-kolleg zu Berlin.
    1993   Variable rules. Handout from Rutgers Optimality Archive. ROW-1
    ms.   *Paradigms and opacity.* Stanford: CSLI Publications.
Lahiri, Aditi
    1991   Anteriority in sibilants. *Proceedings of the Twelfth International Congress of Phonetic Sciences.* Vol 1. 384–388. Aix-en-Provence: Université de Provence.
    1999   Speech recognition with phonological features.' In John Ohala et al. (eds), *Proceedings of the Fourteenth International Congress of Phonetic Sciences.* 715-722. Berkeley: University of California.
Lahiri, Aditi and Vincent Evers
    1991   Palatalization and coronality. In Carole Paradis & Jean-François Prunet (eds.), *The special status of coronals: Internal and external evidence.* 79-100. San Diego: Academic Press.
Lahiri, Aditi and Jacques Koremann
    1988   Syllable weight and quantity in Dutch. *West Coast Conference on Formal Linguistics* 7: 217–228.

Lahiri, Aditi and Henning Reetz
    2002   Underspecified Recognition. In Carlos Gussenhoven, Natasha Werner & Toni Rietveld. *Proceedings of Labphon VII: xx-xx.* Berlin: Mouton.

Lausberg, Heinrich
    1969   *Romanische Sprachwissenschaft.* Berlin: De Gruyter.

Mester, Armin
    1994   The Quantitative Trochee in Latin. *Natural Language and Linguistic Theory* 12: 1–61.

Pellegrini, Giovan Battista
    1977   *Varietà romanze.* Bari: Adriatica.

Prince, Alan and Paul Smolensky
    1993   Optimality theory: Constraint interaction in generative grammar. Ms., Rutgers University & University of Colorado at Boulder.

Reetz, Henning
    1998   Automatic speech recognition with features. Ms., Universität des Saarlandes.
    1999   Converting speeech signals to phonological features. In John Ohala et al (eds), *Proceedings of the Fourteenth International Congress of Phonetic Sciences.* 1733–1736. Berkeley: University of California.

Rohlfs, Gerhard
    1966   *Grammatica storica della lingua italiana e dei suoi dialetti.* Torino: Einaudi.

Rice, Keren
    1996   Default Variability: the Coronal-Velar Relationship. *Natural Language and Linguistic Theory* 14: 493–543.

Rice, Keren and Peter Avery
    1991   On the relationship between laterality and coronality. In Carole Paradis & Jean-François Prunet (eds), *The special status of coronals: Internal and external evidence.* 101–124. San Diego: Academic Press.
    1993   Segmental complexity and the structure of inventories. *Toronto Working Papers in Linguistics* 12: 131–154.

Steriade, Donca
    1987   Redundant values. *Chicago Linguistic Society* 23/2: 339–362.
    1995   Underspecification and markedness. In John A. Goldsmith (ed.), *The handbook of phonological theory.* 114-174. Cambridge, MA: Blackwell.

1997   Phonetics in phonology: the case of laryngeal neutralization. Ms, University of California Los Angeles.

Language index

Alemannic, 273-285, 301, 306. 309, 311, 313
Älvdalen, 95
Anglo Norman, 329

Basque, western, 249, 255, 263, 275, 280
    Antzuola, 263-265, 276-278
    Azkoitia, 265, 266, 280
    Beasain, 266-268, 270, 271, 275, 278
    Bermeo, 251, 252
    Bilbao, 258, 262, 265, 271, 276
    Gernika, 250-256, 258, 261, 263, 268, 270, 271, 274-279
    Getaria, 266
    Getxo, 250-256, 258, 261, 263, 268, 270, 271, 275-280
    Mallabia, 271-276, 278
    Markina, 250, 253, 256, 257, 263, 264, 270, 271, 274, 276, 277, 280

Dutch, 28, 284, 286-290, 292, 293, 295, 296, 298, 299, 310, 312-314, 315, 421
    middle 165, 187, 201, 202, 209, 210, 212, 215, 218, 219, 226, 227, 229, 240, 241, 243, 283, 287, 289, 317
    modern, 206
    old, 277, 280-281, 283

English, 283, 312, 313, 315
    middle 155, 159, 160, 163-165, 168-172, 176, 180, 182-188, 191-193, 220, 322, 336, 336, 337, 342, 375, 377-379
    modern, 160, 162, 163, 165, 166, 168, 170, 174, 176, 180, 182, 184, 186, 189, 190
    old, 145-148, 150, 154, 156-158, 170, 171, 182, 185, 186, 191-193, 316, 322, 332, 336, 337, 351-353, 358, 360-362, 364-368, 376, 377
    Present Day, 331-335, 342, 349, 352-354, 357, 361, 362, 368
Estonian, 47-51, 53-56, 59, 61-65

Finnish, 199

Gallo-Italian, 419, 420, 430
German, 283-286, 289, 290-311, 313, 314
    Swiss, 279, 280, 301, 305
Germanic, West, 283, 286-288, 290-293, 296, 312, 313, 315
Göta, 95
Grison, 284, 292, 293, 295-300, 303, 309, 311

Hindi, 405, 407, 412, 413, 416, 417

Italian, 420, 422, 428-431, 433, 452

Korean
    middle, 69, 71, 73-80, 85-89, 91, 92, 94, 95
    modern, 69, 71, 73, 76-80, 82, 85-89, 91, 92

Latin, 324, 419, 420, 422-425, 427-430, 432, 435
    classical 395, 397, 398, 399, 411, 416
    early classical (Plautinian), 395, 400, 402, 407-410, 412, 413
    preclassical, 409, 410, 411
    vulgar, 421, 429

Ligurian, 419, 420, 422, 424, 430, 439, 447
   Miogliola, 419-431, 433, 434, 436, 439-441, 447-451

Malayalam, 421

Norwegian, 91
   east, 113
   south, 132
   west, 132

Old Norse, 94

Palestinian Arabic, 404

Romance, 419, 420, 430

Spanish, 249, 257-265, 275, 276, 278, 280, 281

Swedish, 97

Thurgovian, 284, 292, 293, 296, 298-309

Turkish, 402, 403, 418

Weert, 7-13, 15, 17-19, 21, 23-26, 28, 30-36, 38-40, 41, 44, 48, 50-52

Subject index

absence of lexical tone contrast, 14
accent, 47, 55, 61, 64
   compensatory retraction, 256
   lexical, 93
   pitch, 92, 96
   retraction, 256
accent I, 7-13, 16, 18-20, 23-35, 41, 92
accent II, 7-13, 16, 18-20, 23-29, 31, 33-35, 41, 42, 92
   connective, 92
acute, 92
alliteration, 156
ambisyllabicity, 76, 81-84, 425, 432
analogical levelling, 283
analogous, 316
analogy, 316
application domain, 284
association, 102

Beowulf, 149-158
bimoraic syllables, 24, 25
bilingualism, development of, 357
blame English stress on the French analysis, 357
borrowing, 357

Canterbury Tales, 159, 160, 163, 165, 169, 170, 173
catalexis, 424
catastrophe model, 357
central, 91
Chaucer, 330
Chaucer's meter, 159, 163, 164, 185
clash foot-extrametricality, 402
compensatory lengthening, 67, 69, 71, 85, 86
compound, 148, 151
   verbs, 320
compounds (and metre), 218

consonant voicing, 12, 26, 28
consonantal endings, 153
continuous column constraint, 179, 188
contrastive vowel length, 286
counting-from-the-left reanalysis, 266
curl, 103

definite articles, 226
degemination, 420, 430
derived accent, 250-253, 256, 258
derived environment, 303
development of bilingualism, 357
diachronic, 91
diacritic, 169, 170
dialect, 7
dialectology, 131
directional asymmetry, 405, 412, 413, 416
   in free foot-extrametricality, 405
   receives a principled explanation in OT, 412
   unexplained in a derivational theory, 412
disyllabic inversion, 163
disyllabic sequence, 49, 50, 55, 62
domain-final lengthening, 170
dominating node principle, 442-444
doubling proces, 291
duration, 47, 49, 51, 52, 54, 56-60, 61
Dutch
   heffingenvers, 201
   iambic metre, 205
   metrical tradition, 201
   Renaissance poetry, 202

Ellesmere, 168
end-stress,

on native items, 357
variant driven by sociolinguistic considerations, 363
English wordstress, 211
enjambement, 170
evolution
　Preclassical to Plautinian or Early Classical Latin, 392
　from unmarked phrase-final to unmarked postinitial accent, 275
exceptional alternating singular–plural pair, 287
extrametricality, 320, 324
　theory, 402
　foot, 384-386, 390, 395, 398, 402-404, 408, 413, 416
　revoking, 424, 425, 430

final defooting, 322
　in clash, 403
four metrical positions, 155
free foot-extrametricality, 402, 404, 405, 412, 413
function words, 215, 243
fundamental frequency, 53, 56, 59-62

ge-, 327
gemination, 284
　in West Germanic, 288
generative metrics, 160, 161
Germanic
　foot, 322, 368
　stress rule, 172
grave, 92
grids, 151

headless lines, 163
heavy syllables, 318
heffingenvers, 201
Hengwrt, 168, 169
Het Leven van St. Lutgart, 201, 203

high vowel deletion, 146, 150
historical persistence of leftmost primary stress, 350
homophonous pairs, 326

iambic alexandrine, 203
iambic metre, 205
iambic pentameter, 197
iambic poetry, 244
Icus in Old English meter, 146
influence from the Spanish intonational system, 265
influence of Spanish prosody, 257
initial inversion, 238
initial strengthening, 67, 73, 75, 83, 84, 86
inseperable prefixed verbs, 318
interpolation, 102
intrinsic properties of high vowels, 30
isogloss, 124
-iz/-az-nouns, 298

Kaluza's Law, 145-151, 153, 154, 157

Leichtschlussdehnung, 301
length, contrast, 23
length, opposition, 67, 68, 70, 72, 81
level stress, 161, 171
Levins 1570, 325
lexical accent, 252-256, 270
lexical prominence is shifted to the syllable where a rise, 265
lexical strata, 332
lexical stress, 419, 422, 425, 429, 432
lexical tone, area, 36
lexical tone, contrast, 7, 8, 10, 11, 13, 14, 17, 19, 25, 26, 34, 35, 42, 43
lexicon, 199, 243, 331
loan words, 315

Subject index 461

long vocalic elements, 23
long vocalic, 153
lowering of high short vowels in open syllables, 30

meter, 155
    four-position, 158
    quantitative, 155
    syllabic, 155
metric foot, 49, 52, 53, 55, 63
metrical phonology, 173, 177, 188
metrical rules of metrics, 243
Middle Dutch word stress, 208
Middle English stress, 159
minimal pair, 12, 14, 15, 22, 35
modification of the constraint Non-Finality, 413
moraic count, 147, 151
moraic trochee, 324
morphology, 319

non-derived, 305
Nonfinality, explains the directional asymmetry of previous foot-extrametricality, 413
Nonfinality, generalizes over syllable-extrametricality and foot-extrametricality, 413
Norman conquest, 315
nuclear phonology, 78, 81

obstruent lenition, 420, 430, 431
OED, 327
Old English stress rule, 329
open syllable lengthening, 170, 187, 283, 323
optimization of the prosodic structure, 323
overlong, 48, 51-55, 62-64

parametric system, 243
parametric theory of metre, 199
persistence of the old, 370

phrase-final accent, 249, 258
pitch, 47, 52, 53, 55, 56, 61
    lexical, 92
    rises and falls as cues for the position of the accent in Spanish and in Basque, 260
pitch-accent, 249, 250, 251, 255, 257, 258, 260, 262, 268, 275
pitch-contours, 258
position of prosodically prominent syllable
    signaled by fall, 261
    signaled by rise, 260
position, 156
post-initial accent, 249, 258, 265-267
post-initial accentuation, 249, 265
post-particle, 318
preantepenultimate stress, 395, 404, 405, 407, 409, 411, 412, 414
prefix boundary, 330
prefixed nouns, 330
prefixed verbs, 310
prefixed words, 315
Principle of Closure, 243, 244
Prokosch' law, 323
prominence mismatch, 161, 176, 182, 184
prosodic change, 47, 67, 72, 74, 77, 79, 81, 86
prosodic rules of metrics, 243
prosody, 47, 49, 65
    in metre, 201

quantity, 48, 148, 146
quantity-sensitive patterns, 357
quaternary pattern, 402, 405
quaternary stress system, 400

ratio, 51, 61, 62
reanalysis, 283
reinterpretation, 203
    of surface pitch patterns, 271

of the predictable rise, 263
resolution, 146-152, 154, 164, 200, 213, 243
   suspension, 154
restructuring, 290
rhythm rule, 166, 177
rise shifted to the syllable with lexical prominence, 265
rising cadences, 163-165
Romance
   loan words, 159-160
   loans, 170-172
   stress rule, 174, 172, 182, 184, 329
rural variety, 32

schwa, 224
   apocope, 12, 26, 27, 29
   final loss in Middle English, 220
   in Middle Dutch, 220
   syllable, 226, 230
schwebende Betonung, 161, 171
scribal diacritic, 168
second consonant shift, 284
secondary stress, 145, 146, 148, 159, 151, 156
Sente Lutgart, 338
separable prefixed verbs, 318
short vocalic element, 23, 26, 30, 33
short vowel, 147, 149, 150, 153
Sievers' five types, 156
spreading, 102
stem
   extension, 296
   levelling, 306
stem-final sonorant consonant, 302
stress, 47, 49, 53, 55, 56, 63, 64, 156, 209, 214
   clash, 94, 151
   doubles, 159, 160, 165-173, 176, 182-186, 186
   English 202
   Middle English, 159

   lexical stress, 419, 422, 425, 429, 432
   quaternary, 399, 400, 401, 402, 416
stress-timed language, 155
strong-stress meter, 155
superheavy syllables, 318
suspension of resolution, 154
syllabic length, 150
syllable, 47-61, 63, 64
   count, 156
   count in Old English meter, 154
   cut, 67, 71, 77, 79, 80, 82, 83, 86
   long, 146, 147, 151, 153
   monomaraic, 24
   short, 147, 148, 151, 152
   (super)heavy, 318
syllable-closing proces, 284
synalepha, 231, 243, 244
syncope, 244, 399, 416
   in Middle Dutch, 240
syntax, 319
systematic quaternary stress excluded by modified NonFin, 401

theme extension, 296
tonal accent distribution, 26
tonal opposition, 67, 68
tone, 67-72, 74-76, 79, 82-86
   accent, 91
   boundary, 92
   lexical, 92
   prominence, 92
   shift, 103
trisyllabic shortening, 322
TSS, 323
typology, 91

underspecification, 420, 421, 436, 442, 446, 452

verse
   accentual, 201
   alliterative, 160, 172, 173, 185
virgule, 168-170, 173, 183, 186
vocalic system of Weert, 21
vowel
   height, 29
   length, 68, 70, 73, 77, 79, 80, 85
   length contrast, 8, 10, 33, 34
   long, 149, 150, 153

weight, 322
weight-by-stress principle, 333
weight-sensitive Romance stress rule, 329
word order, 318
wordstress, 215